Ulysses Unbound

Common sense suggests that it is always preferable to have more options than fewer, and better to have more knowledge than less. This provocative book argues that, very often, common sense fails. Sometimes it is simply the case that less is more; people may benefit from being constrained in their options or from being ignorant.

The three long essays that constitute this book revise and expand the ideas developed in Jon Elster's classic study *Ulysses and the Sirens*. It is not simply a new edition of the earlier book, though; many of the issues merely touched on before are explored here in much more detail.

The first chapter is a survey of the ways in which and the reasons for which an individual might limit his or her freedom of action, with examples ranging from religious fundamentalism to addiction. The second chapter criticizes Elster's own influential theory that political constitutions can be regarded as precommitment devices. His view is now that in politics people mainly want to bind others, not themselves. The third chapter discusses constraints in the creation of works of art, with examples taken from novels, films, and jazz.

In the conclusion Elster shows how these seemingly disparate examples reveal similar patterns, so much so that he proposes a new field of study: constraint theory.

The book is written in Elster's characteristically vivid style and will interest professionals and students in philosophy, political science, psychology, and economics.

Jon Elster is Robert K. Merton Professor of Social Science at Columbia University. His most recent book with Cambridge was *Alchemies of the Mind*.

Ulysses Unbound

Studies in Rationality, Precommitment, and Constraints

JON ELSTER

Columbia University

CAMBRIDGE
UNIVERSITY PRESS

PUBLISHED BY THE PRESS SYNDICATE OF THE UNIVERSITY OF CAMBRIDGE
The Pitt Building, Trumpington Street, Cambridge, United Kingdom

CAMBRIDGE UNIVERSITY PRESS
The Edinburgh Building, Cambridge CB2 2RU, UK   http://www.cup.cam.ac.uk
40 West 20th Street, New York, NY 10011-4211, USA   http://www.cup.org
10 Stamford Road, Oakleigh, Melbourne 3166, Australia
Ruiz de Alarcón 13, 28014 Madrid, Spain

First published 2000

Printed in the United States of America

Typeface Palatino 10/12 pt.   *System* LATEX 2_ε [TB]

A catalog record for this book is available from the British Library.

Library of Congress Cataloging in Publication Data
Elster, Jon, 1940–
Ulysses unbound : studies in rationality, precommitment, and
constraints / Jon Elster.
p.   cm.
Includes bibliographical references (pp. 283–300) and index.
ISBN 0-521-66213-3 (hardbound)
1. Rationalism – Psychological aspects.   2. Reasoning (Psychology)
3. Psychology – Philosophy.   I. Title.
BF441.E45   2000
128'.4 – dc21   99-34103
CIP

ISBN 0 521 66213 3 hardback
ISBN 0 521 66561 2 paperback

For Aanund, Steve, and Tom – partners in self-binding

Contents

Contents

Preface and Acknowledgments

The title essay of *Ulysses and the Sirens* (1979, rev. ed. 1984) was a discussion of precommitment or self-binding, in which I tried to characterize the concept and illustrate it with examples from various domains of human (and animal) behavior. In the present volume I take a fresh look at the question.

In Chapter I, I make a stab at a more systematic analysis than the one I provided in the earlier treatment. The main analytical idea is a distinction between reasons for precommitment and devices for precommitment. As it turns out, some of the phenomena I discuss appear both as reasons and as devices. People may precommit themselves against anger, but also precommit themselves to anger to get their way.

Chapter II reflects a change in my views about *constitutions* as precommitment devices. I have been much influenced by a critical comment on *Ulysses and the Sirens* by my friend and mentor, the late Norwegian historian Jens Arup Seip: "In politics, people never try to bind themselves, only to bind others." Although that statement is too stark, I now think it closer to the truth than the view that self-binding is the essence of constitution-making. Ulysses bound *himself* to the mast, but he also put wax in the ears of the rowers. Similarly, Plutarch tells us, "The friends of Satyrus the Samian, when he was to plead, stopped up his ears with wax, that he might not spoil his case through temper at the insults of his enemies" (*On the Control of Anger*).

Chapter III explores the idea that self-imposed or externally imposed limitations may enhance the value of *works of art*. In art, as elsewhere, less can be more. Artistic choice, to be meaningful, cannot be exercised in a field of possibilities unlimited. Although my expertise in this field is far from extensive, to put it mildly, I hope the application of some rudimentary economic ideas, notably that of

ix

maximization under constraints, may prove useful to readers who know more about aesthetics than I do.

The ideas in Chapters I and II have been developed in close and regular collaboration with several groups of colleagues. The general framework of these chapters owes much to the discussions in the Working Group on Intertemporal Choice, organized by George Loewenstein and supported by the Russell Sage Foundation. Members included George Ainslie, Robert Frank, the late Richard Herrnstein, George Loewenstein, Walter Mischel, Drazen Prelec, Howard Rachlin, Thomas Schelling, and Richard Thaler. Their influence will be evident, notably in Chapter I. The influence of Aanund Hylland and Ole-Jørgen Skog has also been considerable. Douglass Baird and Richard Epstein advised me on the use of law as a precommitment device.

After the fall of Communism in 1989, I worked closely with Stephen Holmes, Aanund Hylland, Claus Offe, Wiktor Osiatynski, Ulrich Preuss, and Cass Sunstein in studying the creation of new political systems in Eastern Europe. By observing the process of constitution-making in Eastern Europe I was led to think about constitutions more generally, from Athenian democracy through the Federal Convention to the present. My work on constitutionalism has been supported by the Center for the Study of Constitutionalism in Eastern Europe at the University of Chicago Law School and by the IRIS project at the University of Maryland. I have also benefited much from discussing the politics of precommitment in the "Chicago–New York group on political theory": Robert Barros, James Fearon, Russell Hardin, Bernard Manin, Pasquale Pasquino, Adam Przeworski, and Susan Stokes. I am grateful, finally, to Mogens Herman Hansen for his comments on an article closely related to the discussion of Athenian politics in Section II.6.

The ideas about art developed in Chapter III have evolved in a more haphazard manner. I am grateful to G. A. Cohen, Hans Fredrik Dahl, Jakob Elster, Martin Elster, James Fearon, Claudine Frank, Joseph Frank, Diego Gambetta, Karen Marie Ganer, Alastair Hannay, Stein Haugom Olsen, and Thomas Pavel for their comments on early (in some cases very early) versions of that chapter. I also benefited much from discussing this chapter in a group that included Brian Barry, John Ferejohn, Stephen Holmes, Bernard Manin, Pasquale Pasquino, Adam Przeworski, Jack Rakove, and John Roemer.

I received written comments on earlier versions of this book from George Ainslie, Tyler Cowen, James Fearon, Robert Frank,

Brian Glenn, Avram Goldstein, Olav Gjelsvik, David Chambliss Johnston, David Laibson, David Laitin, Jørg Mørland, Claus Offe, Wiktor Osiatynski, John Roemer, Michel Troper, Ignacio Sanchez-Cuenca, Ole-Jørgen Skog, Arthur Stinchcombe, and Cass Sunstein. Their comments, while sometimes chastising and critical, were enormously helpful. I am particularly grateful to Robert Frank for detailed written comments on Section I.5, to John Alcorn for numerous observations, and to Ulrich Preuss, who took the time to write an essay on precommitment in response to the manuscript. I am also grateful for the comments by two anonymous reviewers, one of whom in particular forced me to rethink many issues. Finally, I want to thank Aida Llabaly for helpful and competent assistance, my research assistants Mark Groombridge and Joshua Rosenstein, as well as Cheryl Seleski and the marvelously efficient library staff at the Russell Sage Foundation, which provided me with a fellowship to finish this book.

The book is dedicated to Stephen Holmes, Aanund Hylland, and Thomas Schelling. My discussions with them over the last twenty years have helped me flesh out – and revise – the sometimes programmatic and sketchy arguments of the earlier book.

Chapter I

Ulysses Revisited: How and Why People Bind Themselves

I.1. INTRODUCTION: CONSTRAINT THEORY

In this chapter I discuss why individuals may want to restrict their freedom of choice and how they achieve this end. Broadly speaking, they may want to protect themselves against passion, preference change, and (two varieties of) time-inconsistency. They do so by removing certain options from the feasible set, by making them more costly or available only with a delay, and by insulating themselves from knowledge about their existence.

In this section, I want to locate constraints that individuals impose on themselves within the broader field of what one might call "constraint theory." At a very general level, the present book illustrates the proposition that sometimes *less is more* or, more specifically, that sometimes there are benefits from having fewer opportunities rather than more. This idea must be seen on the background of the standard case, in which the exact opposite is true. Prima facie it would seem that nobody could have a motivation for discarding options, delaying rewards, or imposing cost on themselves. And in most of everyday life this intuition is obviously correct. Most people would rather have more money than less, more occupational options rather than fewer, rewards sooner rather than later, a larger range of potential marriage partners rather than a smaller one, and so on. Much progress in human history has in fact taken the form of removing material or legal restrictions on choice. Moreover, even when we don't benefit from having more opportunities, they usually do not harm us either, since we can always choose not to take them up (the "free disposal" axiom of general equilibrium theory). If I find some of the free meals offered by airlines unappetizing, I don't have to eat them.

1

I. Ulysses Revisited

In this book I discuss nonstandard cases in which the "more is better" assumption is invalid. It can be so for one of two reasons. On the one hand, the individual might benefit from having *specific* options unavailable, or available only with a delay, or at greater cost, and so on. (Although I always eat the meals the airlines offer me, I would pay them a bit extra for not serving me.) This is the topic of Chapters I and II. On the other hand, the individual might benefit just from having *fewer* options available, without the desire to exclude any specific choices. This is the main topic of Chapter III, where I argue both that artists need constraints and that the choice of constraints is largely arbitrary. True, the first reason for wanting to be constrained can apply here too, as when a film director decides to shoot in black and white so as not to be tempted by the facile charms of color photography. Yet the second reason for artistic precommitment is usually more important. The decision by a writer to use the format of the short story rather than the novel is not dictated by the desire to exclude any specific words or sentences, only by the desire to use fewer of them.

This second reason might also apply to social life more broadly. Erich Fromm argued that with the rise of the modern world and the progressive removal of restrictions on action, there has also emerged a "fear of freedom" – a fear of having too much choice, too many options, being subject to too little authority.[1] Along similar lines, Tocqueville said, "For my part, I doubt whether man can support complete religious independence and entire political liberty at the same time. I am led to think that if he has no faith he must obey, and if he is free he must believe."[2] The implication is not that people would *choose* to limit their options, but that they would benefit from having fewer rather than more. Many who like me grew up in the relatively austere 1940s and 1950s believe that children and teenagers in later decades would have benefited from having fewer opportunities and less money to spend. And there is a great deal of folklore to the effect that rich kids suffer irreversibly from having too many options, and that individuals who are very richly endowed in talents end up being jacks of all trades and masters of none. Although these beliefs may partly be sour grapes, casual observation suggests that they are not always only that.

At the same general level, the idea that less is more is susceptible of another interpretation, namely, that *ignorance is bliss*. Again, this

1. Fromm (1960).
2. Tocqueville (1969), p. 444. See also Elster (1999a), Ch. I.5.

idea must be considered on the background of a standard assumption to the contrary, namely, that *knowledge is power*.[3] In this case, too, historical progress has often taken the form of gaining new knowledge that enhances our mastery over nature, including, sometimes, human nature. Because this knowledge can also have destructive consequences, one might ask whether it might not sometimes be better to abstain from acquiring it. In *De Finibus* (V.xviii) Cicero has Antiochus interpret the Sirens episode of the *Odyssey* in this perspective:

> So great is our innate love of learning and of knowledge that no one can doubt that man's nature is strongly attracted to these things even without the lure of any profit. . . . For my part, I believe Homer had something of this sort in view in his imaginary account of the songs of the Sirens. Apparently it was not the sweetness of their voices or the novelty and diversity of their songs, but their professions of knowledge that used to attract the passing voyagers; it was the passion for learning that kept men rooted to the Sirens' rocky shores.

Cicero does not suggest, however, that Ulysses bound himself to the mast in order to remain ignorant, nor that the knowledge the Sirens offered would have been dangerous to him. Hence the analogy that is sometimes drawn between the Sirens episode in the *Odyssey* and the Fall in Genesis is somewhat halting.[4] The Serpent seduced Eve by offering her intrinsically corrupting knowledge, whereas the Sirens (in this reading) used the prospect of knowledge merely as a means of enticing their victims to the rocky shores.

In *Forbidden Knowledge*, Roger Shattuck pursues the theme of dangerous knowledge and blissful ignorance through a number of historical and fictional examples. From the history of science, he cites notably the moratorium on DNA recombinant research in the 1970s and objections to the Human Genome Project, arguing that there may be non-obscurantist reasons for blocking or halting the progress of knowledge. [5] Or consider another example: some years ago voices in the Norwegian government opposed exploratory oil drilling north of 62 degrees latitude. To those who argued that it could do no harm and might be useful to know whether there was oil in that region, these critics replied that if one found oil there would be an irresistible pressure on politicians to begin exploitation immediately. The critics

---

3. For a discussion of opposite proverbial sayings of this kind, see Elster (1999a), Ch. I.3.
4. For this analogy see Montaigne (1991), p. 543, and Shattuck (1996), p. 28.
5. Shattuck (1996), pp. 186–95, 210–17.

lost, and were proven right. I discuss half a dozen cases of this general kind at various places in this chapter. By and large, however, the emphasis in the book is on constraints that take the form of making known options less available rather than that of blocking knowledge about their existence.

The book as a whole is concerned with two types of beneficial constraints. First, there are constraints that benefit the agent who is constrained but that are not chosen by the agent for the sake of those benefits. This is the topic of I.5, and a central issue in Chapters II and III. The constraints may be chosen by the agent for some other reason, chosen by some other agent, or not be chosen by anyone at all but simply be a fact of life that the agent must respect. I shall refer to these as *incidental constraints*. Let me give two brief examples, both from the "fact of life" category. One concerns the need to shoot films in black and white before the invention of color photography. It has been argued, as we shall see in Chapter III, that this constraint made for greater artistic creativity. A similar argument has been applied to the social sciences. In a comment on James Coleman's work, Aage Sørensen claims that the invention of high-power computers came at the detriment of sociological theory, when and because "the data limitations and computational limitations that inspired Coleman to enormous creativity and imagination in developing and applying the models were removed."[6]

Second, there are constraints that an agent imposes on himself for the sake of some expected benefit to himself. This is the main topic of the present chapter, and an important topic of Chapters II and III as well. In *Ulysses and the Sirens* I referred to this phenomenon as "precommitment" or "self-binding." Others have used the terms "commitment" or "self-commitment." In the present volume, I often retain my earlier terminology. When the emphasis is on the constraints that are created rather than on the act of creating them, I refer to them as *essential constraints*.

Essential constraints are defined in terms of *expected* benefits, incidental constraints by the *actual* benefits they provide to the agent. (I ignore cases in which A constrains B with the intention of benefiting B but no benefits are in fact provided.) Whereas the establishment of essential constraints is always explained by the expectation of benefit, the actual benefits of incidental constraints may or may not enter

6. Sørensen (1998), p. 255.

into their explanation. In I.5 I discuss the view that emotional constraints on behavior emerge from natural selection by virtue of their beneficial impact on reproductive fitness. If that view is correct, the effects of the constraints have explanatory force. In Chapter II, I mention that consequences of constitutional arrangements that were not in the minds of the framers may come to be acknowledged at a later time, and then serve as reasons to maintain those arrangements if the grounds on which they were originally adopted no longer obtain. In that case, too, the effects of the incidental constraints would have explanatory force.

Because of the pervasive use of functional explanation in the social sciences, it is easy to commit one of two closely related fallacies: to confuse incidental and essential constraints, and to assume without argument that the benefits of incidental constraints always tend to explain them.[7] The human mind, it seems, is simply very reluctant to admit the idea of accidental or non-explanatory benefits.[8] In II.1 I mention some of my own past confusions, and I am not alone in this respect. Thus one task of the present book is to demarcate, as clearly as I can, intentional self-binding from other ways in which beneficial constraints can come about. Another task is to examine whether there can be constraints that are, as it were, essentially incidental. An agent might be *unable to make himself unable* to act in a certain way, and yet find himself constrained, to his benefit, by the force of circumstances or through an act of another agent.

As mentioned, the present chapter is mainly concerned with essential constraints, or self-binding in the standard intentional sense. More specifically, I shall discuss an agent's desire to create obstacles to his or her future choice of some specific option or options. In this perspective, precommitment embodies a certain form of *rationality over time*. At time 1 an individual wants to do A at time 2, but anticipates that when time 2 arrives he may or will do B unless prevented from doing so. In such cases, rational behavior at time 1 may involve precautionary measures to prevent the choice of B at time 2, or at least to make that choice less likely. The present chapter is a survey of the why and how of precommitment – of the *reasons* why people might want to precommit themselves and of the *devices* they have at their disposal.[9]

---

7. Elster (1983a), Ch. 2.   8. Elster (1983b), Ch. II.10.
9. In this book I assume a simple conflict between a short-term and a long-term interest. In the model presented by Ainslie (1992), the mind contains a whole population of

Reasons for precommitment

Devices for precommitment	Overcome passion	Overcome self-interest	Overcome hyperbolic discounting	Overcome strategic time-inconsistency	Neutralize or prevent preference change
Eliminating options	I.2 I.7		I.3 I.7	I.4	I.6
Imposing costs	I.2 I.7	I.5	I.3 I.7	I.4	
Setting up rewards	I.7		I.7		
Creating delays	I.2 I.7		I.3	I.4	
Changing preferences	I.2 I.7				
Investing in bargaining power				I.4	
Inducing ignorance	I.2 I.7		I.3	I.4	I.6
Inducing passion		I.5		I.4	

Table I.1

In I.2 I consider the traditional view that precommitment is an instrument to protect us against passion. Then I discuss the more recent argument that precommitment can help us overcome the problem

interests, with time horizons ranging from fractions of a second to a lifetime. In that case, more complex phenomena become possible, such as alliances between a short-term and a long-term interest against intermediate-range interests. Elsewhere I have used the following example to illustrate this idea: "I wish that I didn't wish that I didn't wish to eat cream cake. I wish to eat cream cake because I like it. I wish that I didn't like it, because, as a moderately vain person, I think it is more important to remain slim. But I wish I was less vain. (But do I think that only when I wish to eat cake?)" (Elster 1989a, p. 37).

of time-inconsistency, be it due to hyperbolic discounting (I.3) or to strategic interaction (I.4). In Section I.5 I consider the argument that passion can serve as such a device. Rather than being an obstacle to the rational pursuit of self-interest (I.2), passion can help us overcome our tendency to act according to immediate self-interest when doing so is against our long-term interest. In I.6, I consider some variations on the "Russian nobleman" case introduced by Derek Parfit, with main emphasis on why fundamentalists might want to insulate themselves from the modern world in order to prevent preference change. In I.7 I survey the numerous forms of self-binding strategies adopted by addicts. In I.8 I discuss some reasons why precommitment, when feasible, might not be desirable; and when desirable, might not be feasible. Here, I also discuss some alternatives to precommitment.

Not all devices for precommitment can serve all reasons for precommitment. Table I.1 indicates some of the main connections between reasons and devices for precommitment, and helps the reader to locate the sections where the various cases are discussed.[10]

I.2. PASSION AS A REASON FOR SELF-BINDING

When we act under the influence of passions, they may cause us to deviate from plans laid in a cooler moment. Knowledge of this tendency creates an incentive to precommit ourselves, to help us stick to our plans. Here, I use "passion" in an extended sense that covers not only the emotions proper such as anger, fear, love, shame, and the like, but also states such as drunkenness, sexual desire, cravings for addictive drugs, pain, and other "visceral" feelings.[11]

From Aristotle to some time in the twentieth century, the most frequent antonym of passion was *reason*, understood as any impartial – dispassionate or disinterested – motivation.[12] A person who wishes to behave justly toward others but fears that his anger

---

10. In this chapter as well as in the following, I ignore *randomization* as a form of individual or collective precommitment, to avoid repeating what I have written elsewhere on the topic (Elster 1989b, Ch. II). A brief survey of the issue is offered in the discussion of randomization in the arts (III.8).

11. For a discussion of the role of emotions in the explanation of behavior, see Elster (1999a), notably Appendix to Ch. IV. For the place of viscerality in the explanation of behavior see Loewenstein (1996, 1999).

12. For a fuller discussion see Elster (1999a), notably Ch. V.

might get the best of him is advised to precommit himself in one of the ways to be discussed shortly. Among modern economists, the most frequent antonym of passion is *rational self-interest*. A person who fears that anger might cause him to act in ways contrary to his self-interest would do well to avoid occasions on which this emotion might be triggered. A reasonable agent precommits himself against anger so as not to hurt others, whereas an agent moved by rational self-interest does so in order not to hurt himself. Later in this chapter, we find examples of precommitment motivated by either of these dispassionate attitudes. As we shall see, other cases also arise. An agent in the grip of passion may precommit himself against another passion, against the rational pursuit of self-interest, or against reason. A rational and self-interested agent may even precommit himself against his own rationality.

EFFECTS OF PASSION

I shall distinguish among four ways in which passions may cause a discrepancy between plans – whether based on reason or on rational self-interest – and behavior. They may do so by distorting cognition (inducing false beliefs about consequences), by clouding cognition (blotting out awareness of consequences), by inducing weakness of will (options with worse perceived consequences are chosen over those with better consequences), or by inducing myopia (changing the decision weights attached to the consequences). Whereas the first two mechanisms involve cognitive irrationality, the last two need not. Whereas the third involves a motivational irrationality, the fourth need not. All but the second leave the agent with some capacity to respond to incentives.

(i) Passion may distort our thinking about the consequences of the behavior. This was in fact Aristotle's definition of emotion: "The emotions are those things through which, by undergoing change, people come to differ in their judgments, and which are accompanied by pain and pleasure, for example, anger, pity, fear, and other such things and their opposites" (*Rhetoric* 1378a 21–22). Although this does not provide a good definition of emotion – there are too many exceptions, some of them noted by Aristotle himself[13] – it accurately

13. Aristotle counts hatred as an emotion (*Rhetoric* 1382a 2–16), but also says that hatred can leave judgment unaffected (*Politics* 1312b 19–34). See also Elster (1999a), Ch. II.2.

8

captures many cases of emotionally induced wishful thinking and self-deception. Emotions can affect "probability and credibility estimates" concerning events outside one's control.[14]

This mechanism may also apply when the passion in question is a craving rather than an emotion. In an example from David Pears, a

driver goes to a party and he judges it best to stop at two drinks in spite of the pleasure to be had from more, because there is nobody else to take the wheel on the way home. Nevertheless, when he is offered a third drink, which, we may suppose, is a double, he takes it. How can he? Easily, if the wish for a third drink biases his deliberation at the party before he takes it. For example, he might tell himself, against the weight of the evidence, that it is not dangerous to drive home after six measures of whiskey, or he might forget, under the influence of his wish, how many drinks he has already taken.[15]

(ii) The passion may be so strong as to crowd out all other considerations.[16] Before an unpleasant encounter, I may resolve to keep my cool. Yet when provoked to anger, I lash out without pausing to consider the consequences. It is not that I do not know the consequences or that I have false beliefs about them: I simply do not, when acting, keep them before my mind. This is Aristotle's conception of weakness of the will (or one of his conceptions), "admitting the possibility of having knowledge in a sense and yet not having it, as in the instance of a man asleep, mad, or drunk. But now this is just the condition of men under the influence of passions; for outbursts of anger and sexual appetites and some other such passions, it is evident, actually alter our bodily condition, and in some men even produce fits of madness. It is plain, then, that incontinent people must be said to be in a similar condition to these."[17]

(iii) I may know even at the time that I am acting against my better judgment. When offered the third drink at the party, the driver may accept it and yet think *as he does so* that he shouldn't. Although the

14. Frijda (1986), pp. 118–21.
15. Pears (1985), p. 12. Along similar lines Rabin (1995) argues that "we may over-eat not because we consciously sanction over-weighting current ... well-being over future well-being, but because we systematically deceive ourselves in ways that support immediate gratification."
16. The passions may also *preempt* all other considerations. As explained in LeDoux (1996) and summarized in Ch. IV.2 of Elster (1999a), there is a direct pathway from the sensory apparatus to the emotional apparatus in the brain that bypasses the thinking part of the brain entirely, so that when the sensory signal arrives to the latter some milliseconds later, the organism has already started to react.
17. *Nicomachean Ethics* 1147a.

reasons against drinking are stronger qua reasons than the reasons for drinking, the latter have a stronger causal efficacy qua sheer psychic turbulence. Something like this is the view of weakness of will that has been made prominent by Donald Davidson and that, in one way or another, is at the center of most recent philosophical discussions of the subject.[18]

A problem with this third view is the difficulty of finding reliable evidence that the agent really thought that, all things considered, he should not take the drink. It is easy enough to find independent evidence that the driver, *before* going to the party, did not want to have more than two drinks. He may have told his wife, for instance, "Stop me if I have more than two drinks." *After* the party, too, he may regret his behavior as contrary to his real interest and take steps to ensure that it doesn't happen again. But how can we know that this all-things-considered judgment exists at the very moment that he is accepting the third drink? By assumption, there is no observable behavior that can support this interpretation. How can we exclude, for instance, the possibility of a last-second preference reversal due to hyperbolic discounting (I.3)? The agent might retain an accurate appreciation of the consequences of his behavior yet weigh them differently from the way he did before. Because Davidson offers a transcendental argument – how is acting against one's better judgment at the time of action *überhaupt möglich*? – it is disturbing that the empirical premise is so hard to establish.[19]

(iv) A person in a state of passion may weigh the consequences of behavior differently from the way he does in a calmer mood. An addict, for instance, may have accurate beliefs about the disastrous effects of the drug on his or her body or purse, and yet ignore them because of an addiction-induced increase of the rate of time discounting.[20] The urgency and impatience often associated with emotion can have the same effect. If I have the choice between seeing

18. Davidson (1970).
19. Cp. Montaigne (1991), p. 1161: "I realize that if you ask people to account for 'facts,' they usually spend more time finding reasons for them than finding out whether they are true. . . . They skip over the facts but carefully deduce inferences. They normally begin thus: 'How does this come about?' But does it do so? That is what they ought to be asking." See also Merton (1987) for the need to "establish the phenomenon" before one sets out to explain it. For a fuller discussion, see Elster (1999d).
20. Becker (1996), p. 210; O'Donoghue and Rabin (1999a); Orphanides and Zervos (1998).

the person I love for ten minutes today and seeing him or her for one hour tomorrow, I might opt for the former option. The effect of passion in such cases is to induce myopia, rather than to distort and cloud cognition or to make us act against our better judgment. Note that the passions that induce myopia may themselves be either durable or transient. In the latter case, a *short-lived* passion causes the agent to have a *shortsighted* idea of his interests. Although the ideas of "momentary passion" and "immediate interest" are conceptually distinct, they are often causally linked (see also II.7).

In self-deception, weakness of will, and myopia – cases (i), (iii), and (iv) – the agent is *reward-sensitive*. This is not to say that he is rational, only that he is capable of exercising choice by weighing consequences against one another.[21] If the delayed negative effects of a certain behavior would be truly disastrous, the agent is less likely to fool himself into believing that they do not exist, less likely to accept them against his own better judgment, and less likely to let them be dominated by short-term reward. It is only in case (ii) that passion makes the agent entirely deaf to incentives beyond the desires of the moment.

PRECOMMITMENT AGAINST PASSION

These differences have obvious implications for strategies of self-binding. When the agent is able to take account of incentives even in the heat of passion, precommitment can take the form of attaching a cost or a penalty to the choice one wants to avoid making. If you think you might get too drunk or too amorous at the office party, you can increase the costs of doing so by taking your spouse along. In *Lucien Leuwen*, Mme de Chasteller takes care to see Lucien only in the company of a chaperone, to make it prohibitively costly to give in to her love for him. By contrast, some passions are so strong that the only practical way of neutralizing them is to avoid occasions that trigger them.[22] In *La Princesse de Clèves*, the princess flees the court for the countryside to avoid the temptation of responding to the overtures of the Duc de Nemours; even later, when her husband is dead and she is free to remarry, she stays away. "Knowing how circumstances affect

---

21. For a fuller discussion, see Ch. 5.1 of Elster (1999b).
22. In Ch. 5 of Elster (1999b) I discuss whether there are cases in which this statement is true even when the word "practical" is omitted.

the wisest resolutions, she was unwilling to run the risk of seeing her own altered, or of returning to the place where lived the man she had loved."[23]

Anger is perhaps the most important of these blind-and-deaf passions. It may be unique among the emotions in its capacity to make us forget even our most vital interests. According to Seneca, anger is "eager for revenge even though it may drag down the avenger along with it."[24] "Who sees not," Hume asked, "that vengeance, from the force alone of passion, may be so eagerly pursued as to make us knowingly neglect every consideration of ease, interest, or safety?"[25] Clearly, if angry people are willing to disregard even a risk to their lives they will not be deterred by any additional disincentives. As we shall see in I.5, this disregard for consequences that characterizes the angry man may also serve his interest, that is, have good consequences. Here I shall focus on the need to contain anger, drawing heavily on various observations in Montaigne's *Essays*.[26]

It is a commonplace that other people can detect that one is angry or in love before one knows it oneself. When one is in love for the first time, as Madame de Rênal in Stendhal's *Le rouge et le noir*, one may live the emotion fully and innocently until one day the realization strikes: "I am in love." There is no self-deception involved, merely unawareness.[27] In anger, too, the emotion often has to reach a certain threshold before awareness occurs. At the same time, episodes of anger are often characterized by a "point of no return" beyond which self-control is of no avail.[28] The reason that anger is so hard to control, according to Montaigne, is that the second threshold occurs before the first. "The infancies of all things are feeble and weak. We must keep our eyes open at their beginnings; you cannot find the danger then because it is so small; once it has grown, you cannot find the cure."[29] In other words, the dynamics of anger (and of love) is subject to the dilemma illustrated in Figure I.1.

If this is right, and I think it often is, a self-control rule such as counting to ten is not likely to be a good remedy against anger. It is an *advice*, and not a very effective one; not a *device*. Although delay

23. Lafayette (1994), p. 108; see also Shattuck (1996), pp. 114–21.
24. *On Anger*, I.i.1.   25. Hume (1751), Appendix II.
26. See also Elster (1996) and Elster (1999a), Ch. II.3.
27. For more extensive discussions of unacknowledged emotions, see Elster (1999a), Chs. II.3, III.2, and IV.2.
28. Frijda (1986), pp. 43–45, 91, 241.
29. Montaigne (1991), p. 1154; see also Ekman (1992), p. 47.

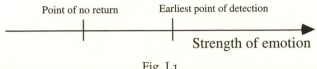

Fig. I.1

devices can be effective forms of precommitment (Chapter II), they have to be set up ahead of time rather than being left to the discretionary control of the agent at the moment he or she needs them. As Thomas Schelling writes, "If I am too enraged to mind my behavior, how can I make myself count to ten?"[30] In theory, delay devices might be used to counteract passion, in the wide sense that also includes cravings for addictive substances. If I want to limit my drinking to social occasions but do not trust myself to do so, I could keep my liquor in a safe with a delaying device so that I would have to set it six hours ahead of time to get access to it. In practice, I have not come across any examples of this strategy. Perhaps it is too expensive – a safe with a timer costs about $1,000 (see also I.8).

Legislation that requires a trial separation before a final divorce might seem to be an exception. The delay allows extramarital passion to calm down and reason to regain the upper hand. Yet with an exception that I discuss later, the delay is always imposed by the state rather than chosen by the spouses themselves at the time of marriage. The legal rights and duties of marriage come as a package. Even when the fact that two people marry shows that they prefer the "delay package" over mere cohabitation, they might have chosen an "instant package" with the possibility of divorce at will had that been available. Marriage would be an essential constraint rather than an incidental constraint only if the delay package was preferred both to cohabitation and to the instant package, because only in that case could restrictions on the freedom to divorce be the *motive* for marrying. Although I have in the past, along with others, used marriage as a standard case of precommitment, I now believe this to be a mistake, or at least misleading.[31]

30. Schelling (1999). Watson (1999) describes "the predicament of self-control" in similar terms: "Techniques of self-control often work by maintaining one's focus against . . . distractions. But employing those techniques already takes an amount of focus that tends to dissolve precisely where it is needed."
31. See also Montaigne (1991), p. 698: "We thought we were tying our marriage-knots more tightly by removing all means of undoing them; but the tighter we pulled the knot of constraint the looser and slacker became the knot of our will and

Gun-control legislation also works by imposing delays between the request for a gun and its delivery.[32] Although these laws serve to protect citizens against fits of murderous passion, it is less plausible to view them as instances of intentional precommitment. Legislators or voters in a referendum are probably much more concerned with protecting themselves and the population at large against others than with self-binding in a literal sense (see also Chapter II). Those who are bound may welcome the ties – or not.

Montaigne noted that when emotions emerge suddenly and strongly we cannot control them, whereas when they are weak enough to be kept under control we may not notice them. He did not think that the problem was necessarily insuperable: "If each man closely spied upon the effects and attributes of the passions which have rule over him as I do upon those which hold sway over me, he would see them coming and slow down a little the violence of their assault. They do not always make straight for our throat: there are warnings and degrees."[33] Yet almost all his practical advice takes a different form: we should avoid the occasions for strong emotions rather than try to stifle them when they arise. "For common souls like ours there is too much strain" in trying to resist or control the emotions.[34]

Emotions are triggered by external events, but only if they come to our knowledge. To prevent the emotions, therefore, we may either ensure that these events do not occur or, if they do, that we do not come to know about them. Montaigne adopted both strategies: "I shun all occasions for annoyance and keep myself from learning about things going wrong."[35] Concerning the first strategy, he refers to the example of King Cotys: "He paid handsomely when some beautiful and ornate tableware was offered to him, but since it was unusually fragile he immediately smashed the lot, ridding himself in time of an easy occasion for anger against his servants." For himself, he adds, "I have likewise deliberately avoided confusions of interests; I have not sought properties adjoining those of close relatives or belonging to

---

affection. In Rome, on the contrary, what made marriages honoured and secure for so long a period was freedom to break them at will. Men loved their wives more because they could lose them; and during a period when anyone was quite free to divorce, more than five hundred years went by before a single one did so." Montesquieu makes the same argument in *Lettres persanes* (Letter 116). See also Phillips (1988), Ch. 5.2.

32. I am grateful to David Laitin for bringing this issue to my attention.

33. Montaigne (1991), p. 1219.   34. Ibid., p. 1148.

35. Montaigne (1991), p. 1075.

folk to whom I should be linked by close affection; from thence arises estrangement and dissension."[36] In *On Anger*, Seneca offers similar advice:

> While we are sane, while we are ourselves, let us ask help against an evil that is powerful and oft indulged by us. Those who cannot carry their wine discreetly and fear that they will be rash and insolent in their cups, instruct their friends to remove them from the feast; those who have learned that they are unreasonable when they are sick, *give orders that in times of illness they are not to be obeyed.*[37]

The second strategy is to shield oneself from knowledge of events that might make one angry or otherwise emotionally disturbed.[38] Referring to an old man whose servants abuse him without his knowing it, Montaigne observes that it "would make a good scholastic debate: whether or not he is better off as he is."[39] I suspect Montaigne would say that he isn't, and that the key factor is that the old man did not *deliberately* blind himself to what his servants were doing. This is what Montaigne himself did: "I prefer people to hide my losses and my troubles from me. . . . I prefer not to know about my estate-accounts so as to feel my losses less exactly. Whenever those who live with me lack affection and its duties I beg them to deceive me, paying me by

---

36. Ibid., pp. 1147–48.   37. *On Anger*, III.xiii.5; my italics.
38. Tyler Cowen (personal communication) notes that some investment theories say that one should never look at one's portfolio. Whereas this advice could be based on the tendency to discount the future hyperbolically (see discussion at the end of I.3) or by a tendency to place excessive emphasis on recently acquired information (Bondt and Thaler 1985), it could also be justified by a tendency to react emotionally to good or bad news.
39. Montaigne (1991), p. 442. This observation prompts a couple of comparative remarks. First, note that the issue raised by Montaigne differs from the question whether it would be better to believe one's servants to be honest while in reality they are not or to believe them dishonest while in reality they are honest. Thus Gibbard (1986), p. 169, comments, "A jealous husband may . . . prefer a 'fool's hell' in which his suspicions rage but his wife is in fact faithful, to a 'fool's paradise' in which his suspicions are allayed but in fact he is unknowingly cuckolded." Second, we may compare Montaigne's dilemma with a similar conundrum raised by Tocqueville (1969, p. 317) in his discussion of American slavery. Tocqueville notes that "the Negro . . . admires his tyrants even more than he hates them and finds his joy and pride in a servile imitation of his oppressors" and asks whether he should "call it a blessing of God, or a last malediction of His anger, this disposition of the soul that makes men insensible to extreme misery and often even gives them a sort of depraved taste for the cause of their afflictions." Tocqueville and Montaigne both make the point that if well-being is bought at the cost of autonomy the price may be too high.

putting a good face on things."[40] Seneca provides another example: "The great Gaius Caesar ... used his victory most mercifully; having apprehended some packets of letters written to Gnaeus Pompeius by those who were believed to belong either to the opposing side or to the neutral party, he burned them. Although he was in the habit, within bounds, of indulging in anger, yet he preferred being unable to do so."[41]

Another situation where ignorance may be bliss is in matters of marital faithfulness. Montaigne writes, "Curiosity is always a fault; here it is baleful. It is madness to want to find out about an ill for which there is no treatment except the one which makes it worse and exacerbates it."[42] In fact,

We should use our ingenuity to avoid making such useless discoveries which torture us. It was the custom of the Romans when returning home from a journey to send a messenger ahead to announce their arrival to their womenfolk so as not to take them unawares. That is why there is a certain people where the priest welcomes the bride and opens the proceedings on the wedding-night to remove from the groom any doubts and worries about whether she came to him virgin or already blighted by an *affaire*.[43]

This is not like avoiding going on the scales to see if one has gained weight, or neglecting to make an appointment with a doctor to find out if one has some dread disease. Those self-deceptive practices are matters of individual information-avoidance, whereas Montaigne here is referring to custom and public policy.

The phenomenon of *regret-avoidance* can be an instance of either strategy. Consider an example suggested by Robert Sugden (personal communication). Suppose first that a driver who sees that traffic is very dense on the highway is deliberating whether to leave it for a smaller road. As the smaller road crosses the highway some miles further away, he knows that he will learn whether his decision was justified, and that if traffic on the highway is in fact going smoothly he

---

40. Montaigne (1991), pp. 731–32. There is another element at work too: "When I am on my travels, whoever has my purse has full charge of it without supervision. He could cheat me just as well if I kept accounts, and, unless he is a devil, by such reckless trust I oblige him to be honest" (pp. 1078–79). By "consciously [encouraging his] knowledge of his money to be somewhat vague and uncertain" (p. 1079), he worries less *and* ensures that there is less to be worried about. See also note 111.
41. *On Anger*, II.xxiii.4.   42. Montaigne (1991), p. 982.
43. Ibid., p. 983.

will feel regret. The regret is a possible cost associated with the choice of the small road that comes on top of the cost of being delayed. On some occasions, anticipation of regret may tip the balance in favor of staying on the highway.[44] Suppose next, however, that there is another small road, which is more circuitous than the first one but which does not cross the highway. The driver might then be tempted to take the slow road, anticipating that if he takes the fast road he might learn – to his regret – that traffic on the highway is in fact so smooth that he would have been better off staying there. Sometimes, people take action to avoid learning whether they have grounds for regret.

Let me mention some further strategies for containing the passions. One is to fight emotion with emotion. When the Argonauts sailed in the waters later visited by Ulysses, Orpheus sang so divinely that none of them listened to the Sirens. Or one might try to fight anger with some other emotion such as fear. In *On Anger*, Seneca raises a possible objection to his claim that it is impossible to retain one's anger: "Do not men sometimes even in the midst of anger allow those whom they hate to get off safe and sound and refrain from doing them injury?" and responds as follows: "They do; but when? When passion has beaten back passion, and either fear or greed has obtained its end. Then there is peace, not wrought through the good offices of reason, but through a treacherous and evil agreement between the passions."[45]

There is a related, but ambiguous, suggestion in Descartes' *Les Passions de l'âme*. He argues that some individuals are never in a position to use their willpower, "because they never let their will fight with its own weapons, using only those with which some passion provides it to resist other passions" (Article 48). Does he mean that these individuals can mobilize (occurrent) emotions at will to fight other emotions? Or that they can deliberately cultivate certain emotional dispositions that will trigger the occurrent emotions that are needed to fight others? The former idea is implausible: by and large, I side with the traditional view that occurrent emotions are involuntary rather than actively chosen.[46] The latter is also somewhat implausible. If emotional dispositions really are within the scope of

---

44. Loomes and Sugden (1987); Bell (1982).
45. *On Anger*, I.viii.7.
46. Elster (1999a), Ch. IV.3.

character planning, wouldn't it make more sense to get rid of those we find undesirable than to create new ones to counteract them?

Many writers within the Buddhist or Stoic traditions have indeed argued that we should fight the passions by getting rid of the tendency to experience them.[47] One of their concerns was to overcome the fear of death, which was also a central theme for Montaigne.[48] In an early essay, "To philosophize is to learn how to die," the emphasis is on how to master the fear of death by anticipating it. In another, "The taste of good and evil things depends on our opinion," he argues, "What we chiefly fear in death is what usually precedes it: pain." Montaigne first claims that this connection is self-deceptive: "It is our inability to suffer the thought of dying which makes us unable to suffer the pain of it . . . As reason condemns our cowardice in fearing something so momentary, so unavoidable, so incapable of being felt as death is, we seize upon a more pardonable pretext." This argument is soon given up, when Montaigne grants "that pain is the worst disaster that can befall our being." In the argument he then goes on to offer, however, the emphasis is more on ignoring or enduring pain when it occurs than on mastering the fear of pain before it occurs.[49]

In the later essays Montaigne came to view things quite differently. "To speak truly, we prepare ourselves against our preparations for death! Philosophy first commands us to have death ever before our eyes, to anticipate it and to consider it beforehand, and then she gives us rules and caveats in order to forestall our being hurt by our reflections and our foresight."[50] In the words of Nico Frijda, the "net effects of anticipation result from the opposing factors of stress produced by anticipatory fear and reduction of surprise with

47. To eliminate the passions, these writers recommended some form of character planning by purely psychic means, the mind acting on itself to change itself (Kolm 1986). Others have advocated or adopted the radical means of cutting off the passions at their physical root. See, for instance, a recent *New York Times* headline (April 5, 1996): "Texas Agrees to Surgery for a Molester. Soon to Leave Prison, Man Wants Castration to Curb His Sex Urge."

48. The main emphasis in these discussions is to eliminate fear as a source of suffering. Yet it is clear that fear was also seen as a source of undesirable behavior. In discussing why wills are rarely drawn up properly, for instance, Montaigne (1991), p. 93, says that it is "No wonder that [ordinary people] often get caught in a trap. You can frighten them simply by mentioning death; and since it is mentioned in wills, never expect them to draw one up before the doctor has pronounced the death-sentence. And then, in the midst of pain and terror, God only knows what shape their good judgement kneads it into!"

49. The quoted passages are in Montaigne (1991), pp. 58–59.

50. Ibid., p. 1190.

its possibilities of anticipatory coping."[51] One might say, therefore, that Montaigne, from viewing the net effect of anticipating death as positive, came to see it as negative. Yet his argument is actually more subtle: the main object of Philosophy is not to enable us to cope with an independently existing threat, but to reduce the fears she has herself created. Philosophers, like doctors or lawyers, pride themselves on their ability to put out the fires they have lit.[52]

PASSIONATE PRECOMMITMENT

Although I have been assuming that the earlier decision to precommit oneself against a later passion is itself a dispassionate one, this is not always the case. Sometimes, people precommit themselves in a moment of passion to prevent themselves from yielding to another passion at a later time. This case is illustrated by the 1997 Louisiana legislation on "covenant marriage," an optional form of marriage that is harder to enter and harder to leave than the regular marriage.[53] Under the traditional system, a couple is entitled to a no-fault divorce after six months of separation. Under the covenant marriage, two years are required. Commenting on the new option, Ellen Goodman cites Amy Wax, a law professor at the University of Virginia, as "worried that newlyweds would 'bind themselves by more stringent terms and live to regret it when Dr. Jekyll turns into Mr. Hyde.'" Goodman also writes, "The covenant marriage mandates premarital counseling. But even Barbara Whitehead, the author of 'The Divorce Culture,' acknowledges ruefully: 'It's impossible to get them to contemplate troubles, adversity, conflict, especially if it's their first marriage and they are fairly young. It's not a teachable moment.'"[54] In a state of infatuation, young people may overestimate the benefits and underestimate the costs of making themselves unable to yield to an extramarital passion later. The fact that by not choosing the covenant marriage when it is available one might send the wrong signal to one's partner might also contribute to excessive use of this option.

---

51. Frijda (1986), p. 293.   52. See also Montaigne (1991), pp. 1160, 1176.
53. In the debates over the British Divorce Reform Act of 1857, Gladstone unsuccessfully argued for a somewhat similar two-track system, according to which couples would have the choice between a Christian marriage without the possibility of divorce and civil marriage (which already existed) with divorce (Stone 1990, p. 379).
54. Goodman (1997).

Another example can be taken from Racine's *Andromaque*. When Hermione learns that Pyrrhus has definitely rejected her, she calls for Orestes and asks him to avenge her:

> While he still lives, fear lest I pardon him.
> Suspect my wavering anger till his death.
> Tomorrow I may love him if today
> He dies not. (1198–1200)[55]

Hermione claims that unless Orestes kills Pyrrhus immediately, she might come to love him again. Hence, the murder is a kind of precommitment: kill him, so that I cannot love him. After Orestes has carried out the assignment and tells Hermione what he has done, she responds as follows:

> *Hermione*
> Why did you murder him? What did he do?
> Who told you to?
>
> *Orestes*
>   God! Did you not yourself
> Here, one short hour ago, ordain his death?
>
> *Hermione*
> Ah! how could you believe my frantic words?
> And should you not have read my inmost thoughts? (1542–46)[56]

First, Hermione tells Orestes to kill Pyrrhus as a precommitment against her possible backsliding. After the deed she tells him that he should have understood that she did not really want to be precommitted, and that her inauthentic self was the precommitting one, not the self against which the precommitment was directed. In her momentary passion for revenge, she precommits herself against her more enduring love.

55. Tant qu'il vivra, craignez que je ne lui pardonne.
    Doutez jusqu'à sa mort d'un courroux incertain:
    S'il ne meurt aujourd'hui, je puis l'aimer demain.
56. *Hermione*
    Pourquoi l'assassiner? Qu'a-t-il fait? A quel titre?
    Qui te l'a dit?
    Oreste
              O dieux! ne m'avez-vous pas
    Vous-même, ici, tantôt, ordonné son trépas?
    Hermione
    Ah! fallait-il en croire une amante insensée?
    Ne devais-tu pas lire au fond de ma pensée?

SECOND-ORDER DESIRES

The idea of precommitment is often linked to that of second-order desires.[57] Suppose a person wants to quit drinking, but finds himself torn between his desire to drink and his desire for all the things that drinking prevents him from doing. This conflict does not necessarily generate a second-order desire not to have the desire to drink. In general, when we desire two incompatible things we decide which desire is the more important and act on it. Thus so far I have been able to handle my desire for butter pecan ice cream without wishing I didn't have it. Suppose, however, that I find myself constantly acting against my better judgment, either in Davidson's sense or in Ainslie's sense (I.3). In that case – but in that case only – it would be rational to form a desire not to have a desire for butter pecan ice cream, and take steps to get rid of it.[58] Second-order desires, rather than being constitutive of what it means to be a person,[59] may simply reflect weakness of will.[60] Moreover, even a weak-willed person would not necessarily form and act on a second-order desire if he or she could deploy some other precommitment strategy. I could ask my wife to throw out butter pecan ice cream whenever she finds it in the fridge rather than try to get rid of my desire for it. What matters is what we do, not what we desire to do.

This statement goes against the view that in matters of personal morality, we should not even desire to do what, all things considered, we think we should not do. We should not wish other people to be less successful, or desire to get even when they insult us, or lust after their spouses. This attitude, which amounts to a self-imposed thought police, can do and has done great harm. I believe that what Kant says about envy is true of a great many other urges: "Movements of envy are ... present in human nature, and only when they break out do

---

57. The following owes much to discussions with Olav Gjelsvik.
58. This is a simplification. Even if I am successful in sticking to my better judgment, the effort to overcome temptation may be so strenuous that I am better off if I reduce it by investing in preference change. (I am grateful to Ole-Jørgen Skog for this point.)
59. This is the view advocated in Frankfurt (1971).
60. By contrast, the *potential* for having such desires may indeed be constitutive of personhood. (I am grateful to David Johnston for this point.) Also, there can be second-order desires without weakness of will if what I wish is to acquire a first-order desire I do not have, such as the desire for listening to classical music, rather than to rid myself of a desire that I do have. (I am grateful to Olav Gjelsvik for this point.)

they constitute the abominable vice of a sullen passion that tortures oneself and aims ... at destroying others' good fortune."[61] Any guilt we might experience in having these feelings is pointless suffering.[62] The remedy is not to go the other extreme and advocate the acting out of all our desires, but rather to recognize the existence of conflicting desires, get our priorities right, and stick to them.

Although this analysis does not need the idea of second-order desires, it may require some kind of asymmetry between the conflicting urges. Suppose I have been a heavy drinker and am trying to quit, judging that my desire to drink is less weighty than my desire for all the things that drinking prevents me from doing. Suppose, moreover, that this is a judgment I make when sober, but that I make the very opposite judgment when under the influence of alcohol. Which self, if any, is right? To a first approximation, we may answer by using the capacity for self-binding as a criterion.[63] If we observe the sober self trying to bind the drunken self but never observe the drunken self trying to bind the sober self, we may reasonably identify the former self with the person's real interest. And there often seems in fact to be an asymmetry of this kind. By virtue of their strength the passions may induce a temporary neglect of the future that prevents the person who is in their grip from responding strategically to strategic moves he or she might later make to curb them. When the person tries to implement his long-term interest, he is aware of the obstacles created by his short-term interest, but not vice versa.[64] This asymmetry has nothing to do with second-order desires: the short-term interest is the object of a cognition, not of a desire.

---

61. Kant (1785), pp. 576–77. A vivid expression of this idea is given by a Tahitian pastor cited in Levy (1973), p. 332: "You think about sleeping with that *vahine*, about committing adultery with that *vahine*, but you do not commit adultery with her – there is no difficulty at all. Because the thought inside of you – all people have had that thought inside of them, there is not one man without that thing inside of him. What can be done? That thought exists within you, because it does not stop. It is the same as some machine that keeps running inside of you."
62. See also Elster (1999a), Ch. III.2.
63. Because of the issues mentioned in note 9, it is valid only to a first approximation.
64. See also Skog (1997), p. 268, for a statement to this effect. Cowen (1991), p. 362, argues, by contrast, that "the actions of an impulsive self are not limited to myopic forms of immediate gratification and may involve sophisticated strategic maneuvers." With the exception of the example from Merton cited later, Cowen's illustrations of this claim are hypothetical and, to my mind, unconvincing. Also, most of his discussion focuses on cases in which strategic action by the impulsive self would be *desirable*, rather than on cases in which it is likely to occur.

I.2. Passion as a Reason for Self-Binding

There are cases, nevertheless, in which cravings or emotions seem to be capable of taking strategic measures to ensure their own satisfaction. A case of this sort arose in the Belgian war trials after World War II. In most of the countries that had been occupied by the Germans, there was a tendency for similar crimes of collaboration to be treated more leniently in, say, 1947 than in 1944 or 1945.[65] Some collaborators were executed for crimes that a few years later would at most have gotten them twenty years in prison.[66] In Belgium, this pattern was anticipated and to some extent taken into account by the organizers of the trials. On the basis of the experience from WWI, "it was believed that after a while, the popular willingness to impose severe sentences on the collaborators would give place to indifference." Hence the Belgians wanted the trials to proceed as quickly as possible, before passion was replaced by a more dispassionate attitude.[67]

A similar case, also related to World War II, was noted by Robert Merton. In Tyler Cowen's summary,

an example of impulsive precommitment is given in Robert Merton's study of social pressures. Merton notes the ephemerality of many persons' desires to contribute to the American war effort during the Second World War. The desire to contribute was strong only immediately after hearing radio appeals for funds. Merton's study of contributors revealed that 'in some instances, listeners telephoned at once precisely because they wished to commit themselves to a bond before inhibiting factors intervened'. After making such telephone calls, persons were required to fulfill commitments that had been undertaken by their impulsive selves.[68]

As these examples show, it is possible for an agent in the heat of passion to precommit himself against the predictable tendency for passion to abate after a while. Instances of such behavior may be rare, but they seem to exist. While they do not refute the overall difference in capacity for self-binding between passion on the one hand and

---

65. Tamm (1984), Ch. 7; Andenæs (1980), p. 229; Mason (1952), p. 187, note 36. The most thorough discussion is in Huyse and Dhondt (1993), p. 231, who consider and reject the hypothesis that the trend is an artifact of the most serious crimes having been tried first. See also Elster (1998).
66. Huyse and Dhondt (1993), p. 125.
67. Huyse and Dhondt (1993), p. 115. I assume that the more lenient attitude that emerged after a few years was based on a genuine desire for justice to be done, whereas what dominated in the initial phases was a desire for revenge disguised (to oneself or to others) as a desire for justice (Elster 1999a, Ch. V.2).
68. Cowen (1991), p. 363, citing Merton (1946), pp. 68–69.

reason or rationality on the other, they suggest that it is less stark than I, for one, have thought in the past.

These are cases of a passionate agent precommitting himself against dispassionateness. Earlier I discussed instances of how passion can induce agents to precommit themselves against passion. Both can be contrasted with the standard case of a dispassionate agent precommitting himself against passion. The case of a rational agent precommitting himself against rationality may also arise. A rational agent may take steps to make himself less rational on some future occasion when being irrational will enable him to get the upper hand in negotiating with other (rational) agents.[69] This idea must not be confused with the suggestion, considered in I.5, that an irrational *disposition* may be useful in dealing with others. Getting drunk on a given occasion if I believe it will help me get my way is not like acquiring a durable disposition toward irascibility or vindictiveness.

I.3. TIME-INCONSISTENCY AND DISCOUNTING

Time-inconsistency, or dynamic inconsistency, "occurs when the best policy currently planned for some future period is no longer the best when that period arrives."[70] To this definition, we may add that the preference reversal involved in time-inconsistency is not caused by exogenous and unforeseen changes in the environment, nor by a subjective change in the agent over and above the reversal itself. The reversal is caused by the mere passage of time. Once we learn that we are subject to this mechanism, we may take steps to deal with it, to prevent the reversal from occurring or from having adverse consequences for behavior.

This general phenomenon can be subdivided into *time-inconsistency caused by hyperbolic discounting*, discussed here, and *time-inconsistency caused by strategic interaction*, discussed in the next section. Apart from a certain formal similarity, the two have little in common. Hyperbolic discounting does not require interaction: it might apply to Robinson on his island before the arrival of Friday. Conversely, strategically induced inconsistency does not require discounting. As we shall see in I.4 and I.5, the two phenomena can interact, but either can exist without the other.

69. Schelling (1960).   70. Cukierman (1992), p. 15.

VARIETIES OF DISCOUNTING

When individuals plan their behavior over time, they typically discount future welfare to a smaller present value. When faced with options whose welfare effects will be felt at various times in the future, they choose the one for which the sum of the present value of these effects is the largest. While there is widespread agreement on this general description,[71] there are two main views about the exact shape of the discounting function. Neoclassical economists usually assume that discounting is *exponential*, in the sense that the welfare t units of time into the future is discounted to present value by a factor of r^t, where $r(<1)$ is the one-period discount factor. Following the pioneering work of R. H. Strotz and George Ainslie, many psychologists and behavioral economists argue that discounting is *hyperbolic*, so that welfare t units into the future is discounted to present value by a factor of $1/(1+kt)$, with $k > 0$.[72] In the following, I shall assume the latter view, which seems to have a great deal of direct and indirect support.[73] Perhaps the central intuition behind this view is that individuals have a strong preference for the present compared to all future dates, but are much less concerned with the relative importance of future dates. If they receive a big sum of money today, for instance, they may decide to spend half of it immediately and allocate the rest evenly over their lifetime.

Time discounting may be undesirable on two very different grounds. First, an individual who discounts the future very heavily, with little ability to defer gratification, is unlikely to have a very good life. That is why we teach our children to be prudent and think about the future (see also I.5). These undesirable effects of discounting

---

71. Among other approaches to discounting, Loewenstein and Prelec (1992) assume that "intertemporal choice is defined with respect to *deviations* from an anticipated status quo (or 'reference') consumption plan." Skog (1997) assumes that discount rates fluctuate stochastically, and shows how this phenomenon, if anticipated, may give rise to precommitment behavior.
72. See notably Strotz (1955–56), Ainslie (1992), as well as the essays in Loewenstein and Elster, eds. (1992). For the present purposes I need not distinguish between hyperbolic discounting and the other non-exponential discounting functions discussed in Phelps and Pollak (1968), Akerlof (1991), Laibson (1994), and O'Donoghue and Rabin (1999a,b). These writers decompose overall discounting into a discounting of all future periods relative to the current period and a standard exponential discounting of all future periods relative to each other.
73. For direct support, see Ainslie (1992) and Laibson (1996a). The indirect support is that many of the precommitment strategies discussed here and in later chapters cannot be explained on the assumption of exponential discounting.

are independent of the exact shape of the discounting function. They may arise for non-exponential as well as for exponential discounting. Second, an individual who is subject to hyperbolic discounting is liable to time-inconsistency. The bulk of the present section is devoted to precommitment behavior motivated by the second problem.

Becker on Endogenous Time Preferences

First, however, let me discuss a recent argument by Gary Becker and Casey Mulligan to the effect that individuals may precommit themselves in response to the problem of high discounting per se. They offer

a model of patience formation that combines the classical economists' insights with a particular view of what it means to be rational, a conception of rationality that is consistent with many kinds of human frailties, including defective recognition of future utilities. Rational persons may spend resources in the attempt to overcome their frailties. This simple idea provides the point of departure for our approach to endogenizing time preferences. Even rational people may 'excessively' discount future utilities, but we assume that they may partially or fully offset this by spending effort and goods to reduce the degree of overdiscounting.[74]

Along similar lines, Becker wrote in the introduction to his most recent book of essays that

People train themselves to reduce and sometimes more than fully overcome any tendency towards undervaluation. The analysis in this book allows people to maximize the discounted value of present and future utilities partly by spending time and other resources to produce 'imagination capital' that helps them better appreciate future utilities . . .

They may choose greater education in part because it tends to improve the appreciation of the future, and thereby reduces the discount of the future. Parents teach their children to be more aware of the future consequences of their choices. . . . Addictions to drugs and alcohol reduce utility partly through decreasing the capacity to anticipate future consequences. Religion often increases the weight attached to future utilities, especially when it promises an attractive afterlife.[75]

---

74. Becker and Mulligan (1997), p. 730.   75. Becker (1996), p. 11.

I.3. Time-Inconsistency and Discounting

In their article, Becker and Mulligan also enumerate various investments that can shape "imagination capital." Besides the purely mental (but not costless) processes of image formation and scenario simulation, these include the purchase of newspapers and other goods that can distract one's attention away from current pleasures and toward future ones; spending time with one's aging parents in order to better appreciate the need for providing for one's own old age; the purchase of disciplinary devices such as a piggy bank or membership in a Christmas club, which help a person sacrifice current consumption; tearing up one's credit cards; investment in schooling, which focuses students' attention on the future; and spending parental resources on teaching one's children to better plan for the future.[76]

Some of these strategies (joining Christmas clubs and tearing up one's credit cards) are more plausibly seen as responses to the problem of time-inconsistency (see the next subsection). To assess the other strategies, let us distinguish among three causes of preference formation.

(1) The preferences of an agent A can be traced back to a rational choice by some other agent B for the purpose of shaping or changing A's preferences.

(2) The preferences of A can be traced back to a rational choice by A for some purpose other than preference-acquisition.

(3) The preferences of A can be traced back to a rational choice by A *for the very purpose of acquiring those preferences.*

Whereas Becker and Mulligan claim to be discussing case (3), most of their examples fall in (1) or (2). Among the examples that do illustrate case (3), the idea that people spend time with their aging parents in order to better appreciate the need for providing for their own old age is in my view nothing short of ludicrous. Nor, to my knowledge, is there evidence that people choose education or religion for the purpose of becoming more oriented to the future. If there is a connection, it is more likely the other way around: people who care more about the future are more likely to choose education or religion.[77]

---

76. Becker and Mulligan (1997), pp. 739–40.
77. Tocqueville (1969), p. 529. Although he also asserts the opposite causal chain (ibid., p. 547), he does not suggest that anyone would *choose* religion because of its spillover effects on discounting in secular matters. In fact, I believe that most religious doctrines would condemn the idea of choosing religion for this reason.

In fact, I believe the idea that people might engage in such behaviors for this purpose is conceptually incoherent. We cannot expect people to take steps to reduce their rate of time discounting, because *to want to be motivated by a long-term concern ipso facto is to be motivated by that long-term concern*, just as to expect that one will expect something to happen *is* to expect that it will happen or to want to become immoral *is* to be immoral.[78] If people do not have that motivation in the first place, they cannot be motivated to acquire it.

Let me expand on this argument, by comparing a cultivated taste for classical music with the putative cultivation of future-oriented time preferences. Considering the first case, I may believe today that I have the choice between two streams of experiences. If I abstain from cultivating a taste for classical music, the stream will be A, A, A .... If I undergo the initially aversive experience of listening to classical music, the stream will be B, C, C .... with B < A < C. A rational agent will make the investment if and only if the discounted value of the second stream is larger than that of the first, which may or may not be the case.

Considering the second case, suppose for vividness that I am offered a "discounting pill" at a price of $100, which will reduce my rate of time discounting. (The pill is a proxy for education, religion, psychotherapy, or any other activity that will affect my rate of

---

78. The first statement is obvious. For the latter, see Elster (1999a), Ch. IV.3. I believe the argument in Mulligan (1997), that parents can invest in becoming more altruistic toward their children, also presupposes the attitude that the investment is supposed to produce: to want to be altruistic *is* to be altruistic. It is instructive to consider two of Mulligan's verbal justifications for his model. First, he notes (p. 73), "Parents are aware of the effects of their actions on their 'preferences' and take those effects into account when determining what actions to take." But this statement, when true, implies the very opposite conclusion of what Mulligan wants it to show. If a selfish person predicts that certain activities will make him more altruistic, he will tend to stay away from them (just as an altruistic person will tend to stay away from activities that will predictably make him more selfish). Second, he argues (p. 77), "People may naturally tend to be selfish, but parents may also spend time and effort in self-reflection in order to overcome such a natural bias." This statement suggests that people may invest resources in overcoming (Davidsonian) weakness of will (I.2). Suppose that I value both my own consumption and that of my children. Faced with the choice between a consumption allocation that gives more to me and one that gives more to my children, I may decide that all things considered I ought to realize the latter, yet I always choose the former. To make myself do what I really want to do, I might then invest resources in strengthening the value I place on the consumption of my children, so that it is less easily undermined by my selfish desires. This is a coherent account, but it does not correspond to Mulligan's formal model. In fact, as far as I know no economic model of (Davidsonian) weakness of will has been proposed.

discounting.) If I take the pill I shall be motivated to save $50 out of my net weekly income of $500. My consumption stream will be 350, 450, 450 .... up to retirement and then continue 450, 450 ... because of the return on my savings. Let us call this stream **I**. If I do not take the pill, I shall spend all my current income on consumption goods. My consumption stream will be 500, 500, 500 .... up to retirement and then continue 100, 100 ... because I would now have to live on welfare thanks to my earlier profligacy. Let us call this stream **II**. Let us finally define stream **III** by a consumption of 450 in each period – a life of prudent saving and comfortable retirement without the initial expense of the pill. By assumption, I preferred **II** over **III**, as I was unwilling to defer gratification without the pill. To take the pill, I would have to prefer **I** over **II** and, by transitivity, to prefer **I** over **III**. As long as the rate of time discounting is positive, this cannot happen, since **I** and **III** differ only in that the first has a lower initial consumption.

HYPERBOLIC DISCOUNTING AND PRECOMMITMENT

I now turn to precommitment against inconsistency. Individuals who discount the future hyperbolically will tend to deviate from their plans unless they take precautionary measures. The person who decided to spread half of his allocation evenly over the rest of his lifetime may decide, at the beginning of the second year, to spend one-half of the half in that year and then allocate the remaining 25% over the rest of his lifetime. If he discounted the future exponentially, no such change of plans would occur.

The problem is set out in a more general form in Figure I.2. At time 1, the agent has a choice between a small reward that will be made available at time 2 and a larger reward that will be made available at time 3. The curves show how these future rewards are discounted (hyperbolically) to present value at earlier times. Before t^*, when the present value curve (II) of the larger reward is above that of the smaller reward (I), the agent intends to choose the larger reward. After t^*, however, the present value of the smaller reward dominates. At time 2, he therefore chooses the smaller reward. With exponential discounting, such preference reversal can never occur: if an option is preferred at one time it is preferred at all other times.

To exhibit pure cases of hyperbolic discounting, we must look for instances that do not involve passions or cravings. Ainslie argues

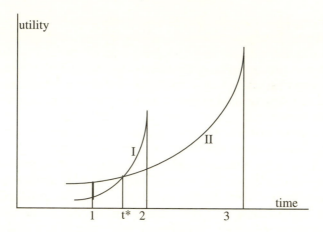

Fig. I.2

that hyperbolic discounting explains why people make resolutions to stop drinking, smoking, or gambling and then fail to carry them out, and in many cases he may well be right. Yet these behaviors are not decisive evidence for hyperbolic discounting, for the deviation from earlier plans could also be due to wishful thinking or to sudden craving triggered by cue-dependence (see I.2 and I.8). More clear-cut cases include procrastination, failure to save for Christmas or for one's old age, failure to go to bed early at night or to get up early in the morning, and failure to do physical exercise. In many of these situations, failure to keep one's resolution is plausibly due to the sheer passage of time. There may not be any passions, urges, or cravings of any kind involved (although in some cases guilt and guilt-induced denial could also contribute to procrastination). And by the argument sketched in I.2, we may reasonably assume that to a first approximation the pre-reversal preference embodies the "real" interest of the person.

The individual who finds that he constantly fails to carry out his plans, and suspects that something like hyperbolic discounting is the culprit, could respond in a number of ways. Here I shall consider only precommitment strategies. In I.8 I consider some of the strategies the person might adopt if self-binding devices are unavailable or have undesirable side effects.

Precommitment strategies include notably the first four devices of Table I.1.

(i) By making the choice of the early, smaller reward physically impossible, one obviously ensures that the larger, delayed reward is chosen.

(ii) By imposing a sufficiently large extra cost on the choice of the early reward, curve I is shifted downward so as to lie entirely below II. The larger reward is always preferred and will also be chosen at time 2.

(iii) By setting up a sufficiently large reward for the choice of the later reward, curve II is shifted upward so as to lie entirely above I. When feasible, this strategy may seem logically equivalent to the previous one, but psychologically the two may have different effects.[79] I postpone discussion of this strategy to I.7.

(iv) By the imposition of a mandatory and sufficiently long delay between the time of choice and the time at which the reward is made available to the agent, curve I is shifted to the right so that the present value of the smaller reward at time 2 is smaller than that of the larger reward. Again, this will ensure the choice of the larger reward.

To illustrate devices (i), (ii), and (iv), consider the problem of inadequate savings.[80] The formerly popular institution of Christmas clubs "offered the unusual combination of inconvenience (deposits were made in person every week), illiquidity (funds could not be withdrawn until late November), and low interest (in some cases, zero interest). Of course, illiquidity was the Christmas club's raison d'être since customers wanted to assure themselves of funds to pay for Christmas presents."[81] These institutions allowed members to pay a premium to protect themselves against their lack of willpower. They

79. There is one sense in which self-imposed rewards and self-imposed costs are conceptually different. One could ask a bank for a loan that is to be paid out only in case one chooses the later reward, and to be repaid (with interest) out of that reward. As Ole-Jørgen Skog has shown (personal communication), this strategy will, for certain parameter constellations, allow for a bootstrapping solution to the time-inconsistency problem. It is doubtful, though, that banks would give such loans without collateral. And if the person has collateral, he or she could also use it to fund self-imposed costs.

80. The second and third devices can also be illustrated by the mirror problem of excessive cash spending. A person might decide not to keep an ATM card and not have a PIN for his credit card, so that he can withdraw cash only during regular banking hours (a delay strategy). Alternatively, he could discard the ATM card but keep the PIN for his credit card, if the bank charges a fee for cash withdrawal on the card (the strategy of self-imposed costs). (I am grateful to John Alcorn for suggesting this example.)

81. Thaler (1992), p. 98.

illustrate the first device, that of making preference reversal physically impossible. Insurance companies may also embody that device, by refusing to reconvert annuities into cash or to have them used as collateral.

But the incontinent saver can also get the *bank* to pay the premium. Many banks allow for higher interest on accounts that can be drawn upon only once or twice a year, more frequent withdrawals being penalized. People who were afraid that they might not stick to their New Year's resolutions to save could use this device to protect themselves, and gain the higher interest as a bonus. This case illustrates the second precommitment device, as does the following proposal. Many people are afraid of going to the dentist. They make appointments, only to break them a day or two before they are due. To overcome this tendency, they might authorize their dentist to bill them thrice the normal fee for a canceled appointment. (See I.5 for the idea that an emotion of shame might act as a similar side bet.)

According to David Laibson,

all illiquid assets provide a form of precommitment .... A pension or retirement plan is the clearest example of such an asset. Many of these plans benefit from favorable tax treatment, and most of them effectively bar consumers from using their savings before retirement. For IRA, Keogh plans, and 401 (K) plans, consumers can access their assets, but they must pay an early withdrawal penalty. Moreover, borrowing against some of these assets is legally treated as an early withdrawal, and hence also subject to penalty. A less transparent instrument for precommitment is an investment in an illiquid asset which generates a steady stream of benefits, but which is hard to sell due to substantial transaction costs, informational problems, and/or incomplete markets. Examples include purchasing a home, buying consumer durables, and building up equity in a personal business.[82]

In Laibson's formal model, illiquid saving instruments are defined by the fact that "a sale of this asset has to be initiated one period before the actual proceeds are received." This illustrates the fourth device. In a footnote, Laibson asserts that the results derived in that model also obtain if there is instead a premium on selling the asset. As explained earlier, precommitment can be achieved either by shifting the present-value curve downward or by shifting it to the right. This equivalence does not always obtain, however. We shall see in Chapter II that

82. Laibson (1997), pp. 444–45.

constitutions sometimes constrain behavior by requiring delays, but virtually never by imposing additional costs.

Laibson also notes that to be effective, these saving schemes require a combination of paternalism and self-paternalism. Even if individuals want to bind themselves, they may be unable to do so unless the government helps them out. "This market failure arises because the schemes are vulnerable to third party arbitrage: any consumer who is engaged in one of these schemes will have an incentive to use a third party to unwind the scheme or arbitrage against the scheme unless the government explicitly forbids such third party contracting."[83] This is not a case of straightforward paternalism, forcing or inducing the citizens to save for their retirement because the government believes that their time horizon is so short that they will not do so voluntarily. Rather, the government subsidizes the rate of interest, penalizes consumption, and forbids arbitrage in order to enable the citizens to do what they really want to do.

To conclude let me mention an important "ignorance-is-bliss" result by Juan Carillo and Thomas Mariotti. They show that in some cases problems created by hyperbolic discounting may be overcome by "strategic ignorance."[84] Specifically, they argue that "there is a tradeoff in the decision to acquire information. On the one hand, under full information, the agent can take the optimal action at the present date. On the other hand, due to perfect recall, this information is shared with all future incarnations." Because the agent can predict that the latter incarnations will be excessively present-oriented from his current point of view, he may not want them to be too well informed. Suppose, for instance, that the agent is afraid of HIV transmission through unprotected sex. Although he does not know how likely it is that the virus will be transmitted by a single act of intercourse, he has an initial subjective probability distribution over this outcome. Given those priors, his optimal action is to abstain from unprotected sex. Yet he also has the option (assumed to be costless) of finding out more, by asking a doctor or consulting statistical tables. He might then rationally decide to abstain from gathering that information, if it might have the effect of lowering the estimate of

83. Laibson (1996a).
84. Carillo and Mariotti (1997). Their model stipulates the two-factor model of discounting offered by Phelps and Pollak (1968) rather than hyperbolic discounting in the strict sense.

transmission and induce a future incarnation to engage in unprotected sex because that will be optimal *from the point of view of that incarnation*.

I.4. TIME-INCONSISTENCY AND STRATEGIC BEHAVIOR

The issue of strategically based time-inconsistency is closely related to the problem of making credible *threats* and *promises*. It is useful, I believe, to discuss these together with *warnings* and *encouragements*, the latter being an admittedly imperfect term for the phenomenon that is related to promises as warnings are to threats. All these phenomena involve a statement, a choice, an event, and an outcome, occurring at four successive moments in that order.

At time 1, the speaker A makes a statement to a listener B to the effect that if B makes a certain choice at time 2, a certain event will happen at time 3. In threats and promises, the event is under the control of A. In warnings and encouragements, it is the result of a causal chain outside A's control. Once B has made his choice and the event has or has not occurred, an outcome is produced at time 4. The two actors rank the possible outcomes according to their respective preference orderings. Although A's preferences could be based on altruistic or malicious concern for B's welfare rather than on A's self-interest, I limit myself to the latter case. Because the outcome occurs after utterance, choice, and event, the time discounting of the two actors can also be relevant. I first discuss strategic time-inconsistency without discounting, then with exponential discounting, and then with hyperbolic discounting. The focus throughout is on the precommitment devices available to A.

CUTTING THE LINES OF COMMUNICATION

First, however, I want to mention and illustrate another aspect of these interactions. In general, B, no less than A, must be supposed to be a strategic agent who is capable of precommitting himself.[85]

---

85. By contrast, I argued in I.2 that in intrapersonal ("multiple-self") precommitment cases, there is usually only one "self" that is capable of precommitting itself against actions that might be undertaken by the others.

If A makes himself unable to abstain from carrying out his threat if B fails to comply, B may make himself unable to comply.[86] This is a classic case of "Chicken," in which the agent who first manages to make a (credible) precommitment strategy known can make the other back down.[87] The special case I shall discuss here arises when B makes himself unable to comply because he makes himself unable to receive messages.

We have already seen several instances of this disabling strategy. When Ulysses tied himself to the mast, he also put wax in the ears of his rowers, to prevent them from hearing the songs of the sirens. In the usual reading (but see I.1 for the different interpretation proposed by Cicero), his intention was to insulate them from noncognitive aspects of the songs, such as the allure of the melody or of the voices of the sirens. We saw how Montaigne advocated a similar strategy to block knowledge about the cognitive content of a message, for the purpose of preventing the emotions that it would predictably trigger. In discussing the work of Carillo and Mariotti, we saw how ignorance might be desirable on purely rational grounds, independently of any direct or indirect emotional impact of the message. In strategic contexts, too, one might want to block the channels of communication, to prevent oneself from receiving a message that would *rationally* induce behavior with adverse consequences. Rather than burning one's bridges, one might cut one's telephone lines.

As usual, Schelling pioneered this approach:

Threats are no good if they cannot be communicated to the persons for whom they are intended; extortion requires a means of conveying the alternatives to the intended victim. Even the threat, 'Stop crying or I'll give you something to cry about,' is ineffectual if the child is already crying too loud to hear it. (It sometimes appears that children know this.) A witness cannot be intimidated into giving false testimony if he is in custody that prevents his getting instructions on what to say, even though he might infer the sanction of the threat itself. When the outcome depends on coordination, the timely destruction of communication may be a winning tactic. When a man and his wife are arguing by telephone over where to meet for dinner, the argument is won by the wife if she simply announces where she is going and hangs up.

---

86. Alternatively, third parties may intervene to prevent B from complying. In Italy, the government freezes all assets of any person whose relative has been kidnapped so that he or she can say, credibly, "I cannot pay you."
87. See, however, Elster (1989c, pp. 170–72), for conditions under which the precommitment game is a Prisoner's Dilemma rather than a game of Chicken.

And the status quo is often preserved by a person who evades discussion of alternatives, even to the extent of simply turning off his hearing aid.[88]

A novel by Stanley Ellin, *Stronghold*, explores this idea to great effect.[89] Four shady characters plan to use the lives of three hostages to extract a large ransom from a man who is the husband of one hostage and the father of the two others, and who also happens to be president of a bank with easy access to cash. Although they must let him leave the house to get the money, they feel confident that they can control the situation by threatening to kill the hostages. The husband of one of the daughters thwarts their purpose, however, by persuading the bank president to disconnect the phone in his home, where the captors keep their hostages. Once the captors discover that they are cut off from the world and unable to communicate demands as well as threats, their plans unravel.

The strategy of cutting off lines of communication can also be deployed by agents in the role of A, namely, when the threat is to *do nothing* in case B engages in behavior with consequences that are undesirable for B as well as for A. (By contrast, when the threat is to do *something* if B engages in a specific behavior, A must learn whether the antecedent is fulfilled before he acts.) As many parents have experienced, the threat that they will not bail out their teenage children if they get into trouble is often lacking in credibility. In a seminal article on time-inconsistency, Kydland and Prescott argued that "the rational agent will know that, if he and others build houses [in a flood plain], the government will take the necessary flood-control measures," even when the socially desirable outcome is not to have houses built there.[90] Similarly, announcements by a government that it will not bail out inefficient firms or banks may not be credible. In a discussion of the recent Asian banking crisis, Shanker Satyanath has shown how this problem can be overcome by lack of reliable private channels of communication from banks to the government. In his summary,

In countries whose political-economic institutional arrangements include reliable private channels of communication from domestic private banks to the government, monetary policy decision makers will rationally accommodate information about the near insolvency of these banks in their interest

88. Schelling (1960), p. 146; see also p. 120.
89. Ellin (1974). Had he read Schelling? I don't know.
90. Kydland and Prescott (1977).

rate choices. .... Accommodation will occur because the government's com-mitment to not accommodate domestic private banks with high solvency problems is incredible on account of the high costs associated with the dis-ruption of a country's financial intermediation capabilities. The anticipation of accommodation reduces the incentives for prudence on the part of do-mestic private banks .... With regard to the counterfactual, where private channels are unreliable, domestic private banks will risk costly bank runs if they try to communicate that they are on the verge of bankruptcy, since this information is potentially observable by the public. .... These banks thus have greater incentive to be prudent and ensure solvency.[91]

In the cases considered by Satyanath, the lack of reliable private channels was an incidental rather than essential constraint. Although the inability of banks to communicate with the government had good consequences for the latter, the arm's-length policy was not estab-lished *for that purpose*. Once the causal mechanism has been discov-ered, however, it can obviously be used as a deliberate precommit-ment device.

Note the crucial feature of Satyanath's argument. The point is not that a system without reliable private channels prevents the banks from informing the government about their problem, as if the phone line had been disconnected. Rather, it is that they cannot inform the government without at the same time informing the public. In the case of the straying teenager, if the parents cannot make themselves incommunicado they might try to set up a system so that the demand for a bailout is automatically made known to his or her peers as well, with the loss of prestige this would entail. Rather than using the crude strategy of making communication physically impossible, they might act on the incentives to communicate.

No Discounting

The problem of strategic inconsistency can be stated as a problem of credibility.[92] As before, suppose that at time 1 A makes a statement about the consequences for B at time 4 if B does X rather than Y at time 2, linking them to an event E that (A claims) will occur at time 3 if and only if B does X. We may then distinguish between two sets of

91. Satyanath (1999).
92. The main intellectual originators of this idea, from very different perspectives, are Schelling (1960) and Kydland and Prescott (1977).

cases. In the first class of cases, E is the result of a causal chain that is outside A's *control*, but about which he may claim to have exclusive *knowledge*. There are four interesting subcases:

Case 1: Warnings. A knows that if B does X an event E (outside the control of either) will occur that is worse for both than if B does Y. It is then in A's interest to inform B about the causal link between X and E. Example: a trade union leader informing (at time 1) the management that if the members are refused a raise (at time 2) their morale will be so demoralized (at time 3) that productivity will suffer (at time 4).

Case 2: False warnings. This is the same case as the first, except that A's statement about a causal link between X and E is false. If B believes the statement, he will never find out that it was false.

Case 3: Encouragements. A knows that if B does X an event E will occur that is better for both than if B does Y. It is then in A's interest to inform B about the causal link between X and E. Example: a trade union leader informing the management that if the members are given a raise their morale will be so enhanced that productivity will go up to an extent that will raise profits more than the wage increase will reduce them.

Case 4: False encouragements. This is the same case as the third, except that A's statement about a causal link between X and E is false. If B believes the statement, he will later find out that it was false.

In the second class of cases, the event E is (known to be) under the control of A. Let us refer to the choice of causing that event as Z and the choice of not causing it as W. Referring to outcomes by the pair of choices that bring them about, we may distinguish among four subcases.

Case 5: Time-consistent threat. B prefers (X, W) over all other outcomes, and prefers (Y, W) over (X, Z). A prefers (Y, W) over all other outcomes, and prefers (X, Z) over (X, W). Example: B is causing a nuisance in the street outside A's house, and A tells him that if B continues to behave in that way (X) he will inform the police (Z).

Case 6: Time-inconsistent threat. B prefers (X, W) over all other outcomes, and prefers (Y, W) over (X, Z). A prefers (Y, W) over all other outcomes, and prefers (X, W) over (X, Z). Example: B is a woman, and A tells her that if she turns down his marriage proposal (X) he will kill himself (Z).

Case 7: Time-consistent promise. B and A both prefer (X, Z) over all other outcomes. Example: A and B can profit from an enterprise that requires an investment of $100,000, and each of them has $50,000 to invest. A tells B that if B invests $50,000 (X), he will do the same (Z).

Case 8: Time-inconsistent promise. B prefers (X, Z) over all other outcomes, and has (X, W) as his least preferred outcome. A prefers (X, W) over all other outcomes, and has (X, Z) as his second-ranked outcome. Example: A and B can profit from an enterprise that requires certain skills and an investment of $100,000. A has the skills, and B the money. A tells B that if B will put up the money (X), A will reimburse B with interest later (Z).

Some comments may be useful. (i) The semantics of "promise" and "warning" are actually more complicated than these explications suggest, as both terms are also regularly used in a nonconditional sense. Warnings, for instance, may enable one's interlocutor to reduce the impact of an unavoidable bad event rather than to prevent it from occurring. (ii) A speaker may not only misrepresent the truth about which event E will occur if B does X, but also disguise the fact that E is actually under his control. He may, in other words, misrepresent a threat as a warning.[93] (iii) As we shall see in I.5, this complication is especially acute if E is a future act by the speaker, presented as an object of prediction rather than of decision. (iv) A listener may deliberately misunderstand a warning as a threat. "In Belgium in 1877 when the Catholic Minister of Justice decided, despite a law which protected the freedom of the voter, not to prosecute the priests who had threatened the punishments of Hell against their parishioners who had voted for the liberal party, Paul Janson ridiculed the Minister: by raising doubts about the gravity of such threats, he was 'really committing religious heresy'."[94] If the priests (as I suspect) had only

---

93. See Elster (1999a), Ch. V.3, for the reasons why a speaker might want to use this strategy.
94. Perelman and Olbrechts-Tyteca (1969), p. 207. Similarly, a president standing for reelection may warn the voters that they will suffer economically if they vote for

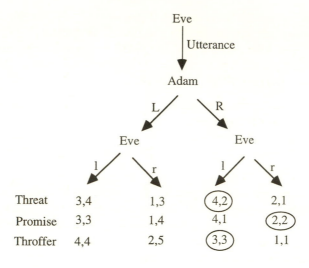

Fig. I.3

been warning their parishioners, there would be no heresy. (v) In repeated interactions, an agent in B's position has a greater incentive
to believe an encouragement than a warning, since he knows it will
be to A's disadvantage at time 5 and later to have been caught lying.

Let me give a stylized example to illustrate threats, promises, and
the mixed cases that are sometimes called "throffers," because they
rely on threats as well as offers.[95] Suppose Adam first has to make
a decision (L or R), then Eve another decision (l or r), and then they
both get payoffs that depend on the choices on both. Prior to Adam's
first move, Eve can make a statement about what she will do if Adam
chooses L or R.

The first number at each end node in Figure I.3 represents the
payoff to Adam and the second the payoff to Eve. (Equilibrium end
nodes are encircled.) In all three cases, Eve's payoffs if Adam goes
left are superior to what she can get if he goes right. She has an incentive, therefore, to induce Adam to move left, using a threat, a

his opponent, but he may not threaten to use the time between early November
and late January to make them suffer.
95. The following draws on Elster (1989c), pp. 272 ff. In that book I also give many
   examples from labor-management bargaining of time-inconsistent threats and
   promises.

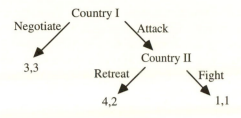

Country I

Negotiate / \ Attack

3,3   Country II

Retreat / \ Fight

4,2   1,1

Fig. I.4

promise, or a throffer. With the first set of payoffs, Eve can threaten to move right if Adam moves right. But this threat is not credible. He knows that she will not cut off her nose to spite her face by moving right; hence he moves right, knowing that she will move left. The outcome will be worse for Eve and better for Adam than it would have been if her threat had been credible. In the second case, Eve can promise to move left if Adam moves left. Once again, however, this promise is not credible. Adam knows that once he has moved left it will be in her interest to move right. As a result he will move right and Eve will move right, leaving them both worse off than if her promise had been credible. Note that this case is an extensive-game version of the standard Prisoner's Dilemma. In the third case, Eve can brand both the carrot and the stick, promising to move left if he moves left and threatening to move right if he moves right. Neither communication is credible; Adam moves right, Eve moves left; he is better off and she is worse off than if the promise/threat had been credible.

To overcome strategic time-inconsistency, an agent may resort to precommitment devices.[96] In the no-discounting case, these include the elimination of options and the imposition of additional costs. The first is proverbially expressed as "burning one's bridges," or one's ships in the French version.[97] It can be illustrated by the game shown in Figure I.4.

96. Time-inconsistency is not the only reason why self-binding (in a very literal sense) can be useful in strategic interaction. Thus when prisoners in the Soviet detention camp system were moved from one site to another, they often insisted on having their hands tied behind their backs and to have this fact explicitly noted in the protocol: "This was the only self-defense the prisoners could muster against the laconic formula 'shot while trying to escape.'" (Werth 1997, p. 154).
97. For historical examples of ship-burning, see Dixit and Nalebuff (1991), p. 169.

In the absence of precommitment, the first country will attack and the second will retreat. By eliminating the retreat option, however, the second country can force the first to the bargaining table. Another classic example is the creation of a doomsday machine, which eliminates the option of not responding to enemy attack and thereby reduces the likelihood of attack.

Following James Fearon, we may distinguish between ex ante and ex post devices for imposing costs on oneself.[98] On the one hand, an actor may adopt what Fearon calls the strategy of "tying hands," that is, by imposing costs that he will incur if he fails to carry out a threat. A classic example is the trade union leader who, by proclaiming publicly that his demand is non-negotiable, raises the stakes by making any concession hurt him more than it would otherwise have done. In international politics, too, political leaders can precommit themselves through such "audience costs," namely, by making strong public statements during a confrontation.[99] On the other hand, he may adopt the strategy of "sinking costs," that is, by imposing costs that he will have to incur regardless of what happens later. This strategy is commonly used by firms to deter entry by a potential competitor. "A firm that buys equipment today signals that it will be around tomorrow if it cannot resell the equipment. Thus, we may conjecture that the buying of equipment – if it is observed by one's rivals – may have strategic effects, and therefore is not a purely internal cost-minimization issue."[100] A firm may also adopt the sunk cost strategy to deter a union, e.g. by building up large inventories that will enable it to weather a strike.

Another example of sinking costs involves the use of the law as a precommitment device. As many writers have observed, the law of contracts is enabling rather than restricting: it allows people to make promises that otherwise would not have been credible. Law can also enhance the credibility of threats. Suppose that you owe me $30,000 but you refuse to pay, and it will cost me $40,000 in legal fees to take you to court to collect the money. Although my threat to take you to court is not credible by itself, I can pay a lawyer a retainer of $10,001,

98. Fearon (1997).
99. See Fearon (1994) for a discussion of such "audience costs" in international politics. He notes that to the extent that the audience is domestic rather than international, authoritarian states are less able to precommit themselves than democratic ones. I return to this idea in Ch. II.9.
100. Tirole (1988), pp. 314–15.

a nonrefundable advance on legal fees of going to court. Now, I gain $30,000 minus the remaining legal fees ($29,999), or $1, by going to court, so that the threat to go to court is now credible. You should then be willing to pay me the $30,000 to avoid your own court costs.[101]

EXPONENTIAL DISCOUNTING

In the standard case of sequential bargaining, two players take turns to make offers and counteroffers.[102] The reason they manage to reach agreement is that bargaining is costly and that they have a common interest in preventing the pie from shrinking while they are bargaining over its division. In labor-management bargaining, the pie might shrink because of loss of production from a strike. In bargaining over a divorce settlement, it might shrink because of the need to pay the lawyers who are actually conducting the negotiation. In the case that concerns me here, the pie shrinks by the mere passage of time. If a bargainer discounts future rewards, he might prefer five dollars today rather than holding out for six tomorrow. If his opponent knows this, a threat to turn down any offer short of six dollars will not be credible. In the standard models of sequential bargaining, the discounting is always assumed to be exponential.

In these models, the standard precommitment devices of eliminating options and imposing costs remain available. In addition, there is now scope for the creation of delays, because a party can get an edge by extending its response time. In wage bargaining, for instance, the more the bargaining pie shrinks during the period when the union considers an offer by the employers, the more the latter have to lose by not giving in to the union's claim and hence the more likely they are to do so.[103] The internal weakness and lack of integration of many unions may, paradoxically, enhance their bargaining power because they can claim, *credibly*, that it will take them a long time to respond to the management's offer. Conversely, the management of a subsidiary

101. I owe this example to James Fearon.
102. Actually, the models do not allow for real-time bargaining. Instead, the bargainers mentally review all possible bargaining scenarios to identify the unique proposal that does not involve noncredible threats or promises. See Ch. 2 of Elster (1989c) for an elementary discussion, and Osborne and Rubinstein (1990) for a more advanced treatment.
103. Barth (1988). See also de Geer (1986), p. 353.

of a multinational firm may gain bargaining power by pointing out that any counterproposal by the union will have to be sent back to headquarters. In either case, the organization has an incentive to set up a slow and cumbersome internal decision-making machinery. The features that are responsible for the delay must be in place before the negotiations begin, and must not be easily modifiable. If the management demands that the union change its bylaws so as to be able to respond more quickly, the union may respond that it would take even longer to consult its members on that issue.

NON-EXPONENTIAL DISCOUNTING

To my knowledge, there is no literature that discusses strategic interaction with hyperbolic discounting. Yet it is easy to see how this issue might arise if we extend the model of threats and promises from four to five periods. Assume that A is subject to naive, hyperbolic discounting. Assume, moreover, that if A keeps his promise he will receive a large payoff at time 5, and a smaller payoff at time 4 if he reneges. At time 1 when the promise is uttered, he may sincerely believe that he will respect it, since from that vantage point doing so would be in his self-interest. Yet as he moves closer to the time when he must make good on his promise, the hyperbolic discounting induces a preference reversal that causes him to break it.

If B could anticipate that outcome, he would not believe the promise. He would choose to do Y rather than X, and A's choice whether to keep his promise would not arise, as it was contingent on X. But suppose B is subject to the same naive hyperbolic discounting. In that case, A's promise might be as credible to B as it is sincere for A. A deal might be struck in good faith on both sides, and then fall apart because A loses the incentive to carry out his promise. In this case, the final outcome differs from what both expected initially. The case of hyperbolically inconsistent threats is different. When A makes his threat, both A and B believe he will carry it out; hence B complies with A's wishes. When the time arrives at which A would have had to carry out the threat had B not complied, A would no longer have wanted to do so, but this counterfactual loss of nerve makes no difference for the outcome.

If A is sophisticated and also believes that B believes that A discounts hyperbolically, A might overcome the time-inconsistency by delaying the smaller reward so that at time 3 he still prefers the larger reward. Because of the general equivalence of delays and self-imposed costs, the latter method could also be used. Needless to say, eliminating the smaller reward altogether would serve the same purpose. Note the different roles of delay in the exponential and non-exponential cases. In bargaining with exponential discounting, threats that would otherwise have been noncredible are made credible by inserting a delay in the decision-process itself. (Recall that this is also how delays might be used to counteract passion.) In bargaining with non-exponential discounting, time-inconsistency is overcome by delaying the rewards that follow the decision. Presumably, response delays could be effective in that case too.

I.5. PASSION AS A DEVICE FOR SELF-BINDING

The idea that precommitment can serve to overcome time-inconsistency problems dates from the 1950s (Strotz and Schelling). When earlier writers – I have cited Seneca and Montaigne – referred to precommitment, it was invariably as a check on passion. Jack Hirshleifer and Robert Frank turn the idea on its head, by arguing that *emotions are solutions rather than problems*; they are precommitment devices that enable agents to overcome time-inconsistency problems. The idea is not a complete reversal of the traditional view. In that view, precommitment was supposed to protect the agent against the effects of *occurrent emotions*. In the more recent view, *emotional dispositions* serve as precommitment devices.[104] According to Frank, emotions solve the self-control problem caused by hyperbolic discounting, as well as the problem of credibility in strategic interaction. According to Hirshleifer, emotions sustain the credibility of threats and promises that would otherwise not be credible. Their arguments rely on two main features of the emotions: their painful or pleasurable qualities and their quasi-automatic action tendencies that can make people act against their rational self-interest.[105]

To the extent that Hirshleifer and Frank rely on the latter feature, their arguments could be said to illustrate the general idea of "the

---

104. As mentioned at the end of I.3, occurrent emotions may also serve as precommitment devices.
105. See Elster (1999a), Ch. IV.2.

rationality of being irrational." Strictly speaking, however, this phrase is meaningless. One might argue that it is rational to make an effort to *appear* to be irrational, that is, to simulate irrational, emotional behavior in order to deter an opponent. The results about reputation-building in games with imperfect information might be extended in this direction.[106] Alternatively, one might argue that it is rational to try to *develop* these emotional dispositions rather than merely faking them.[107] Frank and Hirshleifer adopt neither approach. Their claim is that irrationality is useful, not that it is rational to simulate or develop irrationality. They argue that the emotional dispositions in question evolve through natural selection by virtue of their enhancement of reproductive fitness.

Toward the end of this section I raise some questions concerning the alleged reproductive benefits of these dispositions. Here I want to ask how plausible it is that they could develop, assuming that they have these benefits. By assumption, the emotional disposition will often induce the agent to act against his short-term interest. When others learn that he has this disposition, they will act in ways that promote his long-term interest. Natural selection, however, does not always wait for the long term. Strategies of the kind "One step backward, two steps forward" are not in its repertoire.[108] The first organism to display irrational anger – that is, a tendency to retaliate at no gain and some cost to itself – would be at an evolutionary disadvantage that could not be offset by the advantages that would accrue to its descendants once the behavior was generalized and recognized by others. Although this may not be an insuperable difficulty, it would have to be recognized in a more fully fleshed-out account.

106. Kreps et al. (1982). An argument of this kind would have to take account of the costs of hypocrisy, which may be considerable, not merely by the psychic discomfort it induces (Rabin 1993) but by the effort needed to maintain an emotional appearance across the board.

107. An argument to this effect would have to balance the cost of developing the relevant dispositions against the benefits from having them. Because the costs are incurred early on and the benefits only emerge later, the decision to develop the dispositions might (in the hyperbolic discounting case) be subject to the very problem they are supposed to solve. At time 1 the decision to start developing the disposition at time 2 might look like a good idea, in view of the later benefits it will provide, but at time 2 the costs might loom too large and a preference reversal might take place.

108. Elster (1984), Ch. I. As Dagfinn Føllesdal and Ole-Jørgen Skog (personal communications) have impressed on me, this statement depends on an assumption about the relative speed of two processes (the rate of mutation and the rate of extinction of organisms with deleterious mutations) that is not necessarily satisfied in practice.

FRANK ON STRATEGIC ASPECTS OF EMOTION

Robert Frank argues that emotions serve as solutions to the problem of time-inconsistency. Guilt affects the credibility of promises, whereas anger and envy affect the credibility of threats. The emotions exercise these effects in two ways, by what Frank calls a "sincere-manner" pathway and by a reputational pathway. Whereas the first mechanism generates honest or cooperative behavior in one-shot Prisoner's Dilemmas, the second has implications for iterated games as well as for one-shot games.

The "sincere-manner" pathway involves three premises. First, emotional dispositions are imperfectly indicated to others by the outward expressions of occurrent emotions. Second – and that is why the indication is only imperfect – even those who do not have the dispositions can simulate the expressions. Third, simulators can be detected, at some (fixed) cost to the detectors. Applying these premises to a world in which agents engage in one-shot Prisoner's Dilemma interactions with others, Frank shows that there will be some specific proportion of honest and dishonest individuals in the equilibrium state (frequency-dependent polymorphism). In that state, honest and dishonest individuals have the same expected payoff, so that there is no evolutionary pressure favoring the one or the other group. Moreover, the honest individuals are exactly indifferent between scrutinizing and not scrutinizing their interaction partners,[109] so that there is no evolutionary pressure favoring the one or the other behavior. In Frank's numerical example, a situation in which 75% of the individuals are honest and 75% of those are scrutinizers can perpetuate itself forever.

Note, however, that there is no evolutionary mechanism that can ensure that 75% of the honest will in fact be scrutinizers. Whereas an honest individual who switched to dishonest behavior in equilibrium would be penalized, an honest nonscrutinizer who switched to scrutinizing would not suffer any adverse consequences. The only consequence would be lower payoffs for the dishonest. After a while

---

109. In equilibrium, the sum of the direct and opportunity costs of scrutinizing a potential partner are exactly equal to the expected opportunity cost of not scrutinizing him or her. The latter cost is the probability that a partner chosen at random will be dishonest multiplied by the difference between the cooperative payoff and the "sucker" payoff in the Prisoner's Dilemma. When the proportion of cooperators exceeds the equilibrium share, the probability falls so that scrutiny no longer pays, which allows noncooperators to survive.

this would reduce the number of dishonest, which would reduce the payoffs for scrutinizing and hence induce the honest to stop scrutinizing. This development, in turn, would favor the dishonest, and so on. Although Frank shows that the proportions of honest versus dishonest and of scrutinizers versus nonscrutinizers will both fluctuate around 75% versus 25%, the argument says nothing about the magnitude of the fluctuations or the speed of the correction mechanism. For all we know, the population could be far away from the equilibrium a large proportion of the time.

The central claim in the reputational-pathway argument is that emotions can solve the self-control problem as well as the credibility problem. Actually, as Frank acknowledges in a footnote, the argument for the first conclusion really is that emotions counteract *impatience*, that is, very high rates of time discounting.[110] Whether the discounting is exponential or hyperbolic is inessential. I am not saying that emotions may not have a role in self-control more specifically. Suppose that on February 1 I make an appointment to see my dentist on March 1, because at that date the discounted disutility from future toothaches exceeds the discounted utility of the pain from drilling. Because I discount the future hyperbolically, however, a preference reversal occurs on February 28. I nevertheless go ahead with the appointment because of the anticipation of the shame I would feel from canceling it. Here, shame works in the same way as the premium on withdrawal from a savings account.

This is not, however, the kind of situation Frank has in mind. He considers the role of emotions in reputation-building in repeated interaction. An agent who is given the opportunity of defecting in a Prisoner's Dilemma may know that if he does so he will gain a reputation for being uncooperative that will harm him in the future. If he discounts the future at a sufficiently high rate, however, he may nevertheless go for the quick gain (or "specious reward") and forsake the long-term benefits. Yet if the person "is emotionally predisposed to regard cheating as an unpleasurable act in and of itself – that is, if he has a conscience – he will be better able to resist the temptation to cheat.[111] If the psychological reward mechanism is constrained to

---

110. Frank (1988), p. 82.
111. To bring out the difference between this argument and the argument from Montaigne considered in note 40, consider the choice of cooperation versus defection in the Prisoner's Dilemma. In Frank's analysis, it is the mere fact of defecting that

emphasize rewards in the present moment, the simplest counter to a specious reward from cheating is to have a current feeling that tugs in precisely the opposite direction. Guilt is just such a feeling."[112] This argument applies to impatience as well as to lack of self-control. In fact, each of the many references to "impulse control problems" in Frank's book could be replaced by "impatience" without affecting the argument.

Frank extends the argument to anger and envy. Considering anger, he argues, "Perfectly rational persons with perfect self-control would always seek revenge whenever the future reputational gains outweigh the current costs of taking action. The problem ... is that the gains from a tough reputation come only in the future while the costs of vengeance-seeking occur now. ... Being predisposed to feel anger when wronged helps solve this impulse-control problem."[113] Considering envy, he argues that it is

often prudent to refuse a favorable transaction when the terms are starkly one-sided. By so doing, one can develop a reputation for being a tough bargainer which will mean better terms in future transactions. In this case, too, we have future gains pitted against current costs and the resulting impulse-control problem. Here, someone who feels envious or resentful when he gets less than his fair share taps into the reward mechanism in the current moment.[114]

----

makes one feel bad. According to Montaigne, it is the fact of defecting *after the other person has cooperated* that makes one feel bad. To meet distrust with distrust and trust with trust seems to be a general propensity of human nature. This form of reciprocity differs from that which is embodied in the tit-for-tat strategy in the Prisoner's Dilemma. Tit-for-tat can be a winning strategy when the game is played many times and the two choices in any given game are made simultaneously. The present argument, by contrast, applies to one-shot games in which one party makes a choice, and makes it known, before the other party makes a choice.

112. Ibid. This argument was anticipated by Arthur Lovejoy (1961), p. 80: "The consideration ... that if I eat Welsh rabbit this evening, I shall much regret it tomorrow, may not suffice to deter me from the eating – if I like Welsh rabbit. But the addition of the consideration that those who obtain trivial present pleasure at the cost of future pain are gluttonous fools, or weak-minded, may suffice to turn the scale in favor of abstinence." In the present discussion, I do not question the assumption – common to Frank, Hirshleifer, and Lovejoy – that emotions such as shame or envy can be represented as "psychic costs." In Elster (1999a), Ch. IV.3, I argue, however, that the way emotions enter into the explanation of behavior is considerably more complex.
113. Frank (1988), p. 83.
114. Ibid.

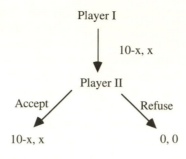

Fig. I.5

We may apply this argument to the Ultimatum Game.[115] As shown in Figure I.5, player I first proposes a division of ten dollars between player II and himself, with x for II and 10 − x for himself. Only whole dollar amounts can be proposed. Player II then is offered the choice between accepting the proposal and ruining the transaction so that neither gets anything.

In experiments with this game, a regular finding is that most people put in the position of player II will reject offers that leave them with less than three dollars out of the ten to be divided. Because most people in the position of player I anticipate this reaction (or because they are altruistic), they tend to offer more than the bare minimum of one dollar that would be expected if both were and knew each other to be motivated only by material self-interest. For some position-II players, their refusal may be caused by anger. For others, envy might be the motivating force. The former choose (0, 0) because the payoffs are modified by the additional benefit from revenge, the latter because they are modified by the additional cost from envy.

Frank's argument can now be reinterpreted in terms of strategic time-inconsistency. In a (one-shot) Ultimatum Game, someone placed in the position of player II might be allowed the option of making a threat before player I makes his proposal, for example, of threatening to refuse any offer giving him less than five dollars. Envy would serve as a straightforward side bet to make the threat credible. Anger, by contrast, would affect the outcome in a more unusual way. It would work – through the pleasures of revenge – by making the less

115. For this game, see Guth, Schmittberger, and Schwartz (1982), Roth (1995), and the comments in Frank (1988), pp. 173–74.

preferred outcome more preferred rather than by making the more preferred outcome less preferred.

For envy or anger to improve the outcome for player II, in material terms and not merely in psychic terms, he must have a *reputation* for being envious or vindictive. This argument must not be confused with the idea that in a finitely iterated Prisoner's Dilemma or Ultimatum Game, backward induction will induce the self-interested behavior in all games unless one of the players believes that the other might be a genuinely irrational person.[116] Frank addresses the question of reputation-building in iterated games with an infinite horizon. In the standard analysis of these games, cooperative or vindictive behavior can be supported as part of an equilibrium in which it is common knowledge that all players are rational and self-interested. Here, a "reputation" for being cooperative or vindictive merely refers to other people's belief about the equilibrium behavior of an agent, not to their beliefs about the agent's motivation. In Frank's analysis, by contrast, beliefs about motivations matter.

To see the difference between Frank's argument and the standard analysis, consider the folk theorem for infinitely iterated games: for any set of reward parameters in a one-shot game and for (essentially) any behavior, there exists a rate of discounting r that will sustain that behavior as an equilibrium strategy in iterated plays of the game.[117] Frank's argument might be stated as asserting that for any r and for any behavior, there exists a modification of the reward parameters through emotional side penalties or side benefits that will sustain that behavior. To be sure, Frank does not state his conclusion in that stark form. I do so merely to indicate how he is essentially turning an old argument on its head. From Descartes onward it has often been argued that prudence or long-term self-interest can mimic morality.[118] Because morality was thought to be more fragile than prudence, many welcomed the idea that the latter was sufficient for social order. By contrast, if one believes that self-interest is likely to be shortsighted rather than farsighted, the moral emotions might be needed to mimic prudence.[119]

Frank does not merely argue, however, that emotions induce *behavior* that is indistinguishable from that which would be induced by

---

116. Kreps et al. (1982).   117. Fudenberg and Tirole (1992), Section 5.1.2.
118. Elster (1984), Ch. II.4.
119. In Ch. IV.3 of Elster (1999a) I discuss how Antonio Damasio (1994) reaches a similar conclusion from very different and (in my opinion) less plausible premises.

long-term self-interest. It is important for his argument that others believe one's *motivation* to be moral rather than prudent. An individual with a reputation for being moral can have an advantage even in a one-shot Prisoner's Dilemma that a merely prudent individual would not.[120] If it is common knowledge that people by and large discount the future heavily and one individual acts as if he does not, others will infer that there is a good chance that he is moral and to be trusted even in situations where cheating would not be detected.

Given the usefulness of being moral, Frank argues that there is no "difficulty seeing why parents might want to install moral sentiments" in their children.[121] He also argues, "The widespread and chronic impulsiveness of criminal offenders may ... be interpreted as support for the claim that emotional competencies underlie moral behavior."[122] But the findings are equally consistent with the claim that criminals discount the future so heavily that moral sentiments of average strength are insufficient to offset their myopia. The only reason to single out morality as an explanatory variable would be if discounting rates were constant across individuals. On that we have some evidence. Small children show clear differences in the ability to delay gratification, correlated in the expected manner with success later in life.[123]

To conclude, Frank claims to address one form of time-inconsistency (hyperbolic discounting), but in fact mainly addresses the other (lack of credibility). Although he makes many general references to the role of emotions in overcoming hyperbolic discounting, his actual argument refers only to their role in counteracting *high* rates of discounting. By contrast, his analysis of reputation-building is really an argument about strategic time-inconsistency. If a person's behavior in iterated games supports an inference to the conclusion that he is swayed by emotions that make him willing to act against his material self-interest, he can make threats and promises in one-shot games that would otherwise not be credible. (If the high rates of discounting are hyperbolically shaped, both forms of time-inconsistency will be

---

120. Frank (1988), p. 91.
121. Frank (1988), p. 93. In his argument, the motivation for parental inculcation of guilt is their desire to promote the welfare of their children. It should be contrasted with the argument in Becker (1996, Ch. 7) according to which parents behave in this way to promote their own welfare – inducing guilt in the children so that they will take care of the parents when they grow old. For a discussion of the latter argument, see Elster (1999a), Ch. IV.3.
122. Frank (1988), p. 162.
123. Mischel, Shoda, and Rodriguez (1989).

combined.) A potentially weak link in Frank's analysis is the assumption that people's beliefs about discounting rates are such as to justify this inference.

HIRSHLEIFER ON STRATEGIC ASPECTS OF EMOTION

In a pioneering article, "The emotions as guarantors of threats and promises," Jack Hirshleifer explicitly argued that emotions can help us overcome the credibility problem.[124] He assumes a sequential game with two actors, who have different emotional makeups and different economic roles. The first actor is purely self-interested or unemotional, whereas the second may be subject to one of the various emotions discussed later. The first actor chooses a point on a joint production frontier, that is, a set of joint payoffs prior to redistribution. The second actor is in charge of redistribution. He can either transfer part of his income to the other or inflict a loss on the other at some cost to himself. Hirshleifer discusses two pairs of emotional responses that might govern the behavior of the second party. The first is a pair of what he calls "action-independent" emotions: benevolence and malevolence. The second are "action-dependent": gratitude and anger. His notion of benevolence turns out to be a preference for equality, that is, the desire to give to those who have less than oneself and to receive from those who have more.[125] The reason why it is called "benevolence" is presumably that only the first of these two wishes can be implemented in behavior. His notion of malevolence, similarly, combines envy toward those who have more and malice toward those who have less. Here, too, only malice has implications for behavior. A malevolent person can make the other person worse off at his own expense, but cannot make himself better off at the other's expense.

The first actor may either overlook the possibility that the second may engage in redistribution or take account of that possibility when he makes his choice. In the first case, he will choose the point on the frontier that maximizes his own income prior to redistribution.

124. Hirshleifer (1987).
125. This statement is a slight simplification. Figure 14.2 (a) in Hirshleifer (1987) indicates that at higher income levels a benevolent person prefers to allocate a given income between himself and the recipient in a way that gives slightly more to himself. The presentation in the text of Hirshleifer's notion of malevolence is subject to a similar simplification.

This point will (in the case envisaged by Hirshleifer) also make the second actor well enough off to transfer some income to the first, who therefore receives an unexpected bonus. The first could have done even better, however, by choosing a point on the frontier that leaves him worse off before redistribution, but makes the second so well off that he will transfer a large sum to the first. If the first is aware of the second's benevolent disposition, he will take the risk of making himself worse off in order to be made better off. In fact, both players end up better off in both material and psychic terms (for the first player these criteria coincide) if the first player is farsighted and sophisticated than if he is naive and myopic. Similarly, if the second player is malevolent the first is better off choosing a point on the frontier where the second is so poor that he cannot afford to hurt the first, even if that point also involves a relatively low income for the first. The outcome makes both players worse off in material and psychic terms than under the income distribution that would have obtained had the second been motivated by rational self-interest. (Note that this is a comparison of two income distributions as evaluated by the same preferences, not of two distributions evaluated by different preferences.)

In my opinion, this story has nothing to do with threats and promises, only with the first player's ability to predict what the other will do. If a benevolent second player announces that the first player will be amply rewarded if he takes the risk, this is more like an encouragement than like a promise. This might seem like a verbal quibble. In the case of threats, however, the flaws in Hirshleifer's analysis turn upon substantive rather than terminological matters. Because the second person is better off *in terms of his malevolent preferences* if the first player believes he is selfish than if he believes him to be malevolent, the second person has no incentive to announce his malicious intentions and every incentive to hide them. Why make a threat (or a warning) if one has nothing to gain if the other believes it?

Hirshleifer's analysis of anger and gratitude also has some quaint aspects. In one of the cases he uses to illustrate the role of these emotions, Hirshleifer assumes that the second person will have no emotional reaction (and thus will not make any transfer) if the first behaves selfishly, that is, if he chooses the point on the frontier that maximizes his income prior to redistribution. If the first player, however, chooses a point that offers less to both, the second will reply by angrily making both of them even worse off. Conversely, if the first player takes the risk of choosing a point that makes him worse off but has the potential for making him better off (after redistribution), the second will be so grateful that he will in fact transfer some income to the first.

But this last claim makes no psychological sense. The second player will not feel any gratitude toward the first if he perceives that the seemingly risky and generous choice was motivated by self-interest.[126] Gratitude presupposes the belief that one's benefactor acted out of sympathy rather than for the sake of gain. Thus the first actor must misrepresent his intention as benevolence in order to gain the benefits from the gratitude of the second. But then the first player cannot make a promise that appeals to the self-interest of the second. The case of threats is even stranger. For the first player to choose a point that makes both worse off, he would have to be malevolent. Hirshleifer assumes that the second will react to malevolence by anger, that is, by doing something that would make them both even worse off. By assumption, the second has the capacity to make them worse off in financial terms, but if the first is malevolent this need not make him worse off in psychic terms. He might in fact *wish* the second to use his resources to make them both worse off.

OBJECTIONS TO THE STRATEGIC ANALYSIS OF EMOTION

Frank and Hirshleifer both argue that negative emotions such as envy or anger could have evolved because they enhance our ability to make credible threats. A problem with their analyses is their tacit assumption that the cost-benefit analysis of emotional dispositions can be analyzed in terms of isolated encounters with other individuals not similarly disposed. In any such encounter, a person known to be envious or angry will indeed get his way. Yet this analysis ignores two other aspects that might well tip the balance in the other direction.

A Mafioso may do very well for himself in encounters with ordinary, law-abiding, rationally self-interested citizens,[127] but very badly

---

126. Kahn and Tice (1973). On the general importance of beliefs about motivations in triggering emotional reactions, see also Elster (1999a), Ch. IV.2. Thus whereas spontaneous expressions of contempt tend to induce shame, deliberate attempts to induce shame tend instead to trigger anger.
127. In Campbell (1995) the Mafioso DiBella gets his wife, Connie, to seduce the lawyer Vollmer, who can get him an important contract. In the reasoning of one of the characters, "Connie DiBella [got] him over that night because she wanted DiBella to know and wanted Vollmer to know that DiBella knew there was a little hanky-

in conflicts with other Mafiosi. Frank is aware of this point,[128] but does not draw the proper implication, namely, that anger or vindictiveness would lose their evolutionary edge, and in fact become counterproductive, if they became fixed in the population. Evolutionary game theorists, therefore, argue that the outcome will be a frequency-dependent equilibrium in which "Hawks" and "Doves" coexist in some determinate proportion.[129] In this equilibrium, each type does exactly as well as the other, because the inability to back down has gains and losses that exactly offset each other. There is no advantage to being emotional.[130]

A second problem can be stated by citing a phrase from Frank and then turning it around: "A person known to eschew self-interest faces opportunities that a pure rationalist does not, even though he gains less than a pure rationalist would in each exchange. The rationalist's problem, which the self-interest model repeatedly overlooks, is that he tends to be excluded from many profitable exchanges."[131] This may be true of positive emotions (honesty and love), but with the negative emotions it's rather the other way around. People will learn to recognize irascible and envious people, and walk around them rather than have any dealings with them. Sometimes one has no choice, but often one can find alternative and more reasonable partners. Irascible and vindictive people will find themselves shunned, which is unpleasant in itself and – more relevantly in the present perspective – detracts from opportunities for mutually favorable interactions with others. They may gain more in each interaction, but have fewer interactions. I am not saying that the net effect of these emotions is negative, only that so far I have not seen anyone even *trying* to argue that it is positive. Moreover, irascible people will not be able to learn that their emotional disposition works against them, and hence will have no incentive to get rid of it or to curb it. They will get positive reinforcement from their encounters with others – being angry

---

panky going on." Knowing that a Mafioso knows you are having an affair with his wife is likely to make you very willing to give him preferential treatment when you are handing out a contract.

128. In Frank (1988), p. 242, he observes that the disastrous outcome of the Falkland war – a bloody and expensive war fought over an intrinsically unimportant piece of real estate – occurred because *both* the British and the Argentines were moved by feelings of moral outrage.

129. Maynard-Smith (1982).

130. In the second edition of his textbook on microeconomics, Frank (1996, Ch. 7) recognizes this point.

131. Frank (1988), pp. 228–29.

works! – but they cannot get any feedback from the encounters they fail to have.

I.6. VARIATIONS ON A RUSSIAN NOBLEMAN

In I.2 and I.5 I have argued that passions can serve both as reasons for precommitment and as devices for precommitment. *Preference change* has a similarly dual status. In I.2 I discussed the idea that we can try to precommit ourselves by changing our preferences. Conversely, we may use a precommitment device to prevent a change of preferences, or at least to disable ourselves from acting on changed preferences. This is the topic of the present section.

<small>RELIGION AND PRECOMMITMENT</small>

In *Ulysses and the Sirens* I cited the following passage from an article by Derek Parfit:

> Let us take a nineteenth-century Russian who, in several years, should inherit vast estates. Because he has socialist ideals, he intends, now, to give the land to the peasants. But he knows that in time his ideals may fade. To guard against this possibility, he does two things. He first signs a legal document which will automatically give away the land, and which can only be revoked with his wife's consent. He then says to his wife, 'If I ever change my mind, and ask you to revoke the document, promise me that you will not consent.' He might add, 'I regard my ideals as essential to me. If I lose these ideals, I want you to think that *I* cease to exist. I want you to regard your husband, then, not as me, the man who asks you for this promise, but only as his later self. Promise me that you would not do what he asks.'[132]

Referring to the same passage, Akeel Bilgrami argues for a theory of *fundamental commitments* that also has clear implications for *pre*-commitment.[133] In his definition, "a desire is a fundamental commitment if we would want it satisfied even if we did not have that desire." The commitment might induce a desire to have or retain a certain desire, if that made its satisfaction more likely, but this would

---

132. Parfit (1973), p. 145; cited in Elster (1984), p. 109. See also Parfit (1984), pp. 327–29. As a solution to the nobleman's predicament, the device is needlessly elaborate: the role of the wife is introduced merely to formulate and discuss *her* predicament.
133. Bilgrami (1996).

be secondary. If the person could choose between, on the one hand, having the desire and not having it fulfilled, and on the other hand, not having it and having it fulfilled, he would prefer the latter.

A desire for ice cream cannot be a fundamental commitment, because our only reason for wanting it to be satisfied is that we have it. By contrast, the Russian nobleman's desire to give his land to the peasants counts as a fundamental commitment. In his case, there is no mention of using precommitment devices to maintain his desire to give his land to the peasantry. He intends to neutralize the effect of a preference change, not to prevent it. Bilgrami discusses Iranian fundamentalists in a similar perspective:

Certain sections of the Iranian government today are precisely arguing against others in the government that in future Iran should have an Islamic way of life (and they should entrench it so that it abides in the future) even though they are happy to admit (perhaps *because* they admit) that in the future due to inevitable modernizing influences from within and from abroad, they might cease to have the desire to live according to Islamic tenets.

Although I find Bilgrami's definition of a fundamental commitment very fruitful, this particular application raises some difficulties. A logical problem is that a country, unlike an individual, cannot use the legal system to bind itself or to entrench a certain lifestyle. There is nobody else that can hold a country to its commitment. (See also Chapter II.) If future Iranians do not want to live according to Islamic tenets, they can and will give them up. A theological question – about which I know nothing – is whether Islamic doctrine would be satisfied by outward observance of the rituals, assuming it could be imposed, without any inward belief. The desire for an Islamic lifestyle might be part of the very lifestyle one wants to see observed. Finally, there is an empirical question whether Bilgrami is right in imputing this argument to these circles in government. Although once again I know nothing about the facts of the case, one could also imagine the fundamentalists trying to prevent the preference changes that Bilgrami describes as inevitable. The key precommitment device here would be *maintenance of ignorance* about the West and its values.[134]

134. As observed by an anonymous author, writing in *The Wall Street Journal* on May 23, 1997, p. A18, the American economic sanctions against Iran may actually serve Iranian interests, by limiting the occasions for value-corroding interactions with the West. If the United States really wants to undermine the Iranian regime, "Washington should now stand aside and let the business emissaries of the 'Great Satan' give the Iranians what they want – and more."

It is of course debatable whether this would be a case of *self*-binding. As with the constitutional precommitments discussed in Chapter II, one could argue that it is rather a case of one generation (or its elite) trying to bind its successors. In some cases, this description would certainly be more accurate. The maintenance of ignorance is then an act of paternalism rather than self-paternalism. Yet the idea of self-binding is not meaningless. You need not know much about Western or modern ideas and values to be able to figure out that if you got to know them better they would undermine your faith. It is not like a man who tries to avoid seeing cats because they make him hysterical, and then discovers that to avoid them he has first to notice them, which makes him hysterical. A better analogy is with somebody who has sufficient experience of how drugs affect him to know that if he took more he would get addicted.[135] Unlike the case illustrated in Figure I.1, the threshold for detection of a danger may come *before* the point of no return.

The Iranian example is a variation on an old theme. Many non-Western or nonmodern societies, or subcultures, have felt threatened by Western or modern values, and deliberately tried to insulate themselves from their influence. Joseph Levenson's *Confucian China and Its Modern Fate* is a classical study of this phenomenon.[136] More recently, indigenous minority groups have demanded to be protected against the majority culture surrounding them. Although liberal societies accord their minority members freedom to maintain their religion or their traditional lifestyle, that freedom may not be a sufficient bulwark against liberalism. To prevent religious or cultural assimilation, the minority may have to precommit itself in ways that reduce the freedom of its individual members.

Often, these actions take the form of restricting the freedom of choice of the younger generation, that is, to protect them from outside influences during a time of life in which they are especially vulnerable. In 1971, the U.S. Supreme Court upheld a decision by the Wisconsin Supreme Court, which had struck down a conviction of three Amish families for refusing to send their children to public school after completion of the eighth grade.[137] (Wisconsin had compulsory schooling until the age of 16.) The majority opinion, written by Chief Justice Burger, accepted the Amish view of "secondary education as

---

135. For a formal model of this phenomenon, see Orphanides and Zervos (1995).
136. Levenson (1968); also Elster (1983b), pp. 154–56.
137. 406 US 205.

an impermissible exposure of their children to a 'worldly' influence in conflict with their beliefs." More specifically, the Court endorsed the idea that "formal high school education, beyond the eighth grade is contrary to Amish beliefs, not only because it places Amish children in an environment hostile to Amish beliefs with increasing emphasis on competition in class work and sports and with pressure to conform to the styles, manners, and way of the peer group, but also because it takes them away from their community, physically and emotionally, during the crucial and formative adolescent period of life."

The minority opinion, written by Justice Douglas, made a distinction among the three Amish children involved in the case. One of them had taken part in the following exchange:

Q. So I take it then, Frieda, the only reason you are not going to school, and did not go to school since last September, is because of *your* religion?

A. Yes.

Q. That is the only reason.

A. Yes. (Emphasis supplied.)

On the basis of her testimony, and his opinion that a child of her age possessed the "moral and intellectual judgment demanded" by the question, Justice Douglas decided that Frieda's decision ought to be respected. By contrast, he dissented as far as the two other children were concerned, because they had not testified that their *"own* religious views are opposed to high-school education" (my italics).

Now we might well doubt whether Frieda's belief that two more years in public school would be an "impermissible exposure to a worldly influence in conflict with her beliefs" was in fact an autonomous one. It is more likely, perhaps, that her fear of the effects of peer pressure was shaped by parental influence. From the present point of view, however, that issue is irrelevant. All that matters is that Frieda expressed a desire to remain ignorant about the modern world, and that the law (or at least Justice Douglas) decided to respect it. Similarly, even if the Russian nobleman had been brainwashed by his fellow radicals into wishing to give away his land, that does not detract from the causal efficacy of his wish. In both cases, the proximate cause is self-paternalism, regardless of the ultimate cause of that motive.

The precommitment strategies of the Amish extend widely beyond education. The use of telephones and electricity is regulated with the same purpose in mind, namely, to prevent preference change that might undermine Amish values.[138] In the case of the telephone, what the Amish fear is not so much contact with the outside world as a change in their internal modes of communication. The maintenance of traditional values by mutual supervision and ostracism (*Meidung*) of deviants presupposes physical interaction. "Visiting over the telephone was not an effective substitute for the monitoring of behavior that traditionally took place in the face-to-face context of community."[139] By contrast, the ban on electricity – except for batteries – is justified mainly by the need for isolation from the outside world.

Reflecting on the church's decision to limit the use of electricity, a member recently said: 'Electric would lead to worldliness. What would come along with electric? All the things that we don't need. With our diesel engines today we have more control of things. If you have an electric line coming in then you'd want a full line of appliances on it. *The Amish are human too, you know.*' Another person noted: 'It's not so much the electric that we're against, it's all the things that came with it – all the modern conveniences, television, computers.'[140]

The case of tourism is more complex.[141] The Amish have largely accepted tourists into their communities, although not into their homes. Donald Kraybill argues, "Tourism, rather than endangering Amish culture, may inadvertently fortify it," because it forces the Amish to maintain the traditional behaviors that the tourists come to observe. Also, "reluctant to admit to pride, there is a quiet satisfaction in knowing that their culture is worthy of such respect. Tourism has bolstered Amish self-esteem."[142] In the long run, however, the perception of being on a stage or in a zoo might come to undermine the commitment. When tradition turns into traditionalism, it dies.

Culture and Precommitment

The belief of Muslims or the Amish in their religion is a fundamental commitment in Bilgrami's sense. A believer desires others to believe,

138. For the regulation of telephones, see Umble (1994) and Kraybill (1989), pp. 143–50. For electricity, see Kraybill (1989), pp. 150–64. Glenn (1999) shows that similar arguments underlie the resistance of the Amish to Social Security.
139. Umble (1994), p. 104.
140. Kraybill (1989), pp. 154–55. The phrase that I have italicized expresses the basic rationale for precommitment: *being weak and knowing it*.
141. On tourism, see Luthy (1994) and Kraybill (1989), pp. 227–34.
142. Kraybill (1989), pp. 232, 233.

and he prefers the state of the world in which they believe and he doesn't to the state in which nobody believes. Can we apply the same criterion to cultural practices and, specifically, to the paradigmatic case of language? There is one clear similarity between the two cases. Someone who speaks (only) a minority language clearly desires that (some) others speak it too, because otherwise the speaker could not communicate with anyone. There is also an obvious difference between the religious and the cultural case. Whereas a believer would prefer the state of the world in which he believes and nobody else does over the one in which nobody does, the analogous preference for a private language would be absurd.[143] A further difference is that most believers would prefer as many people as possible to share their faith,[144] whereas speakers of a minority language typically do not want to become the new majority.

For the desire to maintain a minority language to be a fundamental commitment in Bilgrami's sense, the speaker would have to prefer a state of the world in which his fellow minority members speak it and he doesn't to one in which nobody speaks it. In fact, however, the opposite preference seems more likely.[145]For most individuals, the desire for communication would override the desire to perpetuate a linguistic community to which they do not belong. Yet if their first-ranked option is to perpetuate a community to which they do belong,

---

143. Thus I think Kymlicka (1989, p. 168) gets it wrong when he writes, "We often hear Islamic fundamentalists claim that without restrictions on the freedom of speech, press, religion, sexual practices, etc. of its own members, their culture will disintegrate, thus undermining the self-respect individuals derive from cultural membership." Islam is first and foremost a religion, not a culture. I think Kymlicka makes a similar mistake in his comments on the Pueblo Indians (ibid., pp. 195–98), when he suggests that the only acceptable reason they might have for retaining their religion was that without it their community would disintegrate. But this is putting the cart before the horse: religion cannot be seen as a means to preserve a cultural community if the culture is wholly organized around the religion.

144. But see Harrison (1995) for some exceptions.

145. David Laitin (personal communication) observes that exceptions to this statement are observed in "leaders of the Spanish Basque movement, many of whom don't speak Basque, and want it preserved on the shoulders of other people's children, who feel pressured to send their children to Basque-medium schools. In France, you can see the same phenomenon, with Corsica, Midi, and Alsace, though here it is just a question of an added subject in the schools. Many of the 'nationalists' don't speak the language, but are trying to preserve it by compelling the children of their neighbors to learn it. Of course, bilingualism muddies the waters here, and so there is a disanalogy with religion, where bi-religiosity is not accepted by religious virtuosi."

they could still be motivated to engage in precommitment without commitment in Bilgrami's sense.

The desire to insulate oneself from a larger community can also arise on cultural grounds, somewhat independently of religion and language. To take a personal example, this was one reason why I have twice voted against Norwegian entry in the European community. My fear was that full integration into the European community would entail loss of some cultural and social goods that only small communities can provide. In doing so I knew that a world in which all communities were as small as Norway (4.5 million inhabitants) could probably not produce the technical and scientific achievements from which Norwegians benefit. On Kantian grounds, I should have voted for membership rather than trying to have it both ways – but I am not a Kantian.[146]

I.7. ADDICTION AND PRECOMMITMENT

Addictive behavior, in its full-blown form, is the most striking instance known to me of ambivalence or weakness of will.[147] Many addicts really, strongly want to quit; try again and again; fail again and again; succeed and then relapse; try again, and relapse again. Because the process is typically iterated many times, addicts soon lose any naive beliefs they might have had about how easy it will be to quit. They must confront not only their addiction, but their inability to quit by simply deciding to do so. It is logical, then, to turn to precommitment behavior as a technique for quitting that does not rely merely on their will.

Addicts have in fact developed a number of self-binding strategies. In doing so, they may have a number of goals. First, they may simply

---

146. Some advocates of Norwegian membership believed that *entry* would be an act of precommitment or abdication that – like obtaining a loan from the IMF – would enable the government to resist pressure from trade unions and industry associations. (I thank Ottar Brox for directing my attention to this interpretation.) In Britain, Norman Tebbitt expressed similar concerns over the Maastricht agreement: "There is a principle of British political life that no Parliament can bind a successor Parliament. But once we have given up our own currency, once we have signed up for this federalist Europe, then Parliament has bound its successor. There is no legal way back out of it" (*The Guardian*, November 25, 1991).

147. For a fuller account of addiction, see Ch. 3 of Elster (1999b). In the present discussion, technical details are kept to a minimum.

want to quit. Second, they may want to prevent relapse. Third, they may want to achieve controlled or moderate use. Many of these aims can also be achieved by treatment. In fact, the dividing line between precommitment and treatment is not always easy to draw. The act of seeking treatment may have an aspect of precommitment. Conversely, the treatment may involve the option of using precommitment technology provided by the therapist. Nor is the dividing line between precommitment and public policy always clear. In a referendum on prohibition, some of those who vote in favor may be heavy drinkers who want to limit their own access to alcohol. Although most of those who vote for prohibition probably do so to bind *others* rather than themselves, those motivated by precommitment might, in a given case, be pivotal.

As I shall try to show, there is a very wide range of widely adopted precommitment strategies against addiction. More generally, the struggle for self-control – which may involve the purely cognitive strategies that I discuss in I.8 as well as precommitment strategies – is an absolutely central feature of all the major addictions. The pervasiveness of self-control problems is a major problem, therefore, for all theories that view addiction as initiated by rational choice.[148] Here I shall consider *ten precommitment strategies*:

- throwing away the key
- giving away the key
- imposing costs
- creating rewards
- creating delays
- changing or bolstering beliefs
- changing preferences
- avoiding exposure to cues
- avoiding company
- seeking company

The rationales for these devices are the need to counteract drug cravings and the need to overcome time inconsistency. The cravings may be due to the pull of euphoria or the push from dysphoria; triggered by cues in the environment or by stress; or just arise suddenly

148. See, for instance, Becker and Murphy (1988), Becker (1992), and Orphanides and Zervos (1995, 1998).

in the mind for no particular reason. The time-inconsistency problem mainly arises when there is some natural occasion to consume, such as having dessert at the end of a meal and drinking in the evening or on the weekend. Well ahead of that occasion, one may decide to abstain, and then undergo a preference reversal as in Figure I.2. If all occasions are equally "natural," as is usually the case for cigarette smokers, this problem is less likely to arise.

George Loewenstein (personal communication) has raised the question of craving versus time-consistency with respect to precommitment against caloric foods. If I want to prevent myself from eating dessert, I can choose my restaurant according to one of two strategies. On the one hand, I can decide to go to a restaurant where, if I want dessert, it must be ordered at the beginning of the meal. This would help me overcome my problem of time-inconsistency, if that is what I'm fighting. On the other hand, I can opt for a restaurant where they do not go around with the dessert trolley, but where dessert instead must be ordered from the menu. This would help me overcome my problem of cue-dependent craving, if that is what I'm fighting. As this example shows, the adoption of specific precommitment strategies does not depend only on whether the goal is abstinence, moderation, or relapse-prevention, but also on the nature of the obstacle that prevents me from realizing the goal.

THROWING AWAY THE KEY

In some cases, it may be possible to make the addictive substance physically unavailable, at least for a while. The strategy may be combined with the imposition or utilization of delays. If I know I shall want to drink in the evening but that the liquor stores will be closed, abstaining from keeping liquor in the house will carry me over the dangerous period until next morning when the stores are open and I know I shall not want to drink. These two strategies may also be combined in a different way. Suppose I want to quit smoking and I embark on a long sea voyage where cigarettes will be unavailable. When I touch land again after three weeks, the craving for cigarettes will have subsided to the point where I can keep it in check without precommitment. Here, delays have the function of allowing passion to cool down rather than that of overcoming time-inconsistency.

I. Ulysses Revisited

Giving Away the Key

This strategy is more practicable and more common than the previous one. It amounts to enlisting other people as agents to protect the addict against himself. More specifically (there are other ways of enlisting other people, as we shall see), it amounts to instructing other people to prevent one from having access to the drug. For the strategy to work, the other persons must able to resist or ignore instructions that release them from the promise. In some cases, as we shall see, this condition is not met.

The first instance of this strategy I have come across is in a sworn and witnessed statement made by one James Chalmers of New Jersey in 1795:

Whereas, the subscriber, through the pernicious habit of drinking, has greatly hurt himself in purse and person, and rendered himself odious to all his acquaintances and finds that there is no possibility of breaking off from the said practice *but through the impossibility to find liquor*, he therefore begs and prays that no person will sell him for money, or on trust, any sort of spirituous liquor.[149]

I do not know whether the strategy worked. An instance in which a similar strategy was conspicuously unsuccessful is recorded in Thomas de Quincey's *Confessions of an Opium Eater*, where he writes that Samuel Coleridge

went so far as to hire men – porters, hackney-coachmen, and others – to oppose by force his entrance into any druggist's shop. But, as the authority for stopping him was derived simply from himself, naturally these poor men found themselves in a metaphysical fix, not provided for even by Thomas Acquinas or by the prince of Jesuitical casuists. And in this excruciating dilemma would occur such scenes as the following: –
'Oh, sir,' would plead the suppliant porter – suppliant, yet semi-imperative (for equally if he *did*, and if he did *not*, show fight, the poor man's daily 5s. seemed endangered) – 'really you must not; consider, sir, your wife and –'
Transcendental philosopher – 'Wife! what wife! I have no wife.'
Porter– 'But, really now, you must not, sir. Didn't you say no longer than yesterday –'
Transcendental philosopher – 'Pooh, pooh! yesterday is a long time ago. Are you aware, my man, that people are known to have dropped down dead for timely want of opium?'
Porter – 'Ay, but you tell't me not to hearken –'

149. Cited after Orford (1985), p. 19; my italics.

66

Transcendental philosopher – 'Oh, nonsense. An emergency, a shocking emergency has arisen – quite unlooked for. No matter what I told you in times long past. That which I *now* tell you, is – that, if you don't remove that arm of yours from the doorway of this most respectable druggist, I shall have a good ground of action against you for assault and battery.'[150]

Another precommitment failure is illustrated by Fred Vincy in *Middlemarch*. He "was not a gambler: he had not that specific disease in which the suspension of the whole nervous energy on a chance or risk becomes as necessary as the dram to the drunkard; he had only the tendency to that diffusive form of gambling which has no alcoholic tendency."" Yet he was sufficiently of a gambler to know that he could not trust himself. Having obtained some money from Mr. Featherstone, "he gave four of the twenties to his mother, asking her to keep them for him. 'I don't want to spend that money. I want to pay a debt with it. So keep it safe away from my fingers.'" Yet when the urge to make a speculative venture came over him, "Fred got the eighty pounds from his mother."[151]

A case of successful precommitment is presented by Eliot Gardner and James David, who describe how an inner-city crack user, "Jeannette," kept her habit under control:

One Friday evening, after getting her week's wages, she receives a telephone call from one of her occasional boyfriends, who informs her that he has just acquired some "crack" (free-base) cocaine and some beer, and is planning to party for that night with some friends. Jeannette is invited to "come on over, do a few rocks with us, and have some fun." After some moments of indecision, Jeannette accepts the invitation. She is told to "bring some money, to pay for the crack you use." Jeannette then carefully counts her week's wages, estimates the amount she will need over the coming week for food, rent, and other necessities, and then "pre-commits" herself to use for the crack party only those dollars she will not need for "necessary money" over the coming week. She gives her children to a girlfriend in the same building to watch for the night, and also gives the girlfriend all her "necessary money" for the coming week, telling the girlfriend to "not give it back to me before Monday, no matter how hard I beg."[152]

When her own money is used up, "she is soon back in her own building, begging her girlfriend for the 'necessary money' – screaming and

---

150. de Quincey (1986), p. 145. As a matter of fact, withdrawal from opiates is never deadly.
151. From *Middlemarch*, Chs. 23, 14, 23.   152. Gardner and David (1999), p. 93.

67

threatening when it is refused." The self-binding worked because the person with whom the money was deposited kept her promise of not giving it back. Ideally, the trustee should have something to lose by not keeping the promise. In practice, this may be difficult to achieve. For instance, treating obesity by having one's jaws wired so that one can only take in liquid sustenance is vulnerable to the problem that the person can always ask to be unwired on the grounds that he or she fears asphyxiation by vomiting.

IMPOSING COSTS

There are a number of ways in which addicts can and do impose costs on themselves to make drug use less likely. In virtually all cases they involve the use of other persons. This is true even of disulfiram (Antabuse), a drug that if taken regularly has the effect of making the user violently ill if he takes a drink. "Numerous studies have shown that only a small proportion of those prescribed unsupervised disulfiram will take it regularly and many of these patients would probably do well without disulfiram."[153] Although most users of disulfiram want to avoid drinking altogether, it has also been used to achieve moderate drinking, by adjusting the dosage so that the discomfort occurs only after a couple of drinks. The technique is not risk-free. The drug has side effects, notably drowsiness, which can be kept in check by other potentially addictive drugs, also to be taken under supervision. If the person drinks after having taken the drug, the effect may be fatal. Yet as Colin Brewer dryly notes, "The patient, not the physician, is the person who is supposed to be frightened by the [adverse reaction]."[154]

As with other deterrents, disulfiram works best when it is never triggered. If the fear is strong enough, it may never be triggered. Subcutaneously implanted disulfiram may in fact provide a benign instance of what Gerry Mackie calls a "belief trap."[155] In some countries, it has been widely believed that anyone who drinks when using implanted disulfiram will die.[156] As a matter of fact, implanted disulfiram is pharmacologically inert.[157] The belief – possibly bolstered by

153. Brewer (1993), p. 384.   154. Ibid., p. 388.
155. Mackie (1996).   156. Osiatynski (1997), p. 167.
157. Johnsen and Mørland (1992).

the fact that some alcoholics have died when using disulfiram, though not because they used it – could nevertheless deter people from testing it. Although false, the belief might be therapeutically useful. Thus "following the publication of a controlled study in Norway which found no difference in outcome between placebo and allegedly active disulfiram implants, one of the authors received much criticism from patients who had had implants."[158]

As noted in I.3, a time-tested method of precommitment is to play on "audience effects." One can impose costs on oneself by announcing publicly that one is going to quit, thus raising the stakes by adding shame and loss of prestige to the other costs of relapse. Thomas Schelling provides a more formal or institutionalized example of self-imposed costs:

In a cocaine addiction center in Denver, patients are offered an opportunity to submit to extortion. They may write a self-incriminating letter, preferably a letter confessing their drug addiction, deposit the letter with the clinic, and submit to a randomized schedule of laboratory tests. If the laboratory finds evidence of cocaine use, the clinic sends the letter to the addressee. An example is a physician who addresses a letter to the State Board of Medical Examiners confessing that he has administered cocaine to himself in violation of the laws of Colorado and requests that his license to practice be revoked.[159]

Some contingency contracts used to fight smoking or obesity also involve the imposition of costs on oneself. In weight-reduction programs, for instance, "failure to meet predetermined goals may result in the client forfeiting a sum of money to his or her most disliked organization or political group."[160] As shown by the following passage, this strategy may involve some risks:

Even if a client enter into a contract, there is no guarantee that the contingency will always have the desired effect. The client of a colleague of mine agreed to get rid of a valued possession, an expensive music-box, if she failed to lose what seemed like a reasonable amount of weight. She failed to lose the weight, followed through on the contract, and became doubly upset over what was still further proof to her that she was unable to control herself![161]

158. Brewer (1993), p. 392, citing the first author of Johnsen and Mørland (1992).
159. Schelling (1992), p. 167.   160. Wilson (1980), p. 218.
161. Ibid.

I. Ulysses Revisited

CREATING REWARDS

Rather than overcoming time-inconsistency by attaching costs to the choice of the early small reward, precommitment can be achieved by attaching rewards to the choice of the larger, delayed reward, as shown by the following descriptions.

Contingency contracting has occasionally been employed as the major treatment procedure in smoking cessation programs. The smoker deposits a sum of money (e.g. $100) at the outset and then portions of this money are refunded contingent upon meeting previously stipulated abstinence goals, often extending into a follow up period. In the few systematic evaluations of this method, reasonably good results have been obtained.[162]

In contingency contracting ... the therapist typically arranges a contract in which the specified outcome such as habit change or a designated amount of weight loss is rewarded by return to the client of portions of a refundable money deposit. ... Contracts in which large sums of money ($20 per session) were contingent upon either a prescribed weight loss or changes in eating habits estimated to result in a comparable weight loss produced significantly greater losses (approximately 20 pounds) over a ten-week period than did a treatment at which attendance at treatment sessions only was contracted for.[163]

In a sense, there is no difference between this strategy and the one discussed in the preceding subsection. To create a reward, one must first have the means of doing so. Attaching a reward to the choice of the later reward is then equivalent to imposing a cost on the choice of the earlier reward, since choice of the earlier reward implies forgoing the resources one has attached to the later reward. Yet even though at an abstract level there is no difference between punishing oneself for smoking and rewarding oneself for not smoking, the two procedures have different psychological implications. As people tend to attach less importance to income forgone than to actual losses,[164] the blow to one's self-esteem by failing to abide by the contract may be less if one does not suffer a material loss. Hence we would expect reward-based contracts to be less effective than penalty-based ones.

162. Lichtenstein and Brown (1980), p. 183.   163. Wilson (1980), p. 218.
164. Thaler (1980).

CREATING DELAYS

I have already given some examples of this strategy, and noted that it may be related to passion as well as time-inconsistency. Another example is taken from a study that

examined the effects of an experimental Saturday closing of liquor retail stores in Sweden. They found a decline in the number of arrests for drunkenness by about 10% and also a decline in the number of domestic disturbances, as well as in outdoor and indoor assaults. On the other hand, the evaluation did not demonstrate any effect on total consumption of alcohol.[165]

A Norwegian study yielded similar results. These findings are plausibly explained by assuming that a small subgroup of individuals decide on Friday not to drink on Saturday, change their mind on Saturday, but nevertheless abstain if the liquor store is closed on Saturday. Their change of mind might be a preference reversal induced by hyperbolic discounting, a cue-dependence effect induced by the sight of other Saturday drinkers, or disinhibition caused by drinking beer (which *was* available on Saturdays). Note, however, that, as in the delay strategies discussed in I.2, this is not really a case of *self-binding*. Like gun control and marriage legislation, restrictions on the sale of liquor are more plausibly viewed as devices of social control than as techniques for self-control.

CHANGING OR BOLSTERING BELIEFS

Many of the devices discussed so far – elimination of options, delays, costs – can work simply by virtue of being the object of a belief. If I believe that there are no cigarettes on the ship, that will keep me from smoking even if in fact there is a large cache hidden on board. The false belief that I will die if I drink with implanted disulfiram may be very effective in keeping me sober. If I believe that the risk of getting lung cancer from smoking is much higher than it actually is, that might motivate me to quit whereas a more realistic assessment would not. It might seem, therefore, as if someone resolved on quitting would have an incentive for changing his or her beliefs in some appropriate way. Gordon Winston has argued, in fact, that "protective self-deception" –

165. Edwards et al. (1994), p. 137.

believing that the dangers of addiction are greater than they in fact are – can help one to get off the hook.[166] I have argued elsewhere that this strategy cannot work.[167] It is a conceptual truth that one cannot consciously decide to adopt a belief simply on the grounds that having it would be useful. It is, I believe, an empirical truth that the unconscious mind does not engage in this kind of long-term deceptive or manipulative thinking. Self-deception is a tool of the pleasure principle, not of the reality principle. As a matter of fact, people tend to think the risks of smoking are *smaller* for them than they are for others, not larger.[168] Although Winston argues that one can induce the desired change in beliefs by paying a hypnotist to do so, hypnosis tends in fact to aim at preference change rather than belief change.

Rather than manipulating the belief system to induce irrationally high estimates of the risks involved in addiction, one can try to protect it against self-serving tendencies to form irrationally low estimates. Some ex-smokers who fear they might relapse hang gruesome photographs of the lungs of cancer victims on the walls of their homes and offices. Professional gamblers regularly precommit themselves against wishful thinking. "'Loss of control' is ... recognised by professional gamblers as an occupational hazard against which various precautions can be taken." These include notably prior selection of bets, and avoidance of continuous betting.[169] Also, it is important to avoid the various modes of superstitious thinking that characterize many gamblers.

CHANGING PREFERENCES

Suppose I am free to smoke or to abstain. I want to smoke because I like it, but I also want to abstain, because I care about my health. All

---

166. Winston (1980), pp. 319–20. The "ignorance-is-bliss" theorem by Carillo and Mariotti (1997) mentioned in I.3 might seem to vindicate this claim. Although there is a flavor of similarity between their argument and Winston's, they do not rely on self-deception. When a person decides not to acquire more information about the dangers of an addictive drug, he does not *know* that if he got it, it would show the drug to be more dangerous than he currently believes. In fact, because information about information about X *is* information about X, the idea is meaningless.
167. Elster (1983b), p. 161. See also Elster (1999d).   168. McKenna (1990).
169. Dickerson (1984), pp. 58, 62.

things considered I'd rather abstain, but I am afraid that weakness of will or hyperbolic discounting might get the better of me. In that case, I might form and try to implement a desire to get rid of my desire to smoke. The main tools seem to be hypnosis, aversion therapy, and cue extinction.

A survey of the use of hypnosis to curb smoking, obesity, substance abuse, and alcoholism found very modest success rates.[170] Hypnotic suggestions to induce aversion to alcohol, for instance, "contradict the patient's experience of pleasure or relief from drinking."[171] A more curious idea is the use of "hypnotic suggestions to revivify previous good LSD experiences as an alternative to the actual use of LSD."[172] Aversion therapy uses classical conditioning principles to get the addict to associate the drug with nausea or electrical shocks. William Burroughs, for instance, devised his own technique for pairing a drug with an aversive chemical reaction, by timing an injection of apomorphine to take effect soon after feeling the effects of self-injected morphine.[173] Yet by and large, aversion therapies have had only limited success.[174]

Whereas aversion therapy aims at establishing a negative conditioned response to drugs, cue extinction aims at eliminating positive responses. The addict must be brought or bring himself into the environments or situations traditionally associated with consumption, and then be prevented or prevent himself from consuming. As the connection is broken, the cue-dependent cravings will fade after a while.[175] The process must be systematic and cover all the situations traditionally associated with the drug.[176] According to George Vaillant,

---

170. Brown and Fromm (1987), Ch. 4.   171. Ibid., p. 195.

172. Ibid., p. 191.   173. Callahan (1980), p. 154.

174. Miller and Hester (1980), pp. 31–42; Lichtenstein and Brown (1980), pp. 189–92.

175. Weiss, Mirin, and Bartel (1994), p. 149; Callahan (1980), pp. 158–59; Miller and Hester (1980), pp. 90–91. Miller (1980), pp. 276–77.

176. Thus Goldstein (1994), p. 222, tells "a convincing story from a colleague who had been a nicotine addict but hadn't smoked for years. He had abstained from cigarettes in a variety of situations where he had smoked in the past, and thus he had desensitized himself to a variety of conditioned associations – cigarettes at parties, cigarettes at morning coffee, cigarettes at the desk, and so on. One day he went to the beach and was suddenly overwhelmed by an intense craving to smoke. He found this beyond understanding until he realized that smoking on the beach had been an important pattern at one time in his life, and that he had not had the opportunity to eliminate that particular conditioned association."

one reason abstinence for opiates under parole supervision and abstinence from alcohol under AA supervision are more enduring than abstinence achieved during hospitalization or imprisonment is that the former experiences occur in the community. Thus, abstinence is achieved in the presence of many conditioned reinforcers (community bars, other addicts, community hassles, and so on). For example, AA encourages the alcohol abuser to maintain a busy schedule of social activities and the serving of beverages (coffee) in the presence of former drinkers. Many of the secondary reinforcers are present. Only alcohol is missing. Such 'secondary reinforcers' lose their potency in controlling an addict's behavior most rapidly when such events occur in the absence of reinforcement.[177]

AVOIDING EXPOSURE TO CUES

If the cue-dependence has not been extinguished, the addict should take special care, avoiding exposure to cues associated with consumption when the internal state of the organism is such that craving might easily be triggered. A traditional piece of advice to overweight people, for instance, is "Never shop on an empty stomach." That particular advice, however, is misguided. It turns out that "obese shoppers made more unplanned purchases when they had recently eaten than when they were deprived," the reason being that "the feeling of hunger, for dieters, paradoxically gives them solace, since it tells them they are being successful at avoiding calories." Hence, "it is the normal weight nondieters who should avoid shopping when hungry."[178]

This being said, cue-avoidance is an essential strategy of self-management. Addicts seem to develop these strategies spontaneously, and they are also standard parts of treatment and recovery procedures. People who want to quit smoking often learn that they must stop drinking as well, because alcohol serves as a cue for cigarette craving and also causes disinhibition. (If they go away to an isolated resort, however, they can take alcohol with them as long as they do not also bring cigarettes.) Gambling may be an exception: in most places outside Las Vegas, the everyday environment does not present cues that might trigger the urge to gamble. In the

---

177. Vaillant (1995), pp. 251–2, drawing on Stall and Biernacki (1986).
178. Baumeister, Heatherton, and Tice (1994), p. 177. They report a similar finding about smokers (ibid., pp. 204–5).

case of alcoholism, the fact "that cues influence the desire to drink has not been lost on AA. Their meetings are held in churches or schools, which are places not previously associated with drinking."[179] (Note the stark contrast with the passage from Vaillant cited earlier!) Also, "many dietary regimens include specific training in dealing with food cues."[180] In the case of smoking, the government assists in removing cues: "By effectively eliminating cues to smoke (including advertisements and television portrayals: no one smokes on television), society may reduce the cues that influence smokers to have a cigarette."[181]

Like most forms of precommitment, cue-avoidance is costly. In his "cue-theory of consumption," David Laibson offers a model in which a consumer may be willing to give up part of his income to control the cue process.[182] In a variation of the model he explores the fact that the *means* of (say) smoking, namely, cigarettes, are also *cues* for the craving to smoke. Thus in this case the strategies of cue-management and of option-elimination coincide. As he notes, this desire to reduce the feasible set is not linked to time-inconsistency. He also shows, however, that the interplay of cues and rewards may generate behavior that *appears* to reflect "declining impatience," that is, a less steep trade-off between times t and $t + 1$ than between time 0 and time 1.

AVOIDING COMPANY

Because other addicts provide especially salient cues, it is universally recommended that people who want to stop drinking or smoking avoid places where these activities go on. Once again, the government may come to their assistance. "Polls over the past twenty years have

---

179. Ibid., p. 162.   180. Ibid., p. 182.
181. Ibid., p. 204. The aim of TV advertising for cigarettes was to promote specific brands, not to provide cues to smokers as a collective good for the tobacco industry. The latter was provided as a by-product of profit-seeking by individual firms. (Nor was the ban on TV advertising mainly motivated by the cue-removal effect.) Yet the ban on advertising offered another collective good for the industry: it "would effectively end the possibility that any new competitors would ever enter the cigarette business in the future, however profitable the product, since without television advertising, the introduction of new brands would prove prohibitively expensive" (Kluger 1996, p. 333).
182. Laibson (1996b).

75

consistently shown majority support among smokers for [restrictions on public smoking]. Many smokers view limitations on smoking as a way to help them quit, or at least reduce their consumption, and many also understand the need to control tobacco smoke pollution for the sake of others."[183] According to this argument, smoking in public has two distinct externalities: it can affect the health of others as well as smokers' ability to quit. Whereas the first effect, if proven, would provide a good reason for government intervention, the second is more dubious.

The company of smokers and drinkers may also trigger relapse by peer pressure, which

includes both indirect interpersonal coercion aimed at pressuring the abstinent individual to engage in the addictive behavior and indirect social pressure. Indirect pressure usually occurs as a result of finding oneself in a social context where everyone else is using the substance and not perceiving oneself to be behaving in an appropriate social manner if one does not 'do as the Romans do.'[184]

The latter perception may well be a rationalization, and in fact may be motivated by the desire to have a cigarette or a drink. Again, staying away from others will have costs, especially if a high fraction of the population engages in the activity.[185] Some would-be quitters may be motivated to bear the costs, others may not. One can easily imagine cases in which no single individual is willing to bear the costs in isolation, yet coordinated behavior by all would-be quitters would reduce the costs sufficiently for all of them to be willing to bear them.

Seeking Company

The final set of devices I shall consider involve the deliberate use of other people to limit consumption or prevent relapse. What I have in mind here is not the strategies, discussed earlier, of entrusting control over drug supply or money for gambling to another person, or of asking others to punish one if one deviates. Rather, the idea is that addicts or ex-addicts can use one another as mutual devices for precommitment, by consuming together or abstaining together.

183. Glantz et al. (1996), p. 258.
184. Cummings, Jordan, and Marlatt (1980), p. 304.   185. Moene (1999).

Consider first the idea that the company of others can be a means to controlled use. It is apparently difficult to be a controlled user all by oneself. In one often-cited study, "virtually all subjects . . . required the assistance of other controlled users to construct appropriate rituals and social sanctions out of the folklore of practices of the diverse subculture of drugtakers."[186] In the language of I.2, these seem to be incidental rather than essential constraints. "To a large degree, association with controlled users is a matter of chance rather than of deliberate personal choice."[187] Presumably the controlled users are aware of and welcome the fact that they serve as checks on each other, but that seems not to have been the reason why the collective mode of consumption was chosen in the first place.

Consider next the idea that the company of others can be a means to achieve total abstinence. This is the idea or ideology behind Alcoholics Anonymous. "Each recovering alcoholic member of Alcoholics Anonymous is kept constantly aware, at every meeting, that he has *both* something to give *and* something to receive from his fellow alcoholics."[188] The giving, rather than being a goal of the meetings, is purely a by-product: "Primacy is always given to maintaining one's own sobriety, even as a prior condition to helping others. This kind of enlightened selfishness naturally benefits everyone in the long run."[189] As in the case of controlled usage, keeping company is an equilibrium behavior: it is in the interest of each to come to the meeting if others do so. The strategy may be a subcase of the belief-bolstering strategy discussed earlier, if, as I suspect, a main function of the storytelling ritual at AA meetings is to maintain the vividness of the memory of what it was like to be an alcoholic.

I.8. OBSTACLES, OBJECTIONS, AND ALTERNATIVES

Precommitment, even when desirable, may not be feasible or effective; when feasible and effective, it may not be desirable. In such

---

186. Zinberg, Harding, and Winkeller (1977), p. 127. They note, however, that within the subculture of drug users there are also rituals that exacerbate use rather than moderate it (ibid., p. 126).
187. Ibid., p. 129.   188. Kurtz (1979), p. 215.
189. Royce (1981), p. 248.

cases, individuals with impulse control problems may look for other ways to deal with them.[190]

Obstacles to Precommitment

If we look at the list of devices for precommitment in Table I.1, it is clear that, in a given situation, many of them might simply not be available. To invest in bargaining power, for instance, one must already have some resources. At a very low wage, workers cannot afford to build up the strike fund by virtue of which they could make a credible strike threat to get higher wages. Although they might be able to get their way if they could develop an emotional disposition to strike even when it is not in their interest, the rarity or even absence of such emotional planning suggests that this kind of self-manipulation may simply not be in our repertoire. Trade union leaders can sometimes manipulate their members into a moral frenzy that makes them willing to make pointless sacrifices, but that is another matter.

Maintaining ignorance can also be difficult, for conceptual as much as for physical reasons. One cannot decide to forget; in fact, "there is nothing which stamps anything so vividly on our memory as the desire not to remember it."[191] Although a bargainer might be better off not knowing the amount to be divided by himself and his opponent,[192] he cannot decide to ignore it if in fact he knows it. When one has a suspicion that something is wrong – that one might have an incurable illness or one's spouse have a lover – the deliberate abstention from finding out whether it is founded does not always prevent fear or jealousy. To be effective, the policy of remaining ignorant ("never read your spouse's diary") must be adopted before one has any specific reason for adopting it.

The option of eliminating options by making them physically unavailable may itself be unavailable. If I think I might do something stupid at the office party I can stay away – but not if I'm the boss of the company. To treat my addiction I might want to be admitted to a clinic that will not respond to my request to be let out, but there may not be any such clinics.[193] The Russian nobleman might not be able

---

190. This section owes much to comments by David Laibson. The "social signaling" effect, notably, is due to him.
191. Montaigne (1991), p. 551.
192. Camerer, Loewenstein, and Weber (1989), p. 1244.
193. In Elster (1984), p. 38, I referred to the Norwegian Law of Psychic Health Care

to make a legally enforceable promise to give away his land when he inherits. If I try to precommit myself against my tendency to profligate spending by buying an annuity, I can always finesse the obstacle by using the annuity as collateral for borrowing.[194]

Imposing costs on oneself may also be unfeasible or ineffective. Courts may not honor my contract to pay a large sum of money to a third party if the promise is contingent on my failure to carry out a threat I've made to a second party.[195] If self-deterrence is to be achieved by depositing a large sum of money to be forfeited in case of relapse or to be paid back in installments as a reward for compliance, some people will not be able to lay their hands on an amount that is large enough to make a difference. This middle-class precommitment strategy is simply not available to everyone. Overcoming passion by imposing side bets may not work if the passion makes me deaf and blind to incentives. If I want to quit smoking and try to raise the stakes by telling my friends, it may work the first time but not the third or the tenth time.

OBJECTIONS TO PRECOMMITMENT

Even if there exists a precommitment technology that does work, at least with some probability, its use might require costs greater than the expected benefits. Consider Figure I.2 (p. 30). If time 1 is the latest

with "the unique feature that a person may voluntarily seek irreversible admission to a mental hospital." The law gives the responsible doctor only the right to forbid the patient to leave, however, not the duty to forbid it. For a number of reasons, the doctor may choose not to exercise that right (Helge Waal, personal communication). With regard to the United States, Dresser (1982), p. 792, argues, "A patient and a psychiatrist who contracted for voluntary commitment today would be unlikely to obtain state assistance in enforcing the contract's provisions."

194. The problem can be overcome by depositing one's money in a form that cannot be used as collateral. The FBI undercover agent "Donnie Brascoe" was given the following advice by a Mafioso he met (Pistone 1989, p. 141): "'Donnie, you seem like a pretty sharp guy. I just want to give you a piece of advice. This business we're in, you get old fast, and a lot of things you do now you can't do when you're older. ... So my advice is, Donnie, find somebody you can really trust. Every time you pull a score, take some of that money and give it to that friend and have them keep it for you. And make the rule with the friend that he won't give you any of that money until you like retire. You can't go to this guy tomorrow and ask for a grand or two, because he won't give it to you – that's the rule you've set up.'"

195. See Laibson 1997, p. 448, note 6, for references.

79

possible date for precommitment and if the costs of using the pre-commitment technology exceed the distance between the two curves (the heavily drawn line segment), it will not be in my interest to use it. If I have to pay a therapist to help me change my preferences or modify my emotional reactions, it might not be worth it. If I have to use part of my income today to invest in a strike fund that will enable me to make credible threats and get a greater income in the future, the discounted present value of the increase might not justify the investment. The (actual) cost of imposing (conditional) costs on myself might also be prohibitive. Assuming I could somehow make a legally enforceable promise to pay a third party if I don't carry out a threat, the lawyer's fee might eat up all the gains.

The problem of credible promises poses a special problem. Consider Figure I.3 (p. 40). If Eve could credibly precommit herself to keep her promise to go left if Adam goes left, either by eliminating her option of going right or by attaching a cost to the choice of that strategy, each would stand to gain 1. If the costs to her of precommitting herself are 1.2, she has no incentive to do so, although jointly they would be better off if she did. Adam might, therefore, promise to reimburse her 0.3, so that he would end up with 2.7 and she with 2.1. If that promise is credible, she would make the necessary investment in making her promise credible. To make his promise credible, Adam might have to make an investment of his own. As long as that investment costs less than 0.7, he will make it. If we suppose, for specificity, that the costs to him are 0.6, Adam and Eve will end up with 10% of the benefits from cooperation, the other 90% being invested in credibility.

Precommitment strategies may also be undesirable because of signaling effects. If others observe my precommitment behavior, they will infer that I lack self-control. They may be reluctant, therefore, to have dealings with me on occasions when no precommitment devices are available and my lack of self-control could be costly for them. In many societies, there are norms against total abstention from alcohol as well as norms against drunkenness.[196] Although many who abstain from alcohol do so through personal rules (see next subsection) rather than by precommitment devices, the anti-abstentionist norms presumably cover both categories, and for the same reason. A person who cannot hold his or her liquor cannot be trusted to keep a promise either.[197]

---

196. See Ch. 4.3 of Elster (1999b) for documentation.
197. Although Mischel (1968) shows that people exhibit much less cross-situational

The most important cost of precommitment, however, may be loss of flexibility. Consider again a person who contemplates a voluntary but irreversible hospital treatment of a drug problem, and let us assume, for the sake of argument, that this option is in fact available to him. If he expects that urgent business problems might arise during this period, he might not want to take the risk of being unable to deal with them, knowing that the cynical hospital staff will be deaf to his pleas that *this* is a genuine exception rather than an excuse to indulge in his habit. As Robert Frank says when arguing for the superiority of love over a written marriage contract as precommitment devices, "Any contract lenient enough to allow termination of hopeless marriages cannot at the same time be strict enough to prevent opportunistic switching."[198] Burning your bridges, too, can be a high-risk strategy. By keeping one's options open one may be able to gather new information and make a better decision than by foreclosing them prematurely.[199]

Hence there can be a trade-off between desirability and feasibility. For some addictions, moderate, controlled consumption is the most desirable end. Moderate social drinking, an occasional cigarette after a good meal, or a visit to the race track from time to time may well, for some, be part of their idea of the good life. They have no reason to deny themselves these innocent pleasures, as long as they do not get out of hand. Many never-addicts are able to achieve this goal, at least with regard to drinking and gambling,[200] but ex-addicts can have great difficulties in maintaining controlled use. At the end of a careful discussion of the issue George Vaillant concludes "not that alcohol-dependent individuals never return to social drinking but only that it is a rare and often an unstable state."[201] The issue is controversial, and turns in part on self-fulfilling beliefs about the consequences of relapse. Zero-tolerance beliefs, in particular, "can be compared to a military strategy of putting all one's defenses on the front line, with no reserves. The front line is defended maximally well;

---

consistency than we commonly assume, the false belief in consistency can nevertheless, precisely because it is so common, create this kind of signaling effect.
198. Frank (1988), p. 195.   199. Henry (1974).
200. "Ninety percent of all drinkers drink alcohol when they feel like it but leave it alone when they don't, which leaves about 10 percent drinking out of compulsion. These percentages are almost exactly reversed with smoking: only about 10 percent of the population are thought to be 'chippers', who can take smoking or leave it as they please" (Krogh 1991, p. 3).
201. Vaillant (1995), p. 297.

but if there is a breach, there is no fallback option, and catastrophe ensues."[202]

ALTERNATIVES TO PRECOMMITMENT

If extrapsychic precommitment is unfeasible or undesirable, we may ask whether agents could respond to the challenges of passion, preference change, or time-inconsistency by adopting intrapsychic devices. With regard to passion and preference change, these are not easily neutralized in other ways than by precommitment. Although one may try to counteract emotions by nipping them in the bud or by thinking about something else,[203] I have argued that these techniques are often inadequate. The idea of preventing or neutralizing preference change by purely intrapsychic means seems even less plausible.

With respect to time-inconsistency induced by hyperbolic discounting, however, two intrapsychic strategies are available. The agent for whom precommitment is either unfeasible or undesirable can then turn to the cognitive devices of *sophistication* and *bunching*.[204] In the first approach, the agent views himself as engaged in a strategic game with his future selves, anticipating and shaping their decisions. Rather than assuming naively that his future selves will do what he would like them to do, he takes account of the fact that they will choose according to *their* relative evaluation of the options. Ted O'Donoghue and Matthew Rabin have shown that in some cases this sophisticated approach results in higher welfare compared to that of a naive agent, whereas in other cases sophistication can make things worse.[205]

Specifically, O'Donoghue and Rabin show that sophisticated individuals can mitigate their tendency to procrastinate if they can anticipate it fully. They illustrate the idea by the following example.

Suppose you usually go to movies on Saturdays, and the schedule at the local cinema consists of a mediocre movie this week, a good movie next week, a great movie in two weeks, and (best of all) a Johnny Depp movie

---

202. Ibid., p. 25.   203. Ainslie (1992), pp. 133–42.

204. The term "sophistication" is perhaps unfortunate. *All* devices for self-control – whether extrapsychic or intrapsychic – presuppose that the agent is *aware* of the inconsistency he or she is trying to neutralize.

205. O'Donoghue and Rabin (1999a). The passages cited subsequently occur on pp. 109, 110, and 110–11 of this article.

in three weeks. Now suppose you must complete a report for work within four weeks, and to do so you must skip the movie on one of the next four Sundays. When do you complete the report?

O'Donoghue and Rabin show that a naive subject will write the report on the last Saturday, whereas a sophisticated agent will write it on the second Saturday.

In this case, sophistication helps. In other cases, naive subjects do better than sophisticated subjects. "Suppose you have a coupon to see one movie over the next four Saturdays, and your allowance is such that you cannot afford to pay for a movie. The schedule at the local cinema is the same as for the above example. . . . Which movie do you see?" Naive subjects will behave as follows. "On the first two Saturdays, [naive subjects] skip the mediocre and good movies incorrectly believing they will wait to see the Johnny Depp movie. However, on the third Saturday, they give in to self-control problems and see the great movie." Sophisticated choosers do worse.

The period-2 sophisticate would choose to see the good movie because he correctly predicts that he would give in to self-control problems on the third Saturday, and see merely the great movie rather than the Johnny Depp movie. The period-1 sophisticate correctly predicts this reasoning and behavior by his 2-period self. Hence, the period-1 sophisticate realizes that he will merely see the good movie if he waits, so he concludes he might as well see the mediocre movie now. . . . Knowing about future self-control problems can lead you to give in to them today, because you realize you will give in to them tomorrow.

In other work, O'Donoghue and Rabin show that the last conclusion also applies to addiction.[206] The idea is confirmed by clinical evidence from treatment of addicts, which suggests that they often have a fatalistic attitude: "Since I know I'm going to relapse sooner or later, I might as well begin today."[207]

206. O'Donoghue and Rabin (1999b). The opposite conclusion – sophistication helps – is obtained if we assume, realistically, that the rate of time discounting is endogenous, that is, that addicts discount the future more heavily than nonaddicts, but that only sophisticated agents anticipate this effect. (For the idea of endogenous rates of discounting see also Orphanides and Zervos 1998.) Sophistication also helps if we assume that the highs from addiction diminish as one grows older, but that only sophisticated individuals are able to anticipate this effect.
207. Helge Waal (personal communication). Strictly speaking, this fatalistic attitude does not amount to sophisticated choice as defined here. The addicts' prediction about what they will do is not based on an anticipation of what it will be rational

Needless to say, these arguments do not imply that naiveté could ever be adopted as a precommitment device to protect oneself from addiction and other undesirable effects of sophistication (see the comments on Winston earlier). Even when naiveté, ignorance, innocence, spontaneity, and the like have good consequences, they cannot be deliberately chosen for that reason.[208] The result by Carillo and Mariotti discussed in I.3 is only an apparent exception. They show that an agent may rationally decide not to find out what the truth is on a certain topic, not that he may rationally decide to ignore a truth that he is already aware of.[209]

For more than twenty years George Ainslie has explored the idea that one can overcome the effects of hyperbolic discounting by "personal rules" or "bunching."[210] If an agent knows that he will be exposed to a series of choices each of which has the structure shown in Figure I.2 and is aware of his tendency to hyperbolic discounting, he may induce the choice of the delayed, larger rewards by framing the situation as a *choice of successions* rather than as a *succession of choices*. He may, that is, view himself as having the choice between choosing the early small reward now and on all later occasions, and choosing the large reward now and on all later occasions, ignoring scenarios in which the small reward is chosen on some occasions and the large reward on others. The idea is to set up a mental domino effect, by which one choice acts as a precedent for all later choices. Ainslie argues that this strategy of bunching choices together in a single decision is not only *effective* in overcoming the problem of hyperbolic discounting, but also *rational*.

The effectiveness of bunching is undeniable. Just as a person may manage to cooperate with others by asking, "If not me, who?" he can manage to cooperate with himself by asking, "If not now, when?"[211] For many people, abstention is easier than moderation because it can be sustained by a bright line. The cost of personal rules can be

---

for them to do in the last period of their planning horizon, but on the idea that since most addicts seem to relapse, they are likely to do so as well.

208. Elster (1983b), Ch. II.   209. See also note 166.

210. The fullest statement is in Ainslie (1992).

211. See, however, Skog (1999), who shows that if the number of future periods that are bunched together is small enough, an addict may form a resolution to quit only to find that it dissolves when the moment of choice approaches, thus reproducing the problem of time-inconsistency that motivated the bunching in the first place.

considerable, however.[212] There is a risk that the rigid pattern of rule-following behavior may spread from one sphere of life to others, if the agent wants to strengthen his resolve by extending precedent-setting across spheres. Within a given sphere, the strategy of never suffering a single exception may lead to a great deal of pointless self-denial. The response to this solution-induced problem is to find personal rules or bright lines that allow for moderate indulgence. Norman Zinberg describes how drug users, notably heroin users, achieve moderate or controlled consumption through self-imposed rules such as the following:

- Never use in a strange place.
- Never use with strangers.
- "Snort" only.
- Special schedule for use (for example, after work only).
- Plan in advance for use.
- Don't share "works."
- Clean up surroundings before use.
- Never use alone.
- Copping rules (for example, know your source personally).
- Budget funds for drug use.
- Don't mix drugs.
- Don't use for depression.
- Don't use if you're driving.[213]

The rationality of bunching is more questionable. The everyday Kantianism underlying the question "If not me, who?" definitely re-lies (in my opinion) on a form of magical thinking,[214] and the same is arguably the case for the analogous belief in the causal effect of precedents.[215] Also, if the moderate personal rules turn out to be un-stable and easily invaded by exceptions of all sorts so that the only choice left to the agent is an all-or-none decision, the cost of curtail-ing pleasurable spontaneous activities may be so severe that the agent

---

212. See notably Ainslie (1992), Ch. 6.4.   213. Zinberg (1984), p. 80.
214. Quattrone and Tversky (1986); Elster (1989c), pp. 195–200. Hurley (1989), pp. 150–51 argues, however, that cooperation in the one-shot Prisoner's Dilemma is ratio-nal. Sen (1987), pp. 81–88, makes a similar, although weaker suggestion. I confess to being unable to understand their arguments.
215. See Elster (1989c), pp. 201–2, and Bratman (1995) for claims that the belief in the causal efficacy of precedent is a form of magical thinking. In a reply to criticisms, Ainslie (1994) maintains that the belief is straightforwardly rational.

may rationally decide that it's not worth it. Suppose that the only way I can bring myself to do strenuous physical exercise is by doing it every day without exception, even on occasions when for some reason it's quite unpleasant. Suppose also that it's true, as I read somewhere, that for each hour of physical exercise one's expected life span is extended by fifty minutes. I might then, quite rationally, decide that the costs of exercising every day exceed the benefits.[216]

I conclude by asking whether the problem of strategic time-inconsistency can be solved in other ways than by precommitment. In a discussion of this issue, Avinash Dixit and Barry Nalebuff describe what they call "the eightfold path to credibility":

1. Establish and use a reputation.
2. Write contracts.
3. Cut off communication.
4. Burn bridges behind you.
5. Leave the outcome to chance.
6. Move in small steps.
7. Develop credibility through teamwork.
8. Employ mandated negotiating agents.[217]

Although most of these strategies require precommitment in one way or another, some are more ambiguous. When Dixit and Nalebuff observe that the emotion of pride can have reputation-building effects and hence serve "the implicit social aim of improving the credibility of our manifold daily relationships,"[218] they are either relying on unsupported functionalist reasoning or on a variant of the Hirshleifer-Frank argument discussed in I.5. When they observe that to avoid the unraveling of trust from backward induction that might undermine the strategy of moving in small steps "there should be no

---

216. Let me spell it out. For each daily hour of exercise my expected life span is extended (let us assume) by fifty minutes. On most days, the exercise involves fifteen minutes of pain followed by forty-five minutes of pleasure, leaving a net effect of pleasure. On some days, the exercise involves uninterrupted pain. On all days, the delay of the long-term benefits induces procrastination through hyperbolic discounting. Even on good days, the delay of the short-term benefits induces procrastination through the same mechanism. If I could trust myself to identify the bad days in a non-self-deceiving way, I could abstain on those occasions, get the short-term net benefits on the other days, and slightly lower long-term benefits. If I cannot trust myself, so that I must choose between always exercising and never doing so, I might decide that the pain of exercising on bad days offsets the sum of long-term and short-term benefits.
217. Dixit and Nalebuff (1991), p. 162.   218. Ibid., p. 165.

clear final step,"[219] they are not pointing to a feature of the situation that it is in anyone's power to bring about. They tend to confuse, in other words, credibility-enhancing features of the situation that are deliberately created for that purpose, and those that exist for other reasons yet with the same effect. Although there may be a sense in which the latter, incidental constraints may be viewed as "alternatives" to precommitment, it is not the sense I have been considering in these last pages. By the nature of the case, interpersonal credibility problems cannot be overcome through purely intrapsychic devices.

219. Ibid., p. 176.

Chapter II

Ulysses Unbound: Constitutions as Constraints

II.1. INTRODUCTION

Many writers have argued that political constitutions are devices for precommitment or self-binding, created by the body politic in order to protect itself against its own predictable tendency to make unwise decisions.[1] In an early discussion of the problem, Spinoza made an explicit analogy between individual and political precommitment:

[It] is by no means contrary to practice for laws to be so firmly established that even the king himself cannot repeal them. The Persians, for example, used to worship their kings as gods, yet even their kings had no power to repeal laws that had once been established, as is clear from Daniel Chapter 6, and nowhere, as far as I know, is a king appointed unconditionally, without any explicit terms. This, in fact, is contrary neither to reason nor to the absolute obedience due to a king; for the fundamental laws of the state must be regarded as the king's permanent decrees, so that his ministers render him complete obedience in refusing to execute any command of his which contravenes them. We may clarify this point by reference to Ulysses, whose comrades did execute his command in refusing, in spite of all his orders and threats, to untie him from his ship's mast while he was enchanted by the Siren's song: and it is put down to his good sense that he thanked them afterwards for carrying out his original intention so obediently. Even kings have followed the example of Ulysses; they usually instruct their judges to have no respect for persons in administering justice,

---

1. In this chapter, Roman numerals refer to the proceedings at the Constitutional Convention in Philadelphia, published in volumes I, II, and III of Farrand, ed. (1966). Arabic numerals refer to the proceedings of the first French Assemblée Constituante, as published in *Archives Parlementaires. Série I: 1789–1799*, Paris 1875–1888. *Procès-verbal des conférences sur la vérification des pouvoirs*, Paris 1789, is cited as "P."

not even the king himself, if by some odd mischance he commands something which they know to contravene established laws. For kings are not
gods, but men, who are often enchanted by the Siren's song. Accordingly, if
everything depended on the inconstant will of one man, nothing would be
stable.[2]

According to John Potter Stockton, "Constitutions are chains with
which men bind themselves in their sane moments that they may
not die by a suicidal hand in the day of their frenzy."[3] (But see II.9
for a very different use of the suicide metaphor.) Similarly, Friedrich
Hayek cites the view that a constitution is a tie imposed by Peter
when sober on Peter when drunk.[4] In a more recent statement, Cass
Sunstein writes, "Constitutional precommitment strategies might
serve to overcome myopia or weakness of will on the part of the
collectivity."[5] In the present chapter I discuss the meaning and usefulness of this view.

As explained in I.1, I shall distinguish between constitutions as
essential constraints on behavior and constitutions as incidental constraints. On the one hand, we may ask whether existing provisions
were established for the *purpose* of restricting the freedom of action of
the individuals who voted for them and that of similarly placed individuals in the future. When the Hungarian constituent parliament in
1989–90 voted to create a very powerful constitutional court with the
power to strike down parliamentary legislation, it was an explicit act
of self-limitation.[6] (Instructive contrasts are with Romania, where the
assembly in 1991 voted itself the power to overrule the constitutional
court, and with Poland, where the constituent Sejm in 1992 refused to
give up its power to overrule the court.) Decisions by a majority in a
constituent parliament to restrict the executive may also be instances
of self-binding, if the executive springs from that very same majority.
An example is when the Czech constituent parliament in 1992 voted
a provision that forbids the government from instructing the central
bank.

On the other hand, we may ask whether existing constitutional
provisions as a matter of fact tend to have salutary restraining *effects*

---

2. *Tractatus Theologico-Politicus* VII.1. I am indebted to Etienne Balibar for indicating
   this passage to me.
3. In a debate over the Ku Klux Klan Act of 1871, as cited in Finn (1991, p. 5).
4. Hayek (1960), p. 180.   5. Sunstein (1991b), p. 641.
6. As is typical in these cases, the motives behind the decision were actually a bit more
   complicated (see II.12).

on a subset of the political actors, regardless of why and by whom the constraints were set up in the first place. Although requirements of a supermajority for amending the constitution have never been established for the purpose of preventing cycling majorities, they may have this effect (II.9). Although requirements that constitutional amendments be passed by two successive legislatures have never been adopted for the purpose of overcoming time-inconsistency due to hyperbolic discounting, they may have this effect (II.7).

It is easy to confuse these two approaches, and to indulge in un-supported functional explanation. In *Ulysses and the Sirens*, which among other things was a crusade against this mode of explanation, I made exactly this mistake when I argued that the system of periodical elections "can be interpreted . . . as the electorate's method of binding itself and of protecting itself against its own impulsiveness."[7] Obvi-ously, no electorate ever did anything of the kind. If voters lack the means to recall their representatives at will, the explanation surely has more to do with the motives of politicians than with those of the voters. Yet the confusion is not totally unredeemable. In some cases, the effects of incidental constraints explain the maintenance of institu-tions that were originally introduced for quite different reasons. The shifting justifications for bicameralism are a case in point. Although often introduced by elite minorities to control popular majorities, this device may be retained as a form of democratic self-control by virtue of its delaying and cooling-down properties (II.6).

In exploring these ideas, I shall use the same methodology as in Chapter I, by considering reasons for precommitment as well as devices for precommitment. A comparison between Table II.1 and Table I.1 shows formal differences as well as similarities between constitutional precommitment. Some devices that are available for individual self-binding are not available for the collective case, and vice versa. Some reasons why individuals might want to precom-mit themselves have no analogue in the constitutional case, and vice versa.

I now proceed as follows. In II.2 I discuss whether the idea of a society "binding itself" is at all meaningful, and conclude that in a certain sense or under certain conditions we may answer in the

---

7. Op. cit., p. 90; irrelevant italics deleted. I was not the first to indulge in such reason-ing. Later I cite interventions by Lally-Tolendal in the French Assemblée Constitu-ante of 1789 (8, pp. 517–18) and of Madison at the Federal Convention (I, pp. 430–31) that rest, I believe, on the same fallacy.

Reasons for precommitment

		Overcome passion and interest	Overcome hyperbolic discounting	Overcome strategic time-inconsistency	Ensure efficiency
	Imposing costs	(II.3)		(II.3)	
Devices for precommitment	Eliminating options	II.6			
	Creating delays	II.5 II.7 II.6 II.8	II.8		
	Requiring supermajorities	II.5 II.7			II.10
	Separation of powers	II.7 II.9		II.9	II.9

Table II.1

affirmative. In II.3 I give a brief survey of the main features of constitutions that are relevant for my purposes here. In addition to my main topic, written constitutions, I also consider unwritten constitutional conventions. In II.4 I consider some aspects of the constitution-making process that are especially important for the present analysis, notably whether the framers of the constitution always have the autonomy of decision required to bind themselves (or others). As in II.7, the analysis is carried out through case studies of the American assembly of 1787 and the French assembly of 1789. In II.5 I discuss the relation between constitution-making and parts of the ordinary machinery of government, as two means of obtaining essentially the same results. In II.6 I consider Athenian democracy as a system of constraints on majoritarian decision making. In II.7 through II.10 I consider four reasons for constitutional precommitment, corresponding to the columns of Table II.1. In II.11, I discuss why such precommitment, when desirable, might not be feasible; and when feasible, might not be desirable. In II.12, finally, I try to pull together the various considerations – conceptual, causal, and normative – that tend to cast into question the idea of constitutions as precommitment devices.[8]

II.2. DISANALOGIES WITH INDIVIDUAL PRECOMMITMENT

In *Ulysses and the Sirens* I noted that the Ulysses metaphor for constitution-making is only partially valid, and in particular that the idea of society binding "itself" is a controversial one.[9] Yet I do not think I fully understood the extent of the disanalogy between individual and collective self-binding. As in many other cases, the transfer of concepts used to study individuals to the behavior of collectivities, as if these were individuals writ large, can be very misleading.[10] For one thing, constitutions may bind others rather than being acts of self-binding. For another, constitutions may not have the power to bind in the first place.

CONSTITUTIONS MAY BIND OTHERS

In the early phases of the making of the first French constitution, there was a bitter if mainly tacit struggle between the king and the constituent assembly. Louis XVI implicitly threatened the assembly in July 1789 by concentrating troops around Versailles, where the assembly was meeting, and in September by giving a regiment in Flanders marching orders on Paris. His actions triggered decisive events in Paris on July 14 and October 5–6 that, in retrospect, were turning points in the revolution. The victorious assembly had not forgotten the lesson when it laid down, in the constitution of September 3, 1791,

---

8. After the manuscript of this book was completed I was happy to see Jeremy Waldron (1999) offering a criticism of the idea of constitutions as precommitment devices (and implicitly of my own writings defending this idea) that largely matches some of the objections offered later. Note, however, that among motives for precommitment he considers only the need to preempt passion, thus neglecting the desire to overcome partisan interest and time-inconsistency as well as the desire to promote efficiency. I imagine that Waldron, too, would be sympathetic to the propositions that incumbent governments should not easily be able to change the rules of the political game in their favor, and that stability of the political framework is desirable to extend the time horizon of the economic and political agents.
9. Elster (1984), p. 93.
10. See Elster (1989a), pp. 176 ff.; see also Holmes (1988), pp. 237–38.

that "The executive power [that is, the king] cannot cause any body of troops to pass or sojourn within thirty thousand toises [about 37 miles] of the legislative body, except upon its requisition or its authorization." This was not an act of *self*-binding. The king obtained a veto *in* the constitution, but after the show of force on October 5–6, 1789, he lost his veto *over* the constitution.[11] Rather than binding himself, the king was bound by the assembly – confirming Seip's dictum that I cited in the Preface.

Suppose next as a putative case of self-binding that the framers by simple majority decide (i) that legislation is constrained by certain rights of property, and (ii) that (i) can be modified only by a two-thirds majority in a following legislature. This is not necessarily an act of *self*-binding. In the first place, it is impossible to accept the view – advocated notably by Sieyes – that once the majority has spoken, its opinion ipso facto becomes the general will.[12] The majority binds the minority, and that's all there is to it. In the second place, if elections to the constituent assembly take place with limited suffrage, the current majority among the framers may represent a minority in the population. Anticipating future extensions of the suffrage, they may then try to limit the freedom of action of future majorities. At the Federal Convention, according to Thornton Anderson, "the Founding Fathers . . . in defending property against anticipated majorities of the propertyless, entailed upon their posterity a system insufficiently flexible to adapt."[13] In the third place, even with universal suffrage the majority may act strategically to bind the minority, by constitutionalizing a law rather than enacting it as ordinary statute. Suppose that 51% of the framers want to protect property, but fear that their view might soon become a minority opinion in the population. In that case, they can entrench their view by using their 51% majority to require a 67% majority to undo the provision. To speak of *self*-binding in such cases is cant.

A subtler example may be taken from Aristotle's *Politics*:

The devices adopted in constitutions for fobbing the masses off with sham rights are five in number. . . . As regard the assembly, all alike are free to attend;

---

11. Castaldo (1989), pp. 277–81.
12. On this point, see Manin (1995), pp. 237–42, notably p. 241, note 36. In the first French constituent assembly (1789–91), the identification of the majority vote with the general will had the practical implication that no records were taken of the number of votes for and against a given proposal (Castaldo 1989, p. 351, note 192).
13. Anderson (1993), p. 15.

but fines for non-attendance are either imposed on the rich alone, or imposed on the rich at a far higher rate. As regards the magistracies, those who possess a property qualification are not allowed to decline office on oath, but the poor are allowed to do so. As regards the law courts, the rich are fined for non-attendance, but the poor may absent themselves with impunity. . . . In some states a different device is adopted in regard to attendance at the assembly and the law courts. All who have registered themselves may attend; those who fail to attend after registration are heavily fined. Here the intention is to stop men from registering, through fear of the fines they may thus incur, and ultimately to stop them from attending the courts and the assembly as a result of their failure to register. Similar measures are also employed in regard to the possession of arms and the practice of athletics. The poor are allowed not to have any arms, and the rich are fined for not having them. The poor are not fined if they absent themselves from physical training: the rich are. (1297a)

The arrangements described in this passage exploit the fact that if one set of individuals can enhance their power by limiting their own freedom, they can also *reduce the power of others by expanding their freedom*. These Greek constitutions forced the rich to participate in public affairs by making it costly for them not to do so, while making it less likely that the poor would participate by reducing the costs to them of abstaining. Whereas the modern constitutions (Australia, Belgium) that make voting mandatory *for all* may properly be seen as mechanisms of self-binding to overcome the collective action problem involved in voting, selective mandatory devices serve to control others rather than oneself.

Constitutions May Not Bind at All

Nor are constitutions acts of self-*binding* in a strict sense (but see later sections for less strict senses). When Ulysses bound himself to the mast and had his rowers put wax in their ears, it was to make it *impossible* for him to succumb to the song of the Sirens. Constitutions are usually designed to make it *difficult* to change their provisions, compared to ordinary legislation, but not impossible. Although some constitutions have provisions that are immune against amendment, even these do not bind in a strict sense, because extraconstitutional action always remains possible. The individual who wants to bind himself can entrust his will to external institutions or forces, outside his control, that prevent him from changing his mind. But *there is nothing external to society*, barring the case of precommitment through international institutions with powers of enforcement such as the International Monetary Fund or the World Bank. And even these cannot make it impossible to act against a precommitment, only make it more costly to do so.[14]

In fact, attempts to bind society very tightly could have the opposite effect, for two reasons. First, the citizens might react to the very idea of being bound.[15] One reason for wanting to break out of a fortress might be that one does not want to live under the authority of a tyrant – defined as someone who would build a fortress to prevent the subjects from leaving. By lowering the drawbridge and offering them the opportunity to leave, the ruler might reduce their desire to use it. Thus it was reported that in the last days of the German Democratic Republic, the leaders contemplated giving the citizens free access to West Berlin in the hope that this might defuse their frustration and make them more inclined to stay. Reflecting on his experience as a member of the constitutional committee of the French parliament of 1848, Tocqueville wrote, in a similar vein, "I have long thought that, instead of trying to make our forms of government eternal, we should pay attention to making methodical change an easy matter. All things considered, I find that less dangerous than the opposite alternative. I thought one should treat the French people like those lunatics whom one is careful not to bind lest they become infuriated by the constraint."[16]

Second, the citizens might find very tight amendment provisions an intolerable obstacle to change. A constitution that imposed a requirement of unanimity for all amendments would probably not last for long. The Norwegian constitution of 1814 prohibited the entry of Jews and Jesuits into the kingdom. (The former provision was abolished in 1851, the latter in 1956.) If that ban had been unamendable, it would eventually either have been disregarded (that is,

---

14. Vreeland (1999) argues, however, that as a matter of fact national governments do not seek assistance from the IMF in order to tie their own hands, but rather to tie the hands of their domestic opponents. The argument obviously fits neatly with Seip's dictum cited in the Preface and with the main thrust of the present chapter.
15. Thus Brehm (1966) shows that if people's preferred option is imposed on them rather than chosen, they may develop a preference for an option that was originally ranked lower.
16. Tocqueville (1990), p. 181.

rendered inoperative by a tacit constitutional convention) or changed by extraconstitutional means. Similarly, entrenched restrictions on suffrage could not have survived the irresistible progress of equality in modern, Western societies. Ulysses would have found the strength to break the ropes that tied him to the mast.

In spite of these disanalogies between the individual and the collective cases, the idea of constitutional precommitment is not meaningless. In a few cases, we may talk about *self*-binding in a literal sense, for instance if a constituent parliament unanimously decides to give up some of its powers to another branch of government. The idea also makes fairly literal sense if the majority in the constituent assembly also expects to be the majority in the first legislature. Cases of this sort from recent constitution-making in Eastern Europe were cited in II.1. Creating a constitution that binds future generations may also, in a looser sense, be seen as an act of *self*-binding, namely, if future political agents are expected to have the same reasons for wanting to be restricted as the founding generation. And although these acts are not binding in an absolute sense, we should remember that individual precommitment need not be absolute either.

II.3. THE NATURE AND STRUCTURE OF CONSTITUTIONS

Except for the discussion of Athenian politics in II.6, my main concern in this chapter is with written constitutions, from the Federal Convention to the present.[17] In all Western societies with the exception of Great Britain (and, more ambiguously, Israel), political life is regulated by written constitutions. In Britain, the constitution is entirely made up of unwritten "constitutional conventions."[18] In other countries, such conventions may supplement and sometimes modify the written constitution.[19] Before I proceed to discuss written constitutions, let me say a few words about unwritten conventions from a precommitment perspective.

---

17. For a survey of constitution-making processes in Europe and North America, see Elster (1995a).
18. Marshall (1984).
19. See, for instance, Heard (1991) on the relation between the written and the unwritten constitution in Canada.

WRITTEN AND UNWRITTEN CONSTITUTIONS

One difference between written constitutions and unwritten ones is that the former are *made,* whereas the latter emerge or *evolve.* Another is that whereas violation of the written constitution may trigger *legal* sanctions, for instance by judicial review of legislation or of executive decrees, those who violate an unwritten convention risk *political* sanctions ranging from electoral defeat to revolution. While broadly accurate, this statement does not hold universally. In Great Britain and other Commonwealth countries, constitutional conventions are sometimes cited by the courts. An interesting illustration was provided by the Canadian Supreme Court in 1981, when it decided (by six votes to three) that there was a constitutional convention requiring the government to seek the consent of the provinces before modifying the constitution, while also deciding (by seven votes to two) that the government was not legally required to do so.[20]

In some cases, conventions emerge when precedents harden into (more or less) binding rules. Thus

> every Canadian minister who did not hold a seat in the legislature at the time of his or her appointment to the Cabinet has tried to win a seat within a short period. Negative precedents involve actors abstaining from visible actions in supposed deference to a rule; no British monarch has refused to sign a bill since 1707. Precedents are most useful only when a consistent pattern of either positive or negative precedents emerges; thus it is generally accepted that the Queen cannot veto a bill and that all ministers must either have a seat in the legislature or obtain one.[21]

Sometimes, a single precedent is enough. A famous example is de Gaulle's decision in 1962 to have an amendment of the constitution that created direct election of the president ratified by referendum. Although the 1958 constitution had a place for referenda, they were no part of the formal amendment process. All constitutional scholars at the time agreed that amending the constitution by referendum was unconstitutional.[22] Yet with the help of the tame chairman of the Constitutional Council, de Gaulle was able to override these objections.

---

20. The decision is conveniently available in Bayefsky, ed. (1989), which also provides a full set of supporting documents. For the political and legal context, see Russell (1993) and Heard (1991).
21. Heard (1991), p. 144.
22. Burdeau, Hamon, and Troper (1991), pp. 480 ff.; also Lacouture (1990), vol. III, pp. 572 ff.

Twenty years later, constitutional amendment by referendum had become part of French constitutional jurisprudence. Another example from French constitutional history concerns MacMahon's "loss of the presidency" in 1877. After he abstained from resolving a crisis by using the power of the president to dissolve parliament, that power effectively ceased to be part of the prerogatives of the office.[23] A constitutional convention had been created that lasted until the end of the Third Republic sixty years later. In 1999, American constitutional scholars debated whether conviction of Clinton in the impeachment trial would similarly weaken the power of the presidency.

In other cases, a constitutional convention arises when ordinary legislation takes on a quasi-constitutional status, in the sense that anyone trying to overturn it would incur a serious political risk. In the United States today, there is a constitutional convention that would create severe political costs for anyone who tried to do what President Roosevelt threatened to do in 1937, "packing" the Supreme Court by appointing new judges more sympathetic to the New Deal policies. A more complex case involves Rule 32 (2) of the Standing Rules of the American Senate: "The rules of the Senate shall continue from one Congress to the next Congress unless they are changed *as provided in these rules.*" Although the rule is arguably unconstitutional (it is an attempt by one legislature to bind later legislatures),[24] it now exists as a constitutional convention with the effect, among other things, of creating a 60% majority requirement in the Senate through the practice of filibustering. Also, suppose that the Republicans fail in their ongoing efforts to introduce a balanced-budget amendment and an amendment requiring a two-thirds majority in Congress for tax increases. They might still go ahead and introduce ordinary legislation to the same effect, in the hope that these laws would acquire a quasi-constitutional aura that would prevent later, Democratic Congresses from overturning them.

In practice, deliberate and successful attempts to create a tacit constitutional convention are probably rare. (The 1985 Gramm-Rudman Act, discussed later, was an unsuccessful attempt.) An example may be the statutory regulation of the Norwegian Central Bank. Although the government is allowed to instruct the bank, it must send a message to parliament whenever it does so. This provision was intended to create some de facto independence for the bank, by making government

---

23. Derfler (1983), Ch. 2, notably p. 37.   24. Eule (1987), p. 408.

more reluctant to interfere.[25] It can do so, but at some political costs or risks to itself. Such cases exemplify constitutional precommitment that works by attaching extra costs to the choice of a particular option. (They might not, though, illustrate *self*-binding, but rather one branch of government constraining another.) In Table II.1, uses of this device have been put between parentheses, not because they are rare, but because they fall outside the main line of argument that I am pursuing. The transformation of statutory legislation into a constitutional convention is too heavily dependent on particular political conjunctures to fit in with my main concern here, which is with precommitment devices that operate with some degree of regularity and predictability.

From a normative point of view, one may argue that constitutional amendments should be left to the agents and the procedures explicitly designed in the constitution. Thus Julian Eule argues that the principal objection to the 1985 Gramm-Rudman Act, which stipulated automatic spending cuts for each of the next six fiscal years if the budget deficit exceeded a target amount, was not the one cited by the Supreme Court when it struck the act down, namely, that it violated the separation of powers. Rather, the act was objectionable because it represented an attempt by Congress to bind future Congresses. "Gramm-Rudman is based on the political judgment that it will be far more difficult for future Congresses to repeal Gramm-Rudman than it will be for them to appropriate funds beyond the spending target. . . . This is, I suggest, precisely the sort of extratemporal influence that our temporary agents should not enjoy."[26]

THE STRUCTURE OF WRITTEN CONSTITUTIONS

From now on, then, I mainly consider written constitutions, although I occasionally discuss how unwritten conventions may have similar effects. Substantively, a written constitution regulates the most fundamental features of political life. Procedurally, it is more difficult to change the constitution than to enact ordinary legislation. Legally, the constitution takes precedence over ordinary legislation in the case of conflict. The idea of *constitutionalism*, understood as a general propensity to abide by the constitution and judicial review, cannot

25. Smith (1994), pp. 96–97; see also Willoch (1994).
26. Eule (1987), p. 426, note 215.

be reduced to the mere presence of a constitution with these features. During the Hungarian constitution-making process in 1989–1990 it sometimes happened that when parliament noticed that a constitutional provision it had just adopted was in conflict with existing legislation, it proceeded to change the constitution rather than the statute. When the constitutional court of India has struck down legislation as unconstitutional, parliament has regularly responded by amending the constitution.[27] The Austrian parliament has treated the constitution in an even more cavalier manner.

While such practices are in perfect accordance with the constitution, they may violate constitutionalism. Constitutionalism ensures that constitutional change will be slow, compared to the fast lane of ordinary parliamentary politics. The constitution should be a framework for political action, not an instrument for action. In most countries, the need for a supermajority for constitutional amendment together with the rarity of large majorities in parliament will ensure that constitutions in fact do change slowly. In countries with a long constitutional tradition, powerful unwritten conventions may also deter politicians from constantly tinkering with the constitution to promote short-term or partisan ends. In contrast to the constitutional conventions that can substitute for or supplement written constitutions, one may think of these as *meta-constitutional conventions*. As in the case of violations of constitutional conventions, the violation of meta-constitutional conventions will trigger political rather than legal sanctions – electoral defeat or revolution rather than adverse judicial review.

Constitutions regulate political life, as well as themselves. The first task is carried out by two sets of provisions. First, there is a bill of rights that is intended to protect the citizens from undue interference by the government and to ensure the provision of various procedural and substantive goods. Second, there are provisions regulating what we may call the machinery of government: modes of election and representation, the functions of government, separation of powers, checks and balances, and so on. The self-regulating task of constitutions is also carried out by two sets of provisions. On the one hand, there are rules governing the amendment of the constitution itself. On the other hand, many constitutions contain rules regulating the temporary suspension of the constitution. As the topic of this chapter is precommitment and constitutionalism, I am concerned mainly

27. Rudolph and Rudolph (1987), Ch. 3.

with the features of the constitution itself that make it more resistant to change, that is, with the formal rules governing amendment of the constitution. I shall also discuss the rules for suspending the constitution at moments when Ulysses might want to undo the ties that bind him to the mast. The relation between constitutional self-binding and the machinery of government is the topic of II.5. In II.8 I briefly consider the role of rights as precommitment devices.

Amendment Procedures

With the exception of New Zealand, it is more difficult to amend the constitution than to enact ordinary legislation.[28] (Usually, however, constitutions are *adopted* by simple majority, a rare exception being the recent South African constitution for which a larger majority was required.)[29] The main hurdles for constitutional amendments are

- absolute entrenchment
- adoption by a supermajority in parliament
- requirement of a higher quorum than for ordinary legislation
- delays
- state ratification (in federal systems)
- ratification by referendum

Many constitutions also state that the constitution cannot be amended during a state of emergency. In Germany an amendment, even if passed in the way laid down by the constitution, may be struck down as unconstitutional by the Federal Constitutional Court if it is deemed to be contrary to the fundamental constitutional principles.[30] The same jurisprudence now obtains in India.[31] Conjunctions, disjunctions, and trade-offs among these principles are also observed. In addition, the U.S. Constitution opens the possibility, which has

---

28. Even in New Zealand, the mere fact of naming some clauses "constitutional" rather than statutory may confer some immunity against easy amendment (Eule 1987, p. 394), by virtue of a meta-constitutional convention.
29. For details about the South African case, see Shapiro (1996), p. 216, note 85. In the Assemblée Constituante, delegates from the right tried, unsuccessfully, to impose qualified majorities in voting on the new constitution (Castaldo 1989, p. 129).
30. Finn (1991), p. 190.
31. Rudolph and Rudolph (1987), pp. 110–111; Davis, Chaskalson, and de Waal (1995), p. 37.

never been used, for amending the constitution by calling special constitutional conventions. The frequently made proposal to constitutionalize periodical conventions for revising the constitution has never, to my knowledge, been implemented.[32]

Some constitutions offer absolute entrenchment of rights. Art. 79 (3) of the German constitution says that the basic rights are immune to revision. Similarly Article 57 of the Bulgarian constitution says that fundamental rights are irrevocable.[33] Some constitutions also offer the same protection of the basic form of government, for example, the federal organization of the country (Germany) or the republican form of government (Romania). While the American constitution does not render the equality of the states' votes in the Senate exempt from amendment, it comes close to doing so by stipulating that "no State, without its Consent, shall be deprived of its equal Suffrage in the Senate."

Supermajorities range from unanimity (the *liberum veto* in Poland before 1791),[34] through the requirement of a three-fourths majority (Bulgaria), two-thirds (many countries) to three-fifths (France, the Czech and Slovak Republics). When these numbers refer to the majority of votes rather than of deputies, they are often combined with high quorums, a common combination being a two-thirds quorum and a two-thirds majority. In Canada – a country where the struggle over amendment procedures has been at the heart of politics for several decades – most provisions require the consent of the federal parliament and two-thirds of the provinces, representing

32. In the United States, this idea was advocated by Thomas Jefferson, and criticized to devastating effect by James Madison (Holmes 1988, pp. 215–221). In France, it was discussed at the Assemblée Constituante of 1789–91 (30, pp. 36 ff.). An approximation is found in the Pennsylvania Constitution of 1776, which called for the election every seven years of a Council of Censors to review the constitution and to propose necessary amendments to a specially called convention. The Polish constitution of 1791, which calls for an "extraordinary constitutional diet" every twenty-five years, was in force only for two years. A similar provision existed in the 1921 Polish constitution, whose life also ended before the time was ripe for implementing it.
33. However, Article 158 implies that Article 57 itself is amendable. Similarly, Article 148 of the Romanian constitution and Article 79 of the German constitution, which list the entrenched clauses in the constitution, do not include themselves. For a discussion of this conundrum, see Suber (1990), p. 101 and passim.
34. Wagner (1997), p. 62, asserts that the clause in the American constitution protecting the equality of representation of the states in the Senate is very similar to the *liberum veto*. In theory, though, a state might lose its equal vote in the Senate if (i) this change was approved by the normal amendment procedure and (ii) the state in question voted for it, even if (iii) some other states voted against it.

50% of the population. The amendment procedure itself, however, can be amended only by a unanimous decision of all the provinces.

Delays can be imposed in many ways. In Norway, amendments must be proposed during one parliament and adopted during another. In Sweden, they must be passed by two successive parliaments. In Bulgaria, one path to constitutional amendment is described as follows:

An amendment bill shall be debated by the National Assembly not earlier than one month and not later than three months from the date on which it is introduced. A constitutional amendment shall require a majority of three-fourths of the votes of all Members of the National Assembly in three ballots on three different days. A bill which has received less than three-fourths but more than two-thirds of the votes of all Members shall be eligible for reintroduction after not fewer than two months and not more than five months. To be passed at this new reading, the bill shall require a majority of two thirds of the votes of all Members. (Article 154–155)

Once an amendment has been adopted in parliament, it may be passed on to another instance for ratification. In federally organized countries, endorsement by some proportion of the state legislatures is commonly required. Ratification by popular referendum is optional in some countries, mandatory in others. Again, one may require either a certain percentage of the registered voters to vote for the amendment or impose a combination of participation and majority requirements. Because these processes are time-consuming, they tend to serve as a brake as well.

These hurdles may be combined in several ways. First, by conjunction: the constitution may, as in Norway, require both a delay and a supermajority. In federal systems, one may require that both a majority of the citizens and a majority of the component republics vote in favor. The Swiss constitution of 1848 had a provision of this kind; Canada has a similar, but vastly more complicated system. Second, by disjunction: in France, for example, amendments can be adopted either by simple majority in parliament and then submitted to referendum, or by a three-fifths majority in parliament without referendum. A typical case is the disjunctive trade-off, in which delays may be compressed in exchange for a larger majority. Countries with trade-offs of this kind include France, Bulgaria, Norway (but only with regard to the delegation of national sovereignty), and Finland.

103

Overall, therefore, the most important devices for constitutional precommitment are *supermajorities* and *delays*. As we shall see in II.7 through II.10, the rationales for using the one or the other are quite different. Also, as we shall see in II.5, some of the motives for precommitment may be satisfied by devices not related to the amendment procedure.

SUSPENDING THE CONSTITUTION

I conclude this section with a brief comment on clauses regulating the suspension of the constitution.[35] In an emergency situation, one may want to suspend the constitution if an amendment would be too time-consuming or if only a temporary measure is required. The 1978 Spanish constitution, which distinguishes among states of alarm, emergency, and siege, allows most civil liberties to be suspended in the latter two states. Article 16 of the French constitution of 1958 gives the president unlimited powers during a state of emergency, except the power to change the constitution.[36] Some rights may be protected from suspension during an emergency. Thus Article 48 of the Weimar constitution allowed the president to abrogate habeas corpus, freedom of assembly, and freedom of association, but not freedom of expression and the ban on retroactive legislation.[37] Article 81 of the Bonn constitution stipulates that no legislation amending or suspending the constitution may be passed during an emergency.[38]

35. I am indebted to Bernard Manin for impressing on me the importance of emergency powers provisions in the constitution. For a historical survey of regimes of exception from the Roman dictatorships to the present, see Ch. 2 of Loveman (1993). The bulk of that work is a survey of such regimes in Spanish-American history. Finn (1991) offers a comparison of emergency regimes in Northern Ireland and under the Weimar and Bonn constitutions.

36. Burdeau, Hamon, and Troper (1991), p. 696.

37. Eventually, Article 48, together with Article 25, which authorizes the president to dissolve the Reichstag, became "the instrument through which Weimar's parliamentary democracy was transformed into presidential government" (Finn 1991, pp. 142–43).

38. An earlier draft of the Bonn constitution did allow the government, with the agreement of the president of the two chambers, to suspend certain basic rights in an emergency. "The article was deleted from the Basic Law in its final reading, because it was thought that so long as the occupation powers continued to reserve to themselves responsibility for the Federal Republic's defense and the maintenance of its constitutional order, the exercise of emergency powers by the federal government might lead to confusion" (Golay 1958, p. 132). See also Finn (1991), pp. 193 ff.

Many constitutions ban amendments to the constitution during the state of emergency; some also ban changes in the electoral law. The suspension of the constitution may itself be subject to the constitutional principles of separation of powers and checks and balances. In the Weimar constitution, parliament could abrogate the emergency measures. In France, the Constitutional Court must be officially consulted. I return to the significance of emergency clauses in II.11.

II.4. CONSTRAINTS ON CONSTITUTION-MAKING

The formal process of constitution-making is a relatively recent phenomenon.[39] The first instances occurred in the American colonies after 1776. Shortly thereafter, the United States, France, and Poland adopted written constitutions. Many later constitution-making processes have occurred in waves: in the wake of the 1848 revolutions, after the First and Second World Wars, around 1960 following the rise to independence of many former colonies, and after 1989 following the fall of communism in Eastern Europe and the former Soviet Union.[40] There are of course also many instances of constitution-making that were not part of any wave.

UPSTREAM AUTHORITIES

The central topic of the present chapter is whether these processes should be viewed as acts of constraining others or as acts of self-constraint. A necessary prolegomenon to this question is *whether constituent assemblies might themselves be subject to constraints* that limit their constraining or self-constraining powers. The question arises for the simple reason that constituent assemblies virtually never create themselves. The decision to convene a constituent assembly must be taken by some outside authority. In the United States, it was taken by the Continental Congress; in France in 1789 by the king; in France in 1848 and 1946 by the provisional government; in Japan and West Germany after World War II by the occupying power; in Poland, Hungary, and Bulgaria after 1989 by Round Table Talks between the

---

39. For a survey see Elster (1995a).
40. For explanations of the tendency for constitution-making to come in waves, see Elster (1995a).

old regime and the opposition. Although a self-convening assembly might seem a logical impossibility, the Frankfurt Parliament of 1848 does to some extent fit that description. On March 5, 1848, fifty-one self-selected leaders of the public met in Heidelberg to discuss Germany's future, "without the legitimacy of the state, without explicit authorization from anyone, without a regular selection procedure, empowered only by their own political will."[41] They convened a *Vorparlament* that met in Frankfurt on March 31. That body in turn voted for elections to a constituent assembly and set up a committee to help administer them. The assembly then met on May 18. The making of the 1958 French constitution is another borderline case. Formally, the parliament of the Fourth Republic gave de Gaulle the power to write a new constitution. In reality, he forced the deputies to do so.

Once the decision to convene the constituent assembly has been made, the delegates must be elected or selected. In this case, too, there is a need for an outside authority. The delegates cannot select themselves. Again, there is a considerable range of variation in the selection procedures. In the United States, they were selected by the state legislatures, except for South Carolina, where the legislature authorized the governor to choose the delegates. In France in 1789, they were selected by the three estates. In France and in Germany in 1848, they were directly elected by universal suffrage. This has also been the rule in the making of most twentieth-century constitutions, exceptions being the indirectly elected assemblies that wrote the Indian constitution of 1948 and the German constitution of 1949.

A constituent assembly, in other words, has two upstream authorities or creators: the *convener* and the *selector*. Both will naturally try to influence the final document that the assembly is to produce and/or the procedures it should adopt for its deliberations. In particular, they will want to impose themselves as the final downstream authorities who must ratify the constitution before it can take effect. Equally naturally, the constitution-makers will try to resist attempts to influence the proceedings and their outcome. In France in 1958, Pierre Cot warned de Gaulle that he would be the prisoner of the generals that had brought him to power: "Qui t'a fait roi?"[42] As we know, Cot turned out to be wrong. De Gaulle was largely able to ignore those to whom he owed his power.[43] For reasons to be discussed

41. Huber (1960), p. 593.   42. Comité National (1987–1991), vol. I, p. 125.
43. Although the generals were the source of de Gaulle's power de facto, de jure

shortly, this seems in fact to be the case quite generally. Constituent assemblies tend to view themselves as having what the Germans call "Kompetenz-Kompetenz," the right to define their powers.

As noted earlier, the upstream convener may be a victorious occupying power, as in Germany and Japan after 1945. In Japan, the Americans were pretty much able to impose their constitution.[44] In Germany, the occupying powers met with more resistance. The Germans were able to deflect the American insistence on a strongly decentralized constitution by playing on internal divisions among the Western powers as well as on the rising threat of Communism.[45] Rather than exploring such attempts to impose constitutions from outside, however, I shall discuss the more interesting case of an old regime trying to constrain the new regime to which it is, reluctantly, giving birth. As in II.7, my examples are the Federal Convention in Philadelphia (1787) and the Assemblée Constituante in Paris (1789–91). These are probably the most eminent cases of constitution-making in history, and extremely interesting in a number of respects.[46]

As noted, the decision to convene the assembly must be made by a preexisting authority, which, in our two cases, were the Continental Congress and the king of France. As also noted, the mechanism by which delegates are elected or selected must equally be in existence prior to the assembly itself. In the cases that concern me here, and in most others of interest, these two outside authorities do not coincide.[47] Although Louis XVI decided to convene the Estates General, he could not pick the delegates. When he tried to obtain the power to verify their credentials, he was rebuffed. Whereas the

---

he owed his power to the Parliament of the Fourth Republic. From a technical point of view, his constituent powers were in fact constrained by parliament. Although this was "the first time in [French] constitutional history that the constituent organ was not invested with unconditional authority" (Burdeau, Hamon, and Troper, 1991, p. 449), the constraints were not binding. The only solution excluded by the parliamentary instructions – specifically by the clause "le Gouvernement doit être responsable devant le Parlement" (Comité National 1987–1991, vol. I, p. 125) – was an American-style presidential regime, which de Gaulle had never desired.

44. For a more nuanced analysis, see Koseki (1997).
45. Golay (1958), pp. 17, 8, 110. For the special case of the Central Bank, see Marsh (1992), Ch. 6, especially pp. 149–50.
46. For comparative analyses of these two assemblies, see also Elster (1993b, 1994, 1995b, 1995c).
47. Such coincidence would indicate that we are dealing with a mere puppet assembly, with no will of its own. An example would be the body of sixty-six men convened in China by Yuan Shikai in 1914 to give his rule a semblance of legality through a "constitutional compact."

Continental Congress made the decision to convene the Federal Convention, the state legislatures chose the delegates.[48]

Although the assembly is incapable of deciding the initial convocation and delegation, it can arrogate to itself the power over all other decisions. To varying degrees this is what happened in the two eighteenth-century assemblies. They verified their own credentials, set many of their own rules, sometimes overruling their instructions, sometimes supplementing them. The tension between the assemblies and their conveners – between the creature and its creator – was at the heart of both processes. In Philadelphia, the state legislatures, which were the source of the authority of the delegates, were also perceived by many as a major obstacle to their efforts. In Paris, there was a somewhat similar relationship between the king and the assembly.

The general form of the problem is simple. On the one hand, it seems to be a general principle that if X brings Y into being, then X has an authority superior to that of Y.[49] On the other hand, if Y is brought into being to regulate, among other things, the activities of X, Y would seem to be the superior instance. The paradox can also be summarized in two opposing slogans, "Let the kingmaker beware of the king" versus "Let the king beware of the kingmaker." These relationships obtain both between the assembly and its convener and between the delegates and their constituencies. Collectively, the delegates owe their existence to one institution; individually, to another. These facts are crucial for understanding the debates in both assemblies.

In both cases, the assemblies got the upper hand against their creators. The delegates at the Federal Convention succeeded in replacing the state legislatures with special conventions as the ratifying bodies. Also, they implicitly overruled Congress when they demanded ratification by nine out of the thirteen states instead of the unanimity that governed changes in the Articles of Confederation.[50] The French delegates turned the king's veto *in* the constitution into a merely suspensive one, and his veto *over* the constitution into a vacuous formality. Also, they ignored the instructions of their constituents on a number of crucial issues. This outcome should not surprise us. Almost by definition, the old regime is part of the problem that a constituent

---

48. I am not denying the close ties between the legislatures and Congress. However, the legislatures acting collectively through Congress to call a convention should not be confused with their individual power to select delegates.
49. This principle, however, gives rise to a paradox if the amending clause of a constitution is used to amend itself (Suber 1990).
50. For a full discussion of these and other issues see Ackerman and Katyal (1995).

assembly has to solve. But *if the regime is flawed, why should the assembly respect its instructions?*

Bound Mandates

Following a distinction made by Talleyrand in the Assemblée Constituante (8, p. 201), we may distinguish between three kinds of bound mandates: instructions about how to vote on specific issues; instructions to refuse to debate specific issues; and instructions to withdraw from the assembly in case certain decisions are made. These are all attempts to bind individual delegates. In addition, it was argued, both in Paris and in Philadelphia, that the assembly itself had a limited mandate, in that certain institutions or issues were out of bounds for discussion.

In the French assembly, individual mandates were invoked mainly with respect to three issues: instructions to vote by order or by head, to refuse consent to a loan before the constitution had been adopted, and to support a royal veto in and over the constitution. On all three counts, most delegates eventually decided to ignore their instructions. The main question concerning the collective mandate of the assembly arose in the debate over the royal veto in and over the constitution. For many, it was self-evidently true that the assembly had no mandate to destroy or limit its creator. For others, it was equally evident that the assembly could do anything it wanted, being the embodiment of the will of the nation.

At the Federal Convention, the delegation from Delaware came with instructions not to accept anything short of equality of votes for all states in the new union. Although the instructions themselves (III, pp. 173, 574) did not amount to more than bound mandates of the first kind, the threat to withdraw was nevertheless made at the outset of the convention (I, p. 37). Delegates from the slaveholding states also threatened to withdraw unless they got their way over the slave trade (II, p. 364), but they never referred to any mandate of the first or the third kind.[51] Although threats are more credible if backed by instructions from a superior body (see I.4), the strong interests of the slave states made it believable that they would withdraw if they did

---

51. Two delegates from New York State (Lansing and Yates) actually did withdraw from the convention. This, however, did not amount to withdrawal of the New York *delegation*.

not get their way. For them, a union with strong restrictions on slave-holding and slave trade would be worse than an isolated existence outside the union. In bargaining terms, therefore, they could credibly refuse an option that was worse than their disagreement point.[52]

The Delaware instructions were the only case of individual mandates at the Federal Convention. Far more important was the question of whether the convention itself had a mandate to propose sweeping changes in the constitution. Some delegates to the Federal Convention (for example, see I, pp. 34, 249, 250) claimed that their instructions did not extend to the kind of wide-ranging reform that was emerging. They did not, however, threaten to withdraw on this account. The advocates for a radical change had two replies. James Wilson said, lamely, that "he conceived himself authorized to *conclude nothing*, but to be at liberty to *propose any thing*" (I, p. 253). George Mason argued more robustly that "in certain seasons of public danger it is commendable to exceed power" (I, p. 346). Randolph, similarly, "was not scrupulous on the point of power" (I, p. 255). Bootstrap-pulling can be justified by external circumstances. This kind of statement was also frequent in the French assembly. The exceptional conditions that create the call for a constituent assembly also justify arrogations of power that would appear illegal under normal circumstances. In the constitution-making process the kingmaker should beware of the king.

VERIFYING CREDENTIALS

Once the delegates meet, their credentials must be verified so that the assembly can start working. In Philadelphia, this potentially tricky step caused no problems. The delegates met, read their credentials, and went on with their business. In Paris, the verification debates turned out to be a crucial stage in the self-transformation of the Estates General into the National Assembly.[53] Two issues were at stake. First, the nobility wanted each order to verify the powers of its own

---

52. See also Elster (1995f) for an interpretation of other debates at the Federal Convention in terms of bargaining theory.
53. After initial plenary sessions, these debates took place in a small committee with delegates from the three orders. The transcripts from the debates are relatively full, but do not permit us to identify speakers except by their membership in one of the orders.

delegates, whereas the third estate wanted the verification to take place in a joint session of all three orders.[54] (The clergy said from the beginning that it would go along with any agreement reached by the other two orders.) Second, when the nobility saw that they would not get their way, they accepted a proposal that the king be the arbiter of contested cases. This, too, was unacceptable to the third estate.

The first issue was to a large extent a red herring. Behind it was the much more important question whether the assembly should vote by order or by head. The nobility thought that a joint verification procedure would create a prejudice in favor of the vote by head (P, p. 8). Although the third estate strenuously denied this implication (P, pp. 9, 95), and even claimed (not implausibly) that voting by order would make common verification even more necessary (P, p. 117), there is little doubt that they used this issue to drive in a wedge for the more crucial demand for voting by head. In fact, the ultimate resolution of the crisis came when the third estate unilaterally transformed itself into the National Assembly, and invited delegates from the other orders to join them.

Before that happened, however, the committee had examined the compromise proposal to refer contested cases to the king. The king's commissaries argued (P, p. 160) that having called the assembly into being, the king also had the right to verify the credentials of the delegates in cases of disagreement between the orders. (They actually presented this as a concession, as in the preceding Estates General in 1614 the king had even had the right to decide in cases of disagreement *within* each order.) The spokesmen for the third estate clearly recognized the nature of the dilemma (P, pp. 75, 86–87). On the one hand, it was unacceptable that the credentials of the assembly should be judged by an external power. In the limit, this practice might amount to the king selecting the delegates. On the other hand, self-verification created a vicious circle: how could the assembly verify the credentials without being constituted, and how could it be constituted without a prior verification of the credentials? Their answer to the dilemma was purely pragmatic: "it is impossible to believe that the majority of those who present

54. In this joint session each delegate would have one vote. A compromise suggested by the clergy (P, p. 39) – to have the credentials verified in a vote by order, so that any two estates could block the credentials of a delegate from the third one – was not seriously discussed.

themselves as delegates should not have valid credentials."[55] In the
end, the third estate cut the Gordian knot by simply declaring itself
constituted.

RULES OF DELIBERATION

Another aspect of the constitution of the constituent assembly concerns its internal procedural rules. Both assemblies had to come to
grips with the fact of a preexisting partition of the nation into groups
of unequal size (states and estates, respectively). In both, the question arose whether the assembly should proceed on the principle "one
man, one vote" or "one group, one vote." In both, the convening authorities tried to impose the latter principle. They succeeded in the
American assembly, but not in the French.

In Paris, Necker failed in his attempt to impose the idea that the
traditional method of deliberation and voting by order could not be
changed except by the agreement of each of the three orders and the
approval of the king. Instead the third estate unilaterally imposed
common deliberation and voting by head. This outcome, to be sure,
was clearly what Necker intended to bring about. The doubling of the
votes of the third estate would make little difference if voting were
to be by order. He had hoped, however, that it would be reached by
compromise and negotiation. To that end, he fought, unsuccessfully,
against electoral assemblies that instructed their delegates to vote for
or against voting by head.[56]

Voting in the Federal Convention was by majority vote, each state
having one vote. Although the Pennsylvanians wanted to refuse the
smaller states an equal vote, their proposal was never put on the
table (I, p. 10 n.). When a committee was formed to forge a compromise on the upper house, James Wilson "objected to the committee
because it would decide according to that very rule of voting which
was opposed on one side" (I, p. 515), but to no avail. Yet equality of
votes at the convention could not in itself ensure that the outcome
would be equal representation in the Senate, as decisions were taken

---

55. Even admitting this premise, the dilemma persists. Assume that the assembly has
100 delegates, that three of the credentials are contested, and that the uncontested
delegates are divided 49–48 over the validity of the contested credentials. If in the
vote over one contested case, the other contested cases vote with the minority, the
contested credentials will be approved.
56. Egret (1975), Ch. V, notably pp. 248, 266; also Castaldo (1989), pp. 143–44.

by majority vote among the states and the small states formed a minority. The large states failed in their attempt to impose proportional representation, but not because the rules of voting in the convention made equal representation a foregone conclusion.

The American process had three stages. In the first, we have the convocation of the assembly by Congress. In the second, we have the adoption of a voting procedure to be used at the convention. In the third, we have the adoption of a voting procedure for the future Senate. *In all three stages, the principle "one state, one vote" was followed.* It is tempting to read a causal connection into this fact. The convention adopted the principle for its own proceedings because it was used by the institution that had called it into being. And it proposed the principle for the future because the smaller states at the convention benefited from the disproportionate strength that they derived from its use at that stage. Although the principle cannot by itself explain the final decision of having equal representation in the Senate, it may have been a contributing, perhaps even pivotal factor.[57]

There are two mechanisms that could be at work here. On the one hand, there is the sheer force of precedence and consistency. As William Paterson asked at the convention, "If a proportional representation be right, why do we not vote so here?" (I, p. 250). On the other hand, the equality of votes at the convention increased the voting power of the small states. Since the small states were in a minority, this could not by itself ensure their victory. But the voting procedure at the convention increased their bargaining power for logrolling purposes. Whatever the mechanism, we observe a deep continuity in the American proceedings. The Articles of Confederation shaped the convention. Through the convention, they also shaped the constitution that was finally adopted. The French assembly made a much cleaner break with the past. Once the third estate had obtained the vote by head, there was nothing to stop them.

DOWNSTREAM AUTHORITIES

Consider finally the ratification of the constitution. This act is intended to confer downstream legitimacy on the constitution, to be distinguished from the upstream legitimacy derived from the authorities

---

57. For a discussion of other mechanisms that may have shaped the decision, see Elster (1995f).

who call the assembly into being. Whereas ordinary laws need no legitimacy beyond that of having been adopted by a lawfully elected assembly, the constitution may seem to require a second scrutiny. Because the constitution regulates the most basic aspects of political life and is deliberately constructed so as to be difficult to change, one can argue that there should be an opportunity to scrutinize and if necessary overrule the decision of the constituent assembly. Moreover, the knowledge of that possibility will keep the framers within bounds. Not wanting to be overruled, they will anticipate and feel constrained by the possible censure.

It would seem axiomatic that the authorities who call the constituent assembly into being would also want the right to veto the final document. However, the framers themselves might not accept the authority of their creator, especially if they have already gone beyond their mandate. Instead, they might define themselves as the final and sovereign authority, doing away with any need for ratification. Alternatively, they might appeal directly to the people or to special conventions. These are the outcomes that were observed in, respectively, the French and the American cases.

In France, the right of the king to veto the constitution was a thorny issue, especially in the wake of the decree of August 4, 1789, that abolished all feudal dues. As the king hesitated to give his sanction to the decree, the question arose whether his assent was needed at all. Both the king and the assembly tended to see the other as its creature, invested with powers only through its actions. Mounier argued that since the king had created the assembly, he must also have the right to veto its decision (8, p. 587). In reply, Target argued that a royal veto over the constitution would be absurd, as if "the constituent power had to ask the permission of the constituted power" (8, p. 603). When the issue came up again in the last days of the assembly (30, pp. 127 ff.), the king was left formally free to refuse the constitution. Although some of his advisers urged him to strike a bargain, he opted for unconditional acceptance.[58] It is fair to say that by that time – after the flight to Varennes that undermined his authority – he had no other choice. Reading the debates, there is nothing indicating that they took place under the shadow of future ratification.

That shadow, by contrast, was very much present at the Federal Convention. Although no ratification procedure was laid down in the convocation of the convention, many assumed that the constitution

58. Hampson (1988), p. 182. Actually, a bargain had been struck earlier.

would eventually have to be ratified by the state legislatures. Reasoning from that premise, they argued that the constitution ought to be tailored to be acceptable to those bodies. Charles Pinckney asserted, for instance, that "the Legislatures would be less likely to promote the adoption of the new Government, if they were to be excluded from all share in it" (I, p. 132). Ellsworth argued in similar terms that "if we are jealous of the State [Governments], they will be so of us" (I, p. 374). The constitution would not receive their approval "if on going home I tell them we gave the [General Government] such powers because we could not trust you." Others turned the argument on its head: if the state legislatures had an institutional interest in the outcome, they ought not to be judge in their own cause. Rufus King, for instance, argued for ratification by special conventions on the grounds that "the Legislatures also being to lose power, will be most likely to raise objections" (I, p. 123). In the end, the latter view was adopted. The convention decided that the constitution had to be approved by conventions in nine of the thirteen states. This procedure involved a double break with the Articles of Confederation, which demanded unanimous ratification by the state legislatures for all alterations.

Constituent assemblies thus embody what I have called elsewhere "the paradox of democracy": each generation wants to be free to bind its successors, while not being bound by its predecessors.[59] On the one hand, the assembly wants to free itself from the mandates and constraints that the upstream authorities try to impose on it. On the other hand, it wants to lay down the law for future generations and to make it difficult for them to untie themselves (and to make it difficult for them to bind *their* successors). In one interpretation, constitution-makers regard themselves as superior both to the corrupt or inefficient regime they are replacing and to the interest- and passion-ridden regimes that will replace them. As we shall see, however, more benign interpretations are also possible.

II.5. TWO LEVELS OF CONSTITUTIONAL PRECOMMITMENT

In II.3 I argued that the imposition of delays and supermajorities is at the core of constitutional precommitment. Delays and supermajorities are also, however, used in the ordinary political process. A

59. Elster (1984), p. 93; see also Holmes (1988).

standard argument for bicameralism, as we shall see, is that by slow-
ing down the legislative process it enables passion to cool down and
reason (or interest) to regain the upper hand. Similarly, the need to
have a legislative supermajority to override an executive veto may
reflect concerns that are similar to those underlying the demand
for supermajorities in the amendment procedure. Yet these checks
on the legislature would not have much of a restraining function if
they were not protected in the constitution. They are restrictions that
work only because they are themselves embedded in restrictions. If
the constitutional clause requiring a two-thirds majority in Congress
to override executive veto could be abolished by simple majority
in Congress, there would not be much point to it. Nor would delaying devices be useful if they could be abolished instantly at any
time.[60]

In II.9, I argue that the separation of powers may serve as a precommitment device. By entrusting monetary policy to a central bank and
forbidding the government to instruct it, for instance, the constitution
solves a problem of time-inconsistency that would otherwise arise.
Yet this scheme might have little efficacy if the constitution could be
changed by a simple majority. A government that felt itself intolera-
bly hampered by the bank could then use its parliamentary majority
to abolish its independence. It might refrain from doing so, however,
if the political costs were prohibitive, that is, if the independence of
the bank were upheld by a constitutional convention.

Two Polish Cases

The Polish constitution that was in force between 1989 and 1992 illustrates how supermajority requirement not backed by the constitution
may be vacuous. As a leftover from the earlier Communist constitution, that document allowed parliament to override decisions by the
constitutional court striking down legislation by parliament. This feature embodied the typical Communist fiction of total parliamentary
supremacy. Although the constitution said nothing about the parliamentary majority that was needed, the law on the constitutional
court specifies that a two-thirds majority is required. As that law
could be changed by simple majority, however, the supermajority was

---

60. I am abstracting from the possible restraining effects of meta-constitutional
   conventions.

essentially fictitious. No parliament can bind future parliaments effectively through ordinary legislation.[61]

An even more striking example of such fictitious self-binding was observed in the making of the "Little Constitution" of 1992.[62] In the constitution created by the Round Table Talks in 1989, the Sejm (lower house) needed a two-thirds majority to overrule a veto by the Senate. In its own bylaws, the Sejm also adopted the principle that a simple majority was needed to accept Senate amendments for ordinary legislation and a two-thirds majority for amendments of constitutional laws. This implied that an amended bill that received less than 50% (67% for constitutional laws) but more than 33% of the votes in the Sejm was killed – neither the amended nor the unamended version was passed. To overcome this problem, two solutions were attempted. In July 1992, the Sejm changed its bylaws so that an amended bill was automatically passed unless there was a two-thirds majority against the amendments in the Sejm. This solution eliminated the indeterminacy that was inherent in the earlier system, but at the cost of giving decisive legislative power to the Senate. Half of the Senate, together with one-third of the Sejm, could now decide the fate of any law, including changes in the constitution. The second solution was that adopted in the Little Constitution, in which amendments by the Senate are accepted unless they are rejected by a majority of the deputies in the Sejm. To get the Little Constitution, including this provision, passed, the Sejm first amended its bylaws again. The deputies then reintroduced the original procedure for ordinary statutes, but decided that in the case of constitutional amendments there would be a vote only on whether to adopt the Senate's amendment. If the amendment failed to get two-thirds of the votes, it was rejected, whereas before there had to be two-thirds against it for rejection. Next, the Sejm went ahead and voted down the Senate amendments to the Little Constitution.

Two Levels of Precommitment

Constitutional precommitment, therefore, works at two levels. At a first level, the constitution may design the ordinary *machinery of government* so as to counteract passion, overcome time-inconsistency,

---

61. This is a main theme in Eule (1987).
62. For a fuller exposition, see Elster (1993a).

and promote efficiency. At a higher level, the *machinery of amending* the constitution itself may be designed to be slow and cumbersome. These higher-level constraints have two effects. On the one hand, they act directly on the problems of passion, time-inconsistency, and efficiency. On the other hand, they underwrite and stabilize first-level mechanisms that, in turn, act on the same problems.

A special case arises when the constitution determines whether the political agents shall be allowed or required to precommit themselves. Jean-Jacques Laffont and Jean Tirole discuss this problem in the context of bargaining between a government and a firm over the proceeds from exploiting a natural monopoly such as an oil well.[63] The choice for the benevolent framers is between a constitution that requires the government to make binding long-term (two-period) contracts with the firm and one that forbids long-term contracting. (They do not consider the option of leaving this choice up to the first-period government.) In their model, precommitment is optimal if the probability that governments will be honest is either very low or very high; in the intermediate range, prohibition of precommitment may be desirable.[64] Once again, to be effective the precommitment to or against precommitment needs to be protected from interference by the current majority.

II.6. SELF-BINDING IN ATHENIAN POLITICS

The Athenian political system in the fifth and fourth centuries B.C. was not a constitutional regime, if by that we mean a regime satisfying the substantive, procedural, or legal criteria enumerated in II.3. There was no subset of the laws, that is, that were hierarchically superior to others or more difficult to change.[65] In fact, until about

---

63. Laffont and Tirole (1994), Ch. 16.
64. In their model, the constituent assembly and the government discount the future at the same rate. I do not know how well the results would survive if one assumed that the founders have a lower discounting rate.
65. "In contradistinction to the original Solonian laws, the revised corpus of laws [after 403] came to include quite a number of constitutional laws (that is, norms defining the structure and powers of the organs of government). They did not form a separate and especially protected part of the law-code; the Athenians had no constitution in the formal sense, and, though they sometimes used entrenchment clauses to make it more difficult to reverse a law or a decree, such clauses were not attached to what we call constitutional laws" (Hansen 1991, p. 165). As an

400 B.C. there was no requirement that cases be judged by written, as distinct from unwritten, laws. Yet throughout the period we find procedures in place whose effect – and possibly purpose – was to set up countermajoritarian obstacles to the passions of the majority. Because of the lack of documentary evidence I shall bracket the issue of whether they were intentional precommitment devices or merely incidental constraints on policy-making.

The procedures in question were themselves relatively immune to passion, as they would have to be in order to offer effective protection against impulsive behavior. Throughout the period, a meta-constitutional convention seems to have prevented the assembly from changing the rules in mid-game. In the heat of the moment the Athenians might violate the rules, as we shall see, but not change them. In the fourth century, there was also a formal guarantee against hasty changes. By then, the assembly could pass only decrees. Laws were passed by a smaller body of citizens who had to be at least thirty years old, and by a more elaborate procedure.

THE DANGERS OF POPULAR PASSION

The sources indicate that the Athenians were concerned mainly with ways of counteracting majoritarian *passions*. Because of the nature of direct democracy, there was less need to contain factional *interest*. The Athenians may have had loose political groupings, but no parties that could mobilize voters on the basis of interest.[66] Concerning the importance of majoritarian passions, one should be somewhat wary of the sources, which often have an aristocratic bias (as in the case of Thucydides) or date from several centuries after the events they describe (as in the case of Plutarch). Jennifer Tolbert Roberts argues, for instance, that the widely held view of Athenian democracy as the rule of a mob swayed by emotions is seriously mistaken.[67] In her account, the prosecutions brought against Athenian officials were grounded

instance of entrenchment, Hansen cites a statute (given in Demosthenes 23.62) to the effect that "whosoever, whether magistrate or private citizen, shall cause this ordinance to be frustrated, or shall alter the same, shall be disfranchised with his children and his property." I am not sure how this squares with his statement that "all political decisions in Athens were taken by simple majority" (Hansen 1991, p. 304).
66. Hansen (1991), p. 287.   67. Roberts (1982).

mostly in justified charges of criminal or incompetent behavior, or arose out of substantive policy differences. I have no competence to assess her claim at the general level. Instead, I shall simply cite two well-known cases of mass emotion, and then go on to suggest that parts of the elaborate political system of the Athenians may have served to protect them against this tendency.[68]

The first case (probably circa 440) concerned the *Hellenotamiai*, a board of ten officials who administered the revenues from the Delian League. All we know about this episode is a passage from a speech by Antiphon (5.69–70): "[The] *Hellenotamiai* were once accused of embezzlement, as wrongfully as I am today. Anger swept reason aside, and they were all put to death save one. Later, the true facts became known. This one, whose name is said to have been Sosias, though under sentence of death, had not yet been executed. Meanwhile it was shown how the money had disappeared. The Athenian people rescued him from the very hands of the Eleven [the responsible officials who carried out the sentences]; while the rest had died entirely innocent." There is no need to stress the implicit condemnation of this impulsive action.

The second case (from 406) arose after an Athenian victory in a naval battle at the Arginusae islands. According to Xenophon (*Hellenica* I.6–7), the victorious generals were prevented by a storm from rescuing sailors from disabled vessels in the fleet. Later, eight of the ten generals were charged collectively with treason and sentenced to death, and the six of them who were in Athens executed. I shall outline the main steps in the procedure that led to this outcome.[69] In doing so, I shall refer to the procedure of *graphe paranomon* – prosecution for having made an unlawful proposal in the assembly – which is more fully explained later.

After a preliminary meeting at the assembly, which debated the responsibility of the generals without making any decision, the matter

---

68. The Athenians drew a line, which may be hard to understand for us, between justified and unjustified mass emotions. Herodotus (IX.5) tells a story about Lycidas, a member of the Council of the Five Hundred, who advised the council to accede to a request by the Persians. When the Athenians heard about this, they "were full of wrath, and forthwith surrounded Lycidas, and stoned him to death." Moreover, the Athenian women stoned to death his wife and his children. "The orator found himself punished simply for making a proposal that was not adopted; rather than inducing the horror or remorse of later generations, the case served as an example invoked to obtain the punishment of those who are willing to compromise with the enemy" (Ruzé 1997, p. 439).
69. For a full account see Ostwald (1986), pp. 431–45.

was sent (back) to the Council of the Five Hundred, which prepared cases for the assembly. A member of the council, Callixeinus, persuaded the council to adopt and put before the assembly a proposal to judge the generals immediately, stating that as the assembly had already debated the case no further hearings were required. Euryptolemos and others then stated their intention to bring a *graphe paranomon* against Callixeinus for having made this proposal, presumably on the grounds that the proposal treated "as a judicial procedure what had been merely a deliberative meeting of the Assembly."[70] In the words of Douglas MacDowell, the

consequence of this would be that the proposal could not take effect unless Callixeinus was first tried and acquitted on that charge. Uproar followed. There were shouts that it would be intolerable if the people were not allowed to do what they wished. One speaker suggested that Euryptolemos and his supporters should be tried by the same vote as the [generals], and they felt compelled to withdraw their threat of a *graphe paranomon*.[71]

As Xenophon (*Hellenica* I.7.14–16) continues the story,

When some of the Prytanes [an executive committee of the Council of the Five Hundred that rotated among the ten Athenian tribes] refused to put the question to vote in violation of the law, Callixeinus again mounted the platform and urged the same charge against them; and the crowd cried out to summon to court those who refused. Then the Prytanes, stricken with fear, agreed to put the question – all of them, except Socrates.

Euryptolemos then made another speech, in which he urged that the generals be given time to prepare their defense and be judged individually rather than collectively. Xenophon concludes his account as follows:

When Euryptolemos had thus spoken, he offered a resolution that the men be tried . . . separately; whereas the proposal of the Council was to judge them all by a single vote. The vote being now taken as between these two vote proposals, they decided at first in favour of the resolution of Euryptolemos; but when Menecles interposed an objection under oath [*hypomosia*: see below] and a second vote was taken, they decided in favour of the Council. After this they condemned the generals who took part in the battle, eight in all; and the six who were in Athens were put to death. And not long afterwards the Athenians repented, and they voted that complaints [*probolai*: see below]

70. Ostwald (1986), p. 439.   71. MacDowell (1978), p. 188.

be brought against any who had deceived the people . . . and that Callixeinus be included among them. (*Hellenica* I.7.34–35)

To counteract such outbursts of mass emotions, the Athenians relied on four kinds of devices: the (as far as we know) rarely used device of *anapsephisis* (reconsidering an earlier decision), separation of powers, two-stage procedures, and elaborate mechanisms by which those who whipped up the emotions of the people could be held accountable.

ANAPSEPHISIS

The best-known example of this procedure is from Thucydides's account (3.36 ff.) of the Mytilenian debate.[72] In 428 B.C. the city of Mytilene in Lesbos, a member of the Delian League, rebelled against Athens. The revolt having been crushed, the Athenians "in the fury of the moment determined to put to death . . . the whole adult male population of Mytilene." Thucydides continues:

They accordingly sent a trireme to communicate the decree to Paches [the Athenian general in charge at Mytilene], commanding him to lose no time in despatching the Mytilenians. The morrow brought repentance with it and reflection on the horrid cruelty of a decree which condemned a whole city to the fate merited only by the guilty. This was no sooner perceived by the Mytilenian ambassadors at Athens and their Athenian supports than they moved the authorities to put the question again to a vote; which they the more easily consented to do, as they themselves plainly saw that most of the citizens wished someone to give them an opportunity for reconsidering the matter.

In the ensuing debate, opposite views were defended by Cleon and Diodotus.[73] Cleon opens his speech by saying, "I have often before now been convinced that a democracy is incapable of empire, and never more so than by your present change of mind in the matter of Mytilene." He then goes on to claim, "The most alarming feature in the case is the constant change of measures with which we appear

72. Another apparently inconsistent passage is in Thucydides 6.14, suggesting that reconsideration of a previously passed decree was illegal. Dover (1955) argues that the passages can in fact be rendered consistent with one another; see also Ruzé (1997), pp. 440–43.
73. For an analysis of this debate, see Kagan (1974), pp. 155–63.

to be threatened, and our ignorance of the fact that bad laws which are never changed are better for a city than good ones which have no authority." Diodotus begins by asserting, "I do not blame the persons who have reopened the case of the Mytilenians, nor do I approve the protests which we have heard against important questions being frequently debated. I think the two things most opposed to good counsel are haste and passion; haste usually goes hand in hand with folly, passion with coarseness and narrowness of mind."

Closer analysis of the two speeches shows that what was at stake was not mainly the procedural issue, but whether massacring the Mytilenians would provide an effective deterrence for the future. Cleon's speech suggests, nevertheless, that procedure and deterrence were linked. From the point of view of deterrence, the best would be to massacre the Mytilenians, the second best to have decided not to do so, and the worst to decide to do so and then reconsider, an action that could be interpreted by other states as a sign of weakness. While *anapsephisis* might protect democracy against itself, it could undermine its efficacy in dealing with external enemies. I return to this general tension in II.11.

SEPARATION OF POWERS

In the fifth century, the assembly could arrogate all powers to itself, if it so desired.[74] As in the case of the Arginusae generals, some political trials were conducted in the assembly. Also, the assembly passed laws as well as decrees. After circa 400, the assembly retained the right only to pass decrees, whereas legislation was entrusted to a special body of legislators (*nomothetai*), drawn at random (for each session) from a panel of 6,000 citizens. After this reform, "the *demos* could no longer regard whatever it pleased as valid and binding."[75] Jurors (*dikastai*) were also drawn randomly (for each trial) from the same panel, which was constituted once a year by drawing lots among all citizens who presented themselves. Each of these bodies had 500 members, or sometimes more. After circa 355, the courts had exclusive

74. The need for decisions to be prepared in the Council of the Five Hundred before they came to the assembly or the *nomothetai* might seem to be an exception to this statement (Hansen 1991, pp. 138, 307). Yet as far as I can judge, the argument by Ruzé (1997, Ch. XXII) that the council had rather limited functions seems convincing.
75. Ostwald (1986), p. 522.

jurisdiction over political trials, thus completing the separation of powers.

The overall effect of these changes was to reduce the danger of rash legislation by the assembly. The *dikastai* and *nomothetai* had to be thirty years old, whereas all male citizens above the age of twenty could sit in the assembly. As Mogens Herman Hansen writes, "the reason for the higher age-limit for jurors and magistrates is nowhere expressly stated, but is not hard to guess. Everywhere in Greek literature we come across the idea that wisdom and experience grow with age."[76] It has also been suggested that jurors and (by implication) legislators belonged to the middle and upper classes of the Athenian population.[77] If that was the case, it would provide an additional argument for believing that the juries "acted as a conservative brake on the constitution."[78] In many other societies, both age and wealth have in fact been seen as guarantees of prudent and conservative policy-making.[79] Hansen argues, however, that jurors and (by implication) legislators belonged to the poorer segments of the population.[80] If they were prudent, it was only by virtue of their age.

DELAYING DEVICES

The use of two-stage procedures as a cooling-down device is very common in modern constitutional settings. The Athenians, too, adopted this technique in many of their institutions. It was not possible to raise an issue in the assembly without prior preparation, to force a decision on the spot. All cases had to be discussed in the Council of the Five Hundred before they came to the assembly. According to Hansen, "some decrees, such as treaties and conclusions of peace, seem to have required a debate in two successive sessions of

---

76. Hansen (1991), pp. 89–90.   77. Jones (1957), pp. 36–37.
78. Ibid., p. 124.
79. In bicameral systems, delegates to the upper house have been subject to higher age qualifications. In the current Czech constitution, for instance, senators must be forty years old, whereas members of the lower house must be above twenty-one. In unicameral systems, deputies can be subject to higher age qualifications than the voters. In the current Estonian constitution, for instance, the age limit for voters is eighteen and for deputies twenty-one. In eighteenth- and nineteenth-century constitutions, property and income qualifications were common, justified either as a proxy for literacy or as desiderata in their own right.
80. Hansen (1991), p. 185.

the Assembly; others had to be ratified at a second Assembly meeting, on which occasion there had to be a quorum."[81] The institution of ostracism was subject to the same principle. Once a year, the people met to decide whether to hold an ostracism, that is, to send a citizen into exile for ten years without losing his property or other citizen rights. If the vote was positive, there was another meeting two months later at which each citizen wrote on a fragment of pottery (ostragon) the name of the person he wished to have expelled. Debates were not allowed at either meeting. On the condition that at least 6,000 votes were cast, the person whose name appeared on the largest number of pottery sherds was ostracized.

These forms of institutionalized delay could have undesirable effects. For one thing, "the process could become so complicated and slow as to make it difficult, for example, to mount an effective foreign policy."[82] For another, the interval between two meetings did not necessarily lead to an improved decision. In the case of ostracism, for instance, "the procedural requirement of two meetings meant that the decision was not hasty. But the interval also gave the opportunity for organising the vote."[83] In the last recorded case, the two main candidates for ostracism, Nicias and Alcibiades, turned the tables on the proposer, Hyperboles, by using the interval to gather a majority for sending *him* into exile, an abuse that may have contributed to the demise of the procedure.

ACCOUNTABILITY PROCEDURES

The Athenians had an elaborate system for holding their officials accountable. Generals could be and often were subjected to impeachment. Speakers in the assembly could be held accountable for their proposals, mainly through *graphe paranomon* but also, as in the case of the Arginusae generals, through *probole*. Each of these were legal procedures, and subject to the basic principle of Athenian law that all prosecutions had to be initiated by a private citizen. There were two main kinds of procedures. A *dike* was a suit in a private matter, such as for damage or assault. Here, the accuser usually gained financially if he won and suffered no financial loss if he didn't. A *graphe* was a suit

---

81. Ibid., p. 307.   82. Ibid., p. 308.
83. Sinclair (1988), p. 170.

in (roughly speaking) public matters, such as for impiety or military desertion. With some exceptions, accusers did not gain financially if they won the case. They might be motivated by the public interest, by a desire for revenge, or by envy, but not by material interest. Many prosecutions over matters of state were in fact parts of private feuds rather than public-spirited interventions.[84] By contrast, an accuser who failed to obtain one-fifth of the vote was fined and lost the right to bring similar accusations in the future.

The *probole*, a preliminary accusation that could be brought before the assembly against political leaders who had deceived the public by false statements, does not concern us here. It was a device to protect the citizens against their leaders rather than a device to protect them against themselves. The *graphe paranomon*, by contrast, had exactly the latter character. By means of this procedure, a speaker could be punished for having made an unconstitutional proposal, *even if the proposal had been passed by the assembly*. The procedure is one of the most striking features of Athenian politics. For a contemporary analogue, we would have to imagine a U.S. representative or a senator incurring a crippling fine for having proposed a law voted by Congress and later found unconstitutional by the Supreme Court. In the fourth century, *graphe paranomon* was a centerpiece of Athenian democracy. Hansen notes that

the significance of the *graphe paranomon* can best be set in relief by comparing it with the situation in the modern state in which the right of the courts to oversee legislation has been the strongest. The Supreme Court of the United States has had the power to test and overthrow Congressional Acts since 1803. In the period 1803–96 that power was used 135 times: our sources show us that at Athens that figure was nearly reached in two decades.[85]

Although often described as "indictment for making an illegal proposal," the institution of *graphe paranomon* had in fact a broader scope. A decree proposed in the assembly could be nullified, and its proposer punished, if it (i) violated an existing law, (ii) was procedurally flawed, or (iii) was deemed damaging to the interest of the people.[86] In some of the most famous cases, the accused was charged with having proposed that the assembly bestow honors and privileges on an unworthy person. Although the charges were usually

84. Todd (1993), Ch. 9; Cohen (1995).   85. Hansen (1991), p. 209.
86. Ibid., p. 206.

phrased in legal terms, the real issues were often political or even personal.

A specific feature of the procedure also suggests that the charges more often than not were substantial rather than formal. A *graphe paranomon* was introduced by a *hypomosia*, an allegation under oath that a particular decree was illegal. This could be done either before the decree had been submitted to a vote, or after it had been voted and adopted. If the *hypomosia* occurred before the vote was taken, it was postponed until the court had rendered its verdict. One might expect that after a decision by the court that the proposal was legal, it would be passed on to the assembly for voting. This may not have been the case, however. Hansen argues that if the court decided that the decree was legal, it automatically counted as having passed,[87] a practice that makes sense only if it was assessed on substantial rather than formal grounds.

It is not clear to what extent the *graphe paranomon* actually served its ostensible function, which was to keep policy-making within the bounds of the law rather than to prosecute or persecute particular individuals. To serve the former function, the charge would have to be brought by a citizen who was genuinely motivated by reason rather than by interest or passion. The threat by Euryptolemos to bring a *graphe paranomon* against Callixeinus seems to have been motivated by a genuine concern for the public interest. An example of a (more or less) disinterested *graphe paranomon* that was successfully carried out was the accusation made against Thrasybulus in 403, after the fall of the Thirty Tyrants. Thrasybulus had proposed that all those who had left Athens for Piraeus during their reign be made Athenian citizens when they came back, including foreigners and slaves. "However well intentioned, the proposal will have alarmed the city people: the influx of an unknown number of slaves and of a thousand foreigners would have tipped the electoral balance in their disfavor, and the successful passage of the motion by the Assembly gave their fear substance. In the interest of allaying these apprehensions and of not jeopardizing the reconciliation, Archinus had the decree annulled through a *graphe paranomon*," not on grounds of its content but on a legal technicality.[88]

---

87. Hansen (1991), p. 210. Hansen (personal communication) informs me that his interpretation on this point is controversial.
88. Ostwald (1986), p. 504.

These are both fifth-century cases. Over the course of the fourth century, the *graphe paranomon* increasingly became "a major weapon in political warfare."[89] "Kephalos, a politician at the beginning of the fourth century, boasted that, though he had proposed many decrees, he had never had a *graphe paranomon* brought against him; but the boast of Aristophon, who died in the 330s, was that he had been acquitted in *graphai paranomon* seventy-five times."[90] The best-known of these political cases is a suit brought by Aeschines against Ktesipon for having proposed a decree that the people of Athens should confer a gold crown on Aeschines' old rival Demosthenes. Among the three reasons adduced by Aeschines to show the illegality of this proposal, two are based on technicalities. The third objection, however, is merely pseudolegal. Ktesipon had proposed that the herald should declare that Demosthenes was rewarded by the crown "because he continually speaks and does what is best for the people" (Aeschines 3.49). Yet, Aeschines says, given that "all the laws forbid inserting falsehoods in the decrees of the people" (Aeschines 3.50), he only has to show that the praise given to Demosthenes is false in order to prove that the proposal was illegal. The greater part of his speech, therefore, is devoted to showing that Demosthenes consistently acted against the interest of the people.

Because the *graphe paranomon* could be used irresponsibly, the citizen who brought it was fined and lost some of his civil rights if he failed to get one-fifth of the votes. If the *graphe paranomon* itself is seen as protecting the people against its tendencies to be swayed by demagogues, this penalty clause was a *protection against abuse of the protection device*. In the last years of the democracy, the same clause was attached to *eisangelia*, prosecutions against officials on grounds of religious or political misconduct. This mechanism of *two-step accountability* – holding to account those who hold officials to account – was a unique feature of Athenian democracy.

In discussing these countermajoritarian devices we have noted that even if not necessarily worse than the disease, the remedies might create problems of their own. *Anapsephisis* and two-stage procedures might detract from efficacy in dealing with urgent matters of foreign policy. *Graphe paranomon* could be exploited for private purposes. For a more general discussion of why political self-binding might be undesirable I refer the reader to II.11. Here I only want to emphasize

89. Sinclair (1988), p. 153.   90. MacDowell (1978), p. 51.

that in spite of these problems, the Athenian system of checks and balances was, on the whole, remarkably successful. The Athenians managed to combine extensive democratic participation with a reasonable degree of efficiency and protection against majoritarian passions. Although the system had some pathological features, it is not clear that they were more serious than the pathologies of modern democracies.

II.7. INTEREST AND PASSION IN PHILADELPHIA AND PARIS

In the two late eighteenth-century assemblies, especially the American one, the framers were concerned with the dangers of majority rule. The fear of the Americans was more acute, because they faced a different problem. In both countries, we see a three-stage sequence. In the first stage, there is a strong monarchy that is perceived as arbitrary and tyrannical. In the second, it is replaced by an untrammeled parliamentary regime. In the third, when it is discovered that parliament can be as tyrannical and arbitrary as the king, checks and balances are introduced.[91] In 1787, the Americans went from the second to the third stage. In 1789, the French went from the first to the second stage. The pathologies of the second stage, and the transition to the third stage, came later. This provides the main reason for the difference in tenor in the two debates. The Americans were concerned with protecting themselves against the solution that the French were just in the process of inventing, or reinventing. Although the moderates in the French assembly cited later shared the anti-democratic sentiments of the American framers, they were in a minority.

Passions and Interests

According to Madison, "In all cases where a majority are united by a common interest or passion, the rights of the minority are in danger"

---

91. According to Vile (1967), p. 43, "the use of the power of Parliament by one group of its supporters to threaten other groups had shown to men who had previously seen only the royal power as a danger, that *a parliament could be as tyrannical as a king.*" The statement that I have italicized, although made about England after 1648, is also valid for the United States after 1776 and France after 1791, as well as for Norway after 1814 (Sejersted 1988, pp. 136–37).

(I. p. 135). If the poor or relatively propertyless form a majority, their interest might induce them to enact laws that are contrary to the rights of property. Appropriate countermeasures might include restrictions on the right to vote or on eligibility, as well as strongly protected constitutional limitations ranging from a ban on paper money to the right to full compensation for confiscated property. Also, Madison thought that large constituencies would reduce the scope for interest-based factions. Quite different measures are appropriate, as we shall see, if the majority is led astray by momentary passion rather than by a standing interest.[92]

Looking at the language in the two assemblies, passionate majorities seem to have been perceived as a more serious problem than interested ones.[93] Yet the interests of the *electorate* represent only one part of the problem. Another frequently discussed problem of majority rule was the risk of the emergence of a legislative elite with an interest of its own. As Mirabeau said, elected representatives are "a kind of de facto aristocracy" (8, p. 538) that if unchecked would arrogate all power to itself. As an example of what might happen, he cites "the exclusion of the public from the National Chamber on the simple request by a member of the Assembly, and prohibiting public papers from reporting on their deliberations." At the Federal Convention, Sherman (I, 365) expressed a fear that representatives might develop an esprit de corps that would make them forget their constituents.

These, then, are the two dangers I shall discuss in the following: passionate popular majorities and self-interested representatives. The counteracting devices that were discussed in the two assemblies

---

92. This statement, too, rests on a simplification, by neglecting the phenomenon of "standing passions" such as religious or ethnic fanaticism. I return to that question in II.11.

93. In Philadelphia, we find references to "the turbulence and follies of democracy" (Randolph: I, p. 51), "the fury of democracy" (Randolph: I, p. 59), "the popular passions [that] spread like wild fire, and become irresistable" (Hamilton: I, p. 289), "fickleness and passion" (Madison: I, p. 421), "the turbulency and violence of unruly passion" (Madison: I, p. 430), and to the "precipitation, changeableness, and excesses of the first branch" (Gouverneur Morris: I, p. 512). In Paris, Lally-Tolendal (8, p. 516) refers to the assembly being "entraînée par l'éloquence, séduite par des sophismes, égarée par des intrigues, enflammée par des passions qu'on lui fait partager, emportée par des mouvements soudains qu'on lui communique, arrêtée par des terreurs qu'on lui inspire." Others talk about "les prestiges de l'éloquence, l'effervescence de l'enthousiasme" (Grégoire: 8, p. 567), "les causes d'erreur, de précipitation ou de séduction oratoire" (Sieyes: 8, p. 597), or about "l'erreur, la précipitation, l'ambition" (Robespierre: 9, p. 81).

	Problem of passionate majorities	Problem of self-interested legislators
Bicameralism is the solution	Upper house will slow down the process, and also through wealth or wisdom resist a passionate majority	A divided assembly less likely to become an aristocracy
Executive veto is the solution	Veto can serve as an additional check on dangerous impulses	The executive will resist any legislative self-aggrandizement

Table II.2

include bicameralism and executive veto. These are the main topic of the following discussion. In addition, both assemblies discussed the inclusion of individual rights in the constitution to counteract the various dangers of majority rule.[94] At the first level of constitutional precommitment (II.5), a bill of rights offers absolute protection against majority abuse of the minority by ruling out certain types of legislation altogether. The protection is not stronger than the bill of rights itself, however. At the higher level, therefore, absolute protection requires absolute entrenchment of the rights, that is, total immunity against amendment. As noted in II.3, many modern constitutions do in fact offer such protection.

Traditionally, each of the two devices I consider has been correlated with one of the two dangers. On the one hand, the existence of a second chamber would by a number of mechanisms counteract the passionate impulses of the majority. The built-in delays of bicameralist systems, in particular, were seen as the main protection against impulsive majorities. On the other hand, the executive veto would block the tendency toward legislative tyranny. Even if the veto can be overridden, the need for a supermajority makes it more difficult for the legislature to get its way. But these stark statements need nuances and qualifications. In fact, both devices have been offered as solutions to both problems, as indicated by Table II.2.

94. For a survey, see Elster (1993c). As I argue in Elster (1995b), the two assemblies did not pay much attention to judicial review as a counteracting device.

Before I proceed to discuss the four cases, let me clarify some points. The two societies in question were not direct democracies. Majorities could act only through their elected representatives. When I refer to passion or interest as motivations of the popular majority, I assume that these are faithfully transmitted to and represented in the legislature, notably in the directly elected lower house. When I refer to the interests or passions of the legislators themselves, I have something else in mind. The interest of the legislature is to carve out the largest possible place for itself in the machinery of government. (See II.11 for some examples from recent constitution-making in Eastern Europe.) Also, legislators may act under the sway of passions that arise in the assembly itself, quite independently of their constituencies. Vanity, for instance, may prevent a speaker from backing down from a policy once he has stated it in public.

To this fourfold classification of motives, there corresponds a fourfold classification of constitution-making tasks. From the point of view of the eighteenth-century framers the constitution had to be constructed with two goals in mind. First, the destructive and irrational forces of passion had to be eliminated as much as possible. In the best of cases, passion would be replaced or checked by reason – an impartial concern for the common good. Yet the framers did not proceed from a best-case scenario, at least not in Philadelphia. Instead, they assumed that future voters and politicians, when not in the grip of passion, would be motivated by self-interest. Their second task, therefore, was to design institutions that would give political agents private incentives to act in ways that would at the same time promote the public good. This line of reasoning applies to voters as well as to their representatives. Although I shall mainly consider passionate majorities and self-interested legislators, institutional design can also try to deal with the problems of interested voters and passionate legislators.[95]

A final preliminary comment concerns the distinction between interest and passion. When the American framers opposed private

---

95. As I indicated earlier, Madison was very much concerned with the first of these latter problems. With respect to the second, Benjamin Constant was very preoccupied with "the problem of *amour-propre*, which he thought a peculiarly French flaw," and argued that "institutional devices" were needed to counter it. He advocated, for instance, the British system, which forbade written speeches in Parliament (Holmes 1984, pp. 139–40). See also the comments at the end of this section on the self-binding of the American framers.

interest to the "permanent and aggregate interest of the community," they could mean two different things.[96] On the one hand, private interest often focuses on short-term as distinct from long-term benefits. On the other hand, it focuses on the benefits to an individual or to a group as distinct from benefits to the community as a whole. When Madison and others referred to the dangers of factional strivings, they mainly had in mind the latter aspect of private interest. Examples include the interests of debtors versus creditors, the monied interest versus the landed or manufacturing interests, and so on. Although the dangers of faction could be compounded by myopia, the two are conceptually distinct. Myopia, by itself, is in some ways closer to passion than to interest, if the latter idea is taken in the sense of calm and deliberate consideration of personal advantage. In *The Federalist* No. 6 Hamilton, for instance, refers to "momentary passions and immediate interests" in the same breath. Although a *short-lived* passion is not the same thing as a *shortsighted* interest, Hamilton nevertheless assimilates the two in No. 15, when he opposes "general considerations of peace and justice to the impulse of any immediate interest or passion." Because the framers blurred the distinction to some extent – and because it is in fact somewhat blurred (I.2) – I shall allow myself to do the same when discussing their statements.

BICAMERALISM IS THE SOLUTION TO THE PROBLEM OF PASSIONATE MAJORITIES

This proposition has several aspects. A standard argument (see also II.5) is that bicameralism makes for a slower and more cumbersome process, giving hot spirits time to cool down.[97] When Thomas Jefferson asked George Washington why the convention had established a Senate, Washington replied by asking, "Why do you pour your coffee into your saucer?" "To cool it," Jefferson replied. "Even so," Washington said. "We pour legislation into the Senatorial saucer to cool it." In France, Mounier observed that the majority might

---

96. In this paragraph I follow closely the discussions in White (1987), notably pp. 121–22 and 254–55.
97. For some doubts about the validity of the argument, see Mueller (1996), pp. 192–93.

even need protection against its own temptation to abdicate from power:

A unicameral Assembly . . . might, in a moment of enthusiasm, decide to increase the power of a victorious king or, in difficult circumstances, establish in his favor a dictatorship that could become perpetual. By contrast, two chambers who deliberate separately will ensure the wisdom of their respective resolutions, and give to the legislative body that slow and majestic pace from which it ought never to deviate. (8, p. 555)

This argument does not rely on any special virtues possessed by the senators as compared to the members of the lower house, but appeals merely to the virtues of slowness.[98] It carries over, therefore, to any other delaying or cooling device, such as the need for constitutional changes to be approved by two successive legislatures or the king's suspensive veto.[99] Moreover, the argument does not require the Senate to have a veto or any other kind of formal power over the decision. In Paris La Rochefoucauld proposed a purely consultative Senate or "council":

One might establish a council to examine the projects of law sent to it for comments from the Chamber of representatives. The council of men chosen for this honorable function would have to be consulted twice or thrice before the Chamber of representatives could make a definitive decision. This repeated consultation, together with that in which all the citizens would be involved through the publicity given to the projects by printing and the freedom of the press, would ensure a delay for the legislature sufficient to calm its ardor. (8, pp. 548–49)

Most bicameral systems, however, have also been justified by some qualitative difference between the senators and the representatives

---

98. "By 1784 a South Carolina pamphleteer was contending that the senators were just . . . another representative body, which like the lower house was bound to obey the instructions of its constituents. In fact the senators' position in the legislature possessed no social significance and would be 'entirely useless' if it were not that 'the division in the legislative power seems necessary to furnish a proper check to our too hasty proceedings'" (Wood 1969, p. 239).

99. One might ask whether the same end could not be achieved by a constitutional provision that required several successive readings, at appropriate intervals, of any piece of legislation. However, any such system would create a great deal of frustration among legislators who are confident that they have made up their minds and only want to pass to action; also they might not want to be seen (by themselves or others) as changing their minds.

by virtue of which the upper house would be more prudent and conservative and thus act as a brake on the more impetuous lower house.
A number of screening mechanisms were envisaged. The lower age
limit for senators could be set higher.[100] Senators could be chosen by
indirect elections (the American solution). They could be made subject to longer periods of office, with staggered renewals (also part of
the American solution). More controversially, they may be subject to
stringent eligibility requirements with regard to property or income.
From one perspective, the latter criteria could be used as second-best
approximations for wisdom.[101] From another perspective, of course,
the property criterion served simply to protect property.

BICAMERALISM IS THE SOLUTION TO THE PROBLEM OF SELF-INTERESTED LEGISLATORS

The mechanism behind this argument is a form of "divide and con-
quer": a homogeneous assembly is more likely to form a united front
against the executive than an internally divided one. At the convention, "Mr. Dickinson was not apprehensive that the Legislature com-
posed of different branches constructed on such different principles,
would improperly unite for the purpose of displacing a judge" (II,
p. 429). Mason claimed that a single legislature, as proposed in the
New Jersey plan, contained the seeds of "Legislative despotism" (I,
p. 254). In the Assemblée Constituante, Lally-Tolendal stated the matter quite generally as follows:

A single power will necessarily end by devouring everything. Two powers
will fight until one of them has crushed the other. But three will maintain
themselves in a perfect equilibrium, if they are combined in such a way
that when two are fighting each other, the third, being equally interested
in maintaining the one and the other, will join the oppressed against the
oppressor, and thus restore peace among all. (8, p. 515)

In both assemblies there was apprehension that an upper house
might turn into an aristocracy. In Philadelphia, Gerry said that as

---

100. Clermont-Tonnerre: 8, p. 574; Malouet: 8, p. 591.
101. " 'Integrity,' said Jefferson, was not in his experience, 'the characteristic of wealth.'
     But both Madison and Jefferson were baffled by the apparent inability of the
     people to perceive the truly talented and were thus compelled reluctantly to
     endorse property as the best possible source of distinction in the new republics"
     (Wood 1969, p. 218).

"[the new system] now stands it is as compleat an aristocracy as ever was framed. If great powers should be given to the Senate we shall be governed in reality by a Junto as has been apprehended" (II, p. 286). Wilson similarly said that "he was obliged to consider the whole as having a dangerous tendency to aristocracy; as throwing a dangerous power into the hands of the Senate" (II, p. 522). This argument had an even stronger appeal in Paris, where the very idea of an upper house powerfully reminded people of the old system of orders. However, the argument can be turned on its head. It is precisely in order to prevent the formation of the *legislature as aristocracy* that one must accept an *aristocracy within the legislature*.[102] Although longer terms of office for the Senate may turn their members into an aristocracy, that longer tenure is also needed if it is to be a proper check against the lower branch (Madison: I, pp. 218–19).

The role of bicameralism in checking legislative tyranny was not uncontroversial. Gouverneur Morris argued, "The check provided in the 2d. branch was not meant as a check on Legislative usurpation of power, but on the abuse of lawful powers, on the propensity of the 1st. branch to legislate too much to run into projects of paper money & similar expedients. It is no check on Legislative Tyranny. On the contrary it may favor it, and if the 1st. branch can be seduced may find the means of success" (II, p. 52). The idea that internal division in the legislature might not reduce – might in fact increase – the tendency to legislative tyranny is not one I have encountered elsewhere in the debates. Nor is it particularly plausible. The idea that internal legislative division might not be a *sufficient* deterrent to legislative tyranny is more attractive. Executive veto, as further discussed in the next subsection, may also be required.

Executive Veto Is the Solution to the Problem of Passionate Majorities

An absolute veto for the executive was not seriously discussed in the American assembly. In the French assembly, it was strongly

102. "When in the arguments of the Republicans the upper house became merely a device to check an otherwise unrestrained legislative power, it lost at the same time its embodiment of any kind of aristocracy in the society. Indeed, as Arthur St. Clair, a leading Republican insisted in 1784, 'It is because I abhor every species of aristocracy, that I object to a single branch in the legislature'"(Wood 1969, p. 250).

advocated by some of the "monarchiens," but in the end overwhelmingly defeated. Now, there are two main ways of retaining a form of executive veto even if an absolute veto is rejected. On the one hand, one can allow the assembly to overrule the veto, but require a qualified majority. This was the solution adopted in Philadelphia. On the other hand, one can allow the assembly to overrule the executive by an ordinary majority, but require that the decision be delayed until a later legislature. This was the solution adopted in Paris, allowing the king to veto a proposal in two successive legislatures before the third one could overrule him. In both cases, the solution was defended, among other reasons, for its beneficial impact on passionate majorities.

This argument was made several times in the American debates. According to Madison, "a negative in the Ex: is not only necessary for its own safety, but for the safety of a minority in Danger of oppression from an unjust and interested Majority" (I, p. 108).[103] Gouverneur Morris was more specific. On July 19 he argued that the upper house is needed as a check "on the propensity in the 1st branch to legislate too much to run into projects of paper money and similar expedients" (II, p. 52). Two days later he cited the same phenomena – "emissions of paper money, largesses to the people – a remission of debts and similar measures" (II, p. 76) – as reasons for a strong executive check.[104] Mason similarly argued, "Notwithstanding the precautions taken in the Constitution of the Legislature, it would so much resemble that of the individual States, that it must be expected frequently to pass unjust and pernicious laws" (II, p. 78). In other words, the tripartite system provided a *double check on majority rule*.[105]

In the Assemblée Constituante, the argument took different forms. For many deputies, executive veto was simply seen as a delaying and cooling device – a brake on passionate majorities. For the radical members of the assembly, it was rather a device that allowed the nation to act as a check on its representatives. As La Salle put it, "The suspensive veto is a kind of appeal to the nation, which allows it to intervene as judge between the King and his representatives" (8, p. 529).

---

103. Here and later I blur the distinction between interest and passion.
104. He refers to such measures as "Legislative usurpations," thus contradicting the statement cited earlier (II, p. 52) to the effect that they did not represent usurpation of power but rather abuses of lawful power.
105. In contrast to this conjunctive argument, we may cite the disjunctive reasoning of Duport in the French assembly: "If the brake on the Legislative Body is not a monarch, a single individual, it must be a body of individuals such as a senate or an executive council" (28, p. 264).

The argument came in two versions. Some delegates wanted to leave the decision to the legislature following the final veto (Lameth: 8, p. 572; Grégoire: 8, p. 567). Others wanted primary assemblies to vote directly on the motion that had been opposed by the royal veto (La Salle: 8, p. 534; Pétion: 8, p. 581).

Executive Veto Is the Solution to the Problem of Self-Interested Legislators

The role of the executive veto as a check on the tendency toward legislative tyranny was a permanent theme in the two assemblies. In Paris, Lally-Tolendal, citing England as a precedent, claimed that in 1688 the two chambers of Parliament abdicated some of their powers to the executive in order to prevent legislative tyranny:

> It was in order to defend liberty that the two chambers made the king give his sanction to the *habeas corpus*, and it was also to defend liberty that they united all executive powers in the hand of the king. By removing all means of tyranny from the king, they did not want to reserve any for themselves. In the recent past, the people had recently been oppressed by parliament, just as parliament had been oppressed by the army. The chambers wanted to defend the people against themselves; they would prevent all oppression and limit the freedom of [*enchaîner*] all oppressors. Among the privileges they had usurped and now took away from themselves was the absolute power to legislate all on their own. It was forbidden by law, under penalty of praemunire, to uphold that one or the other of the chambers, or the two of them together, had legislative power without the participation of the king. (8, pp. 517–18)

Many other speakers in the Assemblée Constituante argued for the need for a royal veto to check the tendency toward legislative domination. In doing so, they indulged in considerable amounts of cant, stipulating either a perfect harmony of interest between the king and the people that would enable him to check the aristocratic tendencies of the legislature (Mirabeau: 8, p. 539) or a perfect coincidence between the will of the king and the general happiness (Malouet: 8, pp. 535–36). In the fall of 1789, nobody said outright that even a weak or depraved king would be a useful check on legislative tyranny. After the king's flight to Varennes, it became more difficult to uphold the illusion of his benevolence and wisdom. In the debates on the king's immunity, Duport and Barnave argued that the king could not serve his constitutional function as check on the legislature unless his person was inviolable (28, pp. 263 ff., pp. 326 ff.) "If the monarch depended on the legislative body, it would follow that the latter could destroy its own brake" (Duport: 28, p. 265). I return to this theme shortly.

The Americans also referred to the British experience: "Where the Executive really was the palladium of liberty, *King* and *Tyrant*, were naturally associated in the minds of people; not *legislature* and *tyranny*. But where the Executive was not formidable, the two last were most properly associated. After the destruction of the King in Britain, a more pure and unmixed tyranny sprang up in parliament than had been exercised by the monarch" (Wilson: II, p. 301). Other historical precedents were cited by Gouverneur Morris. Having first reiterated his motion for an absolute veto, which had been defeated a week previously, he went on to say

The most virtuous citizens will often as members of a legislative body concur in measures which afterwards in their private capacity they will be ashamed of. Encroachments of the popular branch of the Government ought to be guarded agst. The Ephori at Sparta became in the end absolute....If the Executive be overturned by the popular branch, as happened in England, the tyranny of one man will ensue – In Rome where the Aristocracy overturned the throne, the consequence was different. He enlarged on the tendency of the legislative Authority to usurp on the Executive and wished the section to be postponed, in order to consider some more effectual check than requiring 2/3 only to overrule the negative of the Executive. (II, pp. 299–300)

To establish the checks enumerated in Table II.2, one must solve two closely related problems that are inherent in any system of checks and balances. First, there is the question of who shall guard the guardians. The checks must themselves be kept in check; otherwise there would not be a system of checks *and balances*. In Paris, defenders of an absolute veto for the king argued that the assembly could always overrule him by refusing to pay taxes (d'Antraigues: 8, p. 544; Mirabeau: 8, p. 539; Mounier: 8, p. 561). In Philadelphia, checks on the executive included overruling his veto by a two-thirds majority, impeachment, and the incentives provided by reeligibility.

Second, there is the question of who shall appoint the guardians and, if necessary, remove them from office. The checks must be genuinely independent of the institutions they are supposed to counteract. I have already cited Duport's observation in the Assemblée Constituante, that the king cannot serve as a brake on the legislature if the assembly can remove him at will. At the Federal Convention, the question arose with regard both to the executive and to the upper house. Regarding the latter, Sherman argued against Randolph's proposal that "the first branch of the fœderal Legislature should have the appointment of the Senators" on the plausible grounds that "if the Senate was to be appointed by the first Branch and out of that Body . . . it would make them too dependent, and thereby destroy the end for which the Senate ought to be appointed" (I, p. 60). Regarding the former, Gouverneur Morris asserted that if the executive is chosen by Congress, "he will be the mere creature of the Legisl: if appointed & impeachable by that body" (I, p. 29). Also arguing against selection of the executive by the legislature, Madison asserted, "The candidate would intrigue with the legislature, would derive his appointment from the predominant faction, and be apt to render his administration subservient to its views" (II, p. 109).

SELF-BINDING IN THE ASSEMBLY

I conclude by noting that the American and French framers also pre-committed *themselves* against the temptations of passion and interest. At the Federal Convention, the framers decided to keep their proceedings closed and secret. The reason, as Madison said later, was that "had the members committed themselves publicly at first, they would have afterwards supposed consistency required them to maintain their ground, whereas by secret discussion no man felt himself obliged to retain his opinions any longer than he was satisfied of their propriety and truth, and was open to the force of argument" (III, p. 379). The framers, in other words, chose secrecy to precommit themselves against their own vanity. By contrast, compared to the French framers the American did not emphasize the vanity motive in the future political agents whose behavior would be regulated by the constitution they were writing.

Unlike the Federal Convention, the Assemblée Constituante functioned also as an ordinary legislature. That arrangement, however, may be undesirable. A main task of a constitutional assembly is to strike the proper balance of power between the legislative and the executive branches of government. To assign that task to an assembly that also serves as a legislative body would be to ask it to act as judge in its own cause. A constitution written by a legislative assembly might be expected to give excessive powers to the legislature (II.11). In the abstract, this problem could be solved by means similar to the ones used in legislative bodies, by checks and balances. A royal veto over the constitution might, for instance, have kept the legislative tendency to self-aggrandizement in check.[106] The Assemblée Constituante adopted another solution, by voting its members ineligible to the first ordinary legislature. It was Robespierre, in his first great speech, who won the assembly for a "self-denying ordinance" – the precommitment of the framers against their self-interest (26, p. 124).

II.8. TIME-INCONSISTENCY, DISCOUNTING, AND DELAYS

In II.3 we saw that many constitutions impose a *delay* between the first proposal of an amendment and its final adoption. In I.3 I argued that delays can serve to overcome the problems associated with hyperbolic discounting. We cannot infer, of course, that delay clauses exist to prevent time reversals caused by hyperbolic discounting. Even after it was identified and characterized by Strotz in 1955, the latter mechanism has never, to my knowledge, been cited as a reason for constitutional precommitment. Delays have been introduced to contain passion, but not to counteract hyperbolic discounting. But although the idea cannot serve as an example of intentional precommitment, it suggests that some delay procedures can serve as incidental constraints that prevent time-inconsistent behavior.

PRECOMMITMENT TO RIGHTS

Consider first constitutional provisions of the inappropriately called "positive rights," such as the right to free health care or free education. It is sometimes assumed that these are forms of social consumption, which must take place at the expense of social investment and efficiency. Developing countries, including countries that are undertaking the transition to a market system, cannot "afford" them. This cannot be the whole truth, because education and health care

---

106. This would hardly be a perfect solution, however. In general, there is no reason to expect the relative strength of the bargaining powers of the executive and the legislature in the constituent body to correspond to the normatively desirable division one might want to write into the constitution.

are also investments in a productive work force.[107] If they are not provided, the reason may be that the government is subject to hyperbolic discounting. The government may fully recognize the value of investments in education and health care, but decide to postpone them until a later date. Yet when that date arrives, priority will again be accorded to a project with immediate benefits. To get around this problem, it might be useful to constitutionalize the rights to education and health care, perhaps even to entrench them as unamendable rights. "People in power almost always want discretion, at least in the short run, and entitlement programs tie their hands. The Bill of Rights is also about tying the government's hands."[108]

PRECOMMITMENT TO A BALANCED BUDGET

In the United States today there is a demand not only for a balanced budget, but for a balanced-budget amendment to the Constitution. (I assume for the sake of argument that a balanced-budget amendment would actually bind Congress.)[109] A main argument for the amendment is that without constitutionalization of this goal, Congress will not be able to resist the many interest groups that lobby for expenditures on this or that activity. Representatives need to be able to tell their constituents that their hands are tied.[110] Yet it is at least conceivable that Congress – or rather individual representatives – also suffers

---

107. If education and health care were seen exclusively in this perspective, these goods would not be provided as they are in Western societies today. More emphasis would be given to treatment of current and future members of the work force. Smoking might be encouraged rather than discouraged (smokers save society a great deal of money by dying early). Funding of the humanities and (probably) the social sciences would suffer. Whereas the existing systems of health care provision can be explained by a combination of security and efficiency considerations, existing systems of education can be explained by a combination of consumption and investment considerations. On these issues, see also Elster (1995d).
108. O'Flaherty (1996), p. 285.
109. For doubts about the enforceability of budgetary precommitments, see Keech (1995), pp. 172–74.
110. Thus Russell Baker: "Then there is the balanced-budget amendment to the Constitution. If enacted, this will force all members of Congress to stop before they spend again. These pathetic wretches are sunk so deep in their vice that they now seek relief by mutilating the Constitution. They propose putting government on the back of government itself so that their inability to control themselves will be restrained" (*International Herald Tribune*, November 30, 1994). Similarly, he explains

from the tendency to procrastinate that is inherent in hyperbolic discounting. Because of the privilege of the present over all future dates, Congress will, like St. Augustine, tell itself that balancing the budget is a good idea – in the future. But when the future arrives, it always does so in the form of a new present, to which the same reasoning then applies. The balanced-budget amendment might overcome this procrastination.

To get the amendment adopted, however, one might have to stipulate that it will only take effect in the next Congress or in an even more distant future.[111] The idea of delay, in fact, serves two functions here. Once the amendment is adopted, a delay *between proposal and adoption* will protect it from being abolished. To get it adopted, an artificial delay might have to be imposed *between adoption and implementation*. The American case is not ideally suited to illustrate the point, because of the variable and uncertain duration of the amendment process. Suppose, therefore, that a balanced-budget amendment was proposed in the Swedish parliament. To be adopted, the amendment must be passed both in the current legislature and at the beginning of the next. The (hyperbolic) discounting of the legislators is such that they prefer at any given time to have a budget deficit in the current legislature and in the next, but then never again. On this assumption the amendment will not pass, unless it is possible to specify that it will take effect only in the fourth legislature.

Delayed Implementation

The framers might also want to write into the constitution a delay between election of a new government and its taking office. In Latin America (Peru, Argentina) and in Eastern Europe (Poland, Hungary), one has recently observed electoral contests between an

---

the line-item-veto bill by the "self-loathing that now afflicts Congress. Congressional members have lately taken to whining about their weakness. They are simply too weak-kneed, they say, to resist doling out federal gravy. A constitutional amendment was passed. Messrs. Gingrich and Dole peddled it like hot gospel. Surely, surely these wretched sinful wastrels who wanted – sincerely wanted – to mend their ways, surely they could control their evil habit if only it were proscribed by that sacred document, the Constitution" (Ibid., March 31, 1995).

111. Tabellini and Alesina (1994), p. 171. In their model, however, the source of the time-inconsistency is uncertainty about the future preferences of the electorate rather than hyperbolic discounting.

efficiency-oriented liberal party that is committed to a policy of initial austerity followed by growth, and a security-oriented populist party that promises high levels of welfare provisions and unemployment benefits. In some cases, the liberal party has a larger initial following in the polls, but as the election approaches it is overtaken by the populist party, which goes on to win the elections. These stylized facts correspond exactly to what we would expect if the voters discounted the future hyperbolically.[112] Moreover, the problem could be overcome by stipulating a delay of, say, six months before the new government took office. Of course, six months might not be enough. Also, six months might be too long, in the sense that the country might not be able to afford a lame-duck government for such a long time. This being said, the problem is a real one and a solution of this sort at least abstractly conceivable.

The idea of a delay between adoption and implementation might also be defended on entirely different grounds. A problem that has plagued most constitutional legislation, whether at the founding stage or in an amendment process, is that framers invariably find themselves in a conflict. On the one hand, the very nature of a constitution requires them to legislate in the interest of all and for the indefinite future. On the other hand, they also have short-term and partisan motives imposed on them by their constituencies. The latter motives would be considerably less important if legislation took place under an artificial veil of ignorance created by a requirement that decisions will not come into effect until, say, ten or twenty years later.

This kind of veil-of-ignorance reasoning was deployed several times at the Federal Convention, most strikingly in an intervention by George Mason:

We ought to attend to the rights of every class of people. He had often wondered at the indifference of the superior classes of society to this dictate of humanity & policy, considering that however affluent their circumstances, or

---

112. More conjecturally (very conjecturally, in fact), hyperbolic discounting might be related to another stylized fact, discovered and analyzed by Stokes (1997, 1999), namely, that immediately after the election many of the governments that were elected on a populist platform begin to implement the liberal program of their rivals. Before the election, there is a preference switch in the electorate; after the election, a policy switch by the government. The two phenomena might be related, if the government believes that in implementing the liberal program it is doing what the voters, in some sense, "really" want and that it has no reason, therefore, to fear defeat in the next election.

elevated their situations, might be, the course of a few years, not only might but certainly would distribute their posteriority through the lowest classes of Society. Every selfish motive therefore, every family attachment, ought to recommend such a system of policy as would provide no less carefully for the rights and happiness of the lowest than of the highest orders of Citizens. (I, p. 49)

Gouverneur Morris argued, in a similar vein, that

State attachments, and State importance have been the bane of this Country. We cannot annihilate; but we may perhaps take out the teeth of the serpents. He wished our ideas to be enlarged to the true interest of man, instead of being circumscribed within the narrow compass of a particular spot. And after all how little can be the motive yielded by selfishness for such a policy. Who can say whether he himself, much less whether his children, will the next year be an inhabitant of this or that state. (I, p. 530)

This argument refers to the thirteen states then in existence, but it was also used to cover the accession of future states. Against Gerry's proposal to "limit the number of new states to be admitted into the Union, in such a manner, that they should never be able to outnumber the Atlantic States" (II, p. 3), Sherman replied, "We are providing for our posterity, for our children and grand children, who would be as likely to be citizens of new Western states as of the old states" (ibid.).

The argument I suggested earlier would reinforce this argument by increasing the uncertainty. If the constitution takes effect tomorrow, I may be able to predict with certainty that my children will be better off under arrangement A than under arrangement B. The fact that the expected utility of my grandchildren and great-grandchildren may be greater under B might not offset that preference. But if the constitution's taking effect is postponed twenty years, the fate of my grandchildren and great-grandchildren may become the more important consideration, for two reasons. For one thing, the veil of ignorance now covers a greater part of the relevant period. For another, if the framers are subject to hyperbolic discounting, the postponement will take the bite out of what I called the "strong preference for the present compared to all future dates" (I.3).

Needless to say, the idea is utopian and probably undesirable on other counts. Demands for constitution-making or constitutional revision tend to arise in times of crisis in which waiting is an unaffordable luxury. Yet I believe that this use of delays might be worthwhile considering in other decision-making contexts. A standard argument for delays is that by providing time to cool down, they counteract the pernicious effects of *passion*. I have argued that by increasing uncertainty, delays also create a veil of ignorance that forces an agent to put himself in everybody's place and thus reduces the importance of *interest*.

II.9. OMNIPOTENCE, STRATEGIC BEHAVIOR, AND SEPARATION OF POWERS

In this section I consider the idea that power, to be effective, must be divided; and that omnipotence, far from being a blessing, can be a curse.[113] I shall mainly discuss the idea in terms of time-inconsistency and credibility, but it is actually more general. Thus one predicament of having too much power is summarized in a dictum offered to Napoleon by one of his advisers, "On ne s'appuie que sur ce qui résiste," a phrase that Tocqueville might have used as an epitaph for his *Ancien Régime*. The following passage gives the flavor of the main argument of that work:

Among the questions addressed to the intendants this one was still found: do the nobles of your province like to stay at home or not? We have the letter of an intendant responding on this subject; he complains that the nobles of his province like to stay with their peasants, rather than fulfilling their duties to the King. But note this well: the province of which he spoke thus was Anjou; later called the Vendée. These nobles, who were criticized for preferring to live with their peasants, who refused, it was said, to do their duty to the king, were the only ones who defended the monarchy in France arms in hand, and were able to die there in combat for it.[114]

Tocqueville's book is a study in *ruin by success*, to use a phrase that Stephen Holmes has coined to summarize the events of 1848 as described by Tocqueville in his *Recollections*.[115] Having reduced the nobility and the bourgeoisie to a state of impotence, the monarchy

---

113. Although the focus here is on institutional factors, the possession of absolute power has also a psychological aspect. The tyrant does not trust or believe anyone; thus Tiberius "hated sycophancy as much as he feared candor" (Veyne 1976, p. 720). Similarly, Herodotus (3.80): the tyrant "is the most inconsistent of all creatures; if you offer him admiration in moderate quantities, he is angry that he is not paid extreme attention, and if someone pays him extreme attention he is angry at him for being a flatterer."

114. Tocqueville (1998), p. 181.

115. Holmes (1992). In the *Recollections*, the pattern noticed by Holmes is that if A allies

had no allies to draw on when it found itself under attack. In the discussion that follows, however, the emphasis will be on division of power among branches of government rather than among classes. Although the two issues were closely linked in the traditional English conception of separation of powers, they are entirely dissociated in modern societies.

THE PARADOX OF OMNIPOTENCE

At the most general level, an omnipotent being is a contradiction in terms. "If an entity has the power to make any law or do any act at any time, then can it limit its own power to act or make law? If it can, then it can't, and if it can't then it can."[116] The paradox, which was originally stated with respect to divine omnipotence, also applies to the political sovereign. Thus according to Hobbes,

The Soveraign of a Common-wealth, be it an Assembly, one Man, is not subject to the Civill Lawes. For having power to make, and repeale Laws, he may, when he pleaseth, free himself from that subjection, by repealing those Lawes that trouble him, and making of new; and consequently he was free before. For he is free, that can be free when he will: Nor is it possible for any person to be bound to himself; because he that can bind, can release; and therefore he that is bound to himselfe onely, is not bound.[117]

As an abstract proposition, the last statement might seem impeccable. Applied to real-life politics it is not, as shown by the passage I cited from Spinoza at the beginning of this chapter. Although the king in question (Darius the Mede) was omnipotent with respect to the laws he could issue, he *lacked the power to retract* the decree his satraps had tricked him into issuing for the purpose of trapping Daniel. The explanation of this irreversibility is not clear from the Biblical text. Nor can we go to other sources, as the very existence of Darius the Mede is shrouded in uncertainty. Very conjecturally, something like a meta-constitutional convention (II.3) could have been at work. If he

himself with B to fight their common enemy C, A should beware of destroying C completely, lest B then turn against him. In the *Old Regime*, the pattern is that if A undermines the power of B and C by divide-and-conquer tactics, he cannot call on their help when attacked by D.

116. Suber (1990), p. 12.
117. *Leviathan*, Part II, Ch. 26. Holmes (1988), who also cites this passage, traces the idea backward to Seneca and forward to Rousseau and others.

had abolished his own decree Darius might have incurred a loss of religious legitimacy. Yet this idea would presuppose that the priesthood was a rival source of power and that the king was not, in fact, omnipotent.

The reason why Hobbes's argument cannot be directly applied to real-life politics derives from the irreversibility of promises. It is not true that "he that can bind, can release," if that statement implies that binding and releasing are equally easy. In politics as elsewhere, to make a promise and then break it is worse than not making it in the first place (see also Cleon's speech in the Mytilenian debate cited in II.6). In the first French constituent assembly, the announcement of the radical measures taken on the night of August 4, 1789, made it impossible to go back. In a wonderful contemporary phrase, "The people are penetrated by the benefits they have been promised; they will not let themselves be de-penetrated."[118] Tocqueville makes a similar point in his analysis of the constitution-making process of 1848. Initially, before the insurrection of June 1848 but apprehensive of its coming, he felt that "what was needed was not so much a good constitution as some constitution or other."[119] Acting under time pressure, he was "much more concerned with putting a powerful leader quickly at the head of the Republic than with drafting a perfect republican constitution."[120] After the June days he stood by this proposal, but now for the reason that "having announced to the nation that this ardently desired right would be granted, it was no longer possible to refuse it."[121] Promises made before the public are often irreversible.

Suppose, however, that we are dealing with a sovereign – such as an absolute monarch, an oriental despot, a politburo, or a junta – that does not have to fear the disappointment of frustrated expectations. Assume, moreover, that he wants to precommit himself to a fixed long-term policy that will create an environment conducive to sustained economic growth. One example is that of China in the 1980s. When the Chinese economy was liberalized and private ownership allowed to develop, the economic agents could not know if this state would last and if they would be allowed to retain their profits. As a consequence their time horizon was shortened, and they often preferred to use their profits for housing or luxury consumption rather

---

118. Cited after Mathiez (1898), p. 265, note 4.
119. Tocqueville (1986), p. 826. The sentence is omitted in the English translation (Tocqueville 1990).
120. Tocqueville (1990), p. 178.   121. Ibid.

than plough them back into business. The Chinese leaders may well have wanted to precommit themselves to a hands-off policy, but there was no way in which they could do so credibly. Because they had all power, they were *unable to make themselves unable to interfere.*[122]

CREDIBILITY

Commitments can be credible when power is divided between the executive, an independent judiciary, and a democratically elected legislature. This is the central part of the story told by Douglass North and Barry Weingast in their reconstruction of English political economy in the seventeenth century. After the glorious revolution, the "threat of removal that was [made credible by the 1648 revolution] limited the Crown's ability to ignore" parliament. At the same time, "the creation of a politically independent judiciary greatly expanded the government's ability to promise to honor its agreements, that is, to bond itself." Finally, "by creating a balance between Parliament and the monarchy – rather than eliminating the latter as occurred after the Civil War – parliamentary interests insured limits on their own tendencies toward arbitrary action."[123]

One can imagine a test, which I lack the competence to carry out, to verify the connection between democracy and effective precommitment. In studies of the relation (further discussed later) between central bank independence and economic growth, the former variable has usually been measured both by formal criteria, such as the independence that the bank possesses by statute, and by behavioral criteria, such as the rate of turnover of bank governors. It has been found that these two aspects of central bank independence are highly correlated within the group of industrialized countries but not within the group of developing countries.[124] It would follow from my argument that they should also be more highly correlated for the group of democratic countries than for the group of nondemocratic countries.

There is a complication, however, due to the fact that some authoritarian regimes may in fact be able to make credible commitments. More specifically, José Campos and Hilton Root argue that the

---

122. Elster (1989c), p. 199.
123. North and Weingast (1989), pp. 817, 819, 829. They do not make it clear whether this was an intentional precommitment or merely an incidental constraint.
124. Cukierman (1992), p. 421, pp. 453–54.

more-or-less authoritarian regimes in high-performing Asian economies gained the necessary credibility through an "implicit constitution" in which the specifically Asian institution of *deliberative councils*
serve as "precommitment devices."[125] These councils are nondemocratic bodies, with members from the public as well as the private sec-
tor. They have quasi-legislative authority to regulate matters within
a given industry or at even higher levels of aggregation. Among their
several functions, perhaps the most important is that of reducing the
freedom of action of the government:

> A dictator, by his nature, does not generally entertain checks (and balances)
> against his authority. But this absence undermines credibility for the long
> term: how do firms know he won't change policies tomorrow? If dictators
> want information to determine the appropriate choice of policies, they must
> ensure that the disclosure of information will not result in the direct (through
> expropriation) or indirect (through adverse changes in policies) confiscation
> of assets. To solve this commitment problem . . . , East Asian leaders traded
> authority for information, in effect tying their own hands by establishing
> institutions that restricted their scope for arbitrary action.[126]

Although the system rests on an unwritten constitutional convention rather than on a written constitution, the basic argument is similar to the one I made earlier. Power, to be effective, must be divided.
In the rest of this section I use the issue of central bank independence
to illustrate this idea.

Independent Central Banks

In recent years there has emerged something like a consensus on the
need for an independent central bank. At least one country (the Czech
Republic) has chosen to write the independence of the bank into the
constitution. In other countries, the independence is either provided
by statute and cemented by a constitutional convention, or grounded
only in a constitutional convention. In the following I shall disregard
these differences, and simply assume that for one reason or another
the bank has a great deal of de facto independence.

The standard argument is that an independent central bank is a
precommitment device to overcome time-inconsistency caused by

125. Campos and Root (1996), p. 103.   126. Ibid., pp. 77–78.

strategic interaction.[127] There are several ways in which such inconsistency may arise. Here, I shall focus on the version of the argument in which the main actors are the government and the public, including employers and a central trade union. I assume that the objective function of the government depends negatively on inflation and positively on the level of employment. I assume, moreover, that this objective function derives from its conception of the public interest rather than from partisan or electoral motives. The government can act directly on the first variable, by using its power to set the rate of monetary expansion and, hence, of inflation. By creating inflation to increase employment (see the later discussion), it can also act indirectly on the second variable. The union cares only about the real wage of its members, which is a function of the nominal wage and the inflation rate. The protocol is such that, first, unions and employers bargain over nominal wages, given their expectations about the rate of inflation. Next, the government sets the rate of monetary expansion and, hence, the actual rate of inflation.

Suppose further that (i) the government announces that it will follow a policy of zero inflation, (ii) the union and the employers believe the announcement and set the nominal wage accordingly, and (iii) the government sticks to the announced policy. The rate of unemployment then produced is called the "natural rate of unemployment." For various reasons, the government may believe that this rate is too high.[128] Assuming (i) and (ii), the government may then decide to create employment by expanding the money supply, which will lead to lower real wages and higher employment. If the union and employers know the objective of the government, however, this policy will not work. Anticipating that the government will use its discretionary control over monetary policy to create more jobs, they will adjust the nominal wage upward to offset inflation. Specifically, they will set the nominal wage in the expectation that the government will set the rate of inflation that is optimal given that nominal wage. Actual and expected inflations will be equal, and the action of the central bank has no effect on employment. The rate of inflation, however, is positive, to the detriment of all.

---

127. See notably Cukierman (1992), on which I draw heavily in the following. The key argument was first stated by Kydland and Prescott (1977). A frontal attack on this line of reasoning is Blinder (1998). I argue later that some of his criticisms are tendentious.
128. Cukierman (1992), Ch. 3.

For the government, the best outcome would be to make a credible announcement of zero inflation and then to proceed to inflate; the next best to make a credible announcement of zero inflation and then proceed not to inflate; and the worst outcome is a credible – because self-fulfilling – announcement of a positive rate of inflation. Because an announcement of zero inflation is never credible, the government is stuck with the worst outcome. The same conclusion is obtained if one examines other reasons why the government might want to expand the supply of money, such as the desire for revenue or the desire to reduce the deficit in the balance of payments. Because all these cases give rise to a dynamic version of the Prisoner's Dilemma,[129] similar to the "Promise" case in Figure. I.3, they are all subject to dynamic inconsistency.

If constitution-makers or legislators come to understand this predicament, they can respond with a policy of precommitment, which might take one of two forms. On the one hand, they might opt for rules rather than discretion and write a specific monetary policy directly into the constitution. This option, on reflection, is either undesirable or unfeasible. A simple mechanical rule such as zero growth of the money supply, while perhaps feasible, would provide too little flexibility for adjustment to unforeseen events. Conversely, a rule that tried to specify optimal responses to all contingencies would be impossibly complex.

On the other hand they might entrust the discretion to an independent central bank rather than to the government. To ensure the real independence of the governor of the bank,[130] a number of measures have been adopted. When the Central Bank of Norway was created in 1816, it was located in Trondheim, several hundred miles from the capital, in order to ensure its independence from the government. More recently, similar reasoning was at the base of the decision to locate the headquarters of the German Bundesbank in Frankfurt rather than in Cologne.[131] In countries with a dual executive, the governor

---

129. Ibid., p. 17.
130. The reason why politicians might want to insulate the bank from their pressure need not be a high-minded motive to promote the welfare of the country. They might also abdicate simply to be able to shift the blame when something goes wrong (Cukierman 1992, p. 213).
131. "As late as September 1956, the chancellor [Adenauer] stirred alarm in Frankfurt by suggesting that the Bundesbank should be set up in Cologne to place it closer to Bonn. In the end, the Bundesbank stayed in Frankfurt, at arm's length from the government" (Marsh 1992, p. 167). Several countries have also located their constitutional courts outside the capital: the German court is located in Karlsruhe,

may be appointed by the president rather than by the government, on the assumption that he or she will then be more likely to be conservative rather than activist, that is, place higher weight on price stability than on employment. The constitution may also explicitly forbid the government from instructing the bank or (as in Norway) require that if it does so, the fact must be made public. Furthermore, one may constitutionalize price stability as the goal of the bank. In the spirit of Schelling, one may also try to strengthen the bank by taking away some of its powers. Thus to protect the bank from informal pressure by the government, one may, as in Argentina, explicitly forbid it to engage in deficit funding.[132]

The creation of independent central banks illustrates the idea of separation of powers as a precommitment device to overcome time-inconsistency. Separation of powers can of course serve other purposes too. By ensuring functional specialization, separation of powers can enhance efficiency. The need for an executive branch of government stems, among other things, from the fact that it would not be efficient to entrust a legislative body with the conduct of war. Also, the separation of powers can reduce corruption and prevent one branch of government from undue interference with the tasks of the others. An instance of the latter idea is the random assignment of judges to cases, to prevent the minister of justice from selecting "reliable" judges for "delicate" cases. A similar argument may in fact be used for having an independent central bank. If the government has direct control over monetary policy, it may use that instrument to enhance its chances of reelection rather than to serve the public interest. In this case, the separation of powers serves to counteract partisan interest. The preceding argument shows, however, that an independent central bank may be required even if the government is motivated solely by considerations of the public interest.[133]

---

the Czech court in Brno, the Estonian court in Tartu, and the Slovakian one in Kosice. I do not know whether the reason, in any of these cases, was an explicit desire to insulate the court from pressure from other branches of government.

132. G. Miller (1993).

133. The version of the Kydland-Prescott analysis criticized by Blinder (1998) comes close to being a caricature. He ridicules their argument by saying, "The vision of highly disciplined and farsighted politicians curing the wayward ways of profligate and myopic central bankers seems a strange role reversal" (p. 46). Three comments seem appropriate. (i) The Kydland-Prescott argument rests on the assumption that politicians and bankers have the *same* values, but may be unable to implement them because of the time-inconsistency problem. One may question this assumption on empirical grounds. Perhaps the need to have an independent

II.10. EFFICIENCY

In II.7 through II.9 I have considered reasons for constitutional pre-commitment – passion and the two forms of time-inconsistency – that have analogues in the individual precommitment cases discussed in Chapter I. What is arguably the most important reason for constitutional self-binding has no parallel, however, in the individual case. This is the idea of using constitutional provisions to eliminate or reduce certain forms of waste and inefficiency that would prevail if all legislation took the form of simple statutes that could be changed by an ordinary majority. I shall distinguish among three varieties of inefficiency that may be remedied in this way: shortening of the time horizon, rent-seeking, and aggregative inconsistency. In all three cases, the main remedy is that of requiring a supermajority for amending the constitution. Although delays and the need to submit amendments to referendum might have some of the same effects, they are unlikely to serve as well. A persistent if slight majority could weather a delay, and a referendum would not be an obstacle if the population at large shares the views of the assembly.

Extending the Time Horizon

Stability is a general means to promote many important ends. Within limits, it is more important to have *some* constitution that is not at the mercy of fluctuating majorities, than to have any particular constitution. As Leibniz said, it does not matter whether the bees escaping from my property belong to me or to my neighbor who catches them, for as long as the laws are fixed I can regulate my behavior by them.[134] Planning and investment by individuals will have

central bank in order to neutralize partisan or myopic governments is more important in practice than the need for independence in order to neutralize time-inconsistency in a nonpartisan and nonmyopic government. But one should not misrepresent the assumption. (ii) Blinder himself acknowledges the possibility that politicians can act in a nonpartisan way when he writes, "Perhaps the principal reason why central banks are given independence from elected politicians is that the political process is apt to be too shortsighted. Knowing this, politicians willingly and wisely cede day-to-day authority over monetary policy to a group of independent central bankers" (p. 61). (iii) Yet how can shortsighted politicians be farsighted enough to protect themselves against their shortsightedness? I touched on that issue in I.3 and discuss it further in II.11.

134. See discussion in Elster (1975), p. 142.

a longer time horizon and bear more fruits if they can be reasonably certain that property rights, including the right to compensation for expropriation, will remain in place. Political parties, too, can operate more efficiently if they can take the framework of elections and institutions for given. As Stephen Holmes notes, "Constitutional rules are enabling, not disabling; and it is therefore unsatisfactory to identify constitutionalism exclusively with limitations on power."[135] One might of course deny that what is good for the existing political parties is also good for society. In the United States, for instance, a thorough shake-up of the political system might allow new political forces to emerge and raise the level of participation above its current dismal level. While this may be true, there is no reason to believe that a system in *constant* change would have these beneficial effects. It would be more likely, I think, to induce fatigue and anarchy.[136]

The stabilizing effect of requiring supermajorities for amending the constitution is arguably the most important aspect of constitutional precommitment. It provides a justification for the seemingly arbitrary procedure of allowing a small majority in the constituent assembly to adopt a document that can be changed only by a substantially larger majority. I am not saying that this procedure is justified in all cases. In II.11, for instance, I discuss the dangers of a majority imposing its will on a minority in matters of religion and ethnicity. Yet I believe the procedure is justified whenever the minority would rather live under a regime that is preferred by the majority and protected by a supermajority requirement than live under its own preferred regime that was not similarly protected. Protestants would certainly prefer to live under a weakly entrenched Protestant system than under a strongly entrenched Catholic system, but defenders of bicameralism might prefer an entrenched unicameral system over unentrenched bicameralism. The argument is related to the idea that even the weak prefer a lawful regime that is biased toward the interests of the strong to a society without any laws altogether, with the difference that here it is the stability of the laws rather than their mere existence that redeems them in the eyes of those who would have preferred a different set of laws.

---

135. Holmes (1988), p. 227.
136. Holmes (1993), Ch. 6 (criticizing Roberto Unger).

REDUCING TRANSACTION COSTS

Richard Posner has observed that supermajorities are also useful in reducing transaction costs. Simple majority voting tends to encourage rent-seeking. "If the vote of a simple majority could change the basic form of government or expropriate the wealth of a minority, enormous resources might be devoted to seeking and resisting such legislation."[137] Note that this statement suggests or presupposes that there is a systematic and substantial difference in rent-seeking potential between constitutional matters and matters that are subject to ordinary legislation. To my knowledge, that claim has not been tested. In any case, it seems clear that the statement, if valid, appeals to constitutions as incidental rather than essential constraints. This is even more true of the third argument from efficiency.

ELIMINATING CYCLES

We know from the Condorcet paradox and Arrow's theorem that with simple majority voting, cyclical majorities can arise. This *aggregative inconsistency*, although different from time-inconsistency, is no less undesirable in its subversive effects. It has been shown that if we impose relatively weak restrictions on the admissible combinations of individual preferences, requirement of a 64% majority or more ensures that social preferences will never be cyclical.[138] They might, however, in many cases be incomplete, if no proposal can gather the requisite majority.[139] In ordinary legislation without a status quo, such as the vote of the annual budget, this problem would be very serious. In the constitutional context, with a well-defined status quo, incompleteness is less of a problem.

II.11. OBSTACLES AND OBJECTIONS

As in the case of individual self-binding (I.8), constitutional precommitment, when desirable, may not be feasible or effective; when feasible and effective, it may not be desirable.

---

137. Posner (1987), p. 9.   138. Caplin and Nalebuff (1988).
139. I owe this observation to Aanund Hylland.

PRECOMMITMENT MAY NOT BE FEASIBLE

With regard to the first issue, the distinction between essential and incidental constraints is relevant. There are cases in which a polity might benefit from constraints and yet is unlikely to impose those constraints on itself. Unless the constraints are imposed from the outside or by a subset of the polity, the normatively desirable self-binding may not, in fact, take place. I shall discuss this problem with regard to three sets of problems that constitutions might be designed to overcome: standing passions, impulsive passions, and interest.

Standing passions include national, ethnic, and religious animosities; strong commitments to equality or hierarchy; and other emotional dispositions that are widely shared and deeply entrenched in the population. Because these passions can induce oppression of minorities and cause severe social conflicts, it would be desirable to have some constitutional protection against them, in the form of entrenched minority rights or power sharing among groups. I agree, therefore, with Cass Sunstein when he writes, "Constitutional provisions should be designed to work against precisely those aspects of a country's culture and tradition that are likely to produce harm through that country's political processes."[140] Yet those provisions are also *the least likely to be adopted*, precisely because culture and tradition work against them. In democratic societies, at least, there is no reason to expect the framers to be exempt from the array of prejudices that animate the population at large.

This is not a merely abstract worry. Given the strong anti-Turkish feelings in Bulgaria, for instance, it would indeed be desirable to have strong protection of ethnic minorities written into the constitution. Yet because the majority in the constituent assembly also harbored those sentiments, the 1991 Bulgarian constitution contains the weakest protection of minority rights among all the new constitutions in Eastern Europe. Ethnically based parties are banned, and minorities are only given the right to be taught their own language rather than to be taught (all subjects) *in* their own language. To take another example, a main reason for the failure of the 1931 Spanish constitution was its stringent anticlerical clauses.[141] If the small Republican majority in the constituent assembly (the constitution was adopted by a

140. Sunstein (1991a), p. 385.   141. Bonime-Blanc (1987), pp. 102–103.

55% majority) had pulled its punches, later developments might have been different.

Tocqueville's skepticism toward precommitment may be understood in this perspective. In *Democracy in America*, he writes

A single fact is enough to show that the stage is not very popular in America. The Americans, whose laws allow the utmost freedom, and even license of language, in other respects, nevertheless subject the drama to a sort of censorship. Plays can only be performed by permission of the municipal authorities. This illustrates how like communities are to individuals: without a thought they give way to their chief passions, and then take great care not to be carried away by tastes they do not possess.[142]

I read the first part of the last sentence as expressing the idea I argued for earlier: people do not precommit themselves against their strong, standing passions. The second part can be illustrated by the idea of an ethnically homogeneous community passing laws ensuring the rights of ethnic minorities. It is obvious that to be free to do things one does not want to do is less valuable than being free to do what one wants.[143] Similarly, to be prevented from doing bad things one wouldn't want to do anyway is less useful than being prevented from doing bad things one might actually be tempted to do. The problem is that when these are *permanent* temptations there is less incentive to set up barriers against them.

An exception might arise if the majority perceives that it will incur costs if it acts on its prejudices against the minority, for example, by stirring up social unrest that will affect the productive capacities of the country or its position on the international scene.[144] Two further factors might, however, work in the opposite direction. In the first place, it is in the nature of passions that they can induce people to act against their self-interest. In the second place, if there is a history of past oppression the dominant group might be afraid to relax its grip on the minority. Claus Offe, for instance, refers to "the logic that Bulgarians apply against their Turkish minority, and which Hitler proclaimed the day before the German invasion of the Soviet Union in 1941: 'After what we have done to

---

142. Tocqueville (1969), p. 430.
143. This is not to say that the freedom to do what one does not want to do has *no* value; see Elster (1983b), pp. 128–29.
144. I am indebted to James Fearon for pointing out to me that a *permanent* temptation to oppress the minority could be much more costly than a short-lived impulse.

them, we will be devastatingly punished unless we continue doing it.' "[145]

Impulsive passions are triggered by sudden and threatening events, such as an economic crisis, revolution, war or imminent risk of war, and the like.[146] The idea that constitutions ought to protect the citizens against succumbing to such impulses was expressed, as we saw (II.1), by saying that they are chains imposed by Peter when sober on Peter when drunk. Yet the premise of a sober Peter may not be fulfilled in reality. It is an overwhelming empirical regularity that constitutions tend to be written in times of turbulence and upheaval in which passions tend to run high.[147] The occasions for constitution-making include social and economic crisis, as in the making of the American constitution of 1787 or the French constitution of 1791; revolution, as in the making of the French and German 1848 constitutions; regime collapse, as in the making of the most recent constitutions in Southern Europe and in Eastern Europe; fear of regime collapse, as in the making of the French constitution of 1958, which was imposed by de Gaulle under the shadow of a military rebellion; defeat in war, as in Germany after the First or Second World War, or in Italy and Japan after the Second; reconstruction after war, as in France in 1946; creation of a new state, as in Poland and Czechoslovakia after the First World War; and liberation from colonial rule, as in the American states after 1776 and in many third world countries after 1945.

If constitutions are typically written in times of crisis, it is not obvious that the framers will be particularly sober. The French constitution-makers of 1791, for instance, were not famous for their sobriety.[148] In the Assemblée Constituante, it was initially envisaged that the assembly would meet two days a week, and work in

---

145. Offe (1992), p. 23.
146. These passions, to be sure, must be rooted in underlying emotional dispositions, which are, however, much more general than what I called standing passions. The disposition to hate members of another religion or ethnic group is much more specific than the disposition to be afraid of an enemy.
147. Russell (1993), p. 106. Holmes and Sunstein (1995), p. 284, argue that "no group of framers, given the universally acknowledged proneness of all actors to commit colossal blunders in turbulent circumstances, can plausibly monopolize authority over the constitutional framework." In their other writings on constitutional precommitment, however, both Holmes (1988) and Sunstein (1991a,b) ignore or tacitly deny this point.
148. A systematic discussion of the role of the passions in the French Revolution is Tulard (1996). He does not mention fear and vanity, however, although these certainly have considerable power to explain how votes were cast in the various constituent assemblies.

subcommittees (*bureaux*) on the other days.[149] However, the moderates and the patriots had very different opinions about these two modes of proceeding. For Mounier, leader of the moderates, the committees favored "cool reason and experience," by detaching the members from everything that could stimulate their vanity and fear.[150] For the radical Bouche, committees tended to weaken the revolutionary fervor. He preferred the large assemblies, where "souls become strong and electrified, and where names, ranks and distinctions count for nothing" (8, p. 307). On his proposal, it was decided that the assembly would sit in plenum each morning and meet in committee in the afternoon.

The importance of this move, which constituted the beginning of the end for the moderates, was clear.[151] It was reinforced by the move to voting by roll call, a procedure that enabled members or spectators to identify those who opposed radical measures, and to circulate lists with their names in Paris.[152] Thus in the crucial debates on bicameralism and the royal veto – devices partly intended to restrain majoritarian passions (II.7) – many delegates were swayed by passion rather than reason (or interest). The majoritarian rhetoric of the assembly did not go well with the idea that untrammeled majority rule might be dangerous. As we saw at the end of II.7, the French framers were able to protect themselves against their interests, but unlike the American framers they did not take steps to protect themselves against their passions.

The threat to constitution-making created by impulsive passions is more general and pervasive than the problem of standing passions. Whereas there is no general reason to expect a nation to be especially vulnerable to the latter at the constitution-making stage, there is, as I indicated, a systematic tendency for constitutions to

---

149. Great care was taken to form the subcommittees so as to prevent the emergence of factions (Castaldo 1989, p. 120, note 65). They were essentially formed randomly (using an alphabetical order) and renewed each month so that the same deputies would never remain together.
150. Mounier (1989), p. 926.
151. Egret (1950), p. 120. Later, Mounier (1989, p. 927) strongly reproached himself for his inactivity on this occasion. Castaldo (1989), p. 202, note 102, shows that both Egret and Mounier overestimate the political aspects of the demise of the *bureaux*. The assembly did not move to plenary sessions only, but replaced the randomly formed and constantly changing *bureaux* with standing committees organized by subject matter.
152. For similar stratagems in the Frankfurt constituent assembly of 1848, see Eyck (1968), notably pp. 115–16, 120, 153 ff.

be written in turbulent circumstances when judgment is clouded by the passions of the moment. The conditions under which the *need* for constitution-making arises tend to hinder the *task* of constitution-making. Elsewhere I have argued, "Emotions provide us with a sense of meaning and direction to life, but they also prevent us from going steadily in that direction."[153] Although in making this claim I did not have constitution-making in mind, it is perfectly illustrated by that process.

Finally, the interests of the framers may stand in the way of precommitment for the purpose of restraining the interests of future political agents. To take an obvious example, a constituent assembly that also serves as an ordinary legislature may not have an interest in creating checks on the interest of the legislature (II.7). The recent constitution-making processes in Eastern Europe illustrate this point.[154] With some exceptions, the framers in Bulgaria, Czechoslovakia, and its two successor states, Poland and Romania, carefully avoided adoption of some of the devices that might limit the powers of the legislature. None of these countries adopted the constructive vote of no confidence that strengthens the power of the government vis-à-vis the assembly. Except for Czechoslovakia, none of them created a strong constitutional court that might strike down legislation as unconstitutional. Except for the countries that had a bicameral constituent assembly, none of them created an upper house that could act as a counterweight to the lower house. (The Czech Republic also counts as a partial exception.) With the partial exception of Romania, none of them made referendum an important part of the process of amending the constitution. The only constituent assembly in the region that abdicated important powers was the Hungarian one, which adopted the constructive vote of no confidence and created a constitutional court that has been said to be the strongest in the world.

Thus overall I agree with Adam Przeworski and Fernando Limongi when they observe that "advocates of commitment . . . do not consider the political process by which such commitments are established."[155] Yet I cannot agree when they go on to adduce this argument against the possibility of precommitment in general and against anti-discretionary precommitment more specifically. They claim that "the same forces that push the state to suboptimal discretionary interventions also push the state to a suboptimal commitment." But

153. Elster (1989a), p. 70.   154. For details, see Elster (1993a, 1995e).
155. Przeworski and Limongi (1993), p. 66.

161

as a general argument, that cannot be right.[156] For one thing, the forces that push for suboptimal intervention may be triggered by an urgent crisis rather than being permanent features of the political scene. For another, a state may be "pushed" to suboptimal discretionary interventions even when there is no crisis and policy makers are concerned exclusively with the welfare of society (II.9). To be sure, discretionary interventions, such as subsidies to ailing industries, are often the outcome of political pressures, the desire for reelection, and the like. Yet this situation is not necessary for a suboptimal outcome to be produced. The lack of a technology for making a credible binding commitment may have the same result.

Even when a polity does not want to bind itself, others may try to bind it. Their motive may be to promote their own interest, to protect the polity against itself, or both. In the making of the West German constitution of 1949, for instance, the Western occupying powers tried to force upon the country a decentralized structure that would prevent the reemergence of German nationalism.[157] Even more drastically, the Japanese constitution of 1946 was written entirely by the American occupying power. Similarly, a constitution-making minority can try to protect the majority against the standing interests or standing passions that animate it. This was a dominant self-interpretation among the American framers in 1787. In such cases of imposed constitutions we are dealing with incidental constraints, at least if the constraints work to the benefit of the constrained and not only to that of the constrainer.

PRECOMMITMENT MAY NOT BE DESIRABLE

Even when feasible and effective, constitutional precommitment might not be desirable. There are two main problems, one created by the potential for a conflict between precommitment and efficiency, the other by the potential for a conflict between precommitment and democracy.

The first problem can be stated by turning the suicide metaphor on its head. In II.1 I cited the phrase "Constitutions are chains with which men bind themselves in their sane moments that they may not die by a suicidal hand in the day of their frenzy." Against this we

---

156. It may, however, be an appropriate response to Blinder (1998).
157. Golay (1958), p. 5.

may cite a famous dictum by Justice Robert Jackson, to the effect that *the constitution is not a suicide pact.*[158] Tight constitutional self-binding may be incompatible with the flexibility of action required in a crisis. At the Federal Convention in Philadelphia, for instance, George Mason observed, "Though he had a mortal hatred to paper money, yet as he could not foresee all emergences, he was unwilling to tie the hands of the Legislature. He observed that the late war could not have been carried on, had such a prohibition existed."[159] Similarly, when in 1946 the Italian Parliament decided against constitutionalizing monetary stability, one of the objections referred to the need for the government to be free to act in times of war.[160]

Commenting on balanced-budget provisions, Guido Tabellini and Alberto Alesina note:

> Each current majority does not want to be bound by the rule, even though it wants the rule for all future majorities. However, a budget rule taking effect at some prespecified future date would be irrelevant...if the rule can be abrogated by a simple majority.... This problem could be overcome by requiring a qualified majority to abrogate the rule, but this requirement would greatly reduce the flexibility with which to respond to unexpected events. A budget rule could contain escape clauses, such as for cyclical fluctuations of tax revenues or wars. However, since it is very difficult or even impossible to list all relevant contingencies, requiring a very large majority to abandon (even temporarily) the budget balance may be counterproductive.[161]

In wartime, appeal to the emergency powers enumerated in many constitutions may be sufficient to prevent a monetary suicide pact from being carried out. More generally, emergency provisions are specifically intended to be suicide prevention devices. Yet although these provisions can act as a safety valve and thus stabilize the constitution, they may also jeopardize it. Drawing on a variety of emergency provisions from the Roman Republic to the Weimar Republic, Bernard Manin argues that unless they are very carefully designed they can amplify the problems they are supposed to solve.[162] Thus if

---

158. Paraphrase of the dissent of Justice Robert Jackson in *Terminiello v. City of Chicago*, 337 U.S. 1, 37 (1949). A related use of the suicide metaphor occurs in a comment by Robert Reischauer, director of the Congressional Budget Office: "The lesson of the last five years is that process reform, by itself, cannot guarantee that significant deficit reduction takes place. No budget process can force those engaged in it to commit what they regard to be political suicide" (cited from Keech 1995, p. 173).

159. I, p. 309.   160. Spinelli and Masciandaro (1993), p. 217.

161. Tabellini and Alesina (1994), p. 171.

162. Personal communication.

passions and interests constitute first-order problems, constitutions a first-order solution, rigidity a second-order problem, emergency powers a second-order solution, and the coup d'état a third-order problem, third-order solutions may be required. Manin suggests, for instance, that the risk of adventurist exploitation of emergency provisions may be reduced by entrusting the decision to declare a state of emergency to another organ than the one that will exercise the power during the emergency.

In the case of monetary policy, one may imagine sudden shocks to the economy, such as the 1973 quadrupling of oil prices, which are not emergencies in any constitutional sense and yet large enough for rigid adherence to a monetary rule to have a disastrous impact on employment. As noted earlier, society may then be better off by having monetary policy entrusted to the discretion of a central bank governor who, although mainly concerned with price stability, also allows some weight for employment. The constitution might constrain him by emphasizing the goal of price stability, but not to the point of making him into the mere executor of a preset policy. But again there is a risk: the governor might turn out to have unexpectedly and disastrously rigid principles. An example is the governor of the Norwegian Central Bank between the wars, Nicolas Rygg. The memory of his calamitous policies explains why Norway has not followed other countries and established a fully independent central bank. Whereas the German Bundesbank acquired its independence as a response to the inflationary trauma of the 1920s,[163] the 1985 law regulating the Central Bank of Norway "was designed as a social response to a *deflationary trauma.*"[164] Rather than prohibiting the government from instructing the bank, Norway chose the indirect strategy of

---

163. This at least is the traditional story (see, for instance, Marsh 1992, p. 146). Déhay (1998) argues that it presupposes a very selective memory. First, the German Central Bank was actually quite independent during the period of high inflation. Second, the deflationary experience of the 1930s was at least as traumatic as the earlier inflation. Third, the 1957 legislation that established the independence of the Bundesbank is better explained as a compromise between the federal government and the governments of the Länder (it ensured each of these two parties that the bank would be independent of the other) than as an abdication by politicians who had learned not to trust themselves as guardians of monetary policy. Even if Déhay is right, however, the traditional story has by now become a myth that has independent causal force in explaining the maintenance (even if not the origin) of the independence of the Bundesbank.

164. Sejersted (1994).

underwriting bank independence by increasing the political costs to the government of instructing it (II.3).[165]

The conflict between precommitment and democracy arises when the agents that exercise the precommitment functions are insulated from democratic control.[166] Even when decisions made by a constitutional court or a central bank are not inefficient in any of the technical senses of that term – Pareto-inferiority or non-utility-maximizing – they may be radically out of line with the stable preferences of a large majority of the citizens. A constitutional court may prohibit or allow abortion against the stable wishes of a large popular majority. A central bank may choose, for its decisions, a rate of time discounting that differs from that of the majority of the citizens. To the extent that citizens have hyperbolic time preferences and the bank is simply following their long-term time preferences while ignoring the steep short-term trade-off, this divergence does not present a normative problem. In this case, the bank is essentially helping the citizens to exercise self-control (see also I.3). To the extent that the bank tries to correct (what it perceives as) the excessive myopia of the long-term preferences themselves, it is open to criticism on democratic grounds.

ESCAPE HATCHES

If the separation of powers creates a risk of rigid, dogmatic, or democratically unresponsive central bank governors, it may have to be augmented by checks and balances. One might, for instance, have a constitutional provision allowing a supermajority in the legislature to depose the governor. I do not know of any countries that allow for this to happen, but other devices exist that may serve the same purpose. Alan Blinder argues that in the American Federal Reserve system, the risk of "overzealous central bankers" is contained both by "internal systems of checks and balances" that stem from the fact that key decisions are made by a committee rather than by one individual, and by external checks that stem from the fact that Congress can override the decisions of the Federal Reserve Board.[167] Although Congress has never used that power, the mere knowledge that it

165. Smith (1994), p. 98.
166. I am indebted to Bernard Manin and Pasquale Pasquino for many discussions of this issue.
167. Blinder (1998), pp. 21–22, 48, 68.

exists may, by virtue of the "law of anticipated reactions," have had a restraining influence.

The argument can be extended to Supreme Court justices or, in Europe, judges on the constitutional court. Judges, like central bank governors, have been known to hold dogmatic and sectarian principles, with potentially disastrous applications and implications. Thus in an address on March 9, 1937, a month after he had announced his plans to expand the Supreme Court, President Roosevelt said, "The majority of the court has been assuming the power to pass on the wisdom of . . . acts of Congress. [W]e must take action to save the Constitution from the Court."[168] His threat worked, so he did not have to carry it out: the court changed its mind rather than accept the creation of six new judges. In a reply to Roosevelt, A. Mason urged instead an amendment to allow Congress by two-thirds majority to override Supreme Court decisions.[169] As noted earlier, such provisions actually exist in some of the Eastern European constitutions. Also, Article III of the American Constitution assigns jurisdiction to the Supreme Court only "with such Exceptions, and under such Regulations as the Congress shall make." Under a literal interpretation, this clause would enable Congress to emasculate the court entirely. Not surprisingly, the court has eschewed this interpretation, yet the clause may have had some influence through the mere knowledge of its existence.

It might seem that in such cases the necessary check on the checkers already exists, because one can always amend the constitution or change the law. As we have seen, however, amending the constitution can be a very cumbersome procedure. In a given situation, there simply might not be time. Also, the constitutional court may, as in India and Germany, have the option of declaring constitutional amendments to be unconstitutional. Whenever for some reason this check on the court is insufficient, a special procedure for holding the court accountable might be necessary. Similarly, one cannot get rid of an irresponsible central bank governor by changing the laws regulating his or her tenure, unless one is willing to let the changes apply retroactively.

Yet these ways of trying to mitigate the problems of precommitment run into a difficulty that I mentioned at the end of Chapter I, namely, the problem of *how to distinguish genuine exceptions from*

168. Cited after Currie (1990), p. 235, note 158.
169. Ibid., note 159.

spurious ones.[170] In a context where unemployment is seen as the major social issue, there could be a large (if temporary) majority in parliament for deposing a central bank governor who refused to raise the supply of money so as to create more jobs. There is no reliable way in which one could distinguish between the case in which a constitutional court ought to be sanctioned because it acts against the stable preferences of the majority and the case in which it is simply doing its job by acting against its temporary preferences. Even time preferences may be state-dependent.[171] And if any solution to the secondary problem created by precommitment devices would simply re-create the problem that they were supposed to solve in the first place, one might well decide against adopting them.

II.12. ULYSSES UNBOUND

In *Ulysses and the Sirens* I came close to claiming both that constitutions *are* precommitment devices (in the intentional sense), and that societies *ought to* bind themselves by constitutional precommitment devices. As I have been saying in various places earlier, these claims are eminently contestable, on conceptual, causal, and normative grounds.

SOCIETIES ARE NOT INDIVIDUALS WRIT LARGE

Let me first observe that the extension of precommitment theory from individual choice to constitution-making is somewhat peculiar. Other extensions from individual to collective decision-making, such as the application of game theory to relations among states in the international system, rest on an assumption of unitary actors. States, like individuals, are supposed to have consistent and stable preferences and beliefs that fully explain their behavior.[172] In

---

170. Discussing whether Germany should have devalued the mark in 1931, Temin (1991), pp. 72–73, writes that the "German government was bound to preserve the value of the mark in its laws and in the Dawes and Young Plans. Would abrogation of that rule have been seen as the proper response to an emergency or as one more example of German unwillingness to accept the judgment of the war?"

171. Orphanides and Zervos (1998).

172. For a discussion of this assumption and its weaknesses, see Ch. IV of Elster (1989b).

the present case, the basis for the extension is that both the individual and the collectivity are assumed to be divided rather than unitary. As we saw in Chapter I many individual acts of precommitments are undertaken because the individual is in some sense divided, and one part of the self wants to protect itself against another part. Even though the individual is not unitary, there is one part that is in charge and that can engage in long-range planning to restrict the myopic or impulsive action tendencies of other parts. The reason why societies are non-unitary is very different. They are made up of many individuals, none of whom or no subset of whom is "in charge."

In earlier centuries, to be sure, the educated elite tended to think of itself as being in charge, with the task of restricting and restraining the passions of the majority. In Philadelphia, for instance, James Madison argued that an upper house or Senate was necessary because "Democratic communities may be unsteady, and be led to action by the impulse of the moment. Like individuals they may be sensible of their own weakness, and may desire the counsels and checks of *friends* to guard them against the turbulency and violence of unruly passion" (I, p. 430; my italics). In contemporary societies, this analogy to individual self-binding has lost whatever appeal it may have had. Once the dividing lines within societies are seen as horizontal rather than vertical, the idea of constitutional precommitment appears in a different light. No group has an inherent claim to represent the general interest. Society has neither an ego nor an id.

Even considered as a horizontal assemblage of individuals or groups society may have some ability to bind itself, in a sense that is partly literal and partly metaphorical. If the precommitment decision is unanimous, it has better claims to be an act of self-binding than if it is a case of a majority imposing its constitutional views on a minority. And even in the latter case, the minority might prefer the majority's constitution to a purely statutory system. If the problems to which the constitution is offered as a solution can be expected to persist indefinitely, the framers can say with some justification that they are acting on behalf of a temporally extended "self" that also includes future generations. Yet these conditions are far from always met. Frequently, constitutions are imposed on minorities and on future generations in the interest of a majority of the founding generation. Also, many apparent acts of self-binding turn out, on closer inspection, to be motivated by partisan motives.

THE MINORITY PROBLEM

This issue arises most obviously when a part of the population is disenfranchised de jure, but also in fully democratic constitution-making. A minority in the constituent assembly may not have the clout to get protection of its rights and interests written into the constitution. Conversely, as Richard Posner writes, "any minority powerful enough to obtain constitutional protection need hardly fear – one might think – adverse legislation."[173] He goes on to cite, however, various reasons for the opposite view, the most important being that a minority may obtain protection by engaging in constitutional logrolling. Yet this is a contingent matter. The minority may or may not be in a position to make deals. Moreover, if the majority has a strong desire to keep the minority down, as in the Bulgarian and Spanish cases that I cited earlier, it may not want to engage in logrolling on this issue.[174] This is not necessarily a question of passion and prejudice. If the British parliament tomorrow decides to adopt a written constitution, the Conservative party and Labour may unite in writing majority voting in single-member districts into the document, thus perpetuating the marginal role of the Liberal party.

In any case, to engage in vote-trading in a constituent assembly, one needs to be present and to have a vote one can trade. Unless delegates to the constituent assembly are chosen by some form of proportional representation, important minorities might suffer de facto disenfranchisement. If they are not represented, they cannot use their votes in logrolling. In fact, even majorities might be de facto disenfranchised. Before the rise of political parties and the invention of proportional representation, there was no assurance that an assembly would be representative of its electorate. The Frankfurt assembly of 1848, for instance, although elected (in principle) by universal male suffrage, included no peasants, only a few small shopkeepers, virtually no manual workers, and no industrial workers at all. Even in more recent times, there is considerable variation in modes of electing members to constituent assemblies, and no assurance that all sizable minorities will be represented.

---

173. Posner (1987), p. 10.
174. For comments on the Spanish case, see Colomer (1995), p. 79.

II. Ulysses Unbound

The Future-Generation Problem

This issue is least serious when the precommitment takes the form of delaying and stabilizing devices. The need to contain impulsive passions, overcome time-inconsistency, and prevent the waste that would be generated by a constantly changing framework are perennial concerns. It is of more concern when the constitution imposes substantive rights and duties combined with stringent supermajority requirements for amendment. It is arbitrary to let one generation impose a virtual ban on abortion or a right to abortion, a ban on income taxes or a right to bear weapons, unrestrained freedom of contract or a right to an adequate income, on its successors. There is no cant-free way in which these procedures can be referred to as *self-binding*. The fact that a later generation may welcome being bound is neither here nor there, since founding generations will rarely be in a position to anticipate this preference.

Groucho Marx noted that future generations have no bargaining power ("What has posterity ever done for me?"). They cannot engage in vote-trading with the current generations. Their only hope, as it were, is that the framers might be moved by concern for their own descendants to take some account of their interests. As mentioned in II.8, several delegates to the Federal Convention argued that the long-term private interest of families could mimic intertemporal impartiality. Yet even this motivation can only be an imperfect substitute if it goes together, as one would expect, with a positive rate of time discounting.

The Partisan-Motive Problem

This issue can be illustrated by recent examples from Norway, France, and Hungary. In Norway, the extremely large oil revenues provided an irresistible temptation to high-level spending by the state. With the proclaimed motive of ensuring the welfare of future generations, the right-wing "Progress Party" then proposed a constitutional amendment stipulating that oil revenues beyond a certain level be earmarked for future pension payments. A more important motive, however, was to make a bid for the votes of the elderly. The public-interest argumentation would have been more credible if use of the funds were to be restricted for the period beginning twenty or fifty years from now.

The Norwegian attempt failed. A conspicuously successful attempt to present partisan goals in the guise of self-binding is provided by the strengthening of the French Conseil Constitutionnel by President Valéry Giscard d'Estaing in 1974. Up to that point, the council had mainly been an instrument of the government of the day in its dealings with unruly parliaments. The opposition had no power to call upon the council to scrutinize laws for their possible unconstitutionality. As president, Giscard d'Estaing offered this weapon to the opposition on a plate, by allowing any group of sixty deputies or senators to bring a law before the council. His motive, however, was not to restrict his own freedom of action. He foresaw, correctly, that the next parliamentary majority would be socialist; also, correctly again, that one of its priorities would be to nationalize important industries; and finally, once more correctly, that the council would strike down such legislation as unconstitutional.[175] He very deliberately and successfully sought to restrain the freedom of action of his successors. I know of no better illustration of Seip's dictum that I cited in the Preface.[176]

A similar example can be taken from the making of the current Hungarian constitution. As John Schiemann has shown, some Hungarian Communists were in favor of a strong constitutional court because they predicted, correctly, that if parliament were to adopt retroactive legislation or extend the statute of limitations for the purpose of bringing them to justice, these measures would be struck down by the court.[177] One Communist delegate to the Round Table Talks said, "We thought that this was one of the institutions which would later be able to prevent a turning against the constitution, a jettisoning of the institution, the creation of all sorts of laws seeking

---

175. Stone (1992), pp. 70–71. Noëlle Lenoir (personal communication) suggests to me that because Giscard d'Estaing was personally committed to a pluralist system and greater autonomy for state institutions, his political philosophy and his strategic interest may have coincided.

176. In their discussion of "why a stubborn conservative would run a deficit," Persson and Svensson (1989) provide another example of how a government can be motivated to act against its own preferences in order to constrain future opposition governments to act in accordance with them.

177. Holmes and Sunstein (1995), p. 290, argue that a similar motivation was at work in the making of the recent Romanian and Bulgarian constitutions: "The 'deep entrenchment' of constitutional provisions, . . . result[s] from the dominance of ex-Communists, eager to 'lock in' their privileges, over the constitution-making process there." They do not spell out, however, the specific provisions that were intended to have this lock-in effect nor which privileges they were intended to lock in.

revenge."[178] One should add, however, that unlike Giscard d'Estaing they were proved right for the wrong reasons. The Hungarian Communists thought they would be able to appoint "reliable" judges as the first members of the court, as an insurance device in case they should become a minority in the new parliament. The court that was actually appointed had a quite different composition. The principle the judges invoked when striking down the retaliatory legislation, namely, that it violated the principle of legal certainty, was not in any way window dressing for Communist self-protection.[179]

THE MOTIVES OF CONSTITUTION-MAKERS

Much of the work on constitutional precommitment (including my own writings in the past) assumes a dichotomy between *framers* and *politicians*, or between higher-order constitutional politics and routine, day-to-day politics.[180] It is commonly assumed that framers and politicians differ not only with regard to their respective tasks, but also with regard to their motives. The framers are assumed to be exempt from the vices of politicians – impulsive passions, standing passions, and private interests – that constitute the rationale for constitution-making. But this, once again, is cant. The idea that framers are *demigods legislating for beasts* is a fiction. The following comment by A. O. Lovejoy on the Federal Convention in Philadelphia is very much to the point:

This assumption of the disinterestedness of the makers of a Constitution – their exemption from the motivations controlling the political behavior of the rest of mankind – was psychologically indispensable in the Convention; certainly few were likely to admit frankly that their own arguments were simply expressions of the 'spirit of faction.' But that they usually were so in fact is, I take it, now recognized by all competent historians; there are, indeed, few better examples of Madison's thesis – the shaping of political opinions

178. Cited after Schiemann (1998).
179. See notably Schwartz (in press), Ch. 4. I might add that in the making of the Italian constitution of 1947, the Communist leader Togliatti opposed the creation of a constitutional court because he thought it was intended as a weapon against a future majority of the Left (Pasquino 1999). Whether or not he was right in assessing the intentions of his opponents, he was certainly wrong in his electoral predictions.
180. See, for instance, Elster (1984), p. 93, and Ackerman (1991).

by private, class, or sectional interest – than are to be found in the debates of the Convention.[181]

In am not denying that framers can be disinterested and dispassionate – indeed, I think many were so motivated at the Federal Convention. Nor am I claiming that these motivations are indispensable for good constitution-making. The argument from efficiency, for instance, does not presuppose particularly lofty motives. I am simply claiming that much of constitutional politics is similar to routine politics as far as motives are concerned, and that we cannot in general expect imperfect framers to create perfect constitutions that will check the imperfections of future politicians. In fact, in II.11 I argued that constitution-makers are *more* likely to be vulnerable to impulsive passions than those whose behavior they are trying to regulate. At the same time, these are also times in which partisan *interest* may assert itself strongly. The political parties or groupings that are represented in the assembly will know that their future depends heavily on the specific institutional arrangements that are written into the constitution. As these decisions may be hard to reverse, they have a strong incentive to ensure that their interests are respected. It is not at all an accident that in Philadelphia the small states were the strongest advocates of equal representation of the states in the Senate.[182]

The motives of constitution-makers matter for how likely they will be to precommit themselves. If they are self-interested, why should they precommit themselves against their tendency to behave in a self-interested way? This is the point made by Przeworski and Limongi. If they are subject to standing passions, why should they precommit themselves against the tendency to act on this motive? This is the point I made against Sunstein. If they are caught up in an emotional frenzy, how can they embody Peter when sober acting to constrain Peter when drunk? It is mainly if the framers are impartial *and* know that impartiality may be lacking on future occasions that they will have an incentive to precommit themselves. Although this case cannot be excluded, I have argued that there is no reason to think that it is typical or frequent.

181. Lovejoy (1961), p. 52, note 16.
182. As Madison (I, pp. 447–48) pointed out, the small states had actually no reason to fear a combination by the large states against them; see also Barry (1989), pp. 292–96. Yet the fear of small states of such combinations seems to have been genuine enough.

II. Ulysses Unbound

Suicide Prevention or Suicide Pact?

Let me return to the Freudian analogy. A constitution is similar to the superego, in the sense of consisting of rigid, inflexible rules that may prevent sensible, optimal behavior on particular occasions. Just as we have seen that the problems created by a private rule may be worse than those it is set up to solve (I.8), the dangers of a sectarian central bank or a dogmatic constitutional court may be worse than the opportunistic behavior these institutions are set up to prevent. In II.11 I discussed how the constitution might set up escape hatches to cope with these second-order problems, by allowing for suspension of the constitution or parts of it during an emergency and by establishing various kinds of checks on central bankers and supreme court justices. Yet as I also argued there, these safety-valve clauses may interfere with the impact of the constitution on the first-order problems. *If the framers try to prevent the constitution from becoming a suicide pact, it may lose its efficacy as a suicide prevention device.*

Chapter III

Less Is More: Creativity and Constraint
in the Arts

III.1. INTRODUCTION

The French novelist Georges Perec wrote a novel, *La Disparition*, in which the letter "e" was nowhere used, and another, *Les Revenentes*, that did not use vowels other than "e."[1] Ernest Hemingway boasted that he could write a compelling short story in six words: "For sale. Baby shoes. Never used."[2] Also, in a science fiction story I once read the protagonist – a writer of fiction – meets an alien who gives him an "adjective magnet" he can use to clean up his stories. If he holds it at some distance, only the longest adjectives are lifted off the page. Held very close, it even takes monosyllabic ones. In between, presumably, there is a distance that would produce prose of optimal sparseness.

The e-less and e-only novels and the six-word short story are extreme examples of the more general idea that artists may impose constraints on themselves in order to create better works of art. In Perec's case, the constraints were entirely idiosyncratic. In other and more frequent cases the constraints take the form of conventions that define a particular genre. Although freely *chosen*, in the sense that it is up to the artist whether to submit to the laws of the genre, they are not *invented* by the artist. In still other cases the constraints are

1. The object that "disappears" in *La Disparition* is in fact the vowel "e." According to Jacques Roubaud, the group of writers, Oulipo, to which Perec belonged sometimes followed the principle that "a text that is written in accordance with a constraint talks about that constraint" (Oulipo 1988, p. 90). Because this is only "sometimes" the case, the infinite regress that would otherwise arise (the need to refer to the constraint is itself a constraint, to which reference must be made, and so on) is avoided. Unlike *La Disparition*, *Les Revenentes* does not respect the rules of French spelling and syntax and thus cannot really be seen as an exercise in "monovocalic constraint" (Bellos 1994, p. 517).
2. Robbins (1997).

imposed from outside, as when a movie director is given a budget and a date by which the shooting must be done. Imposed and chosen constraints frequently coexist. Because of hard technical constraints, prewar jazz recordings could not exceed three minutes. By virtue of a convention or soft constraint, the typical solo on these records did not exceed thirty-two bars.

When an artist chooses to be constrained, we must assume it is because he believes he will benefit artistically from having a smaller choice set. These are cases of standard or intentional precommitment as defined in Chapter I.1. When the constraints are imposed from the outside, he may or may not benefit. If he does, we are dealing with incidental constraint as defined in I.1. Sometimes, an incidental constraint may turn into an essential one, if the artist chooses to abide by the constraint even when it is no longer mandatory. Film directors may abstain from using sound and color even when these technologies are available.

Constraints must leave room for choice. For there to be something for the artist to *create*, the work of art must not be like a crossword puzzle in which there is one and (ideally) only one arrangement of letters that satisfies all the constraints.[3] The creation of a work of art can in fact be envisaged as a two-step process: *choice of constraints* followed by *choice within constraints*. The interplay and back-and-forth between these two choices is a central feature of artistic creation, in the sense that choices made within the constraints may induce the artist to go back and revise the constraints themselves.

There is one apparent exception to the statement that the constraints must leave room for choice. In many temporally extended works of art – literature, film, and music – the ending provides a deeply satisfying sense of inevitability. Each of the previous developments constrains what can happen next, until at the end only one option is left to the artist. (I simplify: a less simplistic treatment is found in III.4.) This narrowing of possibilities is most clearly, if somewhat mechanically, illustrated by the classical crime novel. Yet this sense of inevitability or uniqueness results of course from choices that the artist made with that very purpose in mind. Another exception to the same statement arises when the constraints are so strong that *no* set of combinations of words, tones, and so on satisfies all of them. In III.7

---

3. Some of the work of the Oulipo group has a faint or not-so-faint flavor of the crossword puzzle. Perec himself was a master constructor of crosswords, producing for instance a seven-by-seven crossword with only a single black cell (reproduced in Lecherbonnier et al. 1989, p. 544).

III.1. Introduction

I suggest that Stendhal's unfinished novel *Lucien Leuwen* may illustrate this case. Rather than creating a situation in which there was only one exit, he painted himself into a corner from which there was no exit.

The claim that art needs constraints is far from novel. It is in fact constitutive of the classical artistic stance.[4] It would be wrong to say that this stance emphasizes form at the expense of expression; rather the claim is that *expression needs form*. In a polemic against free verse, Roger Caillois argued that the complete elimination of the constraints of rhyme and meter would create "a prose without firmness, trying to retain by typographical artifice the prestige which disappeared with the constraints that gave rise to it."[5] Writers of free verse are parasites on bound verse; they want the prestige without the discipline and hard work.

Poetry was never anything but the constraints that elevate it above prose. Without constraints, poetry dissolves and evaporates immediately. What capricious tyrant could have imposed them? In which dark hours could these arbitrary and tiresome restrictions have been conceived? And by what perverted mind? And if constraints were nothing but inconveniences, why would poets unanimously have accepted them from the beginning of time, given that nothing forced them to do so? ... We must get rid of the fantasy of some kind of sinister immemorial plot against the liberty of the inspired. The burdens on poetry are coeval with it and constitutive of it. From them derive its power over memory and its other virtues. One cannot tamper with them without fatal consequences. One would break its chains and its power in one fell stroke.[6]

Marx made a similar argument against the confusion of creativity with unconstrained play:

4. Or, more accurately, constitutive of a weak form of the classical stance. The strong form says that artists should abide by *specific* rules, either because they are necessary to *produce* good art (Haugom Olsen 1998, p. 150) or because they facilitate the *reception* of the work of art (Pavel 1998, p. 375). The weak form says only that artists should be constrained by *some* rules, without claiming that any specific rules are superior to others. Thus the strong classicist might recommend playwrights to respect the unities of time, space, and action because of their natural or intrinsic rightness or the greater ease of the spectator that they permit, whereas the weak classicist would recommend them merely as one device, among others, to focus the artistic imagination by constraining it.
5. Caillois (1978), p. 38. Peyre (1944) is a useful collection of statements of this classical stance.
6. Ibid., p. 37. See also Greenberg (1999), p. 48: "Measure in verse and in music, patterns in ballet, ordered necessities of progression in drama, prose or verse fiction, and movies: These have empowered creation at the same time as they have constrained it – and because they have constrained it."

It seems quite far from [Adam] Smith's mind that the individual, 'in his normal state of health, strength, activity, skill, facility', also needs a normal portion of work and of the suspension of tranquillity. Certainly, labor obtains its measure from the outside, through the aim to be attained and the obstacles to be overcome in attaining it. But Smith has no inkling that *this overcoming of obstacles is in itself a liberating activity.* [Labor] becomes attractive work, the individual's self-realization, which in no way means that it becomes mere fun, mere amusement, as Fourier, with grisette-like naiveté, conceives it. Really free working, e.g. composing, is at the same time precisely the most damned seriousness, the most intense exertion.[7]

A more unusual and perhaps controversial claim is that both choice of constraints and choice within constraints can be represented as a form of maximization. Specifically, artists try to *maximize artistic value.* To defend this claim, I do not necessarily have to offer a theory of value in art. For some of my purposes at least, all I need to show is that artists try to make works of art that are as good as they can make them. In doing so I need not refer to *my* conception of artistic value, only to the conception that guides this or that individual artist. As long as that conception is one that allows for choice, the work can be assessed in terms of the extent to which it achieves the aims of the artist, whatever they are. I must stipulate, to be sure, that they are really trying to make works that are good *as works of art*, rather than works that are good as propaganda or works that will bring them a great deal of money or prestige. Yet once this assumption is satisfied, I need not go on to ask whether their conception of a good work of art is a defensible one.

Yet by adopting this radically subjectivist view of rationality one may not be able to say much that is worth saying. To identify the aspects of the creative process that are common to all who aspire to be artists is only a moderately interesting task. By contrast, to understand the creative process that culminates in a great work of art is a task of consuming interest. To make some headway on it, I shall have to sketch a conception of artistic value, the conception by virtue of which I claim that a given work of art is a good or great work of art. By definition, all artists try to satisfy *their* criteria for a good work of art. I claim that good or great artists try to satisfy *my* criteria, or, to put the point in a more restrained and less megalomaniac manner, that the criteria to be discussed here capture important aspects of what great artists try to achieve.

7. Marx (1973), p. 611; italics added.

III.1. Introduction

In trying to make an argument about artistic value, I am un-equipped to do so in other than a naive and dogmatic fashion. As far as I can judge, aesthetic theory is not a highly developed and consensual discipline.[8] Some critics, for instance, take conceptual art seriously; others do not; and it is not clear to me what would allow us to decide who is right.[9] The subjective experience of a work of art may be too malleable by preconceptions and theories to serve as the touchstone by which those theories are to be evaluated.[10] Moreover – a separate point – there is very considerable disagreement on the artistic value of specific works of art. The world's foremost experts on Vermeer were not only taken in by van Meegeren's fake *Supper at Emmaus*, but believed it was better than other works by Vermeer.[11] The will to find beauty in the work of art may generate what it wants to find.[12] Although I believe that some works of art are transhistorically and transculturally better than others, and that the reason they are better is that they better satisfy the criteria to be discussed here, I do not know how I could convince others who do not share this view. Instead, I proceed inductively, by focusing on works of art that are widely believed to be of great value, to see what they may have in common. Actually, works of art widely believed to be flawed or imperfect play an even larger role in my argument. Often it is easier to identify the relevant criteria by looking at cases in which they are *not* satisfied. Needless to say, I do not pretend that reference to what is "widely believed" lets me off the hook. *How* widely believed?

8. The writings I find most congenial are those of Budd (1985, 1995). Yet his first book is mainly criticism of other writers, and the second often too abstract to be of much help in assessing specific works of art.
9. See Elster (1983b), Ch. II.7, for some comments on this issue; see also Shattuck (1997) and Greenberg (1999).
10. As explained by Rawls (1971) for the somewhat analogous case of ethical theories, aesthetics may have multiple "reflective equilibria." I believe, however, that the problem is more serious in aesthetics, because we have fewer firm intuitions in the aesthetic domain than in the ethical one. For a practical instance of this difficulty, consider Rudolf Arnheim's aesthetic criticism of multidimensional art: "The work of Richard Wagner approaches an equilibrium of music and libretto, but this work is so debatable *and so strongly influenced by theory* that by itself it does not represent a valid counterargument" (Arnheim 1957, p. 223; my italics).
11. See the essays collected in Dutton, ed. (1983). It should be said, however, that the most eminent of these experts was in his eighties and half-blind at the time; yet once he "had authenticated *The Emmaus*, a chain of events was set in motion that led to the painting finally appearing in the place of honor as the most spectacular Vermeer of all, in an exhibition of seventeenth-century work" (Werness 1983, p. 32).
12. Elliott (1972), pp. 119–23; also Walton (1988), p. 353.

179

Believed *by whom*? By a self-appointed elite? And what if there are – as is certainly the case – competing elites?

My adoption of what I called the classical stance might seem to imply an antimodernist attitude. As modernism can mean many things, this implication may or may not follow. Toward the end of III.2 I discuss some varieties of – and arguments for – modernism that I do reject. In III.5 I argue that in the twentieth century, artistic conventions have changed so frequently that artists have not always had the time to exhaust their potential, thus inducing an emphasis on originality at the expense of creativity. In III.8 I discuss and reject – as devoid of artistic value – some of the literary and musical compositions of John Cage. These arguments are not intended to be a blanket condemnation of twentieth-century art, or of nonfigurative paintings, atonal music, experimental literature, and so on. There is no question that I feel more at home with Stendhal than with Robbe-Grillet, or with Lester Young than with Ornette Coleman, but these are personal preferences rather than aesthetic judgments. As Malcolm Budd notes, "You can have good grounds for judging that a work you do not find intrinsically rewarding to experience offers an experience that is intrinsically valuable . . . Moreover, we can sometimes make fairly accurate discriminations of artistic value amongst works none of which interests us."[13] Thus when I discuss constraints on narrative in the nineteenth-century novel I do not claim that these are applicable to all fictional writings – but I do have a preference for works that are written under these constraints.

I now proceed as follows. In III.2 I discuss a case of creativity *without* constraints – daydreaming. The nature and significance of artistic constraints are more fully discussed in III.3. In III.4 I consider the relationship among constraints, aesthetic value, and creativity. In III.5 I distinguish creativity (working within constraints) from originality (changing the constraints), arguing that the latter has no intrinsic relation to aesthetic value. The following sections then offer some illustrations and developments of these ideas. In III.6 I consider the impact of Hollywood censorship (the Hays Code) on the artistic value of films, arguing that in some cases the constraints led directors to reach new levels of sophistication. In III.7 I propose an explanation of why Stendhal left *Lucien Leuwen* in an unfinished state (the last of three planned parts was never written). In III.8 I discuss the role of randomization in artistic creation. In III.9 I use pre-1940 jazz as a

13. Budd (1995), p. 175.

vehicle for developing some of the ideas about aesthetic value and creativity that I set out in III.3 and III.4. In III.10, finally, I discuss the view that rules and constraints hamper artistic creation, and the argument that supreme artistic achievements may depend on breaking the rules rather than respecting them blindly.

III.2. DAYDREAMING: CREATIVITY WITHOUT CONSTRAINTS

According to Allen Parducci, "The great bulk of pleasures and pains seem to occur in my private world of anticipations, memories, and fantasies."[14] There are two reasons why these "secondary" mental states are capable of providing pleasure and pain. On the one hand, they may do so because of the pleasure and pain of the corresponding "primary" states. The memory of a good experience, for instance, is itself a good experience. On the other hand, they may enhance or detract from the value we derive from other primary experiences. For instance, "the expectation of prolonged improvement in the future seems to engender dissatisfaction with one's current state."[15] We may refer to the first mechanism as a *consumption effect* and to the second as a *contrast effect*.[16] Often, a given experience will generate oppositely signed consumption and contrast effects. Although the memory of a meal at a superlatively good French restaurant is a good memory, it may detract from the pleasure we derive from later meals at moderately good French restaurants. In general, we cannot tell which effect will dominate – whether one should seek out extraordinary experiences or avoid them.[17]

THE PLEASURES OF DAYDREAMING

For some people, daydreaming is their most potent source of pleasure. Thurber's "The Secret Life of Walter Mitty" provides an example of

14. Parducci (1995), p. 164.
15. Elster and Loewenstein (1992), p. 227.
16. Ibid. For the special case of memory-generated utility, Tversky and Griffin (1991) used the terms "endowment effects" and "contrast effects." Note that contrast effects should not be confused with withdrawal effects (see also Parducci 1995, p. 57, note 3).
17. See also Elster (1999a), Ch. I.6.

someone whose real life was little more than a pretext for daydreaming. When driving through a storm, he turns into a Navy commander on a ship in a hurricane; when driving past a hospital he becomes a world-famous surgeon, and so on.[18] Moreover, good daydreams do not necessarily produce a negative contrast effect when we come back to reality.[19] Unless the daydream is a replica of an actual experience, it does not belong to the same realm as actuality and hence does not induce a devaluation of reality when we return to it. (Similarly, meals at good Mexican restaurants need not be devalued by the superlatively good French meal.) The converse of this proposition, though, is less welcome. Even when our overall happiness might be enhanced by introducing a negative experience as the lower endpoint of the contextual range, we cannot achieve that result simply by imagining one.[20] Whereas memory and anticipation generate contrast effects by altering upper and lower endpoints, mere daydreams often do not.

This being said, it would at least seem that daydreaming about good things is an unambiguous source of pleasure. This was apparently Freud's view:

Let us take the case of a poor orphan boy to whom you have given the address of some employer where he may perhaps find a job. On his way there he may indulge in a day-dream appropriate to the situation from which it arises. The content of his phantasy will perhaps be something like this. He is given a job, finds favour with his new employer, makes himself indispensable in the business, is taken into his employer's family, marries the charming young daughter of the house, and then himself becomes a director of the business, first as his employer's partner and then as his successor. In this phantasy, the dreamer has regained what he possessed in his happy childhood – the

18. Thurber (1996).
19. Although Parducci (1995), p. 39, asserts that Thurber's story "describes the imaginary triumphs of a man for whom being brought back to his modest reality was experienced as a disappointing letdown," the story actually provides no evidence of a contrast effect. I may add, though, that daydreams can have a negative impact on real-life pleasures by other routes, namely, by filling up time that might have been more productively spent in other ways and by generating goals that are too vast. Thus Perec (1990, p. 31) writes about his daydreaming couple that "between these too grand daydreams in which they wallowed with strange self-indulgence, and their total lack of any actual doing, no rational plan, matching the objective necessities to their financial means, arose to fill the gap. The vastness of their desires paralysed them."
20. Parducci (1995), p. 177. Hence the claim by Markman et al. (1993) that people generate "downward counterfactuals" to feel better about their situation should probably be limited to counterfactuals that were once actual.

protecting house, the loving parents and the first objects of his affectionate feeling.[21]

PREMATURE SATIATION

Freud captured the structure of many daydreams. Yet they harbor a general problem. If the orphan has the occasion to rehearse his daydream, he may become impatient at the thought of spending many years as his employer's partner before becoming his successor. Why not have him die of illness as soon as the marriage is secured? For that matter, why not take an even shorter route to happiness by having the employer adopt him upon discovering that the orphan's father was his long-lost childhood friend? In a wonderful phrase by George Ainslie that has inspired much of the present chapter, daydreams have a "shortage of scarcity" that makes them intrinsically unsatisfactory.[22] Thomas Schelling provides an example:

Daydreams escalate. Before I can spend the $10,000 that my poker partner bet because he thought I was bluffing, I revise the figure to $100,000; then I put it in gold at $40 dollars an ounce, spend a couple of years hiking home from a plane crash in Northern Canada, phone my broker to sell and hit the $800 dollar market, and start plotting to invest my two million in something equally good . . . By then I realize that it is all counterfeit if I can make it up so easily. There is no suspense, no surprise, no danger.[23]

A compelling description of a life of daydreaming is found in Georges Perec's first novel, *Les Choses*, in which a young aspiring couple without the means to satisfy their desires take refuge instead in extravagant daydreams, only to find them turning to ashes in the mouth.

At first it felt as if their sensations were multiplied by ten, as if their faculties of sight and sense had been amplified to infinite powers, as if a magical bliss accompanied their smallest gesture, kept in time with their steps,

---

21. Freud (1908), p. 148.   22. Ainslie (1992), p. 258.
23. Schelling (1986), p. 178. Brian Barry has brought to my attention a strikingly similar passage in Lem (1994): "His depression . . . resulted from his inability to fall asleep if he didn't first lie in bed and fantasize a while. In the beginning he pictured the stocks he bought going up and the ones he sold plummeting. Then he pictured having a million dollars. When he got a million, he pictured two, then three, but after five it lost its charm."

suffused their lives: the world was coming towards them, they were going towards the world, they would go on and on discovering it. Their lives were love and ecstasy. Their passion knew no bounds; their freedom was without constraints.

But they were choking under the mass of detail. The visions blurred, became jumbles; they could retain only a few vague and muddled bits, tenuous, persistent, brainless, impoverished wisps. . . . They thought it was happiness they were inventing in their dreams. They thought their imagination was unshackled, splendid and, with each successive wave, permeated the whole world. They thought that all they had to do was to walk for their stride to be a felicity. But what they were, when it came down to it, was alone, stationary and a bit hollow. A grey and icy flatland, infertile tundra.[24]

Daydreaming is a bit like playing solitaire. Here, too, there is a strong temptation to take shortcuts. If there is one card that blocks the whole solitaire from falling into place, many people will cheat by placing it somewhere else. The next time, there may be two cards that need to be rearranged, and soon cheating is so rampant that no pleasure is obtained from playing. One remedy is to switch from solitaire to a card game played with a partner or partners. Besides providing pleasures of interaction, playing with others helps one avoid the quick gains from cheating and achieve the more durable satisfaction generated from tension and tension resolution. As we shall see, the same strategy can also be made to make daydreams more robust against shortcuts and escalations.

CONSTRAINING DAYDREAMS

First, however, let me consider two other strategies. When a child plays make-believe, "he likes to link his imagined objects and situations to the tangible and visible things of the real world."[25] When playing House, a child will say to another, "Now you're the father," and point to a doll, "Here's our baby," and to a hole in the ground, "Here's the bed." In make-believe play, children pace themselves by the constraint of having to match fictional objects one-to-one with real objects.[26] Freud remarks, "The growing child, when he stops playing, gives up nothing but the links with real objects; instead of

24. Perec (1990), pp. 93–94. 25. Freud (1908), p. 144.
26. Pavel (1986), p. 145.

playing, he now *phantasises.* He builds castles in the air and creates what are called *day-dreams.*"[27] Yet this substitutional strategy may fail, because a castle in the air is even less solid than the sand castles that children build. Because it can be extended and embellished effortlessly and instantly, the pleasure provided by a day-dream is much more fragile.

Second, the daydreamer may try to impose some rules on internal narratives. It helps if one imposes the constraint that the daydream be a plausible continuation of my past life (in counterfactual daydreams) or of my present situation (in subjunctive daydreams).[28] This already excludes daydreaming about the eighteenth century or the twenty-second century. The events in the daydream may be further constrained to come about through my agency rather than ex machina. If I can't afford to buy a lottery ticket, I cannot plausibly imagine winning the big prize. Moreover, I might want to minimize the number of accidents and coincidences in my daydream, to make it as lifelike and therefore vivid as possible. But this amounts to something like a proto-theory of the novel, as formally constrained by certain kinds of plausibility.[29]

Some novels are indeed very close to daydreams. According to Freud, this is in fact the typical case.[30] Like daydreams, he argues, novels are exercises in wish-fulfillment. Although Freud mainly discusses "the less pretentious authors of novels, romances, and short stories" who are not "highly esteemed by the critics," he suggests that "even the most extreme deviations from that model could be linked with it through an uninterrupted series of transitional cases."[31] With respect to the more popular authors, he argues,

One feature above all cannot fail to strike us about the creations of these story-writers: each of them has a hero who is the centre of interest, for whom the writer tries to win our sympathy by every possible means and whom he seems to place under the protection of a special Providence. If, at the end

27. Freud (1908), p. 438.
28. The distinction between the two kinds of daydreams is illustrated by *Madame Bovary.* After discovering that she has married a very limited man, Emma starts daydreaming about the men she might have married. Later, after dancing with a man at a ball, she constructs a fictional world with him at the center.
29. For specifications of rules of plausibility for counterfactual scenarios see Kahneman and Tversky (1982) and Kahneman and Miller (1986).
30. The recent assimilation by Walton (1990) of daydreams, children's make-believe games, and fiction was, as we shall see, anticipated by Freud (1908).
31. Freud (1908), pp. 149, 150.

of one chapter of my story, I leave the hero unconscious and bleeding from several wounds, I am sure to find him at the beginning of the next being carefully nursed and on the way to recovery; and if the first volume closes with the ship he is in going down in a storm at sea, I am certain, at the opening of the second volume, to read of his miraculous rescue – a rescue without which the story could not proceed. The feeling of security with which I follow the hero through his perilous adventures is the same as the feeling with which a hero in real life throws himself into the water to save a drowning man or exposes himself to the enemy's fire in order to storm a battery. It is the true heroic feeling, which one of our best writers has expressed in an inimitable phrase: 'Nothing can happen to *me*!' It seems to me, however, that through this revealing characteristic of invulnerability we can immediately recognize His Majesty the Ego, the hero alike of every day-dream and of every story.[32]

The novel, in Freud's opinion, satisfies *two* daydreams: that of the writer and that of the reader.[33] I believe this characterization captures an important aspect of some novels, even of some very great ones. Stendhal, for instance, used his novels as vehicles for vicarious satisfaction (see III.7). For me – perhaps for other readers – the pleasure of reading them has something in common with the daydream-like experience I had when as a boy I read about the heroic exploits of fictional boys of my own age. Julien Sorel's thought when Mathilde de la Mole finally capitulates – "La voilà, cette orgueilleuse, à mes pieds" – has the triumphant ring of many daydreams. Yet of course there is much more to Stendhal than this; and of course many other novels do not – *pace* Freud – fit into this pattern at all.

Joint Daydreams

But even if novels can serve as daydreams, it does not follow that daydreams can be made more satisfactory by abiding by the rules of the novels. Once again, there is nothing that prevents one from cheating or taking short circuits – to go directly for the reward rather than setting up an obstacle and then overcoming it. To overcome this intrinsic obstacle, one can engage in *joint daydreaming*, as memorably described in Dorothy Parker's "The Standard of Living." In this story,

32. Ibid., pp. 149–50.
33. By contrast, Walton (1990) views fiction exclusively as a substitute for the day-dreams and make-believe games *of the reader*. The function of the *author* is only to *authorize*, that is, to provide props for a specific kind of make-believe game.

two office workers, Midge and Annabel, invent a game that they play on their free afternoons:

Annabel had invented the game; or rather she had evolved it from an old one. Basically, it was no more than the ancient sport of what-would-you-do-if-you-had-a-million-dollars? But Annabel had drawn a new set of rules, had narrowed it, pointed it, made it stricter. Like all games, it was the more absorbing for being more difficult.

Annabel's version went like this: You must suppose that somebody dies and leaves you a million dollars, cool. But there is a condition to the bequest. It is stated in the will that you must spend every nickel of the money on yourself.

There lay the hazard of the game. If, when playing it, you forgot, and listed among your expenditures the rental of a new apartment for your family, for example, you lost your turn to the other player. It was astonishing how many – and some of them among the experts, too – would forfeit all their innings by such slips.

It was essential, of course, that it be played in passionate seriousness. Each purchase must be carefully considered, and, if necessary, supported by argument.

Annabel and Midge are pacing each other, each of them serving as a benign constraint on the other's daydreamings.[34] Yet even this carefully constructed folie à deux unravels the day Annabel and Midge, standing before the window of a jeweler's shop, decide to go in and ask about the price of a pearl necklace. Conjecturing that it might cost a thousand or even ten thousand dollars, they are stunned when the salesman tells them that the price is two hundred and fifty thousand:

'Honestly!', Annabel said. 'Can you imagine a thing like that?'

"Two hundred and fifty thousand dollars!' Midge said. 'That's a quarter of a million dollars right there!'

'He's got his nerve!' Annabel said.

They walked on. Slowly the disdain went, completely and slowly as it drained from them, and with it went the regal carriage and tread. Their

---

34. Walton (1990), pp. 18–19, 68, also discusses joint daydreaming, but for the purpose of expanding rather than restricting the mental creations: "Joint fantasizing allows people to pool their imaginative resources. Together they may be able to think of more exciting things to imagine than they could come up with separately." In the present perspective, this effect of joint daydreaming would make them less satisfactory rather than more, as illustrated perhaps by the joint daydreams in *Les Choses*. By contrast, Walton's objection to joint daydreamings – that they "sacrifice ... the vivacity of spontaneous imaginings" – does not apply to the Annabel–Midge game.

shoulders dropped and they dragged their feet; they bumped against each other, without notice or apology, and caromed away again. They were silent and their eyes were cloudy.

Suddenly Midge straightened her back, flung her head high, and spoke, clear and strong.

'Listen, Annabel,' she said. 'Look. Suppose there was this terribly rich person, see? You don't know this person, but this person has seen you somewhere and wants to do something for you. Well, it's a terribly old person, see? And so this person dies, just like going to sleep, and leaves you ten million dollars. Now, what would be the first thing you'd do?'

The story ends here, but it is easy to imagine that the game would soon lose its zest. Once you have indulged in one escalation, what's there to stop you from going on to another? By contrast, a novelist knows that once the book is in the bookstores, he's stuck with it. The knowledge that he is offered only one chance focuses his mind, whereas the indefinite malleability even of joint daydreams dilutes it.

The Role of the Audience

We can use Dorothy Parker's story to bring out another point about the art of the novel, by imagining the interaction between Annabel and Midge taking a slightly different form, with one of them being the narrator and the other the listener. The narrator would be held to the constraints – to produce a plausible narrative of how one could spend a million dollars on oneself – by the knowledge that the listener might cut her short if she violated the constraints. The novelist, similarly, is constrained by his or her expectations about the expectations of the reader. "The role of the artist, properly understood, requires the artist, in the creation of her work, to adopt or bear in mind the role of the spectator."[35] Once the artist has constructed his idea of the reader, he is constrained to write in a way that the reader will find instructive, entertaining, puzzling, moving, disturbing, and so on. Sometimes, the constructed reader will be identical to the author, shorn of his idiosyncratic personal history. In other cases, the intended reader may be a very different creature, as shown by the many cases of male novelists writing for a female audience. Yet however he is

---

35. Budd (1995), p. 11. This holds for any kind of communication. I tell my doctoral students, for instance, to write for a reader who is ignorant, intelligent, and motivated.

constructed, the intended reader of a text serves to discipline the author.[36]

For the reader to have this disciplining function, the author must believe that the reader's freedom in interpreting the text is less than absolute. To be sure, the author intends the reader to have some freedom. As Laurence Sterne wrote in *Tristram Shandy*,

No author, who understands the just boundaries of decorum and good-breeding, would presume to think all: The truest respect which you can pay to the reader's understanding, is to halve this matter amicably, and leave him something to imagine, in his turn, as well as yourself. For my own part, I am eternally paying him compliments of this kind, and do all that lies in my power to keep his imagination as busy as my own.[37]

Yet, as this passage suggests, the freedom is a gift from the author to the reader rather than an inherent property of the reader. In fact, what Sterne is saying is that *the need to ensure freedom for the reader serves as a constraint on the author.*

Yet there can be too much freedom. By saying "too much," I am implicitly offering a criticism of modernist writings. Wolfgang Iser and Thomas Pavel offer two different – not necessarily incompatible – accounts of the relation between indeterminacy and modernism. Referring to the fact that any act of reading must fill in gaps in the text, Iser asserts that

with 'traditional' texts this process was more or less unconscious, but modern texts exploit it quite deliberately. They are often so fragmentary that one's attention is almost exclusively occupied with the search for connections between the fragments; the object of this is not to complicate the 'spectrum' of connections, so much as to make us aware of the nature of our own capacity for providing links.[38]

In Pavel's analysis, the object of indeterminacy is not so much to enhance the reader's awareness of his own interpretive contribution as to mirror the fragmentary nature of the reality the work describes:

Periods of transition and conflict tend to maximize the incompleteness of fictional worlds, which supposedly mirror corresponding features outside

36. What I call the intended reader is also referred to as a "virtual reader" (Prince 1973).
37. Cited after Iser (1974), p. 31.
38. Ibid., p. 280. In II.8 I cite the theory of "inferential art" as an extreme expression of this view.

fiction. In such situations lurks the temptation to lift gradually all constraints on determinacy and to let incompleteness erode the very texture of fictional worlds. Modernism gladly gives in to this temptation.[39]

Although neither Iser nor Pavel offers these accounts as *defenses* of modernism or of the avant-garde, it may be instructive to see why the cited passages would fail if read normatively. In the first account, modernism fails to provide any reason why the reader should be *motivated* to find connections and to learn about his contribution to the joint enterprise. For the reader to be so motivated, he must believe that once the links have been made, something of interest will emerge *over and above the mere activity of linking*. In the second account, modernism fails because it rests on an erroneous criterion of adequacy of a text to its object. Just as a flawed world is not better represented by a flawed text,[40] a fluid or chaotic world is not better represented by a fluid or chaotic text. The features by virtue of which the world may be fluid or chaotic are very different from those by virtue of which a text may be fluid or chaotic.

III.3. CONSTRAINTS AND CONVENTIONS IN THE ARTS

The restrictions imposed on or chosen by the artist can take many forms. A basic distinction is between *hard constraints* and soft constraints or *conventions*. Hard constraints are formal, material, technical, or financial restrictions on the selection and combination of the constituent units of the given medium. Conventions, as the word indicates, are restrictions that constitute a specific genre such as the sonnet or the classical symphony. I shall discuss them in that

---

39. Pavel (1986), p. 109.
40. An example is provided by the comments on a new edition of Joyce's *Ulysses* made by Fritz Senn, director of the Zürich James Joyce Foundation: "Joyce did take tremendous care with some details, but if he didn't care enough with others, is it someone else's task to change him into a different kind of writer than he is? Why should you change an author when he is not infallible? 'Ulysses' is about a deficient, fallible world" (Sarah Lyall, "'Ulysses' in Deep Trouble Again; A New Edition Purges What May Have Been Joyce's Errors and Enrages Critics," *New York Times*, June 23, 1997). In Elster (1978), p. 91, note 10, I cite several instances of the view that contradictory statements about the world reflect contradictions in the world and are, therefore, somehow more adequate to it than a coherent account would be.

order. (Discussion of what I call formal constraints is postponed until III.4.)

Obvious intrinsic constraints arise in music, where composers must take account of the physical limitations of human performers. Architects, too, are limited by the structural constraints of their material. The intention behind the Beauvais cathedral could not be realized, given the techniques available at the time. More subtle intrinsic constraints derive from the relation to the audience. In the temporally extended arts, such as literature and music, readers or listeners take in one element at a time. If they do so in their private home or in another context where they are free to stop reading or listening when their attention flags, the author or composer is to some extent constrained to keep their attention continuously alive. For a novelist, for instance, it is risky to use strategies of the type "One step backward, two steps forward"– using the first chapters to create the background and then begin to unfold the plot. Unless the presentation of the background is intrinsically interesting, the reader might drop out. The constraint becomes less important if the author or composer can count on having a captive audience. Those who have paid to attend the symphony performance are unlikely to leave at the beginning of the first movement if they find it strange or boring. Although children who are read aloud to may fidget during the opening chapters, they are usually more willing to be bored than they would be if it were up to them when to stop.

Prior to the age of home listening, as provided by radio or recordings, composers could count on having a captive audience in the concert hall. Although freeing them from the constraint of having to provide a continuous stream of satisfaction, this arrangement – like radio broadcasting, but unlike recordings – subjected them to a constraint of non-repeatability. Reading a novel, you can always go back to an earlier passage if you think you missed something. Because instant replay is not possible in live musical performances, composers have an incentive to use repeated variations of the same basic theme. If this – conjectural and at most partial – explanation of why music makes prominent use of repetition has something to it, we would expect oral literature also to be more repetitive than written literature, as indeed seems to be the case.

III. Less Is More

Endgames in literature and music have different structures and impose different constraints on the artist. In novels, what Jane Austen called the "tell-tale compression of the pages,"[41] which allows the reader to infer that the ending is near,[42] is a constraint that makes it more difficult for novelists to use the musical device of false endings.[43] Because this constraint is removed in oral literature, we would expect this genre to use false endings more frequently. I do not know whether that is in fact the case. I raise this possibility simply to suggest how some very elementary aspects of the relation between a work of art and its audience may constrain the artist, assuming of course that the work is in fact shaped by expectations about an audience.

IMPOSED CONSTRAINTS

These are especially important in film. Before 1926–27, there was no sound in films. Before the mid-1930s, color was not easily available. Film directors had no choice but to work under these constraints. At all times, films have budget constraints that create severe limits on the freedom of the director. It may also be limited by the demand that a film make as much money as possible, but that is an *objective* that is to be realized within constraints, not itself a constraint. An independent director may be able to transform the demand into a constraint and substitute his or her own objective, by aiming at some "satisfactory" level of profit rather than maximal profit. A related but partly independent constraint is that films are usually made with a time deadline, for instance because the main actors are booked to make another film at some specific date. British film directors must employ a certain proportion of British actors and crew in order to get subsidies. As further discussed in III.6, the Hays Code set constraints on the portrayal of romantic and sexual relationships. Finally, films

41. *Northanger Abbey*, vol. II, Ch. XVI. In many modern editions, the book is published in one volume together with *Persuasion* and preceding it, thus making the reference to the compression of the pages hard to understand.
42. As Delia Laitin points out to me, paperback novels that append the first pages from the author's forthcoming hardcover novel can produce endings that arrive *too early*, relative to the expectations of the reader.
43. They can and do use the device of *surprising* endings – endings that go against the expectations that are set up by the novel itself, given the conventions of the genre. But that is a more sophisticated issue (Kermode 1967).

like theater may "obey psychological constraints: a play cannot usually sustain the audience's attention for more than a couple of hours; a movie's duration depends on the eye's tolerance to strain."[44]

Many nineteenth-century novelists, including Dickens, George Eliot, and Dostoyevsky, faced the constraint of writing for serialization. An obvious effect of this format is that the writer is under a constant deadline. A more important effect is that it leaves no room for the reworking and reshuffling of dialogue and plot that are otherwise essential parts of the novelist's craft. Proust endlessly rewrote the manuscript to *A la recherche du temps perdu*, and also added much at the proof stage. Serialized authors can either invent the basic plot at the outset, or write it as they go along. (They are not the only ones to face this choice. As we shall see in III.7, Stendhal, who did not write for serialization, adopted the first method in *Le rouge et le noir* and the second in *Lucien Leuwen*.) If they use the second method, they are like the improvising musician for whom a freely invented phrase or even an unintentional mistake comes to serve as a constraint on the next invention (III.8). The risk of losing artistic control is obviously greater the shorter the interval between the installments. This may be why Dickens, for instance, preferred the monthly format to the weekly,[45] which does not exclude that shorter intervals may, qua incidental constraints, provide greater benefits.[46] Artistic control is even more difficult to achieve, of course, in open-ended serializations such as TV soap operas.

Music recording was for a long time constrained by the seventy-eight rpm format and the eight-inch record and thus limited to three minutes. Occasionally producers resorted to twelve-inch records, but as they did not fit on all record players they were commercially less interesting. Longer pieces of music could of course be distributed over several records, but not without interruption of the musical flow and thus loss of aesthetic value. In early jazz, both twelve-inch records

44. Pavel (1986), p. 98.
45. "Dickens's eloquent testimony to his sense of limitation and constraint in the shorter form cannot be overemphasized. During an early stage of the writing of *Hard Times*, he told Forster that 'the difficulty of the space is CRUSHING' for anyone who has 'had an experience of patient fiction-writing with some elbow-room always, and open places in perspective'" (Engel 1967, p. 170).
46. "*Hard Times* satisfies the modern taste (in the arts alone) for economy – in fiction, for spare writing and clearly demonstrable form. Dickens was capable of both, but they were not natural or congenial to him, and he chose to employ them under the duress of limited space" (ibid., p. 172).

and multirecord recordings were extremely rare. In practice, jazz musicians were limited to three minutes. Elsewhere I have argued, "Jazz improvisation at a high level of quality is so hard to sustain that the '78' record with three minutes' playing time was just about optimal."[47] I develop that claim in III.9.

In his study of Fred Astaire's dancing, John Mueller observes that "he was working within considerable constraints, some of them self-imposed."[48] He enumerates five kinds of constraints. First, there are choreographic constraints; for instance, Astaire almost never used falls, and didn't even go down on his knees until his twelfth film. Second, there are emotional constraints that follow from the format of the romantic comedy. Third, there are musical constraints inherent in the popular tunes of his day. "Astaire may have found the popular song's efficiency of form and style in keeping with his economical approach to choreography."[49] Fourth, there were financial constraints. Astaire fully accepted that his films had to make money, but as a constraint rather than as an objective. Finally, the film medium itself imposes constraints. Astaire usually stayed close to his partner, for instance, because the camera cannot deal well with wide spaces. He also used gimmicks – "setting up obstacles that he seems to take a Buster Keaton-like pleasure in overcoming."[50] In Mueller's opinion, though, the choreography sometimes suffered when Astaire concentrated on effect, as in a famous scene from *Royal Wedding* where Astaire dances on the walls and the ceiling.

The performing arts were traditionally subject to the constraint that mistakes could not be corrected: there was no "Undo" button. Modern recording technology has removed this constraint, by allowing for repeated takes of the same piece of music. The making of films routinely involves repeated shots of each scene, of which the best can then be selected for release. Fred Astaire, for instance, sometimes shot his dancing scenes as many as fifty times. Moreover, whereas a live performance must be seamless, technology allows one to take bits and parts from several takes and piece them together

47. Elster (1983b), p. 80.   48. Mueller (1985), p. 19.
49. Ibid. Arnheim (1957), pp. 222–23, offers a more general argument: "Great actors often prefer mediocre plays that allow them to work almost by improvisation and thus to reserve the performance essentially to the expression of body and voice; whereas, on the other hand, their genius often spells danger to the great works of dramatic literature. Similarly, good dancers and the makers of silent films have a preference for simple, clear-cut music, which may not be first-rate."
50. Ibid., p. 22.

into one coherent whole. Astaire had a strong aversion to this practice. He insisted on his dance scenes being shot in one continuous cut or, at least, in a small number of uninterrupted chunks. Before Astaire arrived on the scene, a ninety-second dancing scene might use a dozen shots; with Astaire the norm was two or three shots for a three-minute dance.[51] For instance, "the toss of the cane into the umbrella stand in one solo is seen in a single shot, though it would be far easier to devote one shot to the toss and another to a close-up of the landing."[52]

The person or institution commissioning a work of art is often in a position to impose constraints. A piece of music written for some specific occasion may have to be of a specific duration. In fact, composers may demand constraints. Thus when asked whether he could write music for a circus ballet, Igor Stravinsky is reported to have sent the following telegram: "I accept: how many minutes?"[53] A painter who does a portrait of a patron or his wife is constrained to make them appear in a flattering light – at least in their own eyes. In spite of this constraint, good painters may also manage to communicate something about the subjects that they would not have liked had they seen it – the fact, for instance, that they are not perceptive enough to see it. Just as an author writes for an intended reader, a painter must paint for an intended viewer. In general, there is no reason why the subject of a portrait should be that viewer.[54] Architects almost invariably face heavy constraints – financial, utilitarian, and sometimes aesthetic. If the principal asks the artist to submit several plans, or several artists to submit plans, and then selects one, he is not imposing a constraint but inviting the artist to anticipate his selection criteria.

SELF-IMPOSED CONSTRAINTS

Overall, essential constraints are less important in part than incidental ones, yet they are not insignificant. An important self-imposed constraint is the choice of format. Once the painter has chosen a canvas of a given size, he is stuck with it. The decision to draw with charcoal, which cannot easily be erased, is a bit like Astaire's self-imposed constraint to have his dances shot in one continuous sequence. In both

---

51. Ibid., p. 27.   52. Ibid., p. 34.
53. I owe this story to Edmund Phelps. For other examples, see "Route to Creativity: Following Bliss or Dots?" *New York Times*, September 7, 1999, Section F3.
54. Brilliant (1991), p. 40.

cases, the artist deliberately increases the cost of making mistakes, in the hope that fewer mistakes will ensue. A composer of songs may constrain himself by his choice of text. The strategy of self-binding is also illustrated by the Perec novels that I mentioned at the beginning of the chapter. Other examples include Woody Allen's decision to shoot *Manhattan* in black and white, although color was available, and Mel Brooks's decision to make *Silent Movie*, although sound was available. By letting Marcel Marceau, the mime, speak the only words in the film, Brooks makes it clear that the lack of sound elsewhere was by choice rather than by necessity. Fasting is not like starving.[55]

CONVENTIONS

Yet although such *inventions* of constraints may be infrequent, the *choice* of subjecting oneself to an artistic convention is very common indeed. An alcoholic, for instance, could impose hard constraints on himself by moving to a country where alcohol is totally unavailable. He cannot invent a country with these limitations, but he can choose to live in one. Similarly, an artist can choose to be restricted by working within a genre with conventionally defined rules and norms. This option is in fact much more restraining than freely invented constraints. In poetry, for instance, there is only a finite number of conventional forms (sonnet, ballad, and so on) and a finite number of verse forms (hexameter, alexandrine, and so on). By contrast, the number of self-imposed limitations is very large indeed. If Perec had wanted to write a novel excluding two vowels, he would have had fifteen combinations to choose among; with three vowels, there are twenty possibilities; with consonants also included, the numbers become very large. Thus even if constraints serve to limit the feasible set to a manageable size and thus enable the artist to make meaningful choices, allowing him total freedom to choose the constraints may only re-create the *embarras de richesses* at an earlier stage.

Conventions regulate many aspects of works of art. In music, the conventions are purely formal: there is no musical content that is prescribed or proscribed. In literature, conventions regulate form as well as content. Thus consider two conventions of nineteenth-century (pre-Pirandello) theater. One is that the final resolution of the action does not occur before the very end of the play. The other is that

55. Sen (1993), p. 40.

characters in the play must never appear to be aware of the fact that they are nothing but characters in a play. Toward the end of Ibsen's *Peer Gynt*, when Peer is afraid of drowning, the strange passenger tells him that "one does not die in the middle of the fifth act," thus simultaneously violating the second convention and exploiting the first. In painting, conventions obviously regulate form, but also subject matter: not only in defining the repertoire of subjects, notably in religious painting, but also in creating artificial symbolic meanings for specific elements in the painting. One might not, for instance, suspect the importance of seduction in Vermeer's paintings if one did not know it was conventionally associated with the topoi of wine, music, and letter-writing that they abundantly portray. Noël Carroll argues that "sight gags" in movies were regulated by a convention that the perceptual capacities of the characters in the film are the same as those of the audience. Without this convention, we could not make sense of a gag in a black-and-white movie by Jacques Tati in which a tire with wet leaves stuck to it is confused with a funeral wreath. "In a color film, a tire with wet leaves stuck to it would not be visually confused with a funeral wreath; this sight gag is persuasive only because the film is black and white."[56]

Two Views of Artistic Conventions

Conventions and constraints exist for entirely different reasons. If playwrights in seventeenth-century France wrote in alexandrines and respected the unity of space, time, and action, the explanation is not to be found in technology, money, time, or choice. Instead, the convention obviously had something to do with the expectations of other artists or of the public. There are two ways of looking at the matter. In one view, artistic conventions are like social norms – non-instrumental rules of behavior maintained by the sanctions that others impose on violators. In another view, conventions are like coordination equilibria – useful but arbitrary devices similar to the rule of driving on the right hand of the road. Whereas social norms are enforced by others, coordination equilibria are self-enforcing.

56. Carroll (1996), pp. 56–57. A similar example is the convention that when non-English characters appear in an English novel, they speak as if they were English. Thus in Hill (1998), p. 17, a piece of dialogue between two Italian policemen is reported as follows: "'Well,' he enquired, 'is our peerless poet packed?' He added with a grin, 'Note the alliteration. I worked it up on the way over in the car.'"

Social norms range from the apparently trivial to matters of life and death. They include the rules of etiquette described by Bourdieu and Proust no less than the codes of vendetta still in effect in some Mediterranean countries.[57] They are characterized by four features. First, they are non-outcome-oriented injunctions to act. Second, they are shared with the other members of one's society or of some relevant subgroup. Moreover, all members know that all are subject to the norms, and know that they know this, and so on. Third, because all share the norms, group members can enforce them by sanctioning violators. Sanctions range from various forms of avoidance behavior through social ostracism to outright persecution. Finally, norms are also sustained by the internalized emotion of shame.

An argument for seeing conventions in art as social norms might go as follows. Artists, critics, and audiences view conventions as normatively compelling. They embody the right way of doing things. The unities of time, space, and action, for instance, are seen as natural constraints. Playwrights or painters who violate the conventions are subject to a wide array of penalties and sanctions. Their books are not only not bought but, like Joyce's *Ulysses*, banned. Their paintings are stigmatized as made by *fauves*. Ibsen had to produce a version of *A Doll's House* with a happy ending to get it staged in Germany because his German publisher found it shocking. Similarly, "the eighteenth-century public could not accept the death of Cordelia in *King Lear* and preferred the modified version by Nahum Tate in which Cordelia survives and marries Edgar."[58] Also, "in the neoclassical period Shakespeare stands condemned for introducing an ungrateful, scheming soldier in Iago (for soldiers are typically honest and straightforward)."[59]

In another view, an artistic convention is a special kind of equilibrium, often referred to as a "coordination equilibrium" and characterized by two features.[60] First, as in all equilibria, when all follow the convention, nobody wants to deviate. Second, when all follow the convention, nobody wants anyone else to deviate either. The choice

---

57. Elster (1989c, Ch. III; 1999a, Ch. III).
58. Pavel (1986), p. 34. Schelling (1986), p. 177, argues, if I understand him correctly, that such substitute endings would have to be preemptive rather than reactive. It would not make sense, according to him, for a spectator of the original play to demand a revision so that he or she could watch it with a happy ending. If this reasoning is correct, as I believe it is, "interactive art" would suffer from the same lack of constraints as daydreams.
59. Haugom Olsen (1998), p. 150.   60. Lewis (1969).

between driving on the left side and the right side of the road illustrates this situation. A more fanciful example is provided by the rule that governs the night life of Brooklyn mafiosi: "Everybody who had a girl friend took her out on Friday night. Nobody took his wife out on Friday night. The wives went out on Saturday night. That way there were no accidents of running into somebody's wife when they were with their girl friends."[61] Clearly, all that matters is coordination on one rule. Taking girlfriends out on Saturdays and wives on Fridays would do just as well, as long as everyone did the same. Social disaster would strike, however, if people followed different conventions, because then one might risk meeting a friend with his wife when taking one's girlfriend out. As Harold Macmillan complained, "In the old days you could be absolutely sure that you could go to a restaurant with your wife and not see a man that you knew having lunch with a tart. It was all kept separate but this does not seem to happen these days."[62]

An argument for seeing conventions in art as coordination equilibria might go as follows. Art, like other forms of self-realization, requires competent judges; otherwise it becomes a "private language," a morass of subjectivity.[63] If art varied very widely in form and subject matter, quality would be hard to evaluate and appreciate. Even if each artist worked under tight self-imposed constraints, intersubjective standards would be weak if different artists chose different constraints. However, if all artists work under the same constraints, their works can be compared and standards established by the community of artists and critics. Hence conventions in art possess both features of coordination equilibria. Since each artist wants to be judged by others, he has no incentive to deviate from the common framework that makes competent appreciation and self-realization possible. Since he wants his judges to be competent, he has no reasons for wishing others to deviate either.

The distinction between coordination equilibria and social norms is not a hard-and-fast one. When a convention serves as a coordination equilibrium, it will usually also become a social norm.[64] If we take the example of driving on the right side of the road, those who unilaterally drive on the left not only run the risk of an accident, but

61. Pileggi (1987), p. 90.
62. From an excerpt of his diary, serialized in *The Sunday Times*, June 11, 1989.
63. See Elster (1986a) and Greenberg (1999), p. 47.
64. The following draws on Elster (in press).

also expose themselves to the disapproval of other drivers who might be hurt by their reckless behavior. Similarly, an artist who deviates from a convention imposes a cost on other artists, in the form of the loss of a competent judge. The converse does not hold, however. In the arts and elsewhere, there are many social norms that do not serve to coordinate anything.

III.4. CONSTRAINTS, VALUE, AND CREATIVITY

The process of artistic creation is guided by the aim of *maximizing aesthetic value under constraints*.[65] (From now on I use "constraint" in a broad sense that includes both conventions and constraints as more narrowly defined earlier.) Creativity is the ability to succeed in this endeavor. To explain what I mean by these statements, I shall first say a bit more about constraints; then argue that artists are in fact engaged in a process of maximization; and finally explain what I mean by aesthetic value. On this background I then proceed to discuss the relation among constraints, value, and creativity.

CHOICE OF CONSTRAINTS AND WITHIN CONSTRAINTS

I have argued elsewhere that

any given piece of human behavior may be seen as the end result of two successive filtering devices. The first is defined by the set of structural constraints which cuts down the set of abstractly possible courses of action and

---

65. A thoughtful referee of the present book questioned the value of applying the idea of maximization to artistic creation. The following comments will serve both as a response to the question, and as a preview of arguments developed here. (1) The idea of a maximum implies that in a good work of art, "nothing can be added and nothing subtracted" without loss of aesthetic value. The idea of a good work of art as embodying both fullness and parsimony seems naturally captured by the idea of a maximum. (2) By arguing that artists aim at producing a *local* maximum rather than "the" best work they can make, I believe I can make sense of several properties of works of art and their creation. (a) Many artists experiment with small variations before they decide on the final version. (b) The notion of a "minor masterpiece" has a natural interpretation in this framework. (c) The notion of a "flawed masterpiece" also receives a natural interpretation. (3) By arguing that artists choose both constraints *and* within constraints I aim at imposing some structure on artistic creation, by viewing it as a two-step process. It is not merely a question of artists producing the best work they can, but of choosing a framework that is optimally suited to let them do so.

reduces it to the vastly smaller subset of feasible actions. The second filtering process is the mechanism that singles out which member of the feasible set shall be realized. Rational-choice theories assert that this mechanism is the deliberate and intentional choice for the purpose of maximizing some objective function. [66]

Applied to the present set of issues, this general framework suggests two questions. First, given that some of the constraints may themselves be selected rather than imposed from the outside, what is the mechanism by which they are selected? Second, what is the relation between this mechanism and the one that selects an element from the feasible set? In the case of a work of art, both selections ought, ideally, to take the form of intentional choice for the purpose of maximizing aesthetic value. In practice, as we shall see, it cannot work in this way. Yet to the extent that this idea captures one aspect of artistic creation, it is clear that we are not dealing with two successive and independent filters. Rather, choice of constraints and choice within constraints interact. A writer may initially plan to develop an idea in a full-length novel, and then, finding that it will not sustain that format, turn it into a short story of thirty pages. (Whether for conventional or intrinsic aesthetic reasons, the length distribution of fiction writing seems to be bimodal. The novella format is rarer than either the novel or the short story.) A painter may similarly experiment with the choice of constraints as well as experiment within constraints. He or she may, for instance, experiment with painting the same subject both in a small format and a larger one, and choose the one or the other as a function of the within-constraint experimentation.[67] In the following, though, I disregard this complication.

CREATION AS CONSTRAINED MAXIMIZATION

Whatever it is that the artist is maximizing, he can be aiming only at a *local maximum*. A novelist, for instance, does not set out to create a global maximum, such as *the best* novel of a certain kind. Let me first argue that artists are in fact striving to realize a maximum, and

66. Elster (1984), p. 113.
67. The choice of format follows different rules in the various arts. A painter chooses the size of the canvas before he or she begins to fill it; a writer does not. The size distribution of canvases is unimodal; that of writings bimodal. Music is like writing in the first respect, like painting in the second.

then explain why the maximum they seek must be local rather than global.

One piece of evidence for the view that artists are engaged in maximizing is the widespread belief that in a good work of art nothing can be added and nothing be subtracted (Aristotle, *Poetics* 1451^a 33 – 35). For instance, "each scene in a good film must be so well planned in the scenario that everything necessary, and only what is necessary, takes place within the shortest space of time."[68] This ideal of *simultaneous fullness and parsimony* is but another way of stating the idea of a maximum.[69] Another piece of evidence is the widespread practice of artists of *experimenting with small variations* until they "get it right." Natural selection – the paradigm of a process that tends to produce local maxima – works exactly in this way, by screening successive small mutations until a state is reached in which any further feasible mutation would detract from reproductive fitness. Because of genetic drift and a constantly changing environment, these maxima are not immune to further change, but that is irrelevant to the present argument.

An even better model for artistic creation is provided by Eilert Sundt, a nineteenth-century Norwegian sociologist who applied Darwinian principles to explain the evolution of boat design:

A boat constructor may be very skilled, and yet he will never get two boats exactly alike, even if he exerts himself to this end. The variations arising in this way may be called *accidental*. But even a very small variation usually is noticeable during the navigation, and it is then *not accidental* that the sailors come to *notice* that boat which has become improved or more convenient for their purpose, and that they should recommend this to be *chosen* as the one to *imitate* . . . One may believe that each of these boats is perfect in its way, since it has reached perfection by one-sided development in one particular direction. Each kind of improvement has progressed to the point where further development would entail defects that would more than offset the advantage . . . And I conceive of the process in the following way: when the idea of new and improved forms had first been aroused, then *a long series of prudent experiments*, each involving extremely small changes, could lead to

---

68. Arnheim (1957), p. 23. As he also observes, "To show complete incidents would frequently be dull and inartistic, because superfluous" (ibid.). One difference between romantic films such as *Jules et Jim* and sentimental films such as *The English Patient* is that in the former the camera never dwells on a scene once a point has been made.

69. For a fuller discussion of the idea of local maximum, see Ch. I of Elster (1984).

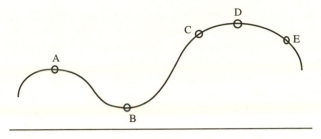

Fig. III.1

the happy result that from that boat constructor's shed there emerged a boat whose like all would desire.[70]

I argue later that in the arts the small variations are partly consciously sought out and partly generated by the unconscious. The selection is always the work of the conscious mind. The practice of experimenting with small variations is in fact extremely common in all the arts. Some artists conform to the dictum "Conception lente, exécution rapide," but for each Picasso, Mozart, or Stendhal there must be ten or one hundred who draft and redraft, discard and start up again, until they think they have it right. In the performing arts, rehearsals and repeated performances have a similar function of honing and fine-tuning. In III.9 I discuss the importance of small variations in jazz, not in improvisation but in building what I call "sculpted solos" over time.

We may interpret some other commonly used expressions as evidence that artists strive for *local* maxima.

In Figure III.1, the vertical dimension represents aesthetic value. The horizontal axis is a quantitative measure of works of art along some relevant dimension. For specificity, we may think of the various points on the curve as representing developments of the same literary theme in works of fiction of various lengths. The short story A and the novel D are both local maxima. In the diagram, the novel is also the global maximum (although of course other novels, differing along other dimensions, might be even better). The short story may be characterized by the common phrase "a minor masterpiece": it is a masterpiece because it is a local maximum, and minor because it is a low-level local maximum. A whole genre in fact may be minor, such as the crime novel, yet within it there may be some masterpieces.

70. Sundt (1976), pp. 211–12.

Insufficiently and excessively developed novels such as C and E may be characterized by another common phrase, "a flawed masterpiece."[71] An insufficiently developed novel might be one in which the tensions of the plot are resolved prematurely, before the groundwork has been laid to make the outcome appear plausible. Imagine a truncated *Pride and Prejudice* in which Elizabeth Bennet accepts Darcy the first time he proposes. An excessively developed plot would be if after the end of the novel as we know it, Jane Austen went on to describe their domestic bliss.[72] (See also the comments on *Scarface* in III.6.) The two flawed masterpieces shown in the diagram are superior to the minor masterpiece. Citing a comment by T. S. Eliot on Akenside, Malcolm Budd writes, "A poet who has nothing worth saying may in one sense write better than another who does have something interesting to say, but what she writes may be a poem of less value."[73] The minor masterpiece is in turn superior to the novella B, which has neither the crispness of a short story nor the richness of a novel.[74] (Here I am assuming that the infrequency of the novella is due to its intrinsic artistic limitations rather than to convention.)

Needless to say, this is all extremely schematic, but I think it captures one aspect of how we (and artists) think about art. The perennial French debate over the respective merits of Racine and Shakespeare, for instance, may be seen in this perspective. For critics such as Gide, the perfection of Racine's plays and the formal flaws of Shakespeare's make them prefer the former. Yet even though Racine's best works probably do embody the idea of a maximum better than almost any other plays, it might be a local rather than a global one. Racine might stand to Shakespeare in the relation of A in the diagram to either C or

---

71. See also the discussion of a "great flawed film" in Truffaut (1985), p. 327.
72. Kermode (1967, p. 23), writing about Dostoyevsky's *The Idiot*, implies that it is excessively developed and would have been better but for the "completely perfunctory and traditional [conclusion], in which he tells you what became of the surviving characters." Similarly, artists who specialize in charcoal drawing, which cannot easily be erased, run the risk of overshooting D in the diagram and going all the way to E by adding too many lines to their portraits. On occasion, they have been saved by the model dying on them when they get to C, which, although suboptimal, is more nearly optimal than E.
73. Budd (1995), p. 105.
74. Rather than saying that the novella has neither the virtues of the short story nor those of the novel one might claim that it manages to have both sets of virtues. This indeed is the suggestion made by Richard Ford (1998), in his editorial introduction to *The Granta Book of the American Long Story*. (Actually, his claim is that the novella is free of the problems that beset, respectively, the short story and the novel.) But if that is so, why are there so few novellas?

D. Similarly, Tyler Cowen (personal communication) asks whether "Dickens's *Bleak House* does not reach higher peaks than anything by Austen, and for reasons related to Dickens's imperfect taste." The implied suggestion is that lack of taste can be a condition for the highest achievements, perhaps because it goes together with a recklessness and willingness to take risks that we do not find in more controlled writers. A weaker statement might be that *Bleak House* is better than any of Austen's novels in spite of (not because of) Dickens's lack of taste. I am not endorsing or disagreeing with any of the value judgments discussed in this paragraph, merely suggesting that the language of local and global maxima seems to be an appropriate one for stating them.

EMOTION AND AESTHETIC VALUE

I now turn to the nature of the maximand, or aesthetic value. Art, as I understand it, can have perceptual, cognitive, or emotional value. Ultimately, however, I believe, the main value of art is emotional. More accurately, perhaps, whereas the value of a work of art can be exclusively emotional, it cannot be exclusively cognitive. Hence I disagree with Noël Carroll when he writes, "Some paintings may be about the nature of painting – maybe much of Frank Stella's work is about the convention of framing; and some films, like *Zorn's Lemma* by Hollis Frampton, may be about the nature of film. These works may be articulated in such a way that they address cognition exclusively."[75] My reasons for disagreeing are simple: if the artist only wants to convey a new cognition, he or she ought to use the medium that is tailor-made for this purpose, namely, that of logical argument and factual exposition. The alternative, it seems to me, would be to say that art can offer "ineffable insights"– a claim that by its very nature does not lend itself to scrutiny or criticism. And can insights be nonpropositional? ("What cannot be said cannot be said, and you can't whistle it either.") And if insights are – as I think – of necessity propositional, do we need art to state them?[76]

---

75. Carroll (1997), p. 193.
76. I am not unaware that in these brief remarks I address, at a very superficial level, issues that have preoccupied the best minds for centuries. To make them slightly less superficial and more clearly relevant, I should make it clear that I do not address notions of *beauty* that might apply both to natural objects such as sunsets and to man-made objects. Moreover, within the class of man-made objects I am

I distinguish between two sources of emotional satisfaction through the arts. On the one hand, *many* works of art can generate non-aesthetic emotions – joy, grief, and the like. On the other hand, *all* works of art, if they have any artistic value at all, induce specifically aesthetic emotions by means of rhythm, echoes, symmetries, contrasts, repetitions, proportion, and similar devices that fall under the general heading of "ordered complexity." The paradigm, for me, is the *Goldberg Variations* as played by Glenn Gould. (It is also a work devoid – for me, at least – of non-aesthetic emotions.) The specifically aesthetic emotions include wonder, amazement, surprise, humor, relief, and release. Some of them may even be akin to the emotion we experience after understanding a mathematical theorem – a feeling of awe before a dénouement that is both surprising ex ante and inevitable ex post. Note, however, that the ability of cognition to generate aesthetic emotions does not vindicate the claim that the sole value of a work of art may be a cognitive one.

In literature and music, sublime artistic effects are created when these two emotional effects go together and reinforce each other. As if by magic, the pleasure of a rhyme that falls into place adds to the poignancy of the words. Although the components are analytically separable, they are not experienced separately.[77] The synergy is beyond exact analysis, but we can recognize it when it works. As Montaigne said, "Just as the voice of the trumpet rings out clearer and stronger for being forced through a narrow tube so too a saying leaps forth much more vigorously when compressed into the rhythms of poetry."[78] For a specific example, consider the following comment on Astaire's dancing:

Astaire is . . . very aware of the drama suggested by the popular-song form. Most of the songs in his films are of the AABA form – that is, made up of one central melodic idea repeated three times, with the third statement separated from the second by a strain (called the "release") of contrasting musical

concerned only with those that are made with the *intention* of inducing an aesthetic experience in an audience.

77. Budd (1995), pp. 53, 153. Fry (1921), pp. 198–99, suggests that the fusion might be illusory. Referring to Giotto's "Pietà," he writes, "My emotion about the dramatic idea seemed to heighten my emotion about the plastic design. But at present I should be inclined to say that this fusion of two sets of emotion was only apparent and was due to my imperfect analysis of my own mental state." For the more general question of whether emotions lose or retain their identity when mixed to form compound emotions, see Elster (1999a), p. 242, notes 7 and 8.

78. Montaigne (1991), p. 164.

material. The dramatic high point in such songs tends to be at the beginning of the final statement of the A strain, its reappearance having been artfully delayed by the release strain. Astaire often makes specific choreographic use of this formal characteristic: it is at this point, for example, that he first firmly clasps his partner close to him in each of two seductive duets, "Change partners" in *Carefree* and "They can't take that away from me" in *The Barkeleys of Broadway*.[79]

A work of art can also help us see or understand the world differently, react to it differently, and understand our own reactions to it differently. A different perception or understanding of the world is valued because it allows us to have emotions that otherwise might have lain dormant or unfocused. Emotions attach to objects; emotional objects exist only qua perceived or conceived; hence new perceptions and conceptions open up the possibility of new emotional attachments. This is not to say that the new understanding may not be valued for itself, on purely intellectual grounds, only that this value is an extra-artistic one that can be found in other mental creations as well. Tocqueville's *Souvenirs* no less than Stendhal's *Lucien Leuwen* helps us understand the nature of the July monarchy, but only the latter is a work of art. (This does not mean that the former has no emotional value.) The substance of the speech of the Grand Inquisitor could easily be rendered into sociological language, but in the context of Dostoyevsky's novel it also acquires emotional significance.

Not every mental creation capable of generating emotional reactions is a work of art. Political speeches and other persuasive messages may produce strong emotions, but that does not make them into art. The difference is not that they are unaccompanied by the specifically aesthetic emotions. In fact, good political rhetoric draws on many of the formal devices that I mentioned two paragraphs earlier. Rather, art and rhetoric differ in the nature of the non-aesthetic emotions they generate. Apart from the epideictic variety (in praise of great individuals or deeds), rhetoric is geared toward generating emotion that will induce action; art is not.[80] From the point of view of the artist, art may be emotion recollected in tranquillity; from the point of view of the reader, viewer, or listener, it is emotion experienced in tranquillity.

The nature of the non-aesthetic emotions generated by art varies across art forms. Painting – notably nonfigurative painting – need

79. Mueller (1985), p. 20.   80. Fry (1921), p. 18.

not generate any such emotions at all.[81] In the case of literature, we are faced – as argued by Robert Yanal – with the apparent paradox that all the following propositions appear to be true, yet at least one of them must be false:

(1) We feel emotions towards the characters and situations of some works of fiction.
(2) We feel these emotions even though we believe that such characters and situations are fictional and not real.
(3) We feel emotions towards characters or situations only when we believe them to be real and not fictional.[82]

As I argue elsewhere,[83] the most plausible resolution of the paradox is by denying (3). Although emotions typically have cognitive antecedents, these need not take the form of full-blooded beliefs that something is the case. As we wait for a child to come home from school, the fleeting thought that he or she might have been in a car accident can trigger strong emotions even when we firmly believe that the chances are virtually nil. Because we do not believe that anything is wrong, we do not call the police; hence the emotion lacks the action tendency that is characteristic of most emotions. Similarly, the emotions we feel when reading about fictional characters do not induce us to take action of any kind; apart from that, however, they may have all the features normally associated with emotions. As suggested by Roger Fry, however, the very lack of an action tendency may enhance the aesthetic value of the emotion. "If the scene presented be one of an accident, our pity and horror, though weak, are felt quire purely, since they cannot, as they would in life, pass at once into actions of assistance."[84]

The issue of non-aesthetic emotions generated by music is much more complex. The best treatment known to me is that of Malcolm Budd in the chapter on music in *Values of Art*, and even that discussion is forbiddingly abstract. In his view, "When you hear music as being expressive of emotion E – when you hear E in the music – you hear the music sounding like the way E feels."[85] Yet as he goes on to say, "The

---

81. Thus whereas Budd (1995) discusses non-aesthetic emotions extensively in his chapters on literature and music, they are only briefly mentioned in his chapter on painting.
82. Yanal (1994), pp. 54–55.   83. Elster (1999a), Ch. IV.2.
84. Fry (1921), p. 13; also Budd (1995), p. 77.   85. Budd (1995), p. 136.

point of resemblance may lie below the level of consciousness (as, perhaps, with the melancholy sound of a minor triad as contrasted with a major triad), so that no matter how well we reflect on how music sounds and how an emotion feels we might be unable to identify a common property that is responsible for the perception of likeness."[86] From this basic observation Budd goes on to discuss a number of different ways in which emotions may infuse and enrich the experience of listening to the music. For my purposes, the most useful point he makes is that whereas the emotional quality of a work of art is one component of its aesthetic value, it is not the only one. Two musical works of different aesthetic value may express the same emotion.[87] Figure III.2 (in Section III.9) is an attempt to illustrate this idea.

CONSTRAINTS AND AESTHETIC VALUE

I now go on to discuss the relation between constraints and aesthetic value. On the one hand, preexisting or preset constraints enhance and stimulate the creative process. On the other hand, the creation of constraints is itself part of that process.

Consider first the capacity of constraints to stimulate creativity. As I remarked in I.1, the main idea is simply that having too many options works against creativity. What matters is to eliminate *some* options, not to eliminate any specific options. From this point of view, it makes little difference whether a writer is constrained by the requirement that verse have eleven syllables (Dante) or twelve (Racine).[88] Neither is intrinsically superior to the other. Yet, not all constraints will do equally well.[89] The constraint of writing a novel without the letter "e" may not make the task of the writer more difficult than writing in the demanding form of *terza rima*. Yet the latter constraint, unlike the former, can contribute directly to aesthetic value, over and above the indirect contribution that follows from the focus-enhancing effect. Because rhythm and meter generate an organized form, they have intrinsic aesthetic potential; the absence of a given letter in the alphabet does not.

I am not claiming that the focus-enhancing effect of constraints depends on their also having independent aesthetic potential. Brevity,

86. Ibid., p. 142.   87. Ibid., p. 146.
88. I am indebted to Pasquale Pasquino for this observation.
89. I am indebted to John Ferejohn and John Roemer for pressing this point on me.

for instance, has no independent aesthetic interest. In jazz, the thirty-two bar solo is not intrinsically superior to a ninety-six bar solo. A superior artist might be able to create a solo of sufficient complexity and structure to fill out ninety-six bars without repeating himself or resorting to clichés. Because of the limitations of the human mind, density – which *is* intrinsically valuable – may de facto require brevity, but in moments of exceptional inspiration these limitations may be transcended. Yet the constraint of the "e"-less novel differs from the brevity constraint. For most writers, having to write around the letter "e" would be an irritating distraction rather than a stimulation, an obstacle to be overcome rather than a challenge to be met. In III.9, I observe that many jazz pianists have performed well on a badly tuned piano simply by avoiding certain keys. I also add, however, that to my knowledge the presence of this constraint did not enhance their performance. I cannot exclude that for some writers, the similar constraint of not using the letter "e" might be the equivalent of having to use verse of twelve syllables, by stimulating their imagination and focusing their attention. Yet even these writers might do better if they subjected themselves to constraints that have independent aesthetic potential as well as the capacity to focus attention.

Constraints must be tight, but not too tight. The search for the right word, tone, and so on is impeded both if the feasible set is too large and if it is too small. As Jacques Hadamard says in a discussion of invention in mathematics, "It is well known that good hunting cartridges are those which have a proper scattering. If this scattering is too wide, it is useless to aim; but if it is too narrow, you have too many chances to miss your game by a line."[90] When the set is very large, the search takes too much time and becomes unmanageable. It is certainly debatable whether the deliberate *expansion* of the feasible set in *Finnegans Wake* was accompanied by an artistic gain; at the very least it is safe to say that in most other hands Joyce's method would be disastrous. For a movie director, an unlimited budget may be disastrous.[91] For a TV producer, having too much time may

90. Hadamard (1954), p. 48.
91. Reviewing Bogdanovich (1997), Clive James (1997), p. 72, writes, "The old guys had to tell a story because they couldn't blow up the world. There were limitations you couldn't spend your way out of, and in overcoming them lay the essence of the craft, its economy, its brio. . . . To accept and transcend limitations can be a source of creative vibrancy, whereas to eliminate it with money almost always leads to inertia."

undermine creativity.[92] Under the heading of "How the absence of limits may itself be a limitation," Paul Griffiths wrote the following in a review of a concert of electronic music organized by the French Institute of Musical-Acoustical Research and Coordination (Ircam):

Its besetting problem remains that it may overfeed what it seeks to support. Necessity, not opportunity, is the mother of invention. The best music, electronic or otherwise, strives at the limit of what is possible, and at Ircam limits are hard to find. On the electronic consoles there are just too many knobs. The point was made clearly at one of the concerts, given at the Théâtre du Châtelet by the ASKO ensemble. At the start was a new work by Luca Francesconi. . . . His 'Sirene/Gespenster' is apparently an approach to an opera on "The Rime of the Ancient Mariner," and the music is appropriately marine, dreamy and a shade sinister. Brass and percussion call from the stage; electronic sounds bathe the space; and from female singers, both soloists and groups, emanate the siren voices. Any 30 seconds of it would have been wonderful, but there were 2,000 (about a half-hour). Contrariwise, the two works of Edgar Varese were bursting with urgency – perhaps partly because they were bursting also the limitations on electronic music 40 and 60 years ago.[93]

Conversely, when the feasible set is very small, it may not contain the right unit. A priori, we would not expect a novel rigorously written under the constraints of *Les Revenentes* to be successful. To the extent that the book is a success, it is perhaps because Perec did not obey other constraints of the French language. Also, the task of translating poetry in a way that reflects both the formal properties of the original and its literal meanings while avoiding artificial turns of phrase, may in some cases be too difficult. As I argue in III.10, creating a psychological drama within the constraint of the silent movie may also be too hard.

This feature of the search for the right unit interacts with two other features. First, when the set is very large the criteria for rightness may

92. Commenting on the sitcom *Seinfeld* (duration twenty-two minutes, excluding commercials) O'Brien (1997), pp. 13, 14, writes, "Its best episodes feel like feature films, and indeed have busier narratives than most features. (The periodic one-hour episodes, by contrast, sometimes go weirdly slack.) . . . Comic opportunities that most shows would milk are tossed off in a line or two. The tension and density of working against the time constraint is a reminder of how fruitful such constraints can be. If Count Basie had not been limited to the duration of a 78 rpm record, would we have the astonishing compression of 'Every Tub' (three minutes, fourteen seconds) or 'Jumpin' at the Woodside' (three minutes, eight seconds)?"
93. *New York Times*, July 3, 1997, p. C11. For an experimental confirmation of the dangers of too much freedom, see Goldenberg, Mazursky, and Solomon (1999).

be somewhat relaxed. Not all novelists are like Flaubert, who polished each phrase to perfection. By contrast, in short stories and even more in poems, optimization at a fine-grained level is very important. Second, and very important, the size of the feasible set is related to artistic motivation. As in all forms of self-realization, motivation is maximized if the task is neither too easy nor too difficult. High-wire performers concentrate better when they have no safety net. As suggested earlier, if Astaire had known that any mistakes he made in a dance sequence could always be edited out by splicing, he would have made more mistakes. Jazz recordings that result from splicing intended to make them better tend in fact to be artistically inferior, even if they allow the performer to erase any technical mistakes he or she might have made.

THE PLACE OF INSPIRATION

So far, I have presented artistic creation as a fully conscious and rational choice within constraints. Needless to say, this cannot be all there is to the story. All artists know that ideas – connections, associations, patterns – often come to them in a completely spontaneous way. They perceive themselves to be mediums or vehicles for ideas that owe nothing to their conscious choice. E. R. Dodds argues that for the Greeks of the Homeric period this experience was one of three sources of their belief in divine agency.

The recognition, the insight, the memory, the brilliant or perverse idea, have this in common, that they come suddenly, as we say, 'into a man's head.' Often he is conscious of no observation or reasoning which has led up to them. But in that case, how can he call them 'his'? A moment ago they were not in his mind; now they are there. Something has put them there, and that something is other than himself.[94]

My conjecture is that inspiration – defined as the rate at which ideas move from the unconscious into the conscious mind – is an inversely U-shaped function of the tightness of the constraints.[95]The "neurons

94. Dodds (1951), p. 11. The other two sources are "the sudden unaccountable feeling of power" and "the sudden unaccountable loss of judgement" (ibid., p. 14).
95. It is also, as persuasively argued by Caillois (1943), pp. 208–209, a function of the artist's past. "When one studies the nature of inspiration it becomes evident that it is never a gift but a restitution. When the poet is surprised by an image, a

for inspiration," if there are such things, fire more intensely when the demands set by the conscious mind are stringent but not too stringent. Exactly how this might happen, I don't know. The main evidence I can offer for the conjecture comes from the phenomenology of artistic creation. It may be what Byron had in mind when he said, "Nothing so difficult as a beginning in poesy, unless perhaps the end": at the beginning the constraints are too weak, and toward the end they are too strong. Most writers know the paralysis induced by the blank page – the ideas simply won't come. A similar paralysis can be induced by the challenge of bringing a complex plot to a satisfactory conclusion. According to Michael Baxandall, "A short history of European art could be written around the 'finishing' agony."[96]

The conscious mind, in this process, does two things. To some extent it works in parallel with the unconscious, by scanning the feasible set for a suitable choice. Writers may resort to a thesaurus or a dictionary of rhymes. Composers and painters may engage in more or less formalized procedures to ensure harmony among the various parts of a composition. Also, the overall design and architecture of the work of art is to a very large extent due to the conscious mind. I return to that issue later.

In addition, and more importantly, the conscious mind plays an important role in scrutinizing, rejecting, or approving the ragbag of ideas thrown up by the unconscious. In *The Dragons of Eden*, Carl Sagan

describes the right hemisphere as a pattern recognizer that finds patterns, sometimes real and sometimes imagined, in the behavior of people as well as in natural events. The right hemisphere has a suspicious emotional tone, for it sees conspiracies where they don't exist as well as where they do. It needs the left hemisphere to analyze critically the patterns it generates in order to test their reality.[97]

This description matches that of Poincaré in his analysis of mathematical invention. He argues that conscious analysis is preceded by an unconscious or subliminal sorting, which is guided mainly by the aesthetic criteria of beauty, elegance, parsimony, and harmony. These

stanza, which some foreign prompting seems to have brought him for no apparent reason and which his own efforts would never have found, it is because he has not stopped to recall how the miracle of today is the reward of his own earlier striving. He does not see the connection between the effort of the past and the facility of the moment."

96. Baxandall (1985), p. 66.   97. Springer and Deutsch (1989), p. 301.

criteria may, however, be misleading. "When a sudden illumination invades the mind of the mathematician, it usually does not deceive him. Yet it can also happen that it is not born out by verification; in almost all these cases we find that the false idea, if it had been true, would have satisfied our natural instinct for mathematical elegance."[98]

Yet there is a difference between the processes described by Sagan and Poincaré and those that are at work in artistic creation. Sagan hits the nail on the head when he suggests that scientists can be misled by patterns into finding conspiracies where none exist. Social scientists may be particularly prone to this fallacy,[99] but in earlier centuries natural scientists also fell victim to the fallacious search for meaning in all things.[100] It would be strange to say, however, that an artist can be misled by beauty or patterns. Obsessional and quasi-hallucinatory works of art, however, such as Alexander Zinoviev's *The Yawning Heights*, Joseph Heller's *Catch 22*, or the paintings of Hieronymus Bosch and Francis Bacon, are not in any way vitiated by their exaggerations or distortions. We appreciate these works, perhaps reluctantly, because they enrich our emotional life, isolating and purifying strands of experience that we usually fail or do not want to acknowledge. This being said, the unconscious mind cannot be trusted to come up with patterns that are consistently satisfactory. It may seize upon similarities and resemblances that, when scrutinized by the conscious mind, turn out to be partial, superficial, misleading, or irrelevant.[101]

FORMAL CONSTRAINTS

I now turn to the use of what I called formal constraints within the work of art itself as a means of enhancing its aesthetic value. This

98. Poincaré (1920), p. 59.
99. In Ch. II.10 of Elster (1983b) I cite Michel Foucault and Pierre Bourdieu as examples of this tendency. More generally, functional explanation and psychoanalytic theory embody the tendency to find meaning everywhere.
100. Many examples in Thomas (1973).
101. I have assumed that the conscious mind is doubly related to the unconscious, by imposing constraints on the search and by scrutinizing the results of the search. Breton (1972, p. 26) offers a formal definition of surrealism in which the conscious mind makes *no* ex ante or ex post contribution: "psychic automatism in its pure state, by which one proposes to express – verbally, by means of the written word, or in another manner, the actual functioning of thought. Dictated by thought, in the absence of any control exercised by reason, exempt from any aesthetic or moral concern." The actual practice of automatic writing, however, was more complex (Abastado 1975, pp. 74–80).

issue is closely related to what I called the specifically aesthetic emotions, generated by formal features of the work. (In III.9 I discuss these emotions in jazz under the heading of "taste.") What I have to say about this topic is limited to temporally extended works of art (notably music, films, and literature) or, more accurately, to works in which the various parts are intended to be perceived in a canonical sequence. (To see the difference between the two characterizations, note that the elements in aleatory music or literature (III.8) are not intended to be perceived in any particular order. Conversely, "in certain Chinese paintings the length is so great that we cannot take in the whole picture at once. Sometimes, the landscape is painted upon a roll of silk so long that we can only look at it in successive segments.")[102]

The formal constraints on the creator stem from his or her anticipation of the perceptions of the audience. Before taking up a new book or sitting down to listen to a piece of music for the first time, the reader or listener faces a very large number of possible experiences. Even if we exclude the combinations of elementary units that violate the constraints of spelling, grammar, and harmony, the remaining number of combinations is incredibly large. And even if we ignore the difference between combinations that tell the same basic story (a phrase that may be narrowly or broadly construed), the remaining number of stories is very large indeed. I shall not define what I mean by a story. As regards literature, on which I focus next, the intuitive idea that I probably share with most readers will be sufficient for my purposes. As regards the notion of a story in music, I refer the reader to some brief comments in III.9.

As the reader plunges into a novel, the universe of possibilities steadily becomes smaller. Some are eliminated simply by virtue of the setting. Once we discover that we are in France in 1830 (and know that we are reading a realistic novel), we can rule out a large number of fictional worlds. Within the world that has been established, the conventions of the genre may enable us to rule out a number of potential developments. Peer Gynt cannot die in the middle of the fifth act; the murder in a crime story must be resolved; a Jane Austen heroine must be married by the end of the book. More interesting, however, is the narrowing down of the feasible set by the self-imposed formal constraints of the narrative. At time 1, the characters are sketchily drawn: they can say or do almost anything. What they then go on to say or do at time 2, however, constrains what they can say or do

102. Fry (1921), p. 21.

215

at time 3, and so on. The constraints derive from conceptions of psychological plausibility or verisimilitude that the novelist can expect readers to share with him or her. A timid person cannot suddenly behave like a rake, even if having him so behave would enable the author to advance the story (III.7).

At the same time, what the characters say and do is the story of the novel. The filling-in of the individual portraits and the development of the story go hand in hand. The utterances and actions of a character have causal effects within the novel as well as outside it. In his marginal notes on *Lucien Leuwen*, Stendhal reminds himself: "When rereading, always ask the double question: how does the hero see these events? How does the reader see them?"[103] Elizabeth Bennet's sparkling wit when talking to Darcy causes the reader as well as Darcy to perceive her "sweetness and archness." Thus it is not only more convincing but also more effective to let the characters in the novel come across to the reader by what they say and do rather than by what the author says about them.[104] It is also, of course, much more difficult. Thus in the early Rex Stout novels featuring Nero Wolfe, the author pulled off the trick of making a purported genius speak like a genius. In the later novels, Stout contented himself by having Archie Goodwin tell us that Wolfe is a genius. When he ceased to impose on himself the constraint of "showing" rather than merely "telling," the novels lost some of their interest. And I do not think mere "telling" could have brought to life Aunt Norris in *Mansfield Park* or Miss Bates in *Emma* in the way Jane Austen does by reporting what they say.

As the characters unfold and the story develops, the constraints become – are made to become – tighter and tighter. At any given point in the novel, there are several things a character can say or do that would be consistent with what the reader knows about him or her. The choice of one particular item in what one might call the "plausible set" can have two consequences. By revealing more about the character it can further reduce the size of the plausible set. By the impact the utterance or action has on others, it changes the situation in which the character will have to choose in the future. The craft of the novelist lies

---

103. Stendhal (1952), p. 1492.
104. If the apparent preference for "telling" over "showing" in Pavel (1986), p. 104, is intended as a general aesthetic judgment, I would disagree. While it may be true that in novels that rely on telling "no detail can be passed over without important loss of information," this responds only to the requirement of *parsimony*. To satisfy the requirement of *fullness* the author must construct the personality of the characters by showing how they talk and behave. Proust was a master of both.

in making artistic choices that will lead the characters, as the result of their own plausible choices, toward a situation where, given what we know about them, there is only one plausible choice they can make, or a unique maximally plausible one. The perceived inevitability of the choice then induces the specifically aesthetic emotion of *release* that we experience when things fall into place. The nature of the choice – the heroine marries, as in Jane Austen, or refuses to marry, as in *La Princesse de Clèves* – induces the appropriate non-aesthetic emotion of happiness, sadness, and so on.

THE PLAUSIBLE SET

The idea of plausibility requires a few additional comments. First, I cannot quite follow Thomas Pavel or Marie-Laure Ryan when they suggest that "the poet must put forward either propositions true in every alternative of the true world . . . or propositions true at least in one alternative of the actual world."[105] But this alternative between inevitability and mere conceivability is too stark.[106] As Ryan herself notes, "Making up improbable events is just too easy to do."[107] In the real world, "man bites dog" is a great news story. In the world of fiction, it is boring.[108] Following Aristotle (*Poetics* 1456[a] 24–25; 1461[b] 13–15), one might perhaps allow for *some* improbable events: the most improbable state of affairs would be if low-probability events never happened. To the question of whether plausibility constrains each step in the development of the novel or only the plot as a whole, my tentative answer is that low-probability events are acceptable for the

---

105. Pavel (1986), p. 46; also Ryan (1991), p. 17. Both quote Aristotle's *Poetics* as asserting that "it is not the poet's business to tell what happened, but the kind of things that would happen – what is possible according to possibility and necessity." Aristotle's actual words, however, refer to what is "possible according to *probability* [eikos] or necessity" (1451[a] 36–37; my italics). Although the Oxford and Loeb translations both use "probability," Bernard Manin and Stephen Holmes suggest to me that "plausibility" might be a better rendering of "eikos" in this context.
106. In Ch. 1 of Elster (1978) I argued that the reduction of all modalities to the stark alternative of the necessary and possible has a certain, if limited, value for the analysis of social phenomena. Looking back, I am struck mainly by the limitations.
107. Ryan (1991), p. 152.
108. Conversely, descriptions of events it would have been boring to witness need not themselves be boring (Spacks 1995, p. 170). In painting, still lifes show especially clearly that an interesting representation need not be the representation of a scene it would have been interesting to witness (Budd 1995, pp. 76–80).

purpose of generating a plot but not for the purpose of helping the author to extricate himself from a mistake in his plotting (ibid., 1460ᵃ 33–35). In the special case of suspense novels or suspense movies, the occurrence of a low-probability event to avert disaster and produce the morally desirable outcome is, of course, mandatory.[109] Yet even here "one can easily go wrong by overadding improbability factors in a suspense sequence, thereby reducing the audience to giddiness."[110]

Second, the criterion of plausibility or verisimilitude may have to be interpreted weakly, as non-implausibility. Dostoyevsky's characters, for instance, are opaque and impenetrable, but not implausible. Julien Sorel's decision to shoot Mme de Rênal comes as a surprise, but is not out of character. Third, as a consequence of the second point, the condition of inevitability is often too strong. T. S. Eliot demands, for instance, "that when the external facts . . . are given, the emotion is immediately evoked. . . . The artistic 'inevitability' lies in this complete adequacy of the external to the emotion."[111] Against this, I would cite a more plausible observation by La Rochefoucauld, to the effect that one and the same external situation may trigger one of two opposite emotional reactions: "Jealousy feeds on doubts, and as soon as doubt turns into certainty it becomes a frenzy, or ceases to exist."[112]

Fourth, another related point, the novel should allow for irrational behavior.[113] To distinguish irrational behavior of the characters from a mere failure of plotting, the author must show us that the behavior, while irrational, is nevertheless intelligible; or more accurately, the irrational behavior must be seen as such.[114] Fifth, the novel allows not only for the unfolding but also for the change of character. The actions of Jane Austen's Emma not only reveal the flaws in her

---

109. Carroll (1996), p. 101. As he also points out (ibid., p. 102), in some suspense movies evil triumphs. Although the viewer usually can anticipate that good will triumph (ibid., p. 106), so that in one sense the outcome is a high-probability event rather than a low-probability event, the existence of movies in which evil triumphs might be used to create an additional suspense about what will *actually* happen in the movie, as distinct from suspense about what can be expected to happen given the events depicted in the movie. One can know that the heroine will not drown and yet be anguished when her death appears inevitable; if one suspects that she might in fact drown the emotion would be a different one.
110. Ibid., p. 106.   111. Eliot (1919), p. 48.
112. *Maxim* 32. See Elster (1999a), Ch. IV.2 for further discussions of one–many relations between the cognitive antecedents of an emotion and the emotion itself.
113. See Livingston (1991), Ch. 5, for an analysis of Zola's *La joie de vivre* in terms of the irrationality of the main character.
114. I am indebted to Thomas Pavel for this clarification.

character but have an impact on and elicit reactions from others that cause her to undertake a painful reassessment of herself. Yet such changes, too, are governed by the demand for verisimilitude: even a change of character must be in character. In most productions of *A Doll's House* (Janet McTeer's recent performance is an exception) Nora's conversion in the last act is not plausibly grounded in her earlier behavior. Sixth, a related point, as Aristotle observed, "Even if inconsistency be part of the man before one for imitation as presenting that form of character, he should still be consistently inconsistent" (*Poetics* 1454ᵃ 26–28). Seventh, a story can lack all deterministic causality and yet be compelling and plausible, if, as in *The Dice Man*, the lack of determinism is itself rooted in the story (III.8). Finally, the novel allows for expansion as well as restriction of the plausible set. If a character initially engages in dissimulation or hypocrisy, readers may be led to form a belief about what he or she can plausibly say or do that unravels when they learn more in a later part of the novel.[115]

Some Implications

Given these caveats, we can draw a few conclusions. First, with the exception indicated earlier the development of the story should not rely on unlikely events or coincidences. In crime stories, the ultimate sign of failure is when the author must introduce a hitherto unknown twin to get out of some corner into which he has painted himself.[116] In *Middlemarch*, the encounter between Raffles and Mr. Bulstrode – a crucial element in the development of the story – is so contrived that it detracts from the otherwise seamless progression of the novel. In fact, the contrivance creates more damage than it does in a more loosely constructed novel such as *La Princesse de Clèves*, which turns on *two* coincidences: the accidental discovery of a letter and an accidentally overheard conversation.[117]

---

115. For a discussion of this "split-level technique" in *Vanity Fair*, see Iser (1974), pp. 111–12.
116. Caillois (1974), p. 182 and passim.
117. I disagree doubly with Shattuck (1996), p. 112, when he asserts, "In a scene that has become famous, the Princess brings herself to confess her love to her husband without naming its object. One implausibility is matched by another: the Duc de Nemours himself is eavesdropping outside the window." First, I do not think the confession is implausible. It is extraordinary, but does not go against anything we know about the Princess or about human nature in general. Second, even if it were implausible, it would not be so by virtue of being an engineered

Second, the development of the story must be "pushed from behind," not only "pulled from ahead," a distinction that has been stated as follows:

> Suppose we want to know 'why' in the early part of Dickens's *Great Expectations*... the six- or seven-year old Pip aids the runaway convict. Two different kinds of answer are possible: (1) according to the logic of verisimilitude (made prominent, in fact, by the text): the child was frightened into submission; (2) according to the structural needs of the plot: this act is necessary for Magwitch to be grateful to Pip so as to wish to repay him; without it the plot would not be the kind of plot it is.[118]

Although the *construction* of the text may be teleological or backward-looking, it should lend itself to a purely causal or forward-looking *reading*.[119] The author, in other words, acts like God in Leibniz's theodicy. Everything that happens in the world can be explained twice over, first as part of a causal chain and then as part of an optimal design. "These are like two kingdoms, one of efficient causes, the other of final causes, each of which separately suffices in detail to give a reason for the whole, as if the other did not exist."[120] A purely teleological development is artistically inferior (Aristotle, *Poetics* 1454[b] 30–35). In III.7 I discuss a blatant example from *Lucien Leuwen*.

Third, some of the ideas from III.3 can be connected to this framework. There, I suggested that insufficient development of a work of art may take the form of a premature resolution of tension. It follows from what I have said here that it may also take the form of setting up a tension without resolving it. Thus when making a film based on *The Big Sleep*, the director discovered that Chandler had neglected to clear up one of the deaths in the novel, leaving it ambiguous whether

---

    coincidence. The teleological device of making a person act out of character detracts much more from the aesthetic value of a novel than the resort to coincidence.

118. Rimmon-Kenan (1983), pp. 17–18.
119. As shown by Genette (1969), pp. 78–86, apropos of Balzac, some causal or forward-looking analyses are nothing but thinly disguised teleological constructions. I cannot follow him, however, when he generalizes this criticism to all novels in which the behavior of the characters is explained by authorial asides. In *Middlemarch*, to take but this case, the motivational analyses are "profits" and not only "costs," to use Genette's language.
120. Leibniz (1705), p. 588. (A post-Leibnizian example is the equivalent of Newtonian and Lagrangian formulations of classical mechanics.) For a brief discussion of the relation between divine creation and artistic invention, see Elster (1986b), pp. 102–103.

it was a murder or a suicide.[121] I also suggested that excessive development can take the form of continuing the novel after the tension has been resolved without setting up a new one. In the present perspective it may also take the form of making the characters say and do things that are redundant with respect to the causal impact both on the reader and on the other characters in the novel.

III.5. ORIGINALITY, AUTHENTICITY, AND CREATIVITY

The notion of originality in art can be understood in many ways.[122] I shall consider two of them. First, an original work can be defined as a genuine, unfaked, authentic one – a work that is what it is alleged to be. Second, a work of art can be called original if it is qualitatively innovative in some sense, breaking with existing conventions and perhaps introducing new ones. I shall focus on the latter meaning, and on the relation between creativity and originality thus understood. First, however, I shall say a few words about originality as authenticity, and its relation to value and constraints.

AUTHENTICITY

Forgeries, that is, works of art falsely presented to be by a specific artist or school, can be great achievements. Van Meegeren succeeded splendidly in his goal of forging paintings by Vermeer, in the sense of being accepted by the best experts at the time.[123] Indeed, when he finally confessed, he had difficulties making the experts believe his confession. It is not clear whether he could have succeeded indefinitely or whether he would eventually have been discovered. It has been argued that forgeries are always discovered in the end, because the forger is too much of his time. On the one hand, he perceives the original from a modern perspective: "Forgeries are generally discovered in the end because they were designed, and

---

121. When asked by Howard Hawks, Chandler responded that he didn't know either (Sperber and Lax 1997, pp. 288–89).
122. A good survey is Vermazen (1991).
123. The essays collected in Dutton, ed. (1983) contain a good deal of discussion of the van Meegeren case and its implications for aesthetic theory.

could only have been designed, to have just those properties that the forger and those in his circle were aware of in the target of the forgery."[124] On the other hand, he has modern conceptions of his own that betray him: "The better forgers, against their intentions, share with their fellow artists the compulsion to impose their own conceptions upon the sight they try to reproduce."[125] The forger fails either by doing too little, that is, by missing some of the qualities in the original, or by doing too much, that is, by adding something of his own.

We need not presuppose that experts will eventually be able to distinguish, by visual inspection alone, the forgery from the original. Detection might spring from technical analysis of paint and canvas, and then be verified by visual means, through newly enlightened eyes. An expert "will not see that the paintings have ... quite different qualities ... unless he already knows which painting is which. Nothing in our argument, however, requires that *this* knowledge be based on visual grounds."[126] Or consider the jazz lover who "was shocked when he heard that Jack Teagarden was not a Negro, [and] he stopped collecting Teagarden records right away."[127] The reaction was probably a form of snobbery,[128] but it is also just possible that knowledge of Teagarden's color enabled him to hear nuances that escaped him before. There are analogues in other, less subjective realms. Once someone has proved a long-standing mathematical conjecture, others may be able to prove it soon thereafter using wholly different techniques of proof.[129] The knowledge that the conjecture is true induces confidence and persistence that would otherwise be lacking. Similarly, once we know that *The Supper at Emmaus* is by van Meegeren and not by Vermeer we can perceive differences that eluded

124. Sparshott (1983), p. 248.   125. Arnheim (1983), p. 242.
126. Sagoff (1983), p. 150.   127. Zwerin (1985), p. 46.
128. When Teagarden arrived in New York in 1927, "black musicians, chronically skeptical of white jazz-men in those musically segregated times, welcomed him into their midst, a few even hinting that no one outside 'the race' could play the blues that well" (Sudhalter 1999), pp. 714–15.
129. An example is the following. In the 1920s the Danish mathematician J. Nilsen proved that all subgroups of free groups are themselves free groups. His proof makes use of complex algebraic methods. A few years later the Norwegian I. Johansson obtained the same result by direct geometrical means. I have been told by Jens-Erik Fenstad (to whom I owe the example) that Johansson would probably not have obtained his result had he not known the theorem to be true. Nahin (1998), p. 15, cites a sixteenth-century instance and compares it to that of sport records: "Within months of Roger Bannister breaking the four-minute mile it seemed as though every good runner in the world started doing it."

us.[130] Yet these comforting arguments cannot be verified empirically, as we cannot have knowledge of the forgeries that have escaped detection.

There are some general reasons, however, why successful forgeries of great artists are likely to be rare. The forger is working under a tighter set of constraints than the original. The composer who would forge a hitherto unknown symphony of Mozart must conform not only to all the conventions within which Mozart himself was working, but also to Mozart's pattern of choices as embodied in the known Köchel numbers. Even a genius has habits, deviations from which can be recognized by experts or computers.[131] Within this double set of constraints the forger must also produce a work of art of sufficient aesthetic value to be plausibly attributed to Mozart. The chances are that anyone sufficiently good to do this would not waste his or her time forging others. Although few artists may be literally inimitable (but see III.9 for a possible exception), some may be so hard to imitate that it is not worth the trouble.

CREATING NEW CONSTRAINTS

To introduce the second conception of originality, let me first distinguish between rebellion and revolution in art. Rebellions violate existing conventions, whereas revolutions abolish them and create new ones. A revolution is usually preceded by a rebellion, but not every rebellion brings about a revolution. It is not even clear that all violations are initiated with revolution in mind. For one thing, there is a phenomenon identified by Roger Caillois and Henri Peyre, further discussed in III.10: the rare and deliberate violation that, for its effects, presupposes that the convention is firmly in place. For another, there is the anarchist rebel who wants to abolish all convention rather than propose a new one. Yet the anarchist may acquire a following against his will, and his rebellion be consolidated into convention. The history of conceptual art from Duchamps to the present illustrates this tendency toward the "institutionalization of the avant-garde."

130. Hadamard (1954), p. 34, assimilates problems concerning the authenticity of pictures to problems of scientific discovery.
131. Literary forgeries can be recognized by computer analysis of vocabulary and syntax. Presumably musical forgeries could be detected in the same way. Painting, however, does not have the digital structure that allows for computerized detection.

Originality, in this second sense, can be defined as a durable break with existing conventions rather than as a momentary departure from them. The emergence of free verse, nonfigurative art, and atonal music are obvious examples from the past century. The question is why artists cannot simply remain content with the medium within which they have been trained. One answer is that "if artists were concerned only with making beautiful pictures, poems, symphonies, etc., the possibilities for the creation of aesthetically pleasing works of art would soon be exhausted. We would (perhaps) have a number of lovely paintings, but we should soon grow tired of them, for they would all be more or less alike."[132] This "exhaustion argument" asserts that after a while there are no more beautiful works of a certain kind to be made, or perhaps that after a while beautiful works of a certain kind lose their power to please. The argument is implausible in either form. It is absurd to argue that the realistic novel went out of fashion when and because all good plots, characters, and dialogues had been invented, and equally implausible to assert that at some time around 1900 readers got tired of realism. As Bruce Vermazen argues, even the most conventional *technique* may have the power of defamiliarizing the *world*, helping us to see it "wie am ersten Tag."[133] Nor do I think that realism went out of business when and because novelists got tired of it.[134]

An alternative account could take off from the Marxist analysis of capitalist relations of production.[135] Among the many things Marx found wrong with capitalism was its alleged inefficiency or suboptimality in developing the productive forces or, in non-Marxist language, technology. In this conception, technical change is a function both of the intensity of search for new techniques and of the efficiency of selecting among the techniques generated by the search. Capitalism, Marx argued, is inherently inferior to communism with respect to the selection of new techniques, being motivated by profit rather than by the desire to reduce human drudgery. At a low level of development of the productive forces, however, capitalism is superior to communism in the intensity of the search for new techniques. Communism, to be viable, presupposes a high level of material welfare, at

132. Lessing (1983), p. 75.   133. Vermazen (1991), p. 274.
134. As suggested by Levenson (1968), vol. 1, p. 41: "An art-form is 'exhausted' when its practitioners think it is."
135. This theory is more fully set out in Ch. 5 of Elster (1985).

which people can spontaneously engage in creative activities, such as artistic, scientific, and technical innovation. By providing the profit motive as a spur to search, capitalism enables mankind to reach that level; but once it is reached, capitalism becomes the ladder it can kick away. The general idea underlying this analysis is that a mode of production remains in existence as long as it is historically progressive, that is, as long as it generates new techniques at a higher rate than any other mode could do. It disappears when and because another mode becomes superior.

The exhaustion argument has a certain resemblance to the Marxist theory. That theory asserts that relations of production change when and because they cease to promote technical change. The exhaustion argument says that conventions change when and because they cease to promote creativity. The value of the comparison is that it suggests an alternative to the exhaustion argument. To see this, note that the Marxist theory compares the actual rate of development of the productive forces with the hypothetical development under another regime, not with their earlier development under the same regime. What induces change is suboptimality, compared to what could be, not stagnation, compared to what has been. The exhaustion argument, as stated and rejected, invokes stagnation as the explanation of new forms of art. The comparison with the Marxist theory suggests that new conventions come into being when and because they promote creativity to a higher extent than the earlier form could do, a development that may but need not go together with stagnation.

We then must ask a further question: what has happened to make the new conventions more fertile than the earlier ones? One answer might be that extra-artistic events, such as the Industrial Revolution or class conflict, create a need for new forms of artistic expression. The confused modernist cliché that "a fragmented society requires a fragmented art" (III.2) expresses this view. Another, more satisfactory answer relies on developments within the arts themselves. The very achievements attained within the old conventions make other conventions the optimal vehicle for further development.[136] As illustrations of this idea one might cite the relation between the late Cézanne watercolors and Cubist painting, or between Lester Young and Charlie Parker. Also, conventions may cease to enhance creativity if they

---

136. This is also analogous to Marx's theory about the development of the productive forces, as interpreted by van Parijs (1984).

get too cluttered up. Often, there is a tendency for more and more details to be regulated by convention, so that the artist experiences a paralyzing lack of breathing space or elbow room.

Trotsky observed, "Societies are not so rational in building that the dates for proletarian dictatorship arrive exactly at that moment when the economic and cultural conditions are ripe for socialism."[137] In other words, socialist relations of production are not established when capitalism has developed the forces of production to a level at which socialism would be optimal for their further development. Similarly, the evolution of art is not so rational that new conventions emerge when and because they are optimal vehicles for further artistic creativity. In the twentieth century, for instance, the most natural explanation for the emergence of new art forms is that many artists labor under a simple conceptual confusion. It is obvious to the most superficial observer that the rate of decay of conventions is much higher today than in any earlier epoch. At the same time, I do not believe that the rate of production of works that will be seen as having durable value is any higher than before. Much of contemporary art (and art criticism) rests on a fundamental misconception – *the overvaluation of originality at the expense of creativity*. Rather than following the imperative "Enchant me!" it obeys Diaghilev's "Astonish me!" As Mette Hjort has argued, the proliferation of new forms may also be due to competition and strategic one-upmanship, rather than to this confusion.[138] In III.8, I discuss the use of randomization in the arts as one example of sterile originality, but there are many others.

Some further observations along these lines are the following.[139] (i) Some artists seek or welcome hard constraints to enhance and focus their creativity. Others invent them for the sake of originality or – a different temptation – virtuosity. (ii) The effort to be original may distract and thus detract from the power to create. In the process of

---

137. Trotsky (1977), p. 334.
138. Hjort (1993). As Thomas Pavel reminds me, one-upmanship in the arts can also stimulate creativity rather than the search for originality. Greek art, for instance, may owe some of its greatness to the search for glory. Aeschylus, for instance, "wrote his plays for performance at a dramatic competition with the hope presumably of securing first prize"; hence when he left Athens for Sicily "it will occasion no surprise that one reason advanced in antiquity for his departure from Athens was professional chagrin, defeat at the hands of the young Sophocles or at the hands of Simonides" (Walcot 1978, pp. 50, 51; see also Elster 1999a, pp. 210–11).
139. This paragraph is indebted to suggestions by John Alcorn.

technical change, innovators may suffer "the penalty from taking the lead," leaving it to imitators to reap the profit.[140] Innovating artists, too, can suffer from being involved in two creative processes at the same time: the creation of constraints and the creation within constraints. (iii) Yet some original works of art are indisputably great works. Sometimes, the two processes of creation enhance each other rather than distract from each other. (iv) Artistic evolution, like other forms of evolution, takes place by adjusting to a moving target. If the time it takes for the artistic community to adjust to a new convention exceeds the time it takes before its willingness to work within the convention is exhausted, each new form of art will be condemned to wither before it can flower, as has been said about capitalism in Russia before the October Revolution.

III.6. THE HAYS CODE

Sections III.6 through III.9 provide four case studies that illustrate some of the ideas developed in the previous sections. The first case is that of constraints on movie-making. I shall focus on content-related constraints as embodied in Hollywood's Production Code ("the Hays Code"), but first say a few words about material constraints. In this section I focus exclusively on the capacity of the constraints to *enhance* the artistic value of the movies, postponing until III.10 a discussion of ways in which they can have negative effects on aesthetic value.

SOUND AND COLOR

In *Film as Art*, Rudolf Arnheim systematically develops the idea that for the movie director, less is more. Although he expected (the essays collected in the book were written between 1933 and 1938) that the combined pressure of the engineer and the public would take movies toward "the complete film" with its superior capacity to imitate nature, he argued that this development would go together with a loss in artistic value. For him, two-dimensional movies were aesthetically more powerful than three-dimensional or stereoscopic movies: "The lack of depth brings a very welcome element of unreality into the film

140. Veblen (1915).

picture. Formal qualities, such as the compositional and evocative significance of particular comparisons, acquire the power to force themselves on the attention of the spectator."[141] Similarly, "the reduction of actual color values to a one-dimensional gray series (ranging from pure white to dead black) is a welcome divergence from nature which renders possible the making of significant and decorative pictures by means of light and shade."[142] Moreover, with a wide screen "formative devices such as montage and changing camera angles will become unusable."[143]

Arnheim's most impassioned argument, however, is for the superiority of silent movies over sound movies. Chaplin, for instance, achieves his most striking effects by replacing the spoken word by pantomime. "He does not *say* that he is pleased that some pretty girls are coming to see him, but performs the silent dance, in which two bread rolls stuck on forks act as dancing feet on the table (*The Gold Rush*). He does not argue, he fights. . . . The incredible visual concreteness of every one of his scenes makes for a great part of Chaplin's art."[144] As a further, striking example he cites a

scene from Sternberg's *The Docks of New York* in which a revolver shot is illustrated by the rising of a flock of birds. Such an effect is not just a contrivance on the part of a director to deal with the evil of silence by using an indirect visual method of explaining to the audience that there has been a bang. On the contrary, a positive artistic effect results from the paraphrase. Such indirect representation of an event in a material that is strange to it, or giving not the action itself but only its consequences, is a favorite method in all art. To take an example at random: when Francesca da Rimini tells how she fell in love with the man with whom she was in the habit of reading, and only says "We read no more that day," Dante thereby indicates, indirectly, simply by giving the consequences, that on this day they kissed each other. And this indirectness is shockingly impressive.[145]

Censorship in the Movies

The example from Dante brings me directly to the main case I want to discuss, the Production Code that regulated Hollywood movies from

141. Arnheim (1957), p. 60.   142. Ibid., p. 66.
143. Ibid., p. 156.   144. Ibid., pp. 106–7.
145. Ibid., p. 107.

1930 (effectively only from 1934) until the 1950s.[146] Movie directors were constrained by the code to use indirect means in representing certain themes, notably sexual ones. In some cases at least, the effect of the constraint was to enhance rather than detract from the artistic value of the representation.

In II.9 I cited Stephen Holmes to the effect that political constitutions can be enabling, not only disabling. In a strikingly similar formulation, Richard Maltby argues that the Hays Code "operated, however perversely, as an enabling mechanism at the same time that it was a repressive one."[147] To see how the code enabled directors to reach artistic heights they might otherwise not have scaled, we may first note the difference among three modes of censorship in the American movie industry before World War II. First, there is *downstream censorship*, as when foreign countries, individual states, or municipalities refused to show movies that were deemed offensive in one way or another.[148] Second, there is *midstream censorship*, which takes place after production but before release, allowing for modifications "in order to assuage the concerns of civic, religious, or manufacturing interests."[149] Finally, there is *upstream censorship*, which took place at "the site of production" rather than at "the site of exhibition." This was how the Hays Code operated. Directors had to submit their scripts ahead of time to the Production Code Administration, and engaged in lengthy negotiations over tiny details. Fritz Lang recounts, for instance, his struggle with the Hays Office over the behavior of a murderer:

After the killing he says something like, "Oh, my God!" *Two* days of violent discussion with the Hays Office: "He cannot say, 'Oh, my God!'" "Why not?" "Well, it *means* 'Oh, my God, help me to get out of murder.'" I said, "OK, I see your viewpoint, what should he say?" So they said, "Good heavens." I said, "Now wait a moment. Even I, as a foreigner, know better than that. I don't want to have the audience laugh at it. 'Good heavens!'" After two days the man who ran the office in those days . . . came up with a solution: instead of "Oh, my God!" it was "Good God" or some such thing – practically the same.[150]

The representation of romantic and sexual relationships was negotiated in an equally fine-grained manner. Over time, the relation

---

146. The full text of the code is reproduced in Belton, ed. (1996). Maltby (1993) is a full historical treatment of its emergence and earlier operation.
147. Maltby (1993), p. 41.   148. Ibid., p. 42.
149. Ibid., p. 43.   150. In Bogdanovich (1997), p. 210.

between director and censor evolved into a game of hide-and-seek, in which the director became ever more skilled at conveying banned facts by indirect means and the censors ever more skilled at detecting (what they thought to be) innuendoes. Fritz Lang tells how the "Hays Office insisted that we couldn't show or glamorize a prostitute – that's impossible. They said she should not swing her purse back and forth. You know how we overcame it? We had to prominently show a sewing machine in her apartment: thus she was not a whore, she was a 'seamstress.'"[151] Yet at the same time as the director tried to veil any reference to prostitution, the censor tried to delete even the most veiled references to it. "In 1935 the Production Administration Office insisted on the removal of one shot, of rain falling on a door, from *The Devil Is a Woman*, because it signified prostitution."[152]

When Darryl Zanuck was planning a movie that mentions an operation, he made it clear to his scriptwriters that they should "stress the point that the operation is not an abortion, but at the same time the audience will guess that it is an abortion." A studio official told him, however, that any references to abortions were out of the question. When Zanuck replied that the movie had no specific reference to abortion, the official countered that "abortion . . . will be the inference which the audience and the censors will draw from the picture" and that "the mere insertion of a medical term for the operation to indicate that it was not an abortion will not be sufficient to escape the fact."[153] The only hope of the director was to write for an audience that was one notch more sophisticated than the censor.

THE BENEFITS OF CENSORSHIP

It was by virtue of this intimate strategic relationship of director, censor, and audience that the code could exercise its benign effects on creativity. Mere downstream or midstream censorship could not have had the same impact. The need for exquisite fine-tuning and indirection brought comedy, in particular, to new levels of sophistication. It does not ring quite true, therefore, when Maltby writes, "As an

151. Ibid., p. 200; see also McGilligan (1997), p. 277.
152. Maltby (1993), p. 66.
153. Maltby and Craven (1995), p. 342.

influence on production, the regulation of movie content through the Production Code might best be understood as a generic pressure, comparable to the pressure of convention in a romantic comedy or a Western."[154] Before the code, movies were certainly subject to the general conventions of the various genres, such as the tripartite structure of comedies (boy and girl meet – they break up – they reunite). Yet these conventions were too general and coarse-grained to represent any kind of *challenge*. In fact, Maltby's own account of the impact of the Code shows that it went beyond that of mere convention:

> The knowing double-entendre, whose greatest exponent was Mae West, 'the finest woman who ever walked the streets,' was a step toward a satisfactory economic solution to the problem of censoring sexuality.... Through the 1930s, Hollywood developed the double-entendre to the point reached by Zanuck in his argument, where the responsibility for the sophisticated interpretation could be displaced entirely onto the sophisticated viewer.... Late 1930s movies reached a particular 'innocence' by presenting a deadpan level of performance that acted as a foil to the secondary 'sophisticated' narrative constructed within the imagination of the viewer.... The more the movie world diverged from what audiences knew went on in the real world, the more the movies took on a comic sophistication of their own. They gained a wit, a knowingness that audiences could take pleasure in, because it revealed and rewarded their own sophistication.[155]

The champagne-like quality of the movies of Ernst Lubitsch, for instance, may owe something to this constraint. In one account, "Lubitsch brought a maturity to the handling of sex in pictures that was not dimmed by the dimness of the censors who took over in the early thirties – indeed he seems to have treated them as rather an amusing challenge – because his method was so circuitous and light that he could get away with almost anything."[156] This may well be an accurate analysis, but it is also imaginable that Lubitsch's creative gifts were *enhanced* – rather than merely *undimmed* – by the censorship.

One instance of the benefits of censorship is reminiscent of the Sternberg example cited from Arnheim. Among the many run-ins that Fred Astaire had with the censors over the years, most were trivial although occasionally mildly harmful in their effect. In one case, the impact, although minimal, was benign. In *Top Hat*, Astaire and

---

154. Maltby (1993), p. 70.   155. Maltby and Craven (1995), p. 342.
156. Bogdanovich (1997), p. 35.

Ginger Rogers, on their way to the park that is the scene of their dance "Isn't it a lovely day to be caught in the rain," are seen in a hansom cab. "Because the play on the word 'damn' in this scene ('Who was the horse's dam?' 'It didn't give a dam.') was found objectionable by Hollywood's censorship office, the film was shot so that Rogers blots out the 'dam' of the response by slamming the trap door of the cab – an improvement over the original."[157] As in Sternberg's movie, the effect is obtained by having the viewer *infer* the punch line rather than by showing it in the obvious, direct way; hence the viewer is made an accomplice to the joke rather than merely its passive audience.

The Hays Code could also have a benign impact outside comedy. In *Key Largo*, starring Humphrey Bogart, Lauren Bacall, and Edward G. Robinson,

Bacall had a difficult scene with Robinson, in which the gangster taunts the young widow with graphic sexual intentions. She responds by spitting in his face, leaving Rocco standing open-mouthed and furious. Huston knew that the language in the scene would cause a problem with the Breen office. Brooks had explicitly "written all the vile things he was saying to her, but John [Huston] told me, 'You know we can't say that crap. So think of something else.'" Brooks suggested that Robinson say the lines, but that they be whispered and the audience not hear them. The scene was made more effective because it gives rein to the viewers' fantasies, but it put an additional dramatic burden on Bacall, whose reaction to Robinson is the dramatic focus.[158]

The idea of leaving something to the viewer's imagination is also central in the argument that the Hays Code, while intended to ban eroticism from the movies, actually enhanced it.[159] George Cukor, for instance, objected strongly to nudity in the movies. "Now, don't get

157. Mueller (1985), p. 80, note 7.   158. Sperber and Lax (1997), p. 414.
159. This view differs from the superficially similar ideas presented by Bataille (1957). According to him, eroticism presupposes – and arises through – the *transgression* of given constraints. Bazin's argument, cited here, is that eroticism arises through the need to *conform* to the constraints. Bataille is closer to (and inspired by) the ideas of Caillois discussed in II.10. If one applied Caillois's theory of *constrained constraint-breaking* to film, eroticism would be generated by the brief sight of a nipple in a film otherwise constrained by the ban on nudity. In Bazin's view, it is the unconditional need to abide by the ban that is the condition for eroticism. I am not saying that this Caillois-like conception of eroticism in the movies bears much resemblance to Bataille's view, except that both emphasize the difference between behavior that ignores constraints – "la liberté première de la vie animale" (Bataille 1957, p. 76) – and behavior that derives its efficacy from the constraints that it violates.

me wrong. I'm not a great moralist or anything. I just think it's awfully easy to do it that way. . . . Just taking the clothes off and clutching and kissing with an open mouth is too simple."[160] In the same interview, he says, "The great rule was that if there was a kiss, the parties had to keep one foot on the floor. But in spite of those restrictions, I have a feeling that it was much more *erotic*, that there was much more of an atmosphere of eroticism."[161] But this isn't quite right. As André Bazin observes in his "Marginal notes on eroticism in the Cinema," the effect was more erotic *because of* the restrictions. Bazin argues, for instance, that the scene from *The Seven Year Itch* when air from the subway grating blows up Marilyn Monroe's skirt "could only be born in the world of a cinema with a long, rich, Byzantine tradition of censorship. Inventiveness such as this presupposes an extraordinary refinement of the imagination, acquired in the struggle against the rigorous stupidity of a puritan code. Hollywood, *in spite and because of the taboos that dominate it*, remains the world capital of cinematic eroticism."[162]

In the cases I have cited the Hays Code raised the level of sophistication of directors, actors, and viewers. Even though some viewers might have *preferred* more direct language, more nudity, and generally fewer indirections, they probably *benefited* from the constraints. (Similarly, Arnheim argues that although viewers prefer sound, color, stereoscopic vision, and wide-screen, they would benefit from their absence.) When given the choice between immediate satiation and delayed gratification, many choose the former, only to regret it. By forcing directors to use indirect means, the Hays Code inadvertently also induced them to raise the level of enjoyment of the audiences.

The code also illustrates the more general idea that from the point of view of the censored, explicit censorship ex ante is preferable to implicit censorship ex post. In many formerly Communist countries, dissidents demanded explicit regulations of what they could and could not say, on the assumption that once the rules were in place they would always be able to write around them.[163] I do not claim, however, that their opinions would have been *more* effective when expressed indirectly. Nor, as we shall see in III.10, do I claim that the Hays Code was invariably benign in its impact on the aesthetic qualities of films.

160. In Bogdanovich (1997), pp. 466, 467.
161. Ibid., pp. 464–65.
162. Bazin (1972), p. 172; my italics. See also his essay on *The Outlaw* (ibid., pp. 163–68).
163. Zinoviev (1979), pp. 306–307, cited and discussed in Elster (1993d), pp. 90–92.

III.7. *LUCIEN LEUWEN* AS AN EMPTY SET

Stendhal's novel *Lucien Leuwen*, published fifty years after he died, is unfinished. In the first part, Lucien leaves Paris to join a regiment in Nancy, where he meets Mme de Chasteller, a young widow, and falls in love with her. In the second part, separated from her by accident, he becomes a functionary in Paris and is sent to the provinces to engage in various electoral shenanigans. In the third, unwritten part, he was supposed to reunite with Mme de Chasteller. It would have been the only one of Stendhal's novels to have a conventional happy ending. I shall suggest an explanation why it was left unfinished: the constraints that Stendhal imposed on himself cannot be satisfied simultaneously. They define an empty set.

The Paradox of Love

The source of the problem lies in Stendhal's paradoxical conception of love.[164] It is an emotion that, in its highest form, is doomed to remain unexpressed. Even if the love is requited, the lovers will never know it. While these statements are not apt descriptions of the love of Julien for Mme de Rênal or of Fabrice for Clélia, they do capture Stendhal's own tormented love for Méthilde, which gave him the raw material for *De l'amour*. As he says in that work, "It is only by loving less that you can have courage towards the one you love."[165] Thus "the prosaic person (*l'âme vulgaire*) calculates the chances of success regardless of the painful risk of defeat, takes a pride in his coarseness and laughs at sensitiveness (*l'âme tendre*), which for all its intelligence is always too ill at ease to say the simple things which are bound to succeed."[166] As we shall see, Lucien's love for Mme de Chasteller is that of an "âme tendre."

Stendhal painted himself into a corner. The woman he loved was tender, proud, and modest. A man who showed any kind of complacent self-assurance or rakish behavior toward her would ipso facto not be worthy of her love. Conversely, a woman who can be seduced by outward self-assurance is ipso facto not a woman

---

164. See Elster (1999a), Ch. II.2, for a fuller discussion of Stendhal's treatment on love, *De l'Amour*, and its relation to *Lucien Leuwen*.
165. Stendhal (1980), Fragment 47.
166. Ibid., Ch. 24. A virtually identical analysis is offered in W. Miller (1993), p. 169.

worth loving. This is not the Groucho Marx syndrome: a woman who would stoop to love *me* is ipso facto not worth loving. Rather the syndrome has the following form: a woman who would accept my advances is not worth loving, since to make advances betrays a calculating spirit and the failure to recognize this fact betrays an inferior spirit. To get out of this predicament, Stendhal turned to the vicarious satisfaction he could find in fiction. As I said, Stendhal's novels are much more than daydreams, but they are also that.

THE NOVEL AS DAYDREAM

In *Lucien Leuwen*, Stendhal gives free rein to his desire for vicarious satisfaction in the love scenes between Lucien and Mme de Chasteller. Paul Valéry reports that reading these scenes "effected in me the miracle of a confusion that I abhor"[167] – that between the emotions of the protagonists and those of the reader. I would add that they also represent a confusion, or fusion, of the emotions of the protagonists and those of Stendhal. In studying this fusion we can draw on Stendhal's marginal comments on the progression of the manuscripts, his difficulties in making the characters go the way he wanted them to, and his plans for their further development. I shall try to argue that in the novel, as in his life, Stendhal got himself into an impossible situation.

Le rouge et le noir was inspired by a *fait divers*, which spared Stendhal the necessity of inventing everything. With *Lucien Leuwen*, he had to invent. His comments on these contrasting creative styles – constrained versus unconstrained – are strikingly contradictory. Early on he writes in the margin of the manuscript, "I cannot create a high-spirited dialogue as long as I think about the plot, whence the advantage of working on a ready-made tale, as Julien Sorel."[168] A few hundred pages later, he writes, "One never goes as far as when one does not know where one is going. This is not like *Julien*, so much the better."[169] Inventing dialogue and story at the same time seems to have intoxicated him, yet if he had written under the constraint of a ready-made story he might not have got himself into the blind alley that the novel turned out to be.

167. Valéry (1957), p. 555. 168. Stendhal (1952), p. 1492.
169. Ibid., p. 1539.

In between the parts of the manuscript where we find these comments, there is the extraordinary interplay between Lucien and Mme
de Chasteller. I shall single out two scenes, which take place on the
following background. Lucien and Mme de Chasteller have come to
love each other deeply, yet are uncertain about one another's feelings.
She fears that he may be no more than a rake, he that she does not
really love him. Whenever he makes a clumsy and tentative advance,
she sees it as a reason for doubting his character; she grows haughty,
he is made desperate. Yet they gradually grow closer to each other.
Lucien writes her a letter; she, after some soul-searching, replies, in
what she believes to be a severe and uncompromising tone. In an
authorial aside, Stendhal comments as follows:

Why note that her reply involved a studied attempt at the haughtiest turns
of phrase? Three or four times Leuwen was urged to abandon all hope, the
very word *hope* was avoided with an infinite adroitness that made Mme de
Chasteller very pleased with herself. Alas, without knowing it she was the
victim of her Jesuitical education; she deceived herself, in applying badly,
and unawares, the art of deceiving others which she had been taught at the
Sacré-Coeur. She *answered*: everything lay in this word, which she preferred
to ignore.[170]

If Mme de Chasteller, in her self-deception, will not admit to herself the significance of replying, Lucien, in his innocence, does not
understand it:

'Ah! So Mme de Chasteller has answered!' is what a young Parisian a little
less well-bred than Leuwen would have thought. 'Her high-mindedness has
decided on it at last. This is the first step. The rest is a matter of form; it will
take a month or two, depending on whether I conduct myself more or less
skillfully, and she has more or less exaggerated ideas as to what ought to be
the defence of a woman of the highest virtue.'

Leuwen, sprawled upon the ground while he read these terrible lines,
hadn't so much as a glimpse of the main point, which should have been:
'Mme de Chasteller has answered!' He was scared by the severity of the
language and the deeply persuasive tone with which she urged him never
again to talk of such feelings.[171]

170. Ibid., p. 959. As an analysis of self-deception, this passage is strikingly similar
to the example in Sartre (1943, pp. 94 ff.) of the woman who lets a man take her
hand, yet refuses to admit to herself the meaning of her act. She finds refuge
in lofty and exalted conversation, as Mme de Chasteller deceives herself by the
severity of her tone.
171. Stendhal (1952), p. 960.

III.7. Lucien Leuwen *as an Empty Set*

This tender and comic ballet goes on for a while, the two lovers almost succeeding in telling each other about their love, yet never quite. At one point Mme de Chasteller scolds him for his frequent visits, which could damage her reputation:

'Well?' said Leuwen, hardly breathing.

So far Mme de Chasteller's manner had been decorous, proper, cold – in Leuwen's eyes at least. The tone of voice with which he uttered the word *well?* might have failed even the most accomplished Don Juan; in Leuwen it was not due to any talent, it was an impulse of nature, it was natural. This simple remark of Leuwen's changed everything.[172]

Mme de Chasteller, moved, almost fails to go on, but Lucien of course fails to see that she fails. We seem to have got no further. Lucien leaves her, "evidently tottering." At this point, Stendhal seems to be on the point of giving up. Lucien really is too clumsy, and Stendhal after all cannot push him in the arms of Mme de Chasteller. He writes in the margin: "Upon which the chronicler says: one cannot expect a virtuous woman to give herself absolutely; she has to be taken. The best hunting dog can do no more than bring the game within gunshot. If the hunter doesn't shoot, the dog is helpless. The novelist is like the dog of his hero."[173] The comment strikingly illustrates the need for the behavior of characters in a novel to be "in character" (III.4). What they do must be plausible, given their behavior up to that point. Lucien's dilemma is that he is both inferior to a "less well-bred young Parisian" *and* superior to "the most accomplished Don Juan." The very superiority of mind that makes him capable of inspiring love also makes him incapable of recognizing it and of expressing his own.[174]

To get out of his predicament, Stendhal engineers a situation in which the love of Lucien and Mme de Chasteller for each other can be shown and understood, and yet not be declared:

Mme de Chasteller took pity on him, and intended to shake his hand in an English fashion, as a sign of friendship. Seeing Mme de Chasteller's hand approach his, Leuwen seized it and raised it slowly to his lips. As he made this movement his face drew very close to that of Mme de Chasteller; he dropped her hand and took her in his arms, pressing his lips to her cheeks. Mme de Chasteller hadn't the strength to resist, and stood motionless as if abandoned in his arms. He embraced her with ecstasy and redoubled his kisses. At

172. Ibid., p. 1035. 173. Ibid., p. 1537.
174. For a similar pattern in *Le rouge et le noir*, see Stendhal (1952), p. 549.

last Mme de Chasteller freed herself gently, but her eyes, brimming with tears, frankly revealed the deepest tenderness. However, she did succeed in saying:

'Goodbye, monsieur . . .'

And as he gazed at her aghast, she added:

'Goodbye, *my dear*, till tomorrow . . . But go now.'[175]

The Dangers of Premature Satiation

There follows a period of extreme happiness, two or three weeks, during which Lucien and Mme de Chasteller are constantly together, innocently but intensely in love. Yet Stendhal must have felt that this was a case of premature satiation. The Lucien who achieves the bliss that he failed to achieve with Méthilde Dembowski is not yet he, Stendhal. Lucien has no character yet, he knows nothing about the world, he has not exposed himself to action, he is pure sensibility. Stendhal and Lucien share the urge to expose themselves to the world and acquire a character. In a diary entry from 1805, Stendhal notes, "In the future, seek all occasions to be in motion, to act incessantly, even for stupid causes."[176] In *De l'amour*, he observes that "Everything can be acquired in solitude, except character"; also, "To have a strong character one must have experienced the effect produced by others upon oneself; therefore others are necessary" (*il faut les autres*).[177] In the novel he has Lucien tell himself, as his reason for leaving Paris, "I need action, and plenty of it. So off to the regiment!"[178]

In Nancy, however, Lucien falls in love, and sees no action to speak of. Stendhal must break up the bliss and throw Lucien into the world. Using a ridiculous and manifestly teleological device (III.4), Stendhal separates the two lovers by making Lucien believe that Mme de Chasteller, whom he has seen daily at close quarters, has suddenly given birth to a child.[179] He returns to Paris to enter the bureaucracy of the July Monarchy. On his travel in the provinces he finally does see action, quite a lot of it in fact, some of which would have been dishonorable had it not been for his fundamental

---

175. Ibid., p. 1037.   176. Stendhal (1981), p. 327.
177. Stendhal (1980), Fragments 1, 92.   178. Stendhal (1952), p. 778.
179. Brombert (1968), p. 105, finds Lucien's gullibility entirely in character and evidence of his "touching blindness." I think it is more plausible to see it as evidence of the problems Stendhal had in constructing his plot.

integrity. So why, having achieved his aim of exposing Lucien to character formation, didn't Stendhal go on to write the Hegelian synthesis?

In *La Création chez Stendhal*, Jean Prévost offers this explanation of the novel's unfinished state:

> To avoid insipidity and the gradual arrival of happiness, Stendhal would have needed a final, real obstacle to put between Mme de Chasteller and Lucien. . . . It only remained to find the *resistance* which would have given substance to the struggle. It was because of lack of having found a real obstacle to put between the two lovers that he left unfinished a book that was so close to being achieved.[180]

But this claim – that the novel was left unfinished because Stendhal simply couldn't think of an obstacle that would serve to separate the lovers – is not very convincing. Mme de Chasteller's grumpy father, for instance, could easily have served this function, as Darcy serves as an obstacle to the marriage of Bingley and Jane Bennet. With a novelist of Stendhal's stature it is intrinsically more plausible to seek the explanation in a structural flaw.

Before I try to identify that flaw, there is an additional point to be made. Stendhal seems almost as enamored of Lucien's witty and worldly father as of Lucien himself. Whereas Lucien has all the awkward grace of a naive and idealistic youth, his father has the uncontrived charm of the born *raconteur* who above all things wants to keep himself entertained. Each of them, in his own way, embodies the ideal of *being natural*, which was, for Stendhal, "the promised land."[181] Leuwen père has the same tender impatience for Lucien as has Stendhal himself. Like Stendhal, he steers Lucien into the right channels by arranging for him to have a post in the bureaucracy, a left-hand mistress and then a right-hand mistress, and so on. (And, like Stendhal, he tells him, "Be free.")[182] Stendhal seems to identify both with the father and with the son. It may not be totally implausible to see a connection between this two-track daydream and an extraordinary exercise in wish fulfillment in which Stendhal grants himself a number of "privileges," one of which is that "four times a year, and each time for an unlimited period, the privileged will be able to occupy two bodies simultaneously."[183]

180. Prévost (1971), p. 313.   181. Starobinski (1961), p. 228.
182. Stendhal (1952), p. 1069.   183. Stendhal (1982), p. 984.

If Stendhal had kept Lucien firmly in his place, the privilege might at least have been granted vicariously. But he did not. He wanted to endow Lucien with both innocence and character. The innocence is the key to his love for Mme de Chasteller, and hers for him; the character is what he sets out to acquire when leaving for Nancy and in fact achieves only after his return to Paris. In the third act, he would then marry Mme de Chasteller and enable Stendhal, by proxy, to have his cake and eat it too. But there is no reason to believe that Mme de Chasteller would recognize in the lucid and worldly cynic who Lucien by that time would have become, the awkward young man whom she had loved. In fact, it is hard to escape the conclusion that Lucien would become more and more like his father.

Stendhal might have achieved the feat of combining innocence and character, being naive and witty, by firmly distinguishing between father and son. This would in fact have enabled him to be two persons simultaneously, to laugh at himself without the object of amusement being infected and corroded by the irony. Yet because Stendhal did not respect the need to keep Lucien separate from his father, the two-track daydream could not be sustained. Alternatively, he could have let Mme de Chasteller undergo a similar *Bildung*, so that when she and Lucien meet again they can laugh affectionately at their earlier selves, as do Elizabeth Bennet and Darcy when the scales fall from their eyes. In his novels, however, Stendhal did not give his heroines that kind of development.

I conclude, therefore, that *Lucien Leuwen* remained unfinished because its separate parts converge to a nonexistent point. There can be no synthesis of innocence and wit, naiveté and cynicism.

III.8. RANDOMIZATION IN THE ARTS

The idea of choice has two antonyms: chance and necessity. Thus to assert the existence of free will against universal determinism, one cannot appeal to quantum mechanics: that would simply be to substitute one opponent for another. It follows that the choice to give up the ability to choose can be accomplished by delegating the outcome to chance as well as to necessity. Whereas the focus in the book so far has been on necessity, I want to say a few words about *precommitment to chance*. Although I shall mainly discuss the use of this device in the arts, let me first say a few words about the use of randomization as a means of self-binding in the contexts discussed in previous chapters.

RANDOMIZATION AND SELF-BINDING

In *The Strategy of Conflict*, Thomas Schelling argued that "the threat that leaves something to chance" is more credible than a threat that leaves the decision to carry it out entirely up to the agent.[184] In the terminology of I.4, this amounts to a mixed threat-and-warning. "If you do not write me a check for ten thousand dollars I shall kill you, and even if I cannot bring myself to do that intentionally I'll be so upset by your refusal that I may just pull the trigger in nervous excitement." An individual may also randomize to protect himself against bias. "The medical experimenter who selects which patients are to receive a new treatment for a disease and which are to receive the standard treatment or none at all, can unconsciously select for the new treatment patients that are healthier and have therefore a better chance of recovery. Randomization prevents the exercise of such bias."[185] In politics, randomization has been used or advocated as a means of precommitting oneself against undue influence. By having elections timed randomly rather than periodically or at the discretion of the government, the framers may "protect themselves" (but see II.2 and II.12) against their tendency to design economic policy with a view to reelection.[186] By choosing political representatives at random and having them serve for a short period, the citizens may protect themselves against their liability to take bribes.[187]

RANDOMIZING AS A TOPIC

Randomization may be used as a *device* in all the arts. In literature it can also serve as a *topic*. Although my interest here is mainly in the former, I begin with a few words about the latter. The paradigmatic example of a work of art in which the plot turns entirely on randomization is Luke Rhinehart's cult novel *The Dice Man*, which portrays and perhaps defends randomization as a way of life. (His recent follow-up, *The Search for the Dice Man*, is less interesting.) The main character of the novel is a psychiatrist who starts making some everyday decisions on a random basis, a practice that then expands

---

184. Schelling (1960), Ch. 8.   185. Suppes (1984), p. 211.
186. Lindbeck (1976).
187. Najemy (1982) describes the importance of this idea in fourteenth-century Florentine politics.

to the point of taking over his life, culminating in a quasi-religious text *The Book of the Die*. Other writers who have made randomization a key element in their stories include Jorge Luis Borges and Shirley Jackson, who both wrote famous short stories titled "The Lottery." The key element in Graham Greene's *The Tenth Man* is the random selection of hostages to be executed. What these literary uses of randomization show is that a story can be compelling and plausible even if events do not follow upon one another in an intelligible order, as long as the non sequitur itself is intelligible.

RANDOMIZING AS A DEVICE

To understand the use of randomization as a device for producing works of art, we must first clarify the concept. To achieve *objective randomness*[188] one needs a stable physical device that generates one of several possible outcomes with known probabilities. Flipping a coin, tossing a die, and spinning a lottery wheel were traditional devices of this kind; modern equivalents are tables of random numbers and computer programs. Typically, these devices are equi-probabilistic, that is, each outcome has the same likelihood of being realized, but in theory as well as in practice they can be designed to yield unequal chances.[189] For many practical purposes, objective randomness can be replaced by *epistemic randomness* – the outcome is random as far as we know. An example may be taken from the first systematic discussion of randomization, Thomas Gataker's *On the Nature and Use of Lots*: "Suppose two by the way contending which way they shall take, put themselves upon the flight of the next fowle that crosseth them, or upon the turning of a stranger, whom they see ride before them, to the right hand or to the left."[190] Artists use objectively as well as epistemically random devices to achieve their ends.

In III.4 I argued that each choice made in the creation of a work of art serves as a constraint on later choices. An artist may decide, however, to generate the constraints randomly rather than intentionally.

---

188. For some complications in the idea of objective randomness, see Elster (1989b), pp. 39–52.
189. Elster (1989b), pp. 47–49. When Boulez (1986), p. 179, writes that the "intrusion of 'chance' into the form of a work of art may manifest itself in circuits using multiple nodal points with different probabilities of triggering," this may be what he has in mind.
190. Gataker (1627), p.16.

Thus Francis Bacon began his pictures by throwing paint at the canvas, so that the resulting blots would serve as constraints on the further work, limiting his freedom and presumably enhancing his creativity. Jackson Pollock's "poured paintings" may be seen as a variant of this idea. Although Pollock said that "with experience it seems possible to control the flow of paint to a great extent" and that "I deny the accident,"[191] these claims do not seem entirely plausible. Rather, I would assume that any accidents that occurred in the pouring of the paint on the canvas were incorporated as constraints on the later stages of the pouring. Although not the object of intention ex ante, they would become the object of intentional attention ex post.

Something similar may occur in the generation of electronic rock music, where the use of feedback almost unavoidably (expect perhaps for Jimi Hendrix and a few other virtuosi) creates an element of unpredictability and randomness. To some extent, it is claimed, this is what generates much of the excitement in this music. The performer must constantly react to, and improvise on the basis of, the unintended sounds generated by the feedback. This constant challenge will focus his attention and creativity better than if he were to generate the musical line all from within himself. Mere routine playing will simply not be possible. If these claims are correct, technical mastery of the feedback effect may actually detract from creativity by removing some of the occasions for improvising.

As a literary example, we may consider randomization in the composition of *Naked Lunch*. "The junkie dealt with the hazy juxtaposition of word and image, and to achieve this effect in *Naked Lunch*, Burroughs had broken down the traditional plot and thought structure of the novel by random sequencing of the book's episodes, which gave the book its dreamy quality."[192] In the traditional conception of the writer's craft, Burroughs would have carefully chosen the sequence so as to achieve this dreamy quality. A conscious choice, however, can leave traces behind itself that testify to a more logical thought than that found in dreams. Watching films or plays one sometimes gets the impression that the stage instructions have called for "disorder," and that the director has tried to carry them out by more or less ingenious attempts to arrange chairs, newspapers, and so on in some casual layout. But the deliberately casual often fails to convince.

191. Cernuschi (1992), p. 128.   192. Schumacher (1992), p. 354.

In this sense, therefore, Burroughs' choice was the right one. However, randomization carries with it a danger of its own, namely, the risk that the observer may read an unintended pattern into the outcome generated by the random process. William Feller, referring to the pattern of German bombing over Britain in World War II, writes, "To the untrained eye, randomness appears as a regularity or tendency to cluster."[193] Similarly, Daniel Kahneman and Amos Tversky write, "Among the 20 possible sequences (disregarding direction and label) of six tosses of a coin, for example, we venture that only HT-THTH appears really random. For four tosses, there may not be any."[194] To use randomization to produce the appearance of chance is a risky business.

JOHN CAGE

A very elaborate experiment in aleatory writing is John Cage's Harvard Lectures *I-VI* (that is their title). To construct his texts or "mesostics" he used a combination of arbitrary constraints and randomization, a flavor of which is conveyed by the following excerpt from his introduction:

Like acrostics, mesostics are written in the conventional way horizontally, but at the same time they follow a vertical rule, down the middle not down the edge as in an acrostic, a string which spells a word or name, not necessarily connected with what is being written, though it may be.... If I am fulfilling some request, the celebration of a birthday, the remembrance of someone who recently died, or the furtherance of some project, I write mesostics. In the writing of the wing words, the horizontal text, the letters of the vertical string help me out of sentimentality.... In taking the next step in my work, the exploration of nonintention, I don't solve the puzzle that the mesostic string presents. Instead I write or find a source text which I then use as an oracle. I ask it what word I shall use for this letter and what one for the next, and so on. This frees me from memory, taste, likes and dislikes.[195]

Cage is better known for his use of random devices in music.[196] His most famous, entirely silent composition work 4'33" consists of

193. Feller (1968), p. 161.
194. Kahneman and Tversky (1982). See also Wagenaar (1988), p. 109.
195. Cage (1990), pp. 1–2. 196. See Revill (1992).

movements (that is, periods of silence) of chance-determined duration. He also used radio and star maps as epistemically random
sources of sound. He justified these practices by the Zen-like idea
that "the highest purpose is to have no purpose at all."[197] The idea
of aesthetic choice is to be banished. At most, choice arises when
the "chance operations yield impossible requirements, in which case
the player is to use his or her discretion, so that chance generates the
conditions in which choice is to be exercised."[198] Such effects were
not, however, seen as desiderata in their own right. Cage objected
to the music by Christian Wolff, whose "success depends on instant
reaction to the unpredictable choices of the other players, involving
a dangerous proximity to improvisation and an interpersonal spontaneity which Cage would never countenance."[199] Nor, presumably,
would he countenance the harnessing of random feedback or intrapersonal spontaneity to artistic purposes.

We learn from the biography of John Cage that he used *I Ching*
to regulate practical matters of everyday life.[200] In college, Cage did
quite badly in the courses in which he just read the assigned materials.
But then, in one course, "instead of following the herd, Cage went into
the library stacks and read the first book written by an author whose
name began with Z, and in an interesting hint of a system he would
apply years later, he read other materials at random, preparing by
that means for his examination in due course. He was given an A."[201]
If one wants to break out of the charmed circle of routine and to go
beyond what one already knows, it would indeed be self-defeating to
try to do this using the knowledge one already has. Instead, one must
expose oneself to the genuinely unexpected, for example, by adopting
a random device. However, it still remains true that the selection of
the set from which the random draw is made must be a conscious
one, and based on knowledge that one already has; otherwise, an
infinite regress arises. A library, after all, is not a random sample of
the universe.

To the extent that it relies on randomizing or on producing periods of silence, Cage's work is entirely unserious. The most chari-
table interpretation is that it is a gigantic and successful put-on.[202]

197. Cage (1961), p. 155.   198. Revill (1992), p. 135.
199. Ibid., p. 211.   200. Revill (1992), p. 132.
201. Revill (1992), p. 34.
202. See also Shattuck (1997) for similar comments on the work of Marcel Duchamp.

He may be of interest to psychologists, as an instance of what happens when someone enacts the precepts of *The Dice Man*, but his work is devoid of aesthetic interest. Among his practices the only one with an aesthetic rationale is the use of self-imposed constraints to avoid sentimentality. By contrast, the use of objective or epistemic randomness to select *within* constraints has no aesthetic justification. It has been suggested that the value of his silent music is that of taking the dictum "Less is more" to its ultimate conclusion,[203] analogously to the Zen idea of one hand clapping. Yet by *removing* choice rather than *restricting* it one destroys creativity rather than enhances it.

One might argue, perhaps, that the very decision to present randomly generated sounds or periods of silence of randomly generated durations is itself a choice that can be assessed from an aesthetic point of view.[204] This argument rests, however, on a confusion between aesthetic experiences and meta-aesthetic statements. What has been called "inferential art"[205] represents the ultimate modernist fallacy (III.2), that of presenting a work of art whose *only* value is to generate reflections on itself.

III.9. CREATIVITY AND CONSTRAINTS IN JAZZ

In this section I discuss the nature of aesthetic value in jazz and the contribution of constraints to such value. For the most part I limit myself to the period between 1936 and 1942, which, for me, represents its highest achievements. The body of recordings of Billie Holiday, Lester Young, and Johnny Hodges with the Basie and Ellington orchestras and in small groups remains unsurpassed, with the important exception of the work of Louis Armstrong from the 1920s. Although I can perceive, intellectually, that Charlie Parker reached the same artistic heights, most of his work does not speak to me. Before proceeding, I should note that I have no musical training; I do not play any instrument; I do not read music. I can only hope that forty years of daily listening to jazz has provided me with what has been called "musical literacy."[206]

---

203. Kostelanetz (1991b), p. 195.   204. Kostelanetz (1991a), p. 108.
205. Ibid., p. 106.   206. As defined by Levinson (1990).

Determinants of Value in Jazz

In general, as I said earlier, value in the arts consists in the experience of aesthetic and non-aesthetic emotions. In the case of jazz, the non-aesthetic emotions in the listener are produced by music that has what I shall call "emotional depth." The aesthetic emotions can arise at two levels. At the simplest level, they are produced by music that possesses what I shall call "taste." At a more advanced level, the aesthetic emotions are produced by the "story" told by the music, often (although not invariably) an improvised story. Although improvisation – the ability to invent a coherent and interesting story around a given musical theme – is often considered the main or even the only aesthetically valuable feature of jazz,[207] I believe that this view is too narrow. The best jazz musicians can show superb taste and emotional depth simply by a straight rendering of a tune, as in Lester Young's solo on "Things 'bout Coming My Ways" (1941) or in many of Armstrong's big-band recordings from the early 1930s. In fact, for musicians such as Armstrong and Hodges a single note is sufficient to convey the depth and control that lie behind it.

As in other art forms, we need to distinguish between creativity and originality (III.5). Lester Young and Charlie Parker were paradigms of originality. Like Armstrong and Hodges, they were also paradigms of creativity. When Young said, "Gotta be original,"[208] it was probably a warning against wholesale imitation rather than an injunction to create an entirely new musical language. It is a striking fact that the most original of these four musicians had the most slavish imitators, Paul Quinichette in the case of Young and Sonny Stitt in the case of Parker, to the point where they can be mistaken for the originals. By contrast, nobody could ever pass himself off for Armstrong or Hodges for even a single note. Their intonation and tone are, I believe, literally inimitable. Be this as it may, my concern here is with the components of creativity listed in the previous paragraph. Originality, as I argued earlier, has no intrinsic aesthetic value.

Before I proceed to a closer discussion of emotional depth, taste, and storytelling, let me briefly consider the role of technical skill in

---

207. Thus for Dodge (1995), p. 250, "The ultimate worth of jazz resides solely in its melodic line." As is clear from his essay on "The psychology of the hot solo" (ibid., pp. 167–72), this remark refers only to improvisation and not to what I call "sculpted solos."
208. Cited in Porter, ed. (1991), p. 135.

high-quality jazz playing. You cannot reach artistic heights without a measure of technical skill, but beyond a certain level skill doesn't matter. (Mezz Mezzrow is the best-known instance of a player who couldn't make it because he fell below that minimal level.) It makes no difference to their achievements whether Armstrong botches an occasional note, whether Hodges is ill at ease when playing at a very fast tempo, or whether Lester Young's skills on clarinet are somewhat rudimentary. Conversely, the virtuosity of Art Tatum may have been more of a handicap than an asset. If you cannot resist the temptation to exploit your skills to form endless and pointless arabesques – and Tatum often could not – it may be better to be less skilled so that you are forced to concentrate on essentials. Count Basie's piano playing is an example. The obsessions of some trumpet players – Roy Eldridge, Cat Anderson, Maynard Ferguson – with achieving high notes has been similarly detrimental to the quality of their work. In their case – unlike Tatum's – I would add that they were also deficient in taste, so that there was not that much to detract from in the first place.

TASTE AND EMOTIONAL DEPTH

I say a bit more about skill later, but let me turn first to taste and emotional depth. Taste – the sense of order, balance, proportion, timing – is an essential prerequisite for the production of the specifically aesthetic emotions (III.4). Fred Astaire had perfect taste; Gene Kelly didn't. Jane Austen had it; Dickens didn't. Among the enemies of taste, two stand out in the present context: the temptation of virtuosity and the demands of an audience. If you can play very high notes or very fast, there is a temptation to display your skills regardless of their musical relevance. The temptation will often be reinforced by an audience that mistakes acrobatics for art. This is especially notable in the work of drummers such as Gene Krupa or Buddy Rich. But the audience may also encourage gimmicks that require no particular skill. When touring with Jazz at the Philharmonic, Lester Young, to his frustration, had to comply with audience demands for deep honks on the tenor sax.[209]

Emotional depth refers to the capacity to generate strong non-aesthetic emotions in the listener. On the one hand, emotional depth is opposed to emotional shallowness. Benny Goodman, for instance,

209. Buchmann-Möller (1990a), pp. 146–47.

was clearly out of his element in the Holiday-Young-Wilson recordings from the 1930s. In the emotionally charged "I Must Have That Man" (1937) his contribution comes as an anticlimax. On the other hand, emotional depth may be opposed to sentimentality, defined by the feature that "the existence or continuation of the emotion is motivated by the satisfaction experienced in feeling the emotion."[210] With a mediocre musician such as Charlie Shavers it is enough to hear a single note (at least when he plays the open horn) to know that he is sentimental rather than emotional.[211]

Jazz has a larger repertoire of emotion-generating devices than most other music forms. In the period I am discussing, jazz playing usually took the form of improvising around *songs* – tunes with lyrics that usually have a clear and strong emotional content. Jazz vocalists communicate this content directly, adapting timbre and phrasing to the emotions expressed in the words. (There are exceptions, as when Billie Holiday sings "Things Are Looking Up" (1937) in a mode that is more wistful than hopeful.) Instrumentalists may also keep the lyrics in mind when they play. Lester Young, in particular, liked to know the words to the tunes he was playing.[212] Similarly, "when improvisations by a well-known trumpeter once strayed too far from the appropriate feeling of a ballad, Art Blakey shouted across the bandstand, 'Think of the lyrics; think of the lyrics.'"[213]

A characteristic feature of jazz, however, is that it tends to blur this distinction between vocal and instrumental performance. Scat singers use nonsense syllables rather than lyrics, to allow the kind of free improvisation that is otherwise reserved for instrumentalists. More important, some vocalists use their voice as an instrument even in straight singing. When Armstrong sings, his intonation is that of a trumpet player. Billie Holiday, too, sometimes has the attack of an instrumentalist. These features are very clear, for instance, in their renderings (1929 and 1936 respectively) of "I Can't Give You Anything But Love." Conversely, some instrumentalists try to mimic the human voice or to achieve a similar sound texture. A well-known example is Bubber Miley's trumpet playing in the early Ellington

---

210. Budd (1995), p. 96. On sentimentality – in music and more generally – see also Tanner (1976–77). For an amusing contrast, compare the truly sentimental rendering of "For Sentimental Reasons" by Helen Ward with Teddy Wilson (1936) with Billie Holiday's *romantic* renderings of "On the Sentimental Side" (1938).
211. See also Sudhalter (1999), p. 493.   212. In Porter, ed. (1991), p. 162.
213. Berliner (1994), p. 255.

band.[214] Even more expressive was the sound of Ellington's trombonist for many years, "Tricky Sam" Nanton, who could cry like a baby on his horn. Also, when Ellington was asked why he didn't have a vocalist, he replied that with Johnny Hodges in the band he didn't need one. Charlie Parker, too, referred to Hodges as the "Lily Pons" of jazz. Hodges's tone – the greatest sound in jazz – conveys emotions of rare intensity and purity.

This mutual influence of vocalist and instrumentalist upon each other offers each of them a greater repertoire for emotional expression. A vocalist can hit a note in a way that underscores the significance of the corresponding word. Conversely, by using a mute brass players can evoke the plaintive, sorrowful, or distressed accents of the human voice. Thus compared to classical singers and instrumentalists, jazz musicians can draw on a much richer array of emotion-expressing devices. Consider also the use of rhythm. When Hodges plays "The Gal from Joe" (1938) or "Jump for Joy" (1941), his glorious sound and the melody could not by themselves convey the feeling of boundless joy: the sprightly bounce is also due to subtle rhythmic devices the dissection of which is beyond my analytical capacity. By contrast, the emotional flatness of Kiri Te Kanawa singing Gershwin is due to her utter lack of sensitivity to rhythm. Also, the uniform perfection of her voice deprives her of an important means of emotional expression. Opera singers cannot let their voices crack or slip to convey emotion, as does Billie Holiday in "I Must Have that Man" (1937). (Later in life, when her voice *always* cracked, that means was no longer available to her.) Finally, the use of blue notes in jazz conveys the emotions of grief and sadness in a most powerful form. Armstrong's "Basin Street Blues" (1929) and Young's "Blue Lester" (1944) are two outstanding examples.

In art, rationalism (taste) and romanticism (emotional depth) are natural allies, with sentimentality as their common enemy.[215] Taste and emotional depth do not, therefore, vary entirely independently of each other. Total lack of taste is incompatible with great emotional force. Otherwise, all the regions in Figure III.2 are illustrated by specific musicians. In addition to the high-taste-high-emotion,

214. See the outstanding analyses of Miley's playing in Dodge (1995), pp. 84–90, 247–59.
215. Thus I remain unconvinced by the defense of sentimentality in Solomon (1997), for whom "our disdain for sentimentality is the rationalist's discomfort with any play of emotion" (p. 226).

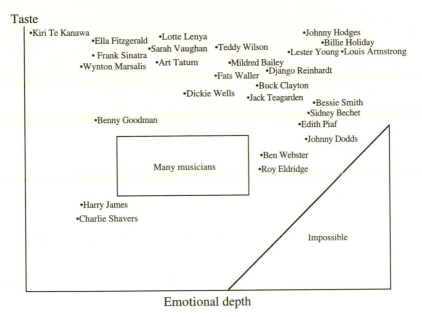

Fig. III.2

high-taste-low-emotion and low-taste-low-emotion musicians mentioned earlier, it includes such high-emotion-low-taste musicians as Roy Eldridge or (at a superior level) Sidney Bechet.[216]

The exact location of individual musicians in this diagram is of course arbitrary (and to some extent dictated by the spatial limitations of the diagram). It is also – a different point – obviously a matter of some controversy. Ella Fitzgerald, for instance, in my opinion has little emotional depth. Her renderings of the standards are the standard renderings, in the sense that she explores and exploits, better than anyone, all the musical possibilities of the songs, with impeccable diction and rhythm. (One must hear her pronouncing "rhythm," in "Fascinating Rhythm" (1959), to grasp the full phonetic potential of that word.) Yet I do not think she gave much attention to the *meaning*

216. The following comment could well apply to Eldridge: "While improvisers strive to project feelings with great conviction, like actors, they must also learn to control them, relating them to other elements of performance. One soloist describes the danger of 'too much emotion' potentially hampering a performance and the occasional need to restrain expression rather than 'overplay a piece for its intended feeling'" (Berliner 1994, p. 259).

of the words and the emotions behind them. An obituary after her death in 1996 cited an apt phrase characterizing her as an "absentee genius." My low assessment of Sarah Vaughan will be even more controversial. I believe that she had essentially the same problem as Tatum.[217] Her vocal gifts were so extraordinary that she was led to do the things that only she could do rather than the things she could do best. Mildred Bailey, who – like Billie Holiday – had a more limited vocal range, goes deeper into her material, notably in recordings with Mary-Lou Williams from 1939.

Telling a Story

Taste and emotional depth are only two of the relevant dimensions of quality in jazz. The third – and the only one in which jazz differs radically from other musical performances – is inventiveness in storytelling. I do not imply that performances of classical music have no element of inventiveness. Just as a judge is more than the passive executor of the law, soloists and conductors are more than transmission belts from composer to audience. Because the actual performance is always underdetermined by the score, musicians must make aesthetic choices that, more than their technical skills, form the basis for our assessment of them. Yet in an obvious sense performers take second place to the composer, whereas in jazz the tune takes second place to the performance. In jazz we cannot tell the dancer from the dance; in the performance of a symphony we can. The distinction is largely a matter of the relative importance of constraints and freedom. In one sense, jazz musicians have more freedom, because they operate under fewer musical constraints. For that very reason, however, they seek or welcome (or should seek or welcome) other constraints that can make their task more manageable. I return to this issue later.

217. Thus I subscribe entirely to the following statement in Green (1991), p. 141: "It is useless your analysts telling you that Ella Fitzgerald or Sarah Vaughan can follow the most intricate chord sequence through to the ultimate flattened fifth in the final tonic chord, hitting resolution after resolution with the same correctitude as any suburban music teacher. When the emotional content is nil, all the correctitude in the world will not save the performance from artistic damnation, an observation that applies more than ever in the world of modern jazz, with its daunting harmonic complexities and its pathetic pursuit of legitimate acceptance." I should add, though, that Green (1991, Ch. 7) has a much more positive assessment of Tatum than I have.

The ability to "tell a story" through melodic innovation[218] is related to taste, but goes well beyond it. Teddy Wilson had supremely
good taste and – in an understated way – considerable emotional
poignancy, but not much of a story to tell. Hodges could, as I indicated, convey both taste and depth in a single note – but one note
tells no story. When I listen to Young's best solos, on "Lady Be Good"
(1936), "Tickle Toe" (both the 1940 and the 1941 versions), both takes
of "When You're Smiling" (with Billie Holiday in 1938) or the 1940
recordings with Benny Goodman and Charlie Christian, it is as if I
am following nonverbal narratives. They contain statements, often
with subordinate clauses, digressions, returns to the main story, am-
plifications of earlier themes, false endings, new starts, and then the
satisfying summing-up when melody lines that have lagged behind
the beat finally catch up with it.[219]

The subjective experience of hearing an extended jazz solo has
the structure of listening to a formal narrative. An analogy could be
Lewis Carroll's nonsense poem "The Jabberwocky," which begins as
follows:

> Twas brillig, and the slithy toves
> Did gyre and gimble in the wabe
> All mimsy were the borogroves
> And the mome raths outgrabe.

Although semantically opaque, the poem has meaning by virtue
of its syntactic structure – unlike some surrealist writings in which
ordinary words are joined together by extrasyntactic means. Similarly, as Kendall Walton has argued, a piece of music may convey "a
very general notion of *returning*, of which not only returns to one's
home but also returns to health, to the scene of a crime, to one's

---

218. See Berliner (1994), pp. 201–205. Because of my lack of musical training, I am
    unequipped to appreciate harmonic innovations.
219. The effect created by catching up with the beat, which is responsible for some of
    the most poignant moments in jazz, is wonderfully described by Dodge (1995),
    p. 169: "Very often the improviser will want his new melodic line, his hot solo, to
    keep on going ahead beyond the limits of a formal section of the original tune. So
    he obeys the demands of his melodic line, not the termination of the section, by
    extending his musical line beyond the normal limit of the section of the accepted
    tune. Having done this for a time, he is naturally way behind the course of the
    melody, but at any point he joins it, with the greatest ease. Like a dog out for
    a walk with its master, running away and continually returning – returning to
    where the master *is*, not to where he left the master!"

former convictions and who knows what else are instances."[220] For each solo by Lester Young one could probably write a verbal narrative with the same structure. Yet although a solo is less than a verbal narrative in that it has no specific subject matter, it is also more because it utilizes rhythm and sound texture to enhance the phrases and transitions that make up the story. The resulting blend of abstractness and concreteness is one of the most attractive features of jazz.

Improvising Versus Sculpting

Creativity in jazz bears a complex relationship to improvisation. An improvised solo of high quality is an extreme feat of creativity, but improvising is not the only way of telling a story. A solo may be "sculpted" – developed and perfected through many performances until it reaches a local maximum. Successful improvisations are permanently adopted and turn into constraints for the new ones, until in the end very little freedom is left. The recent releases of alternate takes from recording sessions of the twenties and thirties, and of radio broadcasts that duplicate tunes also recorded in the studios, make it very clear that solos often were scripted beforehand. In Armstrong's 1924–25 recordings with Fletcher Henderson, for example, he plays "the same" solo on each take. The several versions of Lester Young playing on "One O'Clock Jump" overlap very heavily. Similarly, if we compare Hodges's studio recording of "Blue Reverie" (1937) with the live recording from Carnegie Hall (1938), the solos are virtually identical. If a performer is on the road two days out of three and has the same solo spots in every performance, one can hardly expect him or her to come up with totally new ideas each time. This is probably even more true for singers. Once Billie Holiday had figured out how to render a tune, often deviating drastically from the written score (as in "I'll Get By" from 1937), she stuck to that interpretation. Yet even a sculpted solo can be of the very highest quality. In such cases, the act of creation is spread out over time rather than concentrated in a few minutes.

This does not mean that a sculpted solo is frozen. The Carnegie Hall version of "Blue Reverie" is superior to the studio version. The intonation is stronger, the tone warmer and more intense. Similarly,

220. Walton (1988), p. 356.

there are clear quality differences in successive Armstrong solos on the Henderson sides. One might conjecture, moreover, that a sculpted solo *cannot* become frozen, but will tend to deteriorate. Here we can apply Leibniz' dictum: "We have to move forward if we do not wish to regress: to stand still is impossible." To play "with feeling" may require the exploration of some uncharted territory, even if the deviations from the standard solo are very small. We may compare Hodges on three successive recordings of "Never No Lament" (later known as "Don't Get Around Much Anymore"): the studio version from 1940, the Chrystal Ballroom version from 1940, and the Carnegie Hall version from 1943. While roughly similar, the three solos – all of them very moving – display variations that suggest that Hodges was engaged in a continuous enterprise of exploration and innovation. By the 1960s, his solos were much more set, but even then we find small but significant differences between the Berlin and Stockholm versions (both from 1961) of "On the Sunny Side of the Street." The fine-tuning suggests that he continued to be engaged in a search for the local maximum, or was moving from one such maximum to a nearby one.

At one extreme, therefore, we find the sculpted solo that is part of a standard tune performed by a permanent band, such as the Basie or Ellington orchestra. At the other extreme, we find the solo improvised in recording sessions that bring together musicians who normally do not play together at all. The Billie Holiday–Teddy Wilson sessions from the 1930s fall in this category. In the best of these sessions there is a mix of Basie and Ellington musicians (Young, Hodges, Buck Clayton, Cootie Williams), supplemented by whoever happened to be in town. In an intermediate category we find solos in sessions by small groups consisting of the best musicians in one big band. The Basie sidemen and especially the Ellington sidemen made a number of such recordings. I do not know to what extent they involve sculpted solos. In public performances of the big bands some tunes were usually played by a subset of the whole band, perhaps corresponding to one of these small groups. It is possible, therefore, that some small-group recordings involve sculpted solos. In some cases, the existence of alternate takes is sufficient to exclude this possibility. The wonderful recordings of the Kansas City Six (1938), with Lester Young mainly playing clarinet, all exist with alternate takes that leave no room for doubt about their spontaneity. In other cases, we have independent evidence that a given tune was not part of the standard repertoire.

There are two main criteria, then, for deciding that a given solo is indeed improvised on the spot rather than sculpted over time. If the solo is made within an ad hoc group that was assembled only for recording purposes, it cannot have been the product of long and careful polishing. Also, if the solo exists in alternate takes, any difference between the versions is a pretty good indicator of spontaneity. Sometimes, both criteria are fulfilled. Many of the Holiday–Wilson sessions had alternate takes, resulting, for instance, in wonderful and entirely different solos by Young on "Back in Your Own Backyard" (1938) or "When You're Smiling" (1938). These are among the best jazz recordings ever made, with Young's solos displaying a miraculous combination of freedom and control. Some mathematicians claim that they see proofs as a whole, laid out visually before them. Similarly, these solos convey the impression that the end is invented right from the beginning.[221]

I do not know of any similarly intoxicating solos by Armstrong. His 1926–29 recordings display stunning emotional depth and total musical control, but their dramatic architecture mostly conveys the impression of being sculpted rather than improvised. After 1930, Armstrong essentially stopped telling any musical stories, at least as far as his recorded output shows. He now relied on his unsurpassed musical understanding, which allowed him to present any tune such that his version instantly became *the* version, together with an emotional force that invested even a straightforward statement of the melody with deep meaning. For large parts of his career, this was true also of Johnny Hodges. In a celebrated 1937 version of "The Sunny Side of the Street," and in the even more powerful Cotton Club version from 1938, he does little more than run through the melody with a few minor frills, yet the emotional impact is enormous. Just as "The Gal from Joe" conveys the essence of joy, these performances are distillations of love.

Yet Hodges was also a master improviser. An early example is the soaring solo on "Dear Old Southland" (1933). I cannot believe that this exuberant piece of music could have been rehearsed. Two later examples, and for me perhaps the summit of his achievement, came in a small-group Ellington session from 1938, which included "I Let a Song Go Out of My Heart" and "If You Were in My Place." (They feature a truly awful vocalist who should not, however, allow us to be distracted from Hodges's playing.) In his solos here, he tells stories

221. Green (1991), p. 103.

that are comparable to the best of Young in their complexity and musical interest – and with that wonderful sound in addition. As the complete publication of the Ellington corpus with alternate takes is unfolding, I hope that we may be in for many similar treats.

I conclude with some comments on the role of constraints in jazz. Drawing on Paul Berliner's *Thinking in Jazz*, an exhaustive study of jazz improvisation, we may distinguish among several kinds of constraints: financial, musical, physical, and technical. Some of these have a crippling effect on creativity, others enhance it, and still others may have a more ambiguous impact. In discussing them I shall not stick strictly to the 1936–42 era, but also use examples from the more recent jazz period.

FINANCIAL CONSTRAINTS

All jazz recordings in the period under discussion were commercial: they were made to make money for the recording company. Although the companies were in no position to impose profit-maximization as a goal, they could and did impose financial constraints. The most popular tunes were sometimes given to white performers, with black singers having to work with second-rate material. Yet in the first place this practice was probably less common than has often been assumed,[222] and in the second place a singer like Billie Holiday was able to give an emotional charge to the tritest lyrics. "Songs came to her as competent minor products of the popular music machine of the day, went through the treatment, and emerged as the touching expression of thoughts and emotions their composers had never dreamed of."[223] Yet it would be absurd to claim that she actually sang *better* with low-quality material, along the lines of Arnheim's argument that good actors work better with mediocre plays.

The companies can also try to impose a particular style on musicians, either to cash in on a past success or to move with the trend. On the one hand, "the same medium that helps to create the popularity of improvisers may also constrain their creative activities."[224] Once a

222. Clarke (1994), p. 91, and Nicholson (1995), p. 69, argue, for instance, that the material for the Holiday–Wilson sessions was actually quite good.
223. Green (1991), p. 130. Tanner (1976–77), pp. 141–42, argues that composers of Lieder, too, can transform a sentimental poem into supreme art.
224. Berliner (1994), p. 482.

record has been a hit, the musician must perform the same tune in all live appearances as well, a constraint that can also extend to the style of playing. Thus Lee Konitz said, "I happen to have an identification from the time I played with Miles and a lot of people don't want to hear me playing differently."[225] In these cases, musicians may face the choice between a musically unacceptable compromise and supporting themselves by other means. On the other hand, "record companies can provide the impact for artists to explore a fuller range of expressions. 'My music has always evolved', Walter Bishop Jr. reflects. 'When the record companies told me that they wouldn't record bebop anymore and I was old hat, I found other areas to express myself in'."[226]

The financial constraints of the recording studio may also have a "chilling" effect on the music:

When, as is commonly the case, a company absorbs the costs of recording studio operations and pays improvisers an hourly rate for sessions, it endeavors to limit each album's studio time. Should contracts stipulate that, beyond the initial session payment, a company pay band leaders (and in some cases supporting players) royalties on the basis of record sales, it commonly debits studio charges and numerous other expenses associated with the album's production from the musicians' accounts before allowing them to share in a recording's profits. Aware that performance errors may require recording multiple takes of pieces, each take having direct economic consequences, and aware, too, that they may not have the power to correct problems to their satisfaction in every part, musicians sometimes work out more formal improvisational sketches for recording sessions than for concerts. At the extreme, they occasionally compose complete models for solos and accompanying parts.[227]

MUSICAL CONSTRAINTS

As explained in III.4 for the case of novels, the unfolding of the earlier parts of a work of art may constrain its further development. A similar principle applies to improvisation, but with an additional twist (see also III.8). Jazz musicians develop a repertoire of "musical saves" – devices that will get them out of trouble if they make a mistake. Some of

225. Ibid.   226. Ibid.
227. Ibid., p. 475.

these are simply face savers, as with Dizzy Gillespie's advice: "When you make a mistake, make a loud one, because if you're timid about it, then it really sounds like a mistake."[228] Another, more constructive trick is to repeat the mistake, to make it look intentional. "Reworking a troublesome phrase at separate harmonic positions can provide the solo with a unifying theme. Alternatively, immediate repetition can serve such a phrase as a satisfying tension-building device, with its successful resolution retroactively imbuing the sequence with the character of a planned motive variation."[229] Also, mistakes may be produced deliberately: some

artists feel that realizing their goals depends on having the self-assurance and flexibility to back off from intentional pursuits – to relinquish control. A conga drummer in Chicago once followed this course as he periodically dropped his hands limply onto the drum head from different heights, allowing them to rebound freely, then immediately imitated their complex aleophonic patterns and played off of them.[230]

Unlike the case of electronic rock music, however, the deliberate exploitation of mistakes does not seem to be a central feature of creativity in jazz.

A more subtle constraint arises in the interplay between harmony and melody. It has often been noted that while Lester Young's melodic skills were unsurpassed, his harmonic repertoire was relatively limited.[231] According to Benny Green, these two features of his playing were in fact connected to one another. He argues that it would never "have occurred to [Young's critics] that it was in its very harmonic conventionality that the fascination of Lester Young lay. With the same meagre resources that had been at the disposal of the generation before him, Lester Young evolved a quite original and highly idiomatic style."[232] As the capacity of the human mind is limited and it is better to be a master of one trade than a jack of two,[233] the willingness to work within given harmonic conventions may have been a condition for Young's melodic excellence.

228. Ibid., p. 212.   229. Ibid., p. 215.
230. Ibid., p. 219.
231. Green (1991), pp. 106–110; Schuller (1989), p. 554.
232. Green (1991), p. 110.   233. Elster (1986a).

259

III. Less Is More

PHYSICAL AND TECHNICAL CONSTRAINTS

These form a ragbag of obstacles, ranging from trivial to important. In three amusing examples, musicians were able to bypass technical defects in their instruments simply by playing around them. On one occasion, "a valve of Miles Davis's trumpet became stuck in the midst of an improvisation. Davis simply accepted the loss of its associated pitches as a compositional constraint and formulated the rest of his solo without them."[234] On another, Bud Powell, arriving at a club with an untuned piano, "ran his fingers up and down the keyboard to identify the offending keys. He then proceeded to give a virtuoso performance in which he treated the 'bad notes' as dissonances or special effects – like blue notes – integrating them perfectly with his solo."[235] Art Tatum, too, would choose keys that avoided sour notes on the piano as much as possible.[236] In Powell's case, there is a hint that the added constraint induced him to produce something of value that might otherwise not have happened – although not necessarily of greater value than what would have happened had the piano been properly tuned. To my knowledge, no jazz musician has emulated Perec and *intentionally* deprived himself of some of the technical means normally at his disposal.

Davis, Powell, and Tatum were able to overcome defects in their instruments because of their technical skills. Earlier we have seen that these skills, when defective, may themselves serve as constraints. In the case of instrumentalists, I do not think a general argument can be made that limited skills serve to enhance the quality of playing, by forcing musicians to focus on what to say rather than on how to say it. Although virtuoso skills can tempt a player to engage in playing for effect, they can also be used to convey subtle musical ideas. A possible exception might be Django Reinhardt, whose left hand was crippled after a fire. He "brought out qualities in [his instrument] never seen before in jazz, and exerted considerable influence on subsequent... guitarists. Reinhardt's disability compelled him to play novel harmonies that might, arguably, not have been discovered had his fingers been capable of their full function."[237]

234. Berliner (1994), p. 210.   235. Ibid., p. 455.
236. Stewart (1972), p. 187.
237. Cooke (1998), p. 75. The same may be true of composers. Thus Irving Berlin "couldn't read or write music, and played only the black keys on the piano, in the key of F-sharp. 'The key of C is for people who study music,' he said in a 1948

In the case of vocalists, however, I wonder whether it may not be more than an accident that technical range and emotional depth seem to be inversely related to one another. Earlier I cited Billie Holiday and Mildred Bailey as instances of vocalists who had a limited range but were capable of sustained emotional performances, and Ella Fitzgerald and Sarah Vaughan at the opposite ends of each dimension. (As is clear from Figure III.2, all of them had superb taste.) Among the other great female jazz singers, Bessie Smith also falls into the first category. As one writer has noted, she sang "with a quality of harshness and at the same time with great passion."[238] Among male singers, Armstrong, Jack Teagarden, and Jimmy Rushing would also fall into that category, with the now-forgotten Al Hibbler and Herb Jeffries in the second (unlike Frank Sinatra, they did not even have taste). I conclude, tentatively, that the technical skills that are essential prerequisites for classical singers may actually be a handicap for jazz vocalists.

I tend to disagree with Berliner concerning two constraints that are linked to the technology of studio recordings. In the following passage he seems to argue that splicing and other editing techniques enhance the quality of a performance whereas time constraints work against it:

Many performers and groups take advantage of the studio's editing capabilities because they recognize that the medium of recordings places them in a particularly vulnerable position as artists. Mistakes that passed unnoticed in the heat of live performance can detract from the music when subjected to repeated hearings. For all the value of such technological tools, however, improvisers are sometimes inclined to view them as crutches. Lou Donaldson never evaluates 'musicians from their records. They are made under a different set of circumstances where they can make over what they don't like. You have to hear musicians in person to be able to judge them.' As a trade-off for the advantages they enjoy in the studio, players contend with numerous constraints that distinguish their performances from live events. Until relatively recently, the time constraints of a recording forced musicians to compress the length of presentations substantially.[239]

Although I agree that there is a trade-off, I would locate the costs and benefits in the exact opposite manner. On the one hand, the

interview. 'The fact that I compose only in F-sharp gave me certain harmonies that other writers missed, because they knew more about music'" (Lahr 1999, p. 80).
238. Friedwald (1996), p. 6.   239. Berliner (1994), p. 474.

opportunity to edit and splice is a threat to the artistic concentration that is essential for creativity. Once again, I invoke Astaire's example. On the other hand, the "temporal handcuffs"[240] of the seventy-eight rpm record were in my opinion a boon for creativity. Musical improvisation at a high level requires too much concentration to be sustained for much more than a minute. This opinion goes in the face of much received wisdom. Benny Green, for instance, writes about Young that

The ear-witnesses of Lester in his hey-day have all taken care to lay stress on the apparent inexhaustibility of his creative flow. It is perhaps truer of him than of any of his contemporaries that the limitations of the ten-inch record decimated his prowess for the listener. Mary Lou Williams has even gone so far as to say that "it took Lester maybe four or five choruses to warm up." To consider this statement in the face of some of Lester's delectable four- and eight-bar fragments on the recordings of the mid-1930s inspires the wildest dreams of what might have been and perhaps really was.[241]

The only recording of Lester Young jamming in his hey-day is from the Carnegie Hall concert of 1938. Although his solo here is given high notes by Frank Buchmann-Möller in his discography,[242] he does not single it out as superior to the studio recordings. To my ear, it sounds less focused and coherent than, say, his contributions with Basie on "Tickletoe" (1940) or the master take of "Taxi War Dance" (1939), the 1941 small-group broadcast version of the latter tune (his best ever, in my opinion), the two takes of "Back in Your Own Backyard" (Holiday–Wilson 1938), or the 1940 recordings with Goodman and Charlie Christian. Some might argue, in terms of Figure III.1, that the studio recordings represent points such as A whereas the more extended sessions produce solos located at C or E. This may well be true; we shall never know for sure.

Yet I can invoke the authority of Lester Young himself to support my view. To put his statement into proper perspective, let me first note that classical musicians also improvise. French organ players, for instance, are known for their improvising skills. One "master improviser," Loïc Mallié, confessed that "he found the rigorous structures of jazz, like the 12 bars a blues player has in which to improvise a variation, confining and restrictive."[243] Twelve bars may indeed be

240. Rasula (1995), p. 134.   241. Green (1991), p. 106.
242. Buchmann-Möller (1990b), pp. 46–49.
243. *International Herald Tribune*, June 1–2, 1996.

too little, but the jazz improvisations that I have referred to go well beyond this limit. On the other hand, they should not go too far beyond it. Lester Young is reported to have said, "If you can't say it in 32 bars, maybe you shouldn't say it."[244] Up to a point, more is more; beyond that point, more is less.

III.10. OBSTACLES AND OBJECTIONS

As in previous chapters, I conclude by considering the feasibility and desirability of precommitment and, more generally, the value of being constrained.

OBSTACLES TO PRECOMMITMENT

Although the issue of whether the requisite technology for self-binding is available is less central here than in the earlier chapters, it is not entirely irrelevant. Eighteenth-century and late twentieth-century novelists could not or cannot use the technique of serialization to reduce their freedom. Although an author may publish excerpts from a novel before publication, this is very different from subjecting himself or herself to the rigors of weekly or monthly installments. It would be difficult today to find money for an epic black-and-white movie, and perhaps impossible to find money for a silent black-and-white epic movie. Arnheim's hope that all film forms – with or without color, with or without sound – could exist alongside each other was not realized.[245] In this case, the "shortage of scarcity" is induced by lack of demand. If audiences wanted silent black-and-white movies, they would presumably be produced. In a looser sense, lack of demand may prevent poets from using classical meters or novelists from working within the framework of the realist novel. Yet more strictly speaking, writers are not materially constrained as long as they can afford to buy paper and a pencil. Jazz musicians may be able to play the music they like in clubs even if access to a recording studio depends on their willingness to submit to stylistic constraints.

244. *New York Times Magazine,* June 2, 1996, p. 32.
245. Arnheim (1957), pp. 159–60.

III. Less Is More

HARMFUL EFFECT OF CONSTRAINTS

The question whether and when constraints are desirable is more intricate. In general, the effect of constraints on artistic productions can be benign, neutral, or harmful. In earlier sections, I have given examples and arguments to show that constraints can enhance artistic value. I have also given examples that suggest that constraints may be irrelevant or neutral, when the artist can work around them. Ernst Lubitsch may not have been affected by the Hays Code; Bud Powell, Art Tatum, and Miles Davis may not have been bothered by defective instruments, and Billie Holiday not by inferior song material. In correcting a mistake jazz instrumentalists may simply "accomplish the same developmental goals for which they strive during the normal course of performance."[246]

There is no doubt at all that constraints can be aesthetically damaging. In his book *In Praise of Commercial Culture*, Tyler Cowen argues that technical progress that has removed material constraints on artists enhances aesthetic value and creativity. For instance, new "technologies gave . . . support to French painters and the impressionist. The tin paint tube, introduced in the 1840s, allowed the artist to bring his or her work outside and leave behind the falseness of studio light."[247] More generally, "the successive relaxation of external constraints on internal creativity tends to give rise to a wide gamut of emotions and styles."[248] These external constraints include financial limitations as well as material limitations. "A large market lowers the costs of creative pursuits and makes market niches easier to find."[249] Falling costs of raw materials have a similarly liberating effect. "In the early history of art, paint and materials were very expensive; artists were constrained by the need to generate immediate commissions and sales. When these costs fell, artists could aim more at innovation and personal expression, and less at pleasing buyers and critics. Modern art became possible."[250]

These arguments correspond to the commonsensical observation I made in I.1, that in the normal course of things it is better to have more options than fewer. It is a truth one should keep in mind to avoid absurdly exaggerated praise of constraints. Cowen seems oblivious, however, to the nonstandard idea that art may benefit from being

---

246. Berliner (1994), p. 215.   247. Cowen (1998), p. 117.
248. Ibid., p. 22.   249. Ibid., p. 23.
250. Ibid., p. 20.

constrained. Moreover, he does not really try to show that the removal of constraints enhances the *quality* of art, rather than merely the number of works of art that are made. The relaxation of constraints that enable more artists to realize their ideas may also undermine the focus and concentration that go into the creation of superior works of art. Whether the net effect is beneficial remains to be shown. So far, I have not come across any great movies made with a camcorder.[251]

The Hays Code shows very well how constraints can have harmful as well as valuable effects. Earlier, I cited André Bazin to the effect that censorship could enhance the quality of movies. He adds, however, that "what is gained by such surreptitious transgression can be more than offset by what is lost. The social and moral taboos of the censors are too arbitrary to be able to channel the imagination suitably. Though helpful in comedy or film-ballet, they are just a hindrance, dumb and insurmountable, in realistic films."[252] The careers of Fritz Lang, Howard Hawks, and Orson Welles show that constraints can indeed be fetters rather than spurs on creativity. Both Lang and Hawks had to embed their movies in an artificial plot imposed by the production code. Because Lang's *The Woman in the Window* ended with a suicide, "a story 'solution' discouraged by the Production Code," an ending was added in which the protagonist wakes up to discover that it was all a dream, and then another epilogue was added so that the movie could end on a healthy laugh.[253] In Hawks's *Scarface*, the censors wanted Scarface to pay for his crimes.[254] "And for fully four minutes after the picture, unmatched

---

251. Michael Marriot ("If Only Cecil B. De Mille Had Owned a Desktop Computer," *New York Times*, January 7, 1999) cites an award-winning five-minute parody of American advertising made for $1,700 with digital technology, and goes on to say that the digital video camera "makes it possible for filmmakers to operate more like painters and other artists, first producing their works and then presenting them to the marketplaces of the world. In Hollywood, filmmakers must first present their idea and then try to secure funding." It remains to be seen whether more good movies will result. My bet is that it won't happen.

252. Bazin (1971), p. 172.

253. McGilligan (1997), pp. 310–11. She also describes how Lang made the best out of these constraints, but does not claim that they enhanced the value of the film.

254. Hays's successor, Joseph Breen, had an "obsessive concern" (Schatz 1996, p. 275) with this issue. Thus *The Prisoner of Zenda* "caused problems due to an illegitimate birth that occurred several generations before the story takes place – a seemingly innocuous plot point but a necessary one since it explains the physical similarities between the vacationing Brit and the Ruritanian monarch. Breen was concerned, however, that there was no indication in the story that the long-dead fornicators had suffered 'moral retribution' for their sin" (ibid., pp. 196–97).

for realism, has logically ended, and the audience is walking out of the theatre, you are shown what happens to a bold, bad gunman – the trial, the conviction, the speech by the judge when he pronounces sentence, and all the other details of the hanging process."[255]

In Frank Brady's *Citizen Welles*, memorable descriptions of Welles's struggles with the Hays Office over *The Heart of Darkness*, *The Magnificent Ambersons*, and *Journey into Fear* make it clear that the interference of the censors made for a net loss of aesthetic value.[256] In the last case, notably, the imposed

changes, further demonstrating the omnipotence of the censorious Hays Office, were fatal to the Welles script and the whole theme of Ambler's novel: *Journey* plunged Graham, the innocent, into a world where life is cheap and moral standards are conspicuously lacking. In the book, virtually every gesture, every personal habit of the foreign characters, is suggestive of obscenity. . . . It is this depraved world, as much as the threat of death, that bathes Graham in a perpetual cold sweat.

The devastating effects of censorship can easily be underestimated. In addition to the films that were made under the Hays Code and suffered from the limitations it imposed, the victims of censorship also include the many movies that were never made at all because they would be too obviously incompatible with the code.[257] The cancellation of the projected film version of *The Heart of Darkness*, for instance, was in part due to the ridiculous demands of the censors.[258]

Arnheim's thesis about the superior value of silent movies and black-and-white movies is vulnerable to similar objections. At a general level, his view has been decisively refuted by Noël Carroll,[259] and there is no need to repeat his objections here. Instead I shall discuss a special case, by comparing silent movies and sound movies. There is no question that sound movies are superior in some respects nor, in my opinion, that they are inferior in other respects. To illustrate the advantage of silent movies we may use Carroll's own analysis of the visual gag.[260] As he notes, this device is also available in sound movies; Jacques Tati, notably, made extensive use of it. Yet once sound is available there is an obvious temptation for the director to use

255. McCarthy (1997), p. 148, citing Lincoln Quarberg.
256. Brady (1989), pp. 214–15, 322–23, 330–31.
257. I am indebted to Diego Gambetta for this point.
258. Brady (1989), pp. 213–15.   259. Carroll (1988), Ch. 1.
260. Carroll (1996), Ch. X.

verbal puns instead of visual gags. To avoid this temptation, he or she might decide, therefore, to renounce the use of sound altogether. Arnheim's example from Sternberg, cited in III.6, shows another way in which silent movies can be superior. In this case, the director of a sound movie could not even achieve the effect that Sternberg produced; once you have sound in a movie a gunshot must be heard, unless the director drowns it out by another sound (as in the example from *Top Hat* cited earlier).

As in the case of the Hays Code, the constraints of silent movies may work better for some film genres than for others. For comedy and epic dramas, the need to tell a story merely through images may indeed help to focus the creative powers of the director. In psychological dramas and more generally in any movie that aims at in-depth characterization of individuals and their interaction, a director who tied one hand behind his back by renouncing all use of dialogue would be paralyzed rather than stimulated. The constraints of the silent movie would simply be *too* tight (see also III.4). It is hard, at least for me, to imagine the psychological subtlety and punch of, say, *Fanny and Alexander* or *Dark Eyes* in the silent format.

Film directors nowadays have less choice in these matters. In other art forms, hard constraints are usually freely chosen rather than imposed from outside. If painters decide to use a small canvas or to dispense with colors, they usually do so for a specific artistic purpose and not to meet the expectations of a public. By contrast, the apparently free choice to submit to a convention may be subjectively experienced as a necessity. Up to a point, soft constraints of this kind may have a liberating effect. Yet as noted earlier, the conventions within a given genre often accumulate over time. The main mechanism seems to be that the masters of the genre are taken as normative models, so that their work adds extra constraints to the ones they faced themselves. Over time, the genre may then turn into mannerism, in the generic sense of "excessive or affected addiction to a distinctive manner or method of treatment" (OED).

Transcending the Constraints

When conventions accumulate to reduce the scope of artistic choice, a revolution may be required to liberate creativity. But even before that point is reached, rebellions against convention can serve as a vehicle for creativity. In these cases, constraints are not so much denied as transcended. Although not really a paradox, the idea can be stated in paradoxical terms: *to be bound by conventions is good, to be unbound even better*. Michael Baxandall notes that "many great pictures are a bit illegitimate."[261] In *The Failures of Criticism*, Henri Peyre states the idea in a more general form:

A century of freedom has imbued us with diffidence towards the unrestrained lawlessness of some modern artists and the formlessness of too many plays and novels. In artists, the voluntary acceptance of limits, and even of hurdles over which to practice their bouncing feats, is a sign of ebullient youth, and not of submissive decrepitude. Moreover, is there any keener joy for a writer rigorously trained in artistic discipline, or for a borderline Protestant like Gide or Eliot, than becoming reverently conscious of strict rules which he may some day delight in breaking? After a long century of individualism, many of our contemporaries seem to be overweighed by their absolute artistic freedom which has rendered any revolt insipid.[262]

In a text from 1946, two years after the first edition of *The Failures of Criticism*, Roger Caillois makes the same point. In the passage that I cited in III.1, he asserts that writers of free verse are parasites on bound verse; they want the prestige without the discipline and hard work. But there is another form of parasitism of which he approves, the occasional breaking of a rule by someone who masters it completely and who usually bends to its rigors:

This is how the happy expression of genius and the stunning effects of great art come about. All chains are suddenly broken by a soaring, admirable vigor; here, one wants to say, is nature appearing in its pure splendor, rejecting all showy garments and frills, superb, savage, without collar or make-up. All of this is true, but these revelations must not, cannot be more than flashes. They derive their force and sparkle from their rarity. If you let them set up a permanent home so that nothing else is tolerated, if you remove all barriers and all constraints so that they can burst out at will and unceasingly: then there is no more form and no style. These large leaps themselves, which provided such keen enjoyment, lose all meaning and import. They have no rhyme or reason (*On ne sait plus à quoi ils riment*). As they no longer have any resistance to overcome or any obstacles to confront, they no longer have the relaxed character that made their beauty. They are nothing but elementary turbulence and agitation. They have returned to that primordial chaos from which art could emerge only by inventing shackles and laws for itself.[263]

261. Baxandall (1985), p. 120.   262. Peyre (1967), pp. 226–27.
263. Caillois (1978), pp. 38–39. See also Paulhan (1990), p. 85.

Conventions provide a salutary discipline on the background of which they may be violated with great aesthetic effect, *provided that the violation itself submits to discipline*. Although attractive, this reassertion and revision of the classical doctrine is somewhat unstable, as it can hardly be stated publicly as a prescriptive doctrine without defeating itself.[264] If artists submit to the rules only in order to be able to violate them, they might not be motivated to undergo the strenuous process of internalizing them.[265] The argument that even if they want to paint nonfiguratively painters should first be trained in figurative techniques comes up against a similar problem. For the figurative training to be helpful, it must be taken seriously. For artists to take it seriously, it helps if they believe they will never use any other technique. The tempting idea that one can obtain the benefits of constraints *and* the benefits of violating them may be chimerical.

264. For a somewhat analogous publicity constraint on ethical theories, see Rawls (1971), pp. 177–82.
265. When writing "that the record shows no case of significant innovation where the innovating artist didn't possess or grasp the conventions that he changed or abandoned," Greenberg (1999, p. 53) is making the slightly different point that *permanent* (as distinct from temporary) violation of a convention presupposes, to be successful, that the convention has been fully internalized.

Coda

This book has not been an argument for a thesis but an exploration of some themes. The particular way in which examples and mechanisms are bunched together to yield a "theme" is somewhat arbitrary. In Chapters I and II, the analyses relied on the dual perspective of *rationales* and *devices* for precommitment, a perspective that could also be applied to Chapter III. Rather than pursuing this classification, however, I shall use somewhat different and generally less technical categories to impose some kind of order on the cases covered in the previous chapters. It is emphatically not a summary, but rather a reflection on the case studies. Although at the end of the day I still do not have anything like a systematic account, some of the categories might find a place among the building blocks of a theory of constraints.

TEMPTATIONS

Often, we precommit ourselves in order to avoid temptation, or to make ourselves unable to succumb to it when we meet it. The varieties of temptation I have discussed in this book are numerous and diverse. There is, for instance, the temptation to do nothing or to postpone unpleasant tasks until tomorrow. The smoker who wants to give up cigarettes or the person who thinks he ought to save for his old age are both vulnerable to procrastination. "Give me chastity and continence, but not yet." And then there is the converse temptation, of doing immediately what would give more pleasure if stretched out over longer periods of time. As George Ainslie has argued, many pleasures presuppose the ability to *pace oneself*. Smokers may derive more overall enjoyment from smoking if they smoke less. Those who rely on the pleasures of imagination may find that reading a book is preferable to daydreaming, which is too vulnerable to premature satiation. *Writing* a book is even better. In *Souvenirs d'Egotisme*, Stendhal wrote, "For whoever has tasted the profound occupation of writing, reading is only a secondary pleasure."

There is also the temptation to take the path of least resistance. In art, the striving for effect is a constant temptation if the artist possesses high technical skills or can choose a luxuriously rich medium. For members of backward communities such as the Amish there can be a temptation to make use of the technology of the more advanced environment. Any given piece of technology that is incorporated may have only a negligible impact on the traditional lifestyle, but over time the overall effect of these putatively neutral changes may be corrosive. There can be a "primrose path" to addiction, which also offers salient short-term benefits and more diffuse long-term dangers.

PASSIONS AND CRAVINGS

Whereas temptations are beckoning and seductive, passions and cravings are urgent and compelling. Temptations often use self-deception and wishful thinking as their handmaidens, enabling the agent to overlook the insidious dangers involved. Passions and cravings may be so strong as to crowd out all thoughts about consequences. In a state of violent anger, strong sexual arousal, or cocaine craving, the desire for immediate satisfaction is so intense that considerations about costs and risks hardly arise. Precommitment, in these cases, must be undertaken well ahead of time, and in a cool moment — not, for instance, when one is so infatuated as to want to make it very difficult to break the ties of marriage. It must, moreover, take the form of making certain actions physically or legally impossible rather than of attaching extra costs to them because, by assumption, in the heat of the moment these costs will not have any motivating effect.

The idea of a link between precommitment and passion is a very old one, going back at least to Seneca and Plutarch. In their writings as in virtually all other writers until the past decade, the idea was to precommit oneself *against* passion. Jack Hirshleifer and Robert Frank have argued, however, that the *passions can serve as means of precommitment against temptations*. From a very different perspective, Antonio Damasio also argues that rather than inducing a myopic bias, the emotions enable us to take account of long-term consequences of

271

behavior. Of these various proposals, I believe that the one put forward by Frank – anticipated by A. O. Lovejoy – is the most promising. In his argument, emotions can tip the balance in favor of the distant future by imposing psychological costs of shame and guilt on the choice of short-term reward. Another argument, proposed by Hirshleifer and Frank, can be summarized as asserting that emotionally induced *disregard for consequences can have good consequences* because others will be deterred by the knowledge that one is prepared to act irrationally. In my opinion the idea has little empirical support. Damasio's proposal, too, is essentially speculative.

Enabling

Because we are irrational, temptations, passions, and cravings can lead us astray. Because we can *know* we are irrational, we can use precommitment strategies to protect ourselves. Yet contrary to what I implied in *Ulysses and the Sirens*, the use of precommitment is not necessarily linked to irrationality or imperfection. Even the most rational person may use self-binding techniques to achieve more than he or she could otherwise have done. A simple example of enabling precommitment is the use of contract law to make promises credible. As Stephen Holmes has shown, the idea has important applications in constitutional contexts. Also, there are a number of precommitment strategies that can be used to enhance the credibility of threats. Far from being responses to irrationality, these strategies may include the rational deployment of irrationality, for example, by selecting as negotiator someone who will not back down when he is in a weak position, as a rational person would do. This approach was pioneered by Thomas Schelling in wonderful essays.

Enabling precommitment can also occur in other contexts and for other reasons. When the government abdicates responsibility for monetary policy to a central bank, it is not necessarily because it cannot trust itself to do the right thing. As Finn Kydland and Edward Prescott first pointed out, even a government that is free of myopia and partisanship will do better by renouncing its power to make these decisions. By requiring a supermajority for changing the basic principles regulating political life, constitutions enable economic and political agents to make long-term investment and plans. Precommitment also has an important positive role in art. By throwing away some of their options, artists enable themselves to focus better on the choice among those that remain.

CONSTRAINTS AND CONVENTIONS

At a very general level, devices that limit the freedom of an agent can be classified along two dimensions. First, there is a distinction between the devices that only turn on the expectations of others, and those that do not. Second, there is a distinction between the devices that have been created by the agent and those that he or she simply finds in existence. Although one might coin separate terms for all four cases that arise by crossing these two dichotomies with each other, I have bundled three of them together under the heading of *constraints*, using *convention* for the fourth. A convention is a set of expectations that the agent simply finds in existence. They differ, therefore, from the expectations established by an individual who wants to fortify his resolve to quit smoking by announcing it to his friends. They also differ from hard limitations on his freedom of action that the agent simply finds in existence, as when film directors before circa 1940 were prevented from shooting in color. And finally, of course, they differ from freely chosen hard limitations.

In politics, we encounter constitutional constraints as well as constitutional conventions. The former are embodied in the written constitution as enforced by a constitutional court or some similar organ. The latter are unwritten principles to which political actors conform because they are expected to and because they would suffer politically if they didn't. Whereas there is often a mechanism for undoing a law or a decree that violates the written constitution, there is usually none for undoing an act that violates an unwritten constitution – only a mechanism for punishing its author, for example by not reelecting him. (The Athenian institution of *graphe paranomon* did both – it nullified the law and punished its proposer.) Sometimes, a constraint exists only by virtue of a convention. If the constitution does not contain clauses that make it more difficult to change it than to change other laws, whatever restraining force it has will derive from the convention that constitutions are not to be changed in the middle of the political game.

The freedom of action of artists is also limited by constraints as well as by conventions. Most of the constraints they face are imposed by the technical nature of the medium or by those who fund their work, but some are self-imposed. To work within a given convention is always a decision by the artist. One might ask whether the arts, like politics, provide examples of conventions that mandate the use of certain constraints. To take a hypothetical example, films might be subject to the convention that funeral scenes be shot in black and white. I am not aware, however, of any such cases.

In the case of individual self-control, people often seek to be constrained. A person who is trying to stop or reduce his drinking may try to make alcohol unavailable or take a drug that makes him ill if he drinks (or drinks too much). But in a more metaphorical sense, he can also impose a convention on himself, in the form of a private rule. The rule may take the drastic form of never drinking, or moderate forms such as never drinking before dinner or drinking only in company. It is protected against temptation by the expectation that a single violation will induce a full relapse, somewhat like a tacit price cartel that is glued together by the shared expectation that a single defection will cause universal defection. Although the idea of a self-imposed convention might seem meaningless, given that I defined a convention as a set of expectations that the agent simply finds in existence, we can make some sense of it by viewing the individual as being a succession of selves or, more accurately, as having to make a succession of decisions. Once the expectation that a single violation will trigger full relapse is in place, the agent may take it as a parametric fact rather than as something that can be renegotiated. I do not want, however, to stress the similarity between these intrapersonal conventions and the standard interpersonal case. The analogy, while suggestive and tantalizing, is also imperfect and potentially misleading.

DELAYS

A special case of constraints involves delays, that is, inserting or lengthening a time interval between two decisions in the sequence that leads up to the final action. Traditionally, delays have been assumed to counteract *passion*, by allowing emotions or addictive cravings to cool down and enabling the agent to decide on rational grounds. More recently, it has been shown that delays can be an effective means of resisting the excessive focus on the present that is characteristic of hyperbolic discounting. By using illiquid saving instruments people can protect themselves against their tendency to dip into their savings to finance current consumption.

Delays can have at least three other effects. First, delays can be manipulated to reduce the role of *interest* in decision making. By requiring a time interval between adoption of legislation and its implementation, constitution-makers can make it more likely that future legislators will promote the general good rather than private interest. Second, delays can be useful stratagems in bargaining. If one party is able to create a slow and cumbersome procedure for responding to proposals by the other party, he or she will have a strategic advantage. Finally, the Athenian procedure of ostracism shows that a political leader may use the interval between decisions in a two-stage procedure to stir up passions rather than calming them. Unlike the other effects that I have mentioned, this one would not provide grounds for deliberately adopting a delaying device.

THE ORIGIN AND EXPLANATION OF PRECOMMITMENT

Whereas constraints arise by necessity or choice, conventions *evolve* (except for the intrapersonal case just discussed). The nature of the evolutionary process is ill understood, as is the exact nature of the mechanisms by which conventions regulate behavior. There is probably no general account that will explain both the French constitutional convention that allows the written constitution to be changed by referendum and the convention that a popular tune should have the form AABA.

The paradigmatic case of self-binding – Ulysses having himself tied to the mast – was unambiguously a free choice. When individuals or collectivities constrain themselves in this manner, we must assume that they do so because they believe they will benefit from being bound. (Whether they actually do benefit is another matter.) By contrast, when they are constrained by others or by hard physical or financial limitations, they may not value being bound, and may in fact wish for their freedom. And even when they do prefer being constrained, this is not to say that they have chosen to be constrained. Although one may use the terms "precommitment" and "self-binding" somewhat loosely, to cover all cases of limitations on the freedom of action of an agent that work to the agent's perceived benefit, this will not do for explanatory purposes.

If we disregard non-man-made constraints, we can distinguish several ways in which an agent may become constrained in his actions. (i) The constraints arise because of the benefits to the agent as perceived by the agent. This was the case of Ulysses or of Georges Perec in writing his "e"-only and "e"-less novels. (ii) They arise because of the benefits to the agent as perceived by others. This is paternalistic constraining, in its many varieties. Involuntary hospitalization for mental illness is a standard example. (iii) They arise because of the benefits to others, with benefits to the constrained agent as a side effect. An elite group of founders may write a constitution to benefit themselves, while also believing that the population at large will benefit from being unable to confiscate the property of the elite. In general, however, the side effects may or may not be predicted by the constrainer, and may or may not be valued by the agent who is constrained. As far as I know, the officials in the Hays Office had no idea that they might actually enhance the aesthetic value of movies by censoring them. Today, the American government does not seem to recognize that by imposing economic sanctions on Iran it may actually help that country to maintain its state of isolation and avoid the corrosive influence of Western values.

Binding Oneself or Being Bound

Self-binding is a reflexive operation. An agent, A, binds the same agent, A. In the most literal sense, however, it is very hard to bind oneself. Looking into books on knots and on magicians' tricks, I did not find any instructions for how a person might tie himself into a knot that he could not get out of. It is easy to tie one's feet, but not to tie one's hands with one's hands so tightly that one cannot undo the knot, because after a while the movement of the hands is so constrained that the agent cannot apply the force needed to get the knot really tight. Typically, A needs the assistance of another agent B to bind him. Ulysses had to ask his sailors to tie him to the mast.

Other people can assist in precommitment in a number of ways. As noted, the person who wants to quit smoking can indirectly enlist the support of others by telling them about his intention, hoping to be kept on a steady keel by his anticipation of their disapproval in case of backsliding. Also, rather than throwing away the key an addict might entrust it to another person, who has the right and preferably the duty not to accede to requests to hand it back. The cocaine addict who deposits a self-incriminating letter with the treatment agency, to be sent to his employer if he is found positive on a urine test, must be able to count on the agency to resist his pleas. The person who takes disulfiram to resist the craving to drink usually needs supervision to resist the temptation to skip the medication.

We also find cases of mutual self-binding. Alcoholics Anonymous is based on the idea that the members help each other to abstain. In joint daydreams, the daydreaming partners can help each other resist the temptation to premature satiation. In collective improvisation, each musician constrains the contributions of the others. More generally, artistic conventions may be viewed in this perspective. It is because each artist expects others to respect the conventional laws of a genre that he is motivated to do so himself.

Other people, finally, can try to bind the agent to make it more difficult for him to bind himself (or others). In many cases of constitution-making, we observe that the authorities who convene the constituent assembly or select the delegates also try to constrain the framers. Although these attempts usually fail, they sometimes succeed. In individual behavior, too, the goal of paternalism may be to prevent self-paternalism. Thus marriage counselors may well try to prevent young people from binding themselves through a marriage contract that is very hard to get out of.

BINDING ONESELF OR BINDING OTHERS

When an agent B imposes a constraint on an agent A it may be, as just discussed, because A has asked him to do so. There is a sliding transition from this case to the case in which B binds A because B believes A *would have asked* to be bound had he known all the facts about the case and been capable of making an informed decision. Involuntary hospitalization in a psychiatric hospital is sometimes justified along these lines. In fact, even if A had not been asked to be hospitalized he may later be able to sue B if he is prematurely released.

There is a further sliding transition to cases in which a person binds himself merely for the purpose of creating a constraint that will also limit the freedom of action of others. In the Preface I cited Jens Arup Seip to the effect that "in politics, people never try to bind themselves, only to bind others." Many alleged cases of constitutional self-binding turn out, on closer inspection, to confirm this dictum. An outstanding example was Valéry Giscard d'Estaing's successful attempt to bind the future socialist parliament by ostensibly binding himself. More subtly, in order to gain an ascendancy a person may bind himself and abstain from binding others. Thus in some Greek city states the rich made voting mandatory for themselves but not for the poor, expecting that the poor would in fact not use their political power when they were not required to do so.

MULTIPLE SELVES AND SUCCESSIVE GENERATIONS

As an alternative to the language of "self-binding" one may talk of one self binding another self, typically a self that will exist at a later date. If simply used as a metaphor, this language is harmless enough. If taken literally, however, it raises problems. One may argue, plausibly, that an old man is in a very real sense "another person" from the person he was as a boy. Yet if we disregard invented cases, young people do not actually try to constrain what they will be able to do as they grow old. Many young people say – and some may mean it – that they will kill themselves when they reach a certain age, but none pay a contract killer to make sure the job gets done. When a person actually does take steps to limit his future freedom of action, it is usually because he thinks that *he* – the very same person – might otherwise do something he wouldn't want to do. He binds himself, not another person. The difference matters, because the moral problems that arise when a person tries to bind another do not arise, or arise only in attenuated form, when he tries to bind himself.

The converse case arises when the language of self-binding is applied to what is really a case of binding others. Many writers, including me, have referred to constitution-making as a form of self-binding. Once again, this language may be acceptable as a metaphor but is often problematic if taken literally. When a founding generation limits the freedom of action of later generations, the language of self-binding can be misleading. The moral justification of self-binding in the literal sense does not carry over to this metaphorical sense: the founders cannot claim the right to bind their successors. In some cases, they can be reasonably sure that their successors will want to be bound to certain procedural rules, but the creation of substantive and controversial rights cannot be justified in this way.

Coda

When constraints and conventions are intended to exclude certain actions, they may occasionally exclude too much. Often, there are good arguments for allowing exceptions. To prevent the constitution from becoming a suicide pact, it should contain clauses allowing for emergency powers. Central banks must be allowed to deviate from the goal of monetary stability if the economy is hit by a sudden shock. Rather than becoming a teetotaler, an alcoholic might aim at moderate use. A drug abuser who has agreed to undergo treatment with no possibility of leaving the clinic before the time is up, might plead with the staff that a business necessity has come up that makes it imperative that he be allowed to go away for a few days. From a very different perspective, it has been argued that the deliberate but rare violation of aesthetic conventions could have great aesthetic value.

All arguments for allowing exceptions, however, run into a common problem: how to distinguish genuine exceptions from the temptations or impulses that the constraints were supposed to protect oneself from in the first place. Emergencies that suspend constitutional rights may be used to abolish the constitution. One politician's recession is another's looming depression. Addicts will always be able to find some aspect in which the present occasion is exceptional. And how can an artist know that his violation of a convention is an act of daring imagination rather than mere self-indulgence? To address these second-order problems, various second-order solutions are possible. The problem drinker, for instance, might use a convention to pace himself: never have alcohol in the house except when entertaining guests.

COSTS OF PRECOMMITMENT

Constraints and conventions impose three main costs: loss of flexibility, loss of spontaneity, and loss of decisiveness. The first problem is linked to the need for exceptions, and for a way of distinguishing them from merely unconstrained behavior. But the lack of flexibility may also be so severe as to induce a move to abolish the constraints entirely. In some countries, the disastrous effects of central bank rigidity during the Great Depression triggered legislation that essentially entrusted monetary policy to the discretion of the government. Because of the dangers of rule-utilitarianism in an unpredictable environment, act-utilitarianism may seem like a superior alternative.

Loss of spontaneity is especially important in the arts, where a genuinely powerful imagination may find it intolerable to be shackled by rules. The perennial French debate over the respective merits of Racine and Shakespeare illustrates the point. Against the "perfection" of Racine, there is the "greatness" of Shakespeare. The plays of Racine may represent local maxima of aesthetic value, but Shakespeare's flawed masterpieces might nevertheless be aesthetically superior. The person who tries to overcome a bad habit or an addiction by regimenting himself rigidly might find that his life is desiccated. The ex-smoker who tries to avoid all environments previously associated with smoking may find himself confined to his room.

Finally, the constraints may be so tight as to leave little room for action and innovation. The American constitution, for instance, is often criticized for having a system of checks and balances that is so rigorous that even much-needed reforms are blocked. As an art form develops and ever-new conventions are added to regulate artistic works, creativity may suffer. Beyond a certain point, constraints and conventions cease to be enabling and become stifling.

Being Unable to Make Oneself Unable

Even when unambiguously desirable, self-binding technologies may not be adoptable or available. If precommitment is a device to be adopted by Peter when sober to constrain Peter when drunk, it is not likely to be used if Peter is always drunk, or drunk at the relevant moment. In constitution-making moments, for instance, the framers may be so enthusiastic that they fail to take the proper precautions against the fallibility of human nature. In other cases, the framers may be animated by a standing passion or prejudice that blinds them to the need to protect themselves against it.

Also, the technology may simply not exist. A man may try to save for his old age by creating a retirement fund, only to find that he can use it as collateral to finance additional current spending. If a person tries to back up a threat by contracting with a third party to pay a large sum of money if he fails to carry it out, he may find that the courts refuse to enforce it. A film director who desperately wants to shoot in black and white or without sound may not find anyone who is willing to fund him. When one is angry, it may be difficult to keep in mind the device of counting until ten when angry. The most poignant case is provided by the paradox of omnipotence, the dictator who is able to do everything except make himself unable to interfere with the life of the citizens. How could Ulysses have protected himself against the song of the Sirens had he been so strong that he could break any ties that bound him to the mast?

Some Unexplored and Unresolved Questions

The two issues that I have singled out for more intensive discussion, constitution-making and the creation of works of art, are not the only instances of beneficial constraints. Some of the topics I discussed in the first chapter – savings behavior, industrial organization, international relations, addiction, and religious fundamentalism – could have been considered at equal length. The tendency to procrastinate and techniques for overcoming it would also be fertile topics. As Diego Gambetta has pointed out to me, a full chapter could also have been written on the importance of constraints in *sports*, where there is a ceaseless adjustment of rules so as to make athletes and players bound neither too tightly nor too loosely. Here, the purpose is to make things just difficult enough to present the participants with a challenge that can be met and the spectators with a sight they can enjoy.

This issue – the optimal tightness of the bounds – is one that awaits further study. In the constitutional context, one may ask about the optimal difficulty of amending the constitution, the optimal length and security of tenure for central bankers and judges on the constitutional court, or the optimal supermajority required to override an executive veto. Although there cannot be any answers that are right for all times and places, one might be able to make definite recommendations in the context of specific political systems. In the context of the arts, the issue is partly a matter of the tightness of the constraints and partly a matter of the extent to which the artist should feel free to violate them.

Another issue that remains to be explored concerns the relation between conscious self-binding and unconscious mechanisms of mental adjustment. When a constraint is imposed rather than freely chosen, the agent who is bound may eventually come to welcome it, through the mechanism of dissonance reduction. In 1920, a movie director who had no choice in the matter could develop a philosophy according to which silent movies offer an intrinsically superior medium. Later, when sound becomes available, he might continue to defend the same view because of the need to remain consistent with himself. (The perception of the grapes as sour may persist even when they come within the reach of the fox.) If sound had been available from the beginning, however, the idea of renouncing it might never have crossed his mind. A more general account of constraints would have to incorporate the idea that constraints can *cause* a preference for less over more as well as being the effect of such preferences.

Finally, we should note that the constraints may also induce a preference for what one cannot have or cannot do. Tocqueville remarked that the French had to be kept loosely bound to prevent them from rebelling against the tightness of their chains. When people are constrained from doing what they would not have wanted to do if they were free to do it, they may develop a desire for it. This mechanism may come into play in the case of self-imposed constraints as well. In a marriage undertaken as an act of self-binding, the grass may come to look greener on the other side of the fence. Sometimes, there may not be much of a psychological difference between a constraint imposed by others and one that was imposed by oneself in the past. Some of the temptations against which the agent is supposed to be protected by the precommitment device may owe their existence to the device itself.

References

Abastado, C. (1975), *Le surréalisme*, Paris: Hachette.

Ackerman, B. (1991), *We the People*, Cambridge, Mass.: Harvard University Press.

Ackerman, B., and Katyal, N. (1995), "Our unconventional founding," *University of Chicago Law Review* 62, 475–573.

Ainslie, G. (1992), *Picoeconomics*, Cambridge University Press.

Ainslie, G. (1994), "Is rationality just a bookkeeping system?" Paper read at the American Philosophical Association, Los Angeles, April 2.

Akerlof, G. (1991), "Procrastination and obedience," *American Economic Review* 81, 1–19.

Andenæs, J. (1980), *Det Vanskelige Oppgjøret*, Oslo: Tanum.

Anderson, T. (1993), *Creating the Constitution: The Convention of 1787 and the First Congress*, University Park, Pa.: Pennsylvania State University Press.

Arnheim, R. (1957), *Film as Art*, Berkeley: University of California Press.

Barry, B. (1989), *Democracy, Power and Justice: Essays in Political Theory*, Oxford: Oxford University Press.

Barth, E. (1988), "The sequence of moves in wage bargaining," Working Paper, Institute for Social Research, Oslo.

Bataille, G. (1957), *L'érotisme*, Paris: Editions de Minuit.

Baumeister, R. F., Heatherton, T. F., and Tice, D. M. (1994), *Losing Control: How and Why People Fail at Self-Regulation*, San Diego: Academic Press.

Baxandall, M. (1985), *Patterns of Intention*, New Haven: Yale University Press.

Bayefsky, A., ed. (1989), *Canada's Constitution Act 1982 & Amendments: A Documentary History*, Vols. I–II, Toronto: McGraw-Hill Ryerson.

Bazin, A. (1972), *What Is Cinema?* vol. II, Berkeley and Los Angeles: University of California Press.

Becker, G. (1992), "Habits, addictions, and traditions," *Kyklos* 45, 327–46.

Becker, G. (1996), *Accounting for Tastes*, Cambridge, Mass.: Harvard University Press.

Becker, G., and Mulligan, C. (1997), "The endogenous determination of time preferences," *Quarterly Journal of Economics* 112, 729–58.

References

Becker, G., and Murphy, K. (1988), "A theory of rational addiction," *Journal of Political Economy* 96, 675–700.

Bell, D. (1982), "Regret in decision making under uncertainty," *Operations Research* 30, 961–81.

Bellos, D. (1994), *Georges Perec*, Paris: Seuil.

Belton, J., ed. (1996), *Movies and Mass Culture*, New Brunswick, N.J.: Rutgers University Press.

Berliner, P. (1994), *Thinking in Jazz*, Chicago: University of Chicago Press.

Bilgrami, A. (1996), "Secular liberalism and the moral psychology of identity," unpublished manuscript, Department of Philosophy, Columbia University.

Blinder, A. (1998), *Central Banking in Theory and Practice*, Cambridge, Mass.: MIT Press.

Bogdanovich, P. (1997), *Who the Devil Made It?* New York: Knopf.

Bondt, W. F. M. de, and Thaler, R. (1985), "Does the stock market overreact?" *Journal of Finance* 40, 793–808.

Bonime-Blanc, A. (1987), *Spain's Transition to Democracy: The Politics of Constitution-Making*, Boulder and London: Westview Press.

Boulez, P. (1986), *Orientations*, Cambridge, Mass.: Harvard University Press.

Brady, F. (1989), *Citizen Welles*, New York: Anchor Books.

Bratman, M. (1995), "Planning and temptation," in L. May, M. Friedman, and A. Clark (eds.), *Mind and Morals*, Cambridge, Mass.: MIT Press, pp. 293–310.

Brehm, J. (1966), *A Theory of Psychological Reactance*, New York: Academic Press.

Breton, A. (1972), *Manifestoes of Surrealism*, Ann Arbor: University of Michigan Press.

Brewer, C. (1993), "Recent developments in disulfiram treatment," *Alcohol and Alcoholism* 28, 383–95.

Brilliant, R. (1991), *Portraiture*, Cambridge, Mass.: Harvard University Press.

Brombert, V. (1968), *Stendhal*, Englewood Cliffs, N.J.: Prentice Hall.

Brown, D. P., and Fromm, E. (1987), *Hypnosis and Behavioral Medicine*, Hillsdale, N.J.: Lawrence Erlbaum.

Buchmann-Möller, F. (1990a), *You Just Fight for Your Life: The Life of Lester Young*, New York: Praeger.

Buchmann-Möller, F. (1990b), *You Got to Be Original, Man! The Music of Lester Young*, New York: Greenwood Press.

Budd, M. (1985), *Music and the Emotions*, London: Routledge and Kegan Paul.

Budd, M. (1995), *Values of Art*, London: Allen Lane.

Burdeau, G., Hamon, F., and Troper, M. (1991), *Droit Constitutionnel*, 22ᵉ édition, Paris: Librairie Générale de Droit et de Jurisprudence.

Cage, J. (1961), *Silence*, Middletown, Conn.: Wesleyan University Press.

Cage, J. (1990), *I-VI*, Cambridge, Mass.: Harvard University Press.

References

Caillois, R. (1943), "Pythian heritage (on the nature of poetic inspiration)," *Books Abroad* 17, 207–11.

Caillois, R. (1974), "Le roman policier," in *Approches de l'imaginaire*, Paris: Gallimard, pp. 177–205.

Caillois, R. (1978), *Babel*, Paris: Gallimard.

Callahan, E. J. (1980), "Alternative strategies in the treatment of narcotic addiction: A review," in W. R. Miller (ed.), *The Addictive Behaviors*, Oxford: Pergamon Press, pp. 143–68.

Camerer, C., Loewenstein, G., and Weber, M. (1989), "The curse of knowledge in economic settings," *Journal of Political Economy* 97, 1232–54.

Campbell, R. (1995), *Sauce for the Goose*, New York: The Mysterious Press.

Campos, J. E., and Root, H. L. (1996), *The Key to the Asian Miracle*, Washington, D.C.: The Brookings Institution.

Caplin, A., and Nalebuff, B. (1988), "On 64% majority rule," *Econometrica* 56, 787–814.

Carillo, J., and Mariotti, T. (1997), "Wishful thinking and strategic ignorance," unpublished manuscript, ECARE (Université Libre de Bruxelles) and GEMAQ (Université de Toulouse).

Carroll, N. (1988), *Philosophical Problems of Film Theory*, Princeton: Princeton University Press.

Carroll, N. (1996), *Theorizing the Moving Image*, Cambridge University Press.

Carroll, N. (1997), "Art, narrative, and emotion," in M. Hjort and S. Laver (eds.), *Emotion and the Arts*, Oxford University Press, pp. 190–211.

Castaldo, A. (1989), *Les méthodes de travail de la constituante*, Paris: Presses Universitaires de France.

Cernuschi, C. (1992), *Jackson Pollock*, New York: HarperCollins.

Clarke, D. (1994), *Wishing on the Moon: The Life and Times of Billie Holiday*, New York: Penguin.

Cohen, D. (1995), *Law, Violence and Community in Classical Athens*, Cambridge University Press.

Colomer, J. (1995), *Game Theory and the Transition to Democracy*, Aldershot: Edward Elgar.

Comité National chargé de la Publication des Travaux Préparatoires des Institutions de la Ve République (1987–1991), *Documents pour servir à l'histoire de l'élaboration de la constitution du 4 octobre 1958*, vols. I–III, Paris: La Documentation Française.

Cooke, M. (1998), *The Chronicle of Jazz*, New York: Abbeville Press.

Cowen, T. (1991), "Self-constraint versus self-liberation," *Ethics* 101, 360–73.

Cowen, T. (1998), *In Praise of Commercial Culture*, Cambridge, Mass.: Harvard University Press.

Cukierman, A. (1992), *Central Bank Strategy, Credibility, and Independence: Theory and Evidence*, Cambridge, Mass.: MIT Press.

Cummings, C., Jordan, J. R., and Marlatt, G. A. (1980), "Relapse: Prevention and prediction," in W. R. Miller (ed.), *The Addictive Behaviors*, Oxford: Pergamon Press, pp. 291–321.

Currie, D. (1990), *The Constitution in the Supreme Court: 1888–1986*, Chicago: University of Chicago Press.

Damasio, A. (1994), *Descartes' Error*, New York: Putnam.

Davidson, D. (1970), "How is weakness of the will possible?" reprinted in *Essays on Actions and Events*, Oxford: Oxford University Press, 1980.

Davis, D., Chaskalson, M., and de Waal, J. (1995), "Democracy and constitutionalism: The role of constitutional interpretation," in D. van Wyk et al. (eds.), *Rights and Constitutionalism*, Oxford: Oxford University Press, pp. 1–130.

Déhay, E. (1998), "L'exemple allemand d'indépendance de la banque centrale" (Unpublished Manuscript).

Derfler, L. (1983), *Presidents and Parliaments: A Short History of the French Presidency*, Boca Raton: University Presses of Florida.

Dickerson, M. G. (1984), *Compulsive Gamblers*, London: Longman.

Dixit, A., and Nalebuff, B. (1991), "Making strategies credible," in R. Zeckhauser (ed.), *Strategy and Choice*, Cambridge, Mass.: MIT Press, pp. 161–84.

Dodds, E. R. (1951), *The Greeks and the Irrational*, Berkeley and Los Angeles: University of California Press.

Dodge, R. P. (1995), *Hot Jazz and Jazz Dance*, Oxford: Oxford University Press.

Dover, K. J. (1955), "Anapsephisis in fifth-century Athens," *Journal of Hellenic Studies* 75, 17–20.

Dresser, R. (1982), "Ulysses and the psychiatrists: a legal and policy analysis of the voluntary commitment contract," *Harvard Civil Rights-Civil Liberties Review* 16, 777–854.

Dutton, D., ed. (1983), *The Forger's Art*, Berkeley: University of California Press.

Edwards, G., et al. (1994), *Alcohol Policy and the Public Good*, Oxford: Oxford University Press.

Egret, J. (1950), *La révolution des notables*, Paris: Armand Colin.

Egret, J. (1975), *Necker et la Révolution Française*, Paris: Champion.

Ekman, P. (1992), *Telling Lies*, New York: Norton.

Eliot, T. S. (1919), "Hamlet," in *Selected Prose of T.S. Eliot*, New York: Farrar, Straus and Giroux, pp. 45–49.

Ellin, S. (1974), *Stronghold*, New York: Norton.

Elliott, R. K. (1972), "The critic and the art lover," in W. Mays and S. C. Brown (eds.), *Linguistic Analysis and Phenomenology*, Lewisburg: Bucknell University Press, pp. 117–27.

Elster, J. (1975), *Leibniz et la formation de l'esprit scientifique*, Paris: Aubier-Montaigne.

Elster, J. (1978), *Logic and Society*, Chichester: Wiley.

Elster, J. (1983a), *Explaining Technical Change*, Cambridge University Press.

Elster, J. (1983b), *Sour Grapes*, Cambridge University Press.

Elster, J. (1984), *Ulysses and the Sirens*, rev. ed., Cambridge University Press.

Elster, J. (1985), *Making Sense of Marx*, Cambridge University Press.

Elster, J. (1986a), "Self-realization in work and politics," *Social Philosophy and Policy* 3, 97–126.

Elster, J. (1986b), "Deception and self-deception in Stendhal," in J. Elster (ed.), *The Multiple Self*, Cambridge University Press, pp. 93–113.

Elster, J. (1989a), *Nuts and Bolts for the Social Sciences*, Cambridge University Press.

Elster (1989b), *Solomonic Judgments*, Cambridge University Press.

Elster (1989c), *The Cement of Society*, Cambridge University Press.

Elster, J. (1993a), "Rebuilding the boat in the open sea: Constitution-making in Eastern Europe," *Public Administration* 71, 169–217.

Elster, J. (1993b), "Constitutional bootstrapping in Paris and Philadelphia," *Cardozo Law Review* 14, 549–76.

Elster, J. (1993c), "Majority rule and individual rights," in S. Hurley and S. Shute (eds.), *On Human Rights*, New York: Basic Books, pp. 175–216, 249–56.

Elster, J. (1993d), *Political Psychology*, Cambridge University Press.

Elster, J. (1994), "Argumenter et négocier dans deux assemblées constituantes," *Revue Française de Science Politique* 44, 187–256.

Elster, J. (1995a), "Forces and mechanisms in the constitution-making process," *Duke Law Review* 45, 364–96.

Elster, J. (1995b), "Limiting majority rule: Alternatives to judicial review in the revolutionary epoch," in E. Smith (ed.), *Constitutional Justice under Old Constitutions*, The Hague: Kluwer, pp. 3–21.

Elster, J. (1995c), "Strategic uses of argument," in K. Arrow et al. (eds.), *Barriers to the Negotiated Resolution of Conflict*, New York: Norton, pp. 236–57.

Elster, J. (1995d), "The impact of constitutions on economic performance," in *Proceedings from the Annual Bank Conference on Economic Development*, Washington, D.C.: The World Bank, pp. 209–226.

Elster, J. (1995e), "Transition, constitution-making and separation in Czechoslovakia," *Archives Européennes de Sociologie* 36, 105–34.

Elster, J. (1995f), "Equal or proportional? Arguing and bargaining over the Senate at the Federal Convention," in J. Knight and I. Sened (eds.), *Explaining Social Institutions*, Ann Arbor: University of Michigan Press, pp. 145–60.

Elster, J. (1996), "Montaigne's psychology," *The Great Ideas Today*, Chicago: Encyclopedia Britannica, pp. 108–55.

Elster, J. (1997): Review of Becker (1996), *University of Chicago Law Review* 64, 749–64.

Elster, J. (1998), "Coming to terms with the past," *Archives Européennes de Sociologie* 39, 7–48.

Elster, J. (1999a), *Alchemies of the Mind: Rationality and the Emotions*, Cambridge University Press.

Elster, J. (1999b), *Strong Feelings: Emotion, Addiction, and Human Behavior*, Cambridge, Mass.: MIT Press.

Elster, J. (1999c), "Gambling and addiction," in J. Elster and O.-J. Skog (eds.), *Getting Hooked: Rationality and the Addictions*, Cambridge University Press, pp. 208–34.

Elster, J. (1999d), "Davidson on weakness of will and self-deception," in L. Hahn (ed.), *The Philosophy of Donald Davidson*, La Salle, Ill.: Open House Publishing, pp. 425–42.

Elster, J. (in press), "Rationality, economy, and society," in S. Turner (ed.), *The Cambridge Companion to Weber*, Cambridge University Press.

Elster, J., and Loewenstein, G. (1992), "Utility from memory and anticipation," in G. Loewenstein and J. Elster (eds.), *Choice over Time*, New York: Russell Sage Foundation, pp. 213–34.

Engel, M. (1967), *The Maturity of Dickens*, Cambridge, Mass.: Harvard University Press.

Eule, J. N. (1987), "Temporal limits on the legislative mandate," *American Bar Foundation Research Journal*, 379–459.

Eyck, F. (1968), *The Frankfurt Parliament 1848–49*, London: Macmillan.

Fearon, J. (1994), "Domestic political audiences and the escalation of international disputes," *American Political Science Review* 88, 577–92.

Fearon, J. (1997), "Signaling foreign policy interests," *Journal of Conflict Resolution* 41, 68–90.

Feller, W. (1968), *An Introduction to Probability Theory and Its Applications*, 3d ed., vol. 1, New York: Wiley.

Finn, J. E. (1991), *Constitutions in Crisis*, New York: Oxford University Press.

Ford, R. (1998), "Why not a novella?" editorial introduction to *The Granta Book of Long Stories*, London: Granta.

Frank, R. (1988), *Passions within Reason*, New York: Norton.

Frank, R. (1996), *Microeconomics*, New York: McGraw-Hill.

Frankfurt, H. (1971), "Freedom and will and the concept of a person," *Journal of Philosophy* 68, 56–20.

Freud, S. (1908), "Creative writers and daydreaming," in *The Complete Psychological Works of Sigmund Freud*, London: The Hogarth Press, 1959, vol. IX, pp. 141–53.

Friedwald, W. (1996), *Jazz Singing*, New York: Da Capo Press.

Frijda, N. (1986), *The Emotions*, Cambridge University Press.

Fromm, E. (1960), *Fear of Freedom*, London: Routledge.

Fry, R. (1921), *Vision and Design*, New York: Brentano.

Fudenberg, D., and Tirole, J. (1992), *Game Theory*, Cambridge, Mass.: MIT Press.

Gardner, E., and David, J. (1999), "The neurobiology of chemical addiction," in J. Elster and O.-J. Skog (eds.), *Getting Hooked: Rationality and the Addictions*, Cambridge University Press, pp. 93–136.

References

Gataker, T. (1627), *On the Nature and Use of Lots*, 2nd. ed, London.

Geer, H. de (1986). *SAF i förhandlingar*. Stockholm: SAFs Förlag.

Genette, G. (1969), "Vraisemblance et motivation," in *Figures II*, Paris: Seuil, pp. 71–100.

Gibbard, A. (1986), "Interpersonal comparisons: Preference, good, and the intrinsic reward of a life," in J. Elster and A. Hylland (eds.), *Foundations of Social Choice Theory*, Cambridge University Press, pp. 165–93.

Glantz, S., et al. (1996), *The Cigarette Papers*, Berkeley and Los Angeles: University of California Press.

Glenn, B. (1999), "Collective precommitment from temptation: The case of the Amish," unpublished manuscript, St. Antony's College.

Golay, J. F. (1958), *The Founding of the Federal Republic of Germany*, Chicago: University of Chicago Press.

Goldenberg, J., Mazursky, D., and Solomon, S. (1999), "Creative sparks," *Science* 285, 1495–96.

Goldstein, A. (1994), *Addiction*, New York: Freeman.

Goodman, E. (1997), "Worried About All Those Divorces? Tighten the Knot and Feel Better," *International Herald Tribune*, August 12.

Green, B. (1991), *The Reluctant Art*, New York: Da Capo Press.

Greenberg, C. (1999), *Homemade Esthetics*, Oxford University Press.

Guth, W., Schmittberger, R., and Schwartz, B. (1982), "An experimental analysis of ultimatum bargaining," *Journal of Economic Behavior and Organization* 3, 367–88.

Hadamard, J. (1954), *The Psychology of Invention in the Mathematical Field*, New York: Dover Books.

Hampson, N. (1988), *Prelude to Terror*, Oxford: Blackwell.

Hansen, M. H. (1991), *The Athenian Democracy in the Age of Demosthenes*, Oxford: Blackwell.

Harrison, S. (1995), "Anthropological perspectives on the management of knowledge," *Anthropology Today* 11, 10–14.

Haugom Olsen, S. (1998), "Literary aesthetics," in M. Kelly (ed.), *The Encyclopedia of Aesthetics*, vol. 3, New York: Oxford University Press, pp. 147–55.

Hayek, F. (1960), *The Constitution of Liberty*, Chicago: University of Chicago Press.

Heard, A. (1991), *Canadian Constitutional Conventions*, Toronto: Oxford University Press.

Henry, C. (1974), "Investment decisions under uncertainty: The 'irreversibility effect,'" *American Economic Review* 64, 1006–12.

Hill, J. S. (1998), *Ghirlandaio's Daughter*, New York: St. Martin's Press.

Hirshleifer, J. (1987), "The emotions as guarantors of threats and promises," in J. Dupré (ed.), *The Latest on the Best*, Cambridge, Mass.: MIT Press, pp. 307–26.

Hjort, M. (1993), *The Strategy of Letters*, Cambridge, Mass.: Harvard University Press.

References

Holmes, S. (1984), *Benjamin Constant and the Making of Modern Liberalism*, New Haven: Yale University Press.

Holmes, S. (1988), "Precommitment and the paradox of democracy," in J. Elster and R. Slagstad (eds.), *Constitutionalism and Democracy*, Cambridge University Press, pp. 195–240.

Holmes, S. (1992), "Destroyed by success," unpublished manuscript.

Holmes, S. (1993), *The Anatomy of Antiliberalism*, Cambridge, Mass.: Harvard University Press.

Holmes, S., and Sunstein, C. (1995), "The politics of constitutional revision in Eastern Europe," in S. Levinson (ed.), *Responding to Imperfection: The Theory and Practice of Constitutional Amendment*, Princeton: Princeton University Press, pp. 275–306.

Huber, E. R. (1960), *Deutsche Verfassungsgeschichte seit 1789*, vol. 2, Stuttgart: Kohlhammer.

Hume, D. (1960), *A Treatise on Human Nature*, ed. Selby-Bigge, Oxford: Oxford University Press.

Hurley, S. (1989), *Natural Reasons*, Oxford: Oxford University Press.

Huyse, L., and Dhondt, S. (1993), *La répression des collaborations*, Bruxelles: CRISP.

Iser, W. (1974), *The Implied Reader*, Baltimore: Johns Hopkins University Press.

James, C. (1997), "Hit men" (review of Bogdanovich 1997), *The New Yorker* July 7, 70–73.

Johnsen, J., and Mørland, J. (1992), "Depot preparations of disulfiram: Experimental and clinical results," *Acta Psychiatrica Scandinavica* 86, 27–30.

Jones, A. H. M. (1957), *Athenian Democracy*, Baltimore: Johns Hopkins University Press.

Kagan, D. (1974), *The Archidamian War*, Ithaca, N.Y.: Cornell University Press.

Kahn, A., and T. E. Tice (1973), "Returning a favor and retaliating harm: The effects of stated intentions and actual behavior," *Journal of Experimental Social Psychology* 9, 43–56.

Kahneman, D., and Miller, D. T. (1986), "Norm theory: Comparing reality to its alternatives," *Psychological Review* 93, 126–53.

Kahneman, D., and Tversky, A. (1982), "The simulation heuristics," in D. Kahneman, P. Slovic, and A. Tversky (eds.), *Judgment under Uncertainty*, Cambridge University Press, pp. 201–209.

Kant, I. (1785), *The Metaphysics of Morals*, in *The Cambridge Edition of the Works of Immanuel Kant: Practical Philosophy*, Cambridge University Press, 1996.

Keech, W. R. (1995), *Economic Politics*, Cambridge University Press.

Kermode, F. (1967), *The Sense of an Ending*, Oxford: Oxford University Press.

Kluger, R. (1996), *Ashes to Ashes*, New York: Knopf.

Kolm, S.-C. (1986), "The Buddhist theory of 'no-self,' " in J. Elster (ed.), *The Multiple Self*, Cambridge University Press, pp. 233–65.

Koseki, S. (1997), *The Birth of Japan's Postwar Constitution*, Boulder: The Westview Press.

References

Kostelanetz, R. (1991a), "Inferential art," in R. Kostelanetz (ed.), *John Cage*, New York: Da Capo, pp. 105–109.

Kostelanetz, R. (1991b), "John Cage: Some random remarks," in R. Kostelanetz (ed.), *John Cage*, New York: Da Capo, pp. 193–207.

Kraybill, D. (1989), *The Riddle of Amish Culture*, Baltimore: Johns Hopkins University Press.

Kreps, D., et al. (1982), "Rational cooperation in the finitely iterated Prisoner's Dilemma," *Journal of Economic Theory* 27, 245–52, 486–502.

Krogh, D. (1991), *Smoking*, New York: Freeman.

Kurtz, E. (1979), *Not-God: A History of Alcoholics Anonymous*, Center City, Minn.: Hazelden Educational Services.

Kydland, F., and Prescott, E. (1977), "Rules rather than discretion: The inconsistency of optimal plans," *Journal of Political Economy* 85, 473–91.

Kymlicka, W. (1989), *Liberalism, Community and Culture*, Oxford: Oxford University Press.

Lacouture, J. (1990), *De Gaulle*, vols. I–III, Paris: Seuil.

Lafayette, Mme de (1994), *The Princess of Clèves*, New York: Norton.

Laffont, J.-J., and Tirole, J. (1994), *A Theory of Incentives in Procurement and Regulation*, Cambridge, Mass.: The MIT Press.

Lahr, J. (1999), "Revolutionary Rag," *The New Yorker*, March 8, pp. 77–83.

Laibson, D. (1994), "Self-control and saving" (Ph.D. Dissertation, Department of Economics, MIT).

Laibson, D. (1996a), "Hyperbolic discount functions, undersaving, and savings policy," NBER working paper #5635.

Laibson, D. (1996b), "A cue-theory of consumption," manuscript, Department of Economics, Harvard University.

Laibson, D. (1997), "Golden eggs and hyperbolic discounting," *Quarterly Journal of Economics* 112, 443–78.

Lecherbonnier, B., et al., eds. (1989), *Littérature XXᵉ Siècle*, Paris: Nathan.

LeDoux, J. (1996), *The Emotional Brain*, New York: Simon and Schuster.

Leibniz, G. W. (1705), "Considerations on vital principles and plastic natures," in L. E. Loemker (ed.), *Leibniz: Philosophical Papers and Letters*, Dordrecht: Reidel, 1969, pp. 586–90.

Lem, S. (1994), *Peace on Earth*, New York: Harcourt Brace.

Lessing, A. (1983) "What is wrong with a forgery?" in D. Dutton (ed.), *The Forger's Art*, Berkeley: University of California Press, pp. 58–76.

Levenson, J. (1968), *Confucian China and Its Modern Fate*, Vol. 1, Berkeley: University of California Press.

Levinson, J. (1990), "Musical literacy," *Journal of Aesthetic Education* 24, 17–30.

Levy, R. (1973), *The Tahitians*, Chicago: University of Chicago Press.

Lewis, D. (1969), *Convention: A Philosophical Study*, Cambridge, Mass.: Harvard University Press.

Lewis, M. (1992), *Shame*, New York: The Free Press.

References

Lichtenstein, E., and Brown, R. A. (1980), "Smoking cessation methods: Review and recommendations," in W. R. Miller (ed.), *The Addictive Behaviors*, Oxford: Pergamon Press, pp. 169–206.

Lindbeck, A. (1976), "Stabilization policy in open economies with endogenous politicians," *American Economic Review: Papers and Proceedings* 66, 1–19.

Livingston, P. (1991), *Literature and Rationality*, Cambridge University Press.

Loewenstein, G. (1996), "Out of control: Visceral influences on behavior," *Organizational Behavior and Human Decision Processes* 65, 272–92.

Loewenstein, G. (1999), "A visceral theory of addiction," in J. Elster and O.-J. Skog (eds.), *Getting Hooked: Rationality and the Addictions*, Cambridge University Press, pp. 235–64.

Loewenstein, G., and Elster, J., eds. (1992), *Choice over Time*, New York: The Russell Sage Foundation.

Loewenstein, G., and Prelec, D. (1992), "Anomalies in intertemporal choice," in G. Loewenstein and J. Elster (eds.), *Choice over Time*, New York: Russell Sage, pp. 119–46.

Loomes, G., and Sugden, R. (1987), "Some implications of a more general form of regret theory," *Journal of Economic Theory* 41, 270–87.

Lovejoy, A. O. (1961), *Reflections on Human Nature*, Baltimore: Johns Hopkins Press.

Loveman, B. (1993), *The Constitution of Tyranny*, Pittsburgh: University of Pittsburgh Press.

Luthy, D. (1994), "The origin and growth of Amish tourism," in D. B. Kraybill and M. A. Olshan (eds.), *The Amish Struggle with Modernity*, Hanover: University Press of New England, pp. 113–29.

MacDowell, D. M. (1978), *The Law in Classical Athens*, Ithaca, N.Y.: Cornell University Press.

Mackie, G. (1996), "Ending footbinding and infibulation: A convention account," *American Sociological Review* 61, 999–1017.

Maltby, R. (1993), "The Production code and the Hays office," in T. Balio (ed.), *Grand Design*, Berkeley and Los Angeles: University of California Press, pp. 73–108.

Maltby, R., and Craven, I. (1995), *Hollywood Cinema*, Oxford: Blackwell.

Manin, B. (1995), *Principes du gouvernement représentatif*, Paris: Calmann-Lévy.

Markman, K. D., et al. (1993), "The mental simulation of better and worse possible worlds," *Journal of Experimental Social Psychology* 29, 87–109.

Marsh, D. (1992), *The Bundesbank*, London: Mandarin.

Marshall, G. (1984), *Constitutional Conventions*, Oxford: Oxford University Press.

Marx, K. (1973), *Grundrisse*, Harmondsworth: Pelican Books.

Mason, H. L. (1952), *The Purge of Dutch Quislings*, The Hague: Martinus Nijhoff.

References

Mathiez, A. (1898), "Etude critique sur les journées des 5 & 6 octobre 1789," *Revue Historique* 67, 241–81.

Maynard-Smith, J. (1982), *Evolution and the Theory of Games*, Cambridge University Press.

McCarthy, T. (1997), *Howard Hawks*, New York: Grove.

McGilligan, P. (1997), *Fritz Lang*, New York: St. Martin's Press.

McKenna, F. A. (1990), "Heuristics or cognitive deficits: How should we characterize smokers' decision making?" in D. M. Warburton (ed.), *Addiction controversies*, Chur, Switzerland: Harvood, pp. 261–70.

Merton, R. K. (1946), *Mass Persuasion*, Westport, Conn.: Greenwood.

Merton, R. K. (1987), "Three fragments from a sociologist's notebook," *Annual Review of Sociology* 13, 1–28.

Miller, G. (1993), "Constitutional moments, precommitment, and fundamental reform: The case of Argentina," *Washington University Law Quarterly* 71, 1061–86.

Miller, P. M. (1980), "Theoretical and practical issues in substance abuse assessment and treatment," in W. R. Miller (ed.), *The Addictive Behaviors*, Oxford: Pergamon Press, pp. 265–90.

Miller, W. (1993), *Humiliation*, Ithaca, N.Y.: Cornell University Press.

Miller, W. R., and Hester, R. K. (1980), "Treating the problem drinker: Modern approaches," in W. R. Miller (ed.), *The Addictive Behaviors*, Oxford: Pergamon Press, pp. 11–142.

Mischel, W. (1968), *Personality and Assessment*, New York: Wiley.

Mischel, W., Shoda, Y., and Rodriguez, M. (1989), "Delay of gratification in children," *Science* 244, 933–938.

Moene, K. O. (1999), "Addiction and social interaction," in J. Elster and O.-J. Skog (eds.), *Getting Hooked: Rationality and the Addictions*, Cambridge University Press, pp. 30–46.

Montaigne, M. de (1991), *The Complete Essays*, tr. M. A. Screech, Harmondsworth: Penguin.

Mounier, J. -J. (1989), "Exposé de ma conduite dans l'Assemblée Nationale," in F. Furet and R. Halévi (eds.), *Orateurs de la Révolution Française, I: Les Constituants*, Paris: Gallimard, pp. 908–97.

Mueller, D. C. (1996), *Constitutional Democracy*, Oxford: Oxford University Press.

Mueller, J. (1985), *Astaire Dancing*, New York: Knopf.

Mulligan, K. (1997), *Parental Priorities and Economic Equality*, Chicago: University of Chicago Press.

Nahin, P. (1998), *An Imaginary Tale*, Princeton: Princeton University Press.

Najemy, J. (1982), *Corporatism and Consensus in Florentine Electoral Politics 1280–1400*, Chapel Hill: University of North Carolina Press.

Nicholson, S. (1995), *Billie Holiday*, Boston: Northeastern University Press.

North, D., and Weingast, B. (1989), "Constitutions and commitment: The

293

evolution of institutions governing public choice in seventeenth-century England," *Journal of Economic History* 49, 803–32.

O'Brien, G. (1997), "Sein of the times," *New York Review of Books* August 14, 12–14.

O'Donoghue, T., and Rabin, M. (1999a), "Doing it now or later," *American Economic Review* 89, 103–24.

O'Donogue, T., and Rabin, M. (1999b), "Addiction and self-control," in J. Elster (ed.), *Addiction: Exits and Entries*, New York: Russell Sage, pp. 169–206.

Offe, C. (1992), "Strong causes, weak cures," *East European Constitutional Review* 2, 1, 21–23.

O'Flaherty, B. (1996), *Making Room: The Economics of Hopelessness*, Cambridge, Mass.: Harvard University Press.

Orford, J. (1985), *Excessive Appetites: A Psychological View of the Addictions*, Chichester: Wiley.

Orphanides, A., and Zervos, D. (1995), "Rational addiction with learning and regret," *Journal of Political Economy* 103, 739–58.

Orphanides, A., and Zervos, D. (1998), "Myopia and addictive behavior," *Economic Journal* 108, 75–91.

Osborne, M., and Rubinstein, A. (1990), *Bargaining Theory*, San Diego: Academic Press.

Osiatynski, W. (1997), *Alcoholism: Sin or Disease?* Warsaw: Stefan Batory Foundation.

Ostwald, M. (1986), *From Popular Sovereignty to the Rule of Law*, Berkeley: University of California Press.

Oulipo (1988), *Atlas de Littérature potentielle*, Paris: Gallimard.

Parducci, A. (1995), *Happiness, Pleasure and Judgment*, Mahwah, N.J.: Lawrence Erlbaum.

Parfit, D. (1973), "Later selves and moral principles," in A. Montefiore (ed.), *Philosophy and Personal Relations*, London: Routledge and Kegan Paul, pp. 137–69.

Parfit, D. (1984), *Reasons and Persons*, Oxford: Oxford University Press.

Parijs, P. van (1984), "Marxism's central puzzle," in T. Ball and J. Farr (eds.), *After Marx*, Cambridge University Press, pp. 88–104.

Pasquino, P. (1999), "L'originie du contrôle de constitutionnalité en Italie," unpublished manuscript.

Paulhan, J. (1990), *Les fleurs de Tarbes*, Paris: Gallimard.

Pavel, T. (1986), *Fictional Worlds*, Cambridge, Mass.: Harvard University Press.

Pavel, T. (1998), "Classicism," in M. Kelly (ed.), *The Encyclopedia of Aesthetics*, vol. 1, New York: Oxford University Press, pp. 373–77.

Pears, D. (1985), *Motivated Irrationality*, Oxford: Oxford University Press.

Perec, G. (1990), *Things*, Boston: Godine.

References

Perelman, C., and Olbrechts-Tyteca, L. (1969), *The New Rhetoric*, Notre Dame: University of Notre Dame Press.

Persson, T., and Svensson, L. E. O. (1989), "Why a stubborn conservative would run a deficit: Policy with time-inconsistent preferences," *Quarterly Journal of Economics* 104, 325–45.

Peyre, H. (1944), "Fortune du Classicisme," *Lettres Françaises*, vol. 11, 47–54; vol. 12, 42–51.

Peyre, H. (1967), *The Failures of Criticism*, Ithaca, N.Y.: Cornell University Press.

Phelps, E. S., and Pollak, R. A. (1968), "On second-best national saving and game-theoretic equilibrium growth," *Review of Economic Studies* 35, 185–99.

Phillips, R. (1988), *Putting Asunder: A History of Divorce in Western Societies*, Cambridge University Press.

Pileggi, N. (1987), *Wiseguy*, New York: Pocket Books.

Pistone, J. (1989), *Donnie Brascoe*, New York: Signet Books.

Poincaré, H. (1920), "L'invention mathématique," in H. Poincaré, *Science et méthode*, Paris: Flammarion, pp. 43–63.

Porter, L., ed. (1991), *A Lester Young Reader*, Washington: Smithsonian Institution Press.

Posner, R. (1987), "The constitution as an economic document," *George Washington Law Review* 56, 4–49.

Prévost, J. (1971), *La création chez Stendhal*, Paris: Mercure de France.

Prince, G. (1973), "Introduction à l'étude du narrataire," *Poétique* 14, 178–96.

Przeworski, A., and Limongi, F. (1993), "Political regimes and economic growth," *Journal of Economic Perspectives* 7, 51–69.

Quincey, T. De (1986), *Confessions of an English Opium Eater*, London: Penguin Books.

Quattrone, G., and Tversky, A. (1986), "Self-deception and the voter's illusion," in J. Elster (ed.), *The Multiple Self*, Cambridge University Press, pp. 35–58.

Rabin, M. (1993), "Incorporating fairness into game theory and economics," *American Economic Review* 83, 1281–1302.

Rabin, M. (1995), "Moral preferences, moral constraints, and self-serving biases," manuscript, Department of Economics, University of California at Berkeley.

Rasula, J. (1995), "The media of memory: The seductive menace of records in jazz history," in K. Gabbard (ed.), *Jazz among the Discourses*, Durham: Duke University Press.

Rawls, J. (1971), *A Theory of Justice*, Cambridge, Mass.: Harvard University Press.

Revill, D. (1992), *John Cage*, London: Bloomsbury.

Rimmon-Kenan, S. (1983), *Narrative Fiction*, London: Methuen.

Robbins, A. (1997), "E-Mail: Lean, mean and making its mark," *New York Times*, May 11, page F13.

Roberts, J. T. (1982), *Accountability in Athenian Government*, Madison: University of Wisconsin Press.

Roth, A. (1995), "Bargaining experiments," in J. H. Kagel and A. E. Roth (eds.), *Handbook of Experimental Economics*, Princeton: Princeton University Press, pp. 253–348.

Royce, J. E. (1981), *Alcohol Problems and Alcoholism*, New York: The Free Press.

Rudolph, L. I., and Rudolph, S. H. (1987), *In Pursuit of Lakshmi: The Political Economy of the Indian State*, Chicago: University of Chicago Press.

Russell, P. H. (1993), *Constitutional Odyssey*, Toronto: University of Toronto Press.

Ruzé, F., (1997), *Délibération et pouvoir dans la cité grecque de Nestor à Socrate*, Paris: Publications de la Sorbonne.

Ryan, M. L. (1991), *Possible Worlds, Artificial Intelligence, and Narrative Theory*, Bloomington: Indiana University Press.

Sagoff, M. (1983), "The aesthetic status of forgeries," in D. Dutton (ed.), *The Forger's Art*, Berkeley: University of California Press, pp. 131–52.

Sartre, J.-P. (1943), *L'être et le néant*, Paris: Gallimard.

Satyanath, S. (1999), "Accommodating imprudence: The political economy of information in the Asian banking crisis," unpublished manuscript, Department of Political Science, Columbia University.

Schatz, T. (1996), *The Genius of the System: Hollywood Filmmaking in the Studio Era*, New York: Henry Holt.

Schelling, T. C. (1960), *The Strategy of Conflict*, Cambridge, Mass.: Harvard University Press.

Schelling, T. C. (1986), "The mind as a consuming organ," in J. Elster (ed.), *The Multiple Self*, Cambridge University Press, pp. 177–95.

Schelling, T. C. (1992), "Self-control," in G. Loewenstein and J. Elster (eds.), *Choice over Time*, New York: Russell Sage, pp. 167–76.

Schelling, T. C. (1999), "Rationally coping with lapses from rationality," in J. Elster and O.-J. Skog (eds.), *Getting Hooked: Rationality and the Addictions*, Cambridge University Press, pp. 265–84.

Schiemann, J. (1998), "The constitutional court: Myopic bargains and democratic institutions," unpublished manuscript, Department of Political Science, Columbia University.

Schuller, G. (1989), *The Swing Era*, Oxford: Oxford University Press.

Schumacher, M. (1992), *Dharma Lion: A Biography of Allen Ginsberg*, New York: St. Martin's Press.

Schwartz, H. (in press), *Constitutional Justice in Central and Eastern Europe*, Chicago: University of Chicago Press.

Sejersted, F. (1988), "Democracy and the rule of law," in J. Elster and R. Slagstad (eds.), *Constitutionalism and Democracy*. Cambridge University Press, pp. 131–52.

References

Sejersted, F. (1994), "On the so-called 'autonomy' or 'independence' of central banks," Working Paper #75, TMV Centre for Technology and Culture, University of Oslo.

Sen, A. (1987), *On Ethics and Economics*, Oxford: Blackwell.

Sen, A. (1993), "Capability and well-being," in M. Nussbaum and A. Sen (eds.), *The Quality of Life*, Oxford: Oxford University Press, pp. 30–53.

Shapiro, I. (1996), *Democracy's Place*, Ithaca, N.Y.: Cornell University Press.

Shattuck, R. (1996), *Forbidden Knowledge*, New York: St. Martin's Press.

Shattuck, R. (1997), Review of Calvin Tomkin, *Duchamp: A Biography* and Jerrold Seigel, *The Private Worlds of Marcel Duchamp: Desire, Liberation, and the Self in Modern Culture*, *New York Review of Books*, March 27.

Sinclair, R. K. (1988), *Democracy and Participation in Athens*, Cambridge University Press.

Skog, O.-J. (1997), "The strength of weak will," *Rationality and Society* 9, 245–71.

Skog, O.-J. (1999), "Hyperbolic discounting, willpower, and addiction," in J. Elster (ed.), *Addiction: Exits and Entries*, New York: Russell Sage, pp. 151–68.

Smith, C. (1994), "Norges Banks rettslige selvstendighet," in *Stabilitet og Langsiktighet: Festskrift til Hermod Skånland*, Oslo: Aschehoug, pp. 87–104.

Solomon, R. C. (1997), "In defense of sentimentality," in M. Hjort and S. Laver (eds.), *Emotion and the Arts*, Oxford: Oxford University Press, pp. 225–45.

Spacks, P. M. (1995), *Boredom*, Chicago: University of Chicago Press.

Sparshott, F. (1983), "The disappointed art lover," in D. Dutton (ed.), *The Forger's Art*, Berkeley: University of California Press, pp. 246–63.

Sperber, A. M., and Lax, E. (1997), *Bogart*, New York: William Morrow.

Spinelli, F., and Masciandaro, D. (1993), "Towards monetary constitutionalism in Italy," *Constitutional Political Economy* 4, 211–22.

Springer, S., and Deutsch, G. (1989), *Left Brain, Right Brain*, 3d ed., San Francisco: Freeman.

Stall, R., and Biernacki, P. (1986), "Spontaneous remission from the problematic use of substances," *International Journal of Addictions* 21, 1–23.

Starobinski, J. (1961), "Stendhal pseudonyme," in *L'Oeil Vivant*, Paris: Gallimard, pp. 189–240.

Stendhal (1952), *Romans et Nouvelles*, vol. 1, Paris: Gallimard (ed. de la Pléiade).

Stendhal (1980), *De l'amour*, ed. V. Del Litto, Paris: Gallimard.

Stendhal (1981), *Oeuvres Intimes*, vol. 1, Paris: Gallimard (ed. de la Pléiade).

Stendhal (1982), *Oeuvres Intimes*, vol. 2, Paris: Gallimard (ed. de la Pléiade).

Stewart, R. (1972), *Jazz Masters of the 30s*, New York: Da Capo Books.

Stokes, S. (1997), "Democratic accountability and policy change: Economic policy in Fujimori's Peru," *Comparative Politics* 29, 209–226.

Stokes, S. (1999), "What do policy switches tell us about democracy?" in

References

B. Manin, A. Przeworski, and S. C. Stokes (eds.), *Democracy, Accountability and Representation*, Cambridge University Press, pp. 98–130.

Stone, A. (1992), *The Birth of Judicial Politics in France*, Oxford: Oxford University Press.

Stone, L. (1990), *The Road To Divorce: England 1530–1987*, Oxford: Oxford University Press.

Strotz, R. H. (1955–56), "Myopia and inconsistency in dynamic utility maximization," *Review of Economic Studies* 23, 165–80.

Suber, P. (1990), *The Paradox of Self-Amendment*, New York: Peter Lang.

Sudhalter, R. M. (1999), *Lost Chords*, New York: Oxford University Press.

Sundt, E. (1976), "Nordlandsbåden," in E. Sundt, *Verker i Utvalg*, vol. VII, Oslo: Gyldendal.

Sunstein, C. (1991a), "Constitutionalism, prosperity, democracy," *Constitutional Political Economy* 2, 371–94.

Sunstein, C. (1991b), "Constitutionalism and secession," *University of Chicago Law Review* 58, 633–70.

Suppes, P. (1984), *Probabilistic Metaphysics*, Oxford: Blackwell.

Sørensen, A. B. (1998), "Theoretical mechanisms and the empirical study of social processes," in P. Hedström and R. Swedberg (eds.), *Social Mechanisms*, Cambridge University Press, pp. 238–66.

Tabellini, G., and Alesina, A. (1994), "Voting on the budget deficit," in T. Persson and G. Tabellini (eds.), *Monetary and Fiscal Policy*, Cambridge, Mass.: MIT Press, vol. 2, pp. 157–78.

Tamm, D. (1984), *Retsopgøret efter Besættelsen*, Copenhagen: Jurist- og Økonomforbundets Forlag.

Tanner, M. (1976–77), "Sentimentality," *Proceedings of the Aristotelian Society*, n.s. 77, 127–47.

Temin, P. (1991), *Lessons from the Great Depression*, Cambridge, Mass.: MIT Press.

Thaler, R. (1980), "Towards a positive theory of consumer choice," *Journal of Economic Behavior and Organization* 1, 39–60.

Thaler, R. (1992), *The Winner's Curse*, New York: The Free Press.

Thomas, K. (1973), *Religion and the Decline of Magic*, Harmondsworth: Penguin Books.

Thurber, J. (1996), "The Secret Life of Walter Mitty," in *Thurber: Writings and Drawings*, New York: Library of America, pp. 545–50.

Tirole, J. (1988), *The Theory of Industrial Organization*, Cambridge, Mass.: The MIT Press.

Tocqueville, A. de (1969), *Democracy in America*, New York: Anchor Books.

Tocqueville, A. de (1986), *Souvenirs*, in *Tocqueville*, Collection Bouquins, Paris: Robert Laffont.

Tocqueville, A. de (1990), *Recollections: The French Revolution of 1848*, New Brunswick: Transaction Books.

Tocqueville, A. de (1998), *The Old Regime and the Revolution*, Chicago: University of Chicago Press.

Todd, S. C. (1993), *The Shape of Athenian Law*, Oxford: Oxford University Press.

Trotsky, L. (1977), *History of the Russian Revolution*, London: Pluto Press.

Truffaut, F. (1985), *Hitchcock*, New York: Simon and Schuster.

Tulard, J. (1996), *Le temps des passions*, Paris: Bartillat.

Tversky, A., and Griffin, D. (1991), "Endowment and contrast in judgments of well-being," in R. Zeckhauser (ed.), *Strategy and Choice*, Cambridge, Mass.: MIT Press, pp. 297–318.

Umble, D. (1994), "The Amish on the line: The telephone debates," in D. B. Kraybill and M. A. Olshan (eds.), *The Amish Struggle with Modernity*, Hanover: University Press of New England, pp. 97–112.

Vaillant, G. (1995), *The Natural History of Alcoholism Revisited*, Cambridge, Mass.: Harvard University Press.

Valéry, P. (1957), "Stendhal," in *Oeuvres*, ed. de la Pléiade, vol. 1, Paris: Gallimard, pp. 553–82.

Veblen, T. (1915), *Imperial Germany and the Industrial Revolution*, London: Macmillan.

Vermazen, B. (1991), "The aesthetic value of originality," *Midwest Studies in Philosophy* XVI, 266–79.

Veyne, P. (1976), *Le pain et le cirque*, Paris: Editions du Seuil.

Vile, M. J. C. (1967), *Constitutionalism and the Separation of Powers*, Oxford: University Press.

Vreeland, J. R. (1999), "The IMF: Lender of last resort or scapegoat?" Paper presented at the International Studies Association, Washington, D.C.

Wagenaar, W. A. (1988), *Paradoxes of Gambling Behaviour*, Hove and London: Lawrence Erlbaum.

Wagner, W. J. (1997), "Some comments on old 'privileges' and the 'liberum veto,' " in S. Fiszman (ed.), *Constitution and Reform in Eighteenth-Century Poland*, Bloomington and Indianapolis: Indiana University Press, pp. 51–64.

Walcot, P. (1978), *Envy and the Greeks*, Warminster: Aris and Phillips.

Waldron, J. (1999), *Law and Disagreement*, Oxford: Oxford University Press.

Walton, K. (1988), "What is abstract about the art of music," *Journal of Aesthetics and Art Criticism* 46, 351–64.

Walton, K. (1990), *Mimesis as Make-Believe*, Cambridge, Mass.: Harvard University Press.

Watson, G. (1999), "Disordered appetites," in J. Elster (ed.), *Addiction: Exits and Entries*, New York: Russell Sage, pp. 3–28.

Weiss, R. D., Mirin, M. D., and Bartel, R. L. (1994), *Cocaine*, Washington, D.C.: American Psychiatric Press.

Werness, H. B. (1983), "Han van Meegeren *fecit*," in D. Dutton (ed.), *The Forger's Art*, Berkeley: University of California Press, pp. 1–57.

Werth, N. (1997), "Un État contre son peuple: Violences, répressions, terreurs en Union soviétique," in S. Courtois et al., *Le livre noir du Communisme*, Paris: Robert Laffont, pp. 42–295.

White, M. (1987), *Philosophy, The Federalist, and the Constitution*, New York: Oxford University Press.

Willoch, K. (1994), "Hvor uavhengig bør sentralbanken være?" in *Stabilitet og Langsiktighet: Festskrift til Hermod Skånland*, Oslo: Aschehoug, pp. 105–27.

Wilson, G. T. (1980), "Behavior therapy and the treatment of obesity," in W. R. Miller (ed.), *The Addictive Behaviors*, Oxford: Pergamon Press, pp. 207–37.

Winston, G. (1980), "Addiction and backsliding: A theory of compulsive consumption," *Journal of Economic Behavior and Organization* 1, 295–324.

Wood, G. (1969), *The Creation of the American Republic*, New York: Norton.

Yanal, R. J. (1994), "The paradox of emotion and fiction," *Pacific Philosophical Quarterly* 75, 54–75.

Zinberg, N. (1984), *Drug, Set, and Setting: The Basis for Controlled Intoxicant Use*, New Haven: Yale University Press.

Zinberg, N., Harding, W., and Winkeller, M. (1977), "A study of social regulatory mechanisms in controlled illicit drug users," *Journal of Drug Issues* 7, 117–33.

Zinoviev, A. (1979), *The Yawning Heights*, New York: Random House.

Zwerin, M. (1985), *La Tristesse de Saint Louis*, New York: William Morrow.

Index

accountability, 125–29
addiction, 63–77; *see also* eating disorders
  to alcohol, 65, 66, 68, 71, 73, 74, 77
  to cocaine, 67, 69
  to gambling, 67, 72, 74
  to nicotine, 65, 70, 72, 73, 74, 75, 76
  to opiates, 66–67, 73
  and personal rules, 85
  and sophisticated choice, 83
Aeschines, 128
Ainslie, George, 5 n.9, 21, 25, 84–86, 183, 270
Alcibiades, 125
Alcoholics Anonymous, 74, 75, 77, 277
Alesina, Alberto, 163
Allen, Woody, 196
altruism, 28 n.78
Amish, the, 59–61, 271
anapsephisis, 122–23, 128
Anderson, Cat, 248
Anderson, Thornton, 93
Andromaque, 20
anger, 12–13, 49, 50, 53–55, 56
Antiphon, 120
Antraigues, Comte d', 139
Archinus, 127
Arginusae, 120
Aristotle, 7, 8, 9, 93–94, 202, 217, 219, 220
Armstrong, Louis, 246, 247, 248, 249, 250, 254, 256, 261
Arnheim, Rudolf, 227–28, 233, 263, 266–67
artistic value, 178–79, 200–21
  and cognition, 205
  and constraints, 209–12
  and emotion, 206–9
  in jazz, 247–54
  maximization of, 200 n.65, 201–5

Assemblée Constituante (1789–91), 107–15, 129–41, 159–60
Astaire, Fred, 194–95, 206–7, 212, 231–32, 248, 262
Athens, 118–29
audience (in the arts), 188–89, 191, 195, 215
audience costs, 42, 69
Austen, Jane, 192, 204, 205, 215, 217, 248
authenticity (of works of art), 221–23
aversion therapy, 73

Bacon, Francis, 214, 243
Bailey, Mildred, 252, 261
balanced-budget amendment, 98, 142–43
Balzac, Honoré de, 220 n.119
bargaining, 43–45
Barnave, Antoine-Pierre-Joseph-Marie, 138
Basie, Count, 246, 248
Bataille, Georges, 232 n.159
Baxandall, Michael, 213, 268
Bazin, André, 233, 265
Bechet, Sidney, 251
Becker, Gary, 26–29
belief change, 71–72
belief trap, 68
Berlin, Irving, 260
Berliner, Paul, 257, 261
bicameralism, 90, 124 n.79, 133–35, 155, 160
Big Sleep, The, 220
Bilgrami, Akeel, 57–58
Blakey, Art, 249
Bleak House, 205
Blinder, Alan, 153 n.133, 165
Borges, Jorge Luis, 242
Bosch, Hieronymus, 214

301

Index